Colloquial

Tibetan

Colloquial Tibetan provides a step-by-step course in Central Tibetan as it is spoken by native speakers. Combining a thorough treatment of the language as it is used in everyday situations with an accurate written representation of this spoken form, it equips learners with the essential skills needed to communicate confidently and effectively in Tibetan in a broad range of situations. No prior knowledge of the language is required.

Key features include:

- progressive coverage of speaking, listening, reading and writing skills
- phonetic transliteration of the Tibetan script throughout the course to aid pronunciation and understanding of the writing system
- structured, jargon-free explanations of grammar
- an extensive range of focused and stimulating exercises
- realistic and entertaining dialogues covering a broad variety of scenarios
- useful vocabulary lists throughout the text
- additional resources available at the back of the book, including a full answer key, a grammar section, bilingual glossaries and English translations of dialogues.

Balanced, comprehensive and rewarding, *Colloquial Tibetan* will be an indispensable resource both for independent learners and for students taking courses in Tibetan.

Audio material to accompany the course is available to download free in MP3 format from www.routledge.com/cw/colloquials. Recorded by native speakers, the audio material features the dialogues and texts from the book and will help develop your listening and pronunciation skills.

By the end of this course, you will be at Level B2 of the Common European Framework for Languages and at the Intermediate-High level on the ACTFL proficiency scales.

THE COLLOQUIAL SERIES
Series Adviser: Gary King

The following languages are available in the Colloquial series:

Afrikaans
Albanian
Amharic
Arabic (Levantine)
Arabic of Egypt
Arabic of the Gulf
Basque
Bengali
Breton
Bulgarian
Burmese
Cambodian
Cantonese
Catalan
Chinese (Mandarin)
Croatian
Czech
Danish
Dutch
English
Estonian
Finnish
French
German
Greek
Gujarati
Hebrew
Hindi
Hungarian
Icelandic
Indonesian
Irish
Italian
Japanese
Kazakh
Korean
Latvian
Lithuanian
Malay
Mongolian
Norwegian
Panjabi
Persian
Polish
Portuguese
Portuguese of Brazil
Romanian
Russian
Scottish Gaelic
Serbian
Slovak
Slovene
Somali
Spanish
Spanish of Latin America
Swahili
Swedish
Tamil
Thai
Tibetan
Turkish
Ukrainian
Urdu
Vietnamese
Welsh
Yiddish
Yoruba
Zulu (forthcoming)

COLLOQUIAL 2s series: *The Next Step in Language Learning*

Chinese
Dutch
French
German
Italian
Portuguese of Brazil
Russian
Spanish
Spanish of Latin America

Colloquials are now supported by FREE AUDIO available online. All audio tracks referenced within the text are free to stream or download from www.routledge.com/cw/colloquials. If you experience any difficulties accessing the audio on the companion website, or still wish to purchase a CD, please contact our customer services team through www.routledge.com/info/contact.

Colloquial
Tibetan

The Complete Course for Beginners

Jonathan Samuels

Routledge
Taylor & Francis Group
LONDON AND NEW YORK

First published 2014
by Routledge
2 Park Square, Milton Park, Abingdon, Oxon OX14 4RN

and by Routledge
711 Third Avenue, New York, NY 10017

Routledge is an imprint of the Taylor & Francis Group, an informa business

British Library Cataloguing in Publication Data
A catalogue record for this book is available from the British Library

Library of Congress Cataloging in Publication Data
Samuels, Jonathan, [date]
Colloquial Tibetan : the complete course for beginners / Jonathan Samuels.
pages cm. – (The Colloquial Series)
audio disc ; digital,CD audio 4 3/4 in.
Includes bibliographical references and index.
1. Tibetan language—Textbooks for foreign speakers—English. 2. Tibetan language—Grammar. 3. Tibetan language—Spoken Tibetan. 4. Tibetan language—Sound recordings for English speakers. 5. Tibetan language—Self-instruction. I. Title.
PL3613.S26 2014
495′.486421–dc23

2013012635

ISBN: 978-1-138-95019-1 (pbk)

Typeset in Avant Garde and Helvetica
by Graphicraft Limited, Hong Kong

MIX
Paper from responsible sources
FSC® C013056

Printed and bound in Great Britain by
TJ International Ltd, Padstow, Cornwall

Contents

Acknowledgements

Credit is due to Gareth Sparham; without him, this book might never have been written. A very special thanks goes to Berthe Jansen for providing her support, shrewd observations, and the book's evocative illustrations. I would also like to thank Joanna Bialek for her valuable comments and suggestions. I am grateful to the team at Routledge; including Andrea Hartill, Gary King, and particularly Isabelle Cheng, who have shown commendable patience and flexibility. I am also grateful to my reviewers for their input.

Finally I would like to say that I am indebted to all of those Tibetans who, over the years, with such generous spirit, have allowed me to share in their culture.

Introduction

The Tibetan language

Exact numbers are difficult to come by, but various Tibetan dialects are spoken by more than five, and perhaps up to eight million people, in areas within PRC, India, Nepal, Bhutan and Pakistan, as well as by various Tibetans living in exile, scattered around the world. It is still common for Tibetans to categorise their language into three different forms, corresponding to the three historical provinces of Ü-tsang (often called 'Central Tibet'), Amdo and Kham (both described as 'Eastern Tibet'). In truth however, there are many dozens of dialects, spread over these and other areas, in a complex patchwork which is still being explored. Whilst disputed by some, Tibetan is generally classified in the same language family as Chinese (the Sino-Tibetan family). More specifically, it belongs to a branch called Tibeto-Burman. Thus it is unrelated, for instance, to languages of the Indo-European family, making it quite distinct not only from languages in Europe, but also from those of Northern India, Nepal, etc.

The spoken and written divide

The Tibetan written system is believed to have developed in the seventh century CE. Written Tibetan must to a large extent have reflected the way people spoke in the distant past. However, the evolution of the spoken and written language followed different paths at an early stage. The written language developed into a standard, literary form, whereas the dialects continued to change and diverge. Many of the dialects of Tibetan are not mutually comprehensible, although the literary language the speakers use is the same (so they can all read the same texts, but not necessarily discuss what they mean).

The modern literary movement of more recent decades has meant significant changes to the way Tibetans express themselves in written form, but there is still no great appetite for writing literature, newspapers, or other materials for public consumption in a style which is close to the way that people actually speak (partly because writing in dialects would mean losing the only common language). So the type of language that appears in this book is Tibetan as it is spoken, but hardly ever represented in writing (except the odd informal letter, or in books for learning colloquial Tibetan).

The Tibetan sentences in this book may correspond to the way that people speak, rather than the way things are expressed in literary Tibetan, but there is only one way to spell words (i.e. that of literary Tibetan). Spellings were never really modified to take account of historical changes in pronunciation. So there is often a huge gulf between the way things are spelt and the way they are pronounced, and even Tibetans find spelling challenging. The full transliteration of the Tibetan provided in this book can help the user negotiate this gulf.

The 'dialect' of this book

Because many Tibetan dialects are not mutually comprehensible, it has, for centuries, been necessary for travelling Tibetans (traders, monks, officials, etc.) to speak forms of the language which could cross the dialect divide. The language taught in this book to some extent represents one of these pragmatic hybrids. It can certainly be called a Central Dialect, as it is firmly rooted in the language of the Central, Ü district. But it also incorporates some elements from other areas (particularly from the east and south). It definitely does not claim to be the rather idiosyncratic Lhasa dialect. It is however, undoubtedly the form of the language with the widest spread, and someone speaking it could communicate throughout the Tibet Autonomous Region (Ü-tsang and areas of Kham), as well as right through the diaspora (where this has become the standard form of the language).

A few language features

Central Tibetan is a tonal language. While tone is an essential feature, the system is much simpler than found in other languages in the region (e.g. Mandarin, Cantonese, Burmese, Vietnamese, and Thai). Apart from tone, sounds are also distinguished in terms of aspiration, although again, the system is a simple one. Central Tibetan also has a very extensive system of honorific language, rivalling that of Japanese and Korean. Honorific language is used particularly in formal and polite conversation, and contrasts with the ordinary level of speech.

The scope of this book

This book is described as a 'Complete Course' in the language. It provides more than enough to engage in conversations ranging from basic to medium-advanced. It does not, of course, pretend to cover all aspects of the language (and it envisions a later, more advanced sequel). However, I have tried to ensure that those structures that are not covered here represent *alternative* perspectives; different ways that the speaker might approach a sentence. Not knowing them should not greatly hinder the learner's ability to communicate. Details of some areas that are not dealt with can be found in the Grammar section at the end of the book.

How to use this book

In keeping with the style of the series, the emphasis is upon the original script. The alphabet and letter combinations are explained (together with the sound system) in the 'Pronunciation and the alphabet' section, and Unit 1. Unlike other books teaching colloquial Tibetan, *all* of the dialogues and vocabulary are rendered in transliterated form. So the user does not need to master all of the letter combinations before starting with the dialogues (in Unit 2). Because of the numerous discrepancies between spelling and pronunciation referred to earlier, it is actually advisable, even for those who have gained familiarity with the script, to regularly refer to the transliteration.

Those who want to start with the dialogue material before learning the script can skip most of Pronunciation and the alphabet, and Unit 1. But they should still read the sections within these headed by the symbol ‡. These contain instructions about how to read the transliteration correctly (and no responsibility can be taken for the pronunciation of those who ignore these sections!).

It is the policy of this book to introduce the honorific language gradually, having first given the user a grounding in the ordinary level of the language.

From Unit 8 onwards, translations for the dialogues appear not in the units, but at the end of the book. On some occasions (indicated in the text), the user of the book is advised not to read the translation until completing the whole unit.

Some of the more formal and technical points relating to grammar and language are included in the Grammar section.

I hope that what awaits you proves to be a rewarding experience. Good luck!

Pronunciation and the alphabet: basic sounds and symbols

This section introduces:

- the sound system
- aspiration and tone
- the alphabet
- vowels
- examples of words

‡ The sounds of Tibetan speech

Two key features distinguish Tibetan sounds: aspiration and tone. In many cases, Tibetan uses the same basic consonant sound, but distinguishes different versions of it, depending on whether it is aspirated or non-aspirated, high tone or low tone. The different versions are listed below.

The letter **h** indicates aspiration. So **kh**, for instance, is an aspirated consonant, whereas **k** is not aspirated. In standard British and US English, when k begins a word, such as 'kin', it is aspirated (similar to **kh**). But when preceded by an s, as in 'skin', it is unaspirated (**k**). A similar distinction is noticeable with consonants t and p (comparing, for example, 'till' with 'still', and 'pin' with 'spin').

The distinction is illustrated more clearly when (as below) one compares certain consonants in British English (which are uniformly aspirated), with those in Indian English (which are uniformly non-aspirated). Unless otherwise stated, 'English' means British English.

A dot below the letter (**ṭ**) means that the sound is a retroflex. These sounds will be explained further in Unit 1.

Consonants

k	**kh**	– Indian and British English *c* in 'can't'
ky	**khy**	– Indian and British English *cu* in 'cure'
p	**ph**	– Indian and British English *p* in 'pill'
t	**th**	– Indian and British English *t* in 'tea'
ṭ	**ṭh**	– Similar to Indian and British English *tr* in 'try', but with the tip of the tongue bent back
ts	**tsh**	– Indian and British English *zza* in 'pizza'
c	**ch**	– Indian and British English *ch* of 'chop'
s		– as *s* in English 'sound'
r		– usually soft, like *r* in English 'rope' (only very occasionally heard as a rolled r), but from the front of the tongue, with a slight buzz and aspiration
sh		– as *sh* in English 'shop'
l		– as *l* in English 'limb'
m		– as *m* in English 'me'
n		– as *n* in English 'no'
ng		– as *ng*, at the end of English 'sing'
ny		– as *ny* within English 'Sonya'
w		– as *w* in English 'wick'
y		– as *y* in English 'you'
hr		– combining Tibetan *h* and *r* sounds, but with tip of tongue bent back; this has hints of a Sean Connery 's/sh'
lh		– heavily aspirated *l* (best produced by starting with a *h*-sound, then introducing *l* into it, rather than the other way round)
h		– as *h* in English 'hop'
'		– a glottal stop (abrupt stopping of the sound) as in what happens instead of a *t* in Cockney 'all right?', or at the end of 'uh', in 'uh-oh'

Vowels

a – as *a* in English 'sat'
ä – as *ä* in German 'Geschäft', similar to *e* in English 'left'
e – similar to Tibetan *ä*, but with lips spread wider (i.e. towards a smile)
o – as in English 'pop'
ö – as *ö* in German 'Köln'; more exaggerated than *u* in English 'blur'
u – as *oo* in English 'soon', but shorter
ü – as in French 'une', or *ü* in German 'Übung'
i – as *i* in English 'sip'

Tibetan vowels are generally much shorter than English ones. On the few occasions that they have a longer sound, this will be indicated by the colon symbol. For example **a:** is a long a-sound.

More about some of the above sounds follows in Unit 1. The Grammar section also has further comments about the transliteration system.

‡ Tone

In English, one can use any tone or pitch to say a consonant, vowel or word. Different pitches may indicate something about the speaker's mood or feelings, but the various sounds and words are still recognisable as the 'same' through a whole range of pitches. In Tibetan however, as with other tonal languages, a sound, word, etc. has a fixed tone or pitch. Getting the wrong tone is comparable to pronouncing a sound with the wrong consonant or vowel; it can make it unrecognisable, or even transform it into another word.

The Tibetan tonal system is relatively straightforward. The transliteration system in this book distinguishes between high, low, and neutral tones. A mark above the vowel will indicate which tone the syllable has. For instance **kā**, **ka̱**, **ka** are, respectively, high, low, and neutral-tone versions of syllables with the consonant **k**. There are three consonant sounds towards the end of the above list; **hr**, **lh** and **h**. With the exception of these (which are always high tone), all the consonant and vowel sounds have high, low and neutral tone versions. (Unit 1 has more about these distinctions.)

Tones in Tibetan are a little more varied than the division into high, low, and neutral suggests. A syllable can have certain 'contours' within it (falling, flat, etc.). But whilst one cannot communicate clearly without knowledge of the three-fold distinction, one can without a formal introduction to tone contours. It is better to learn about contours through gradual familiarity with the language.

The alphabet (Audio 1:02)

Basic Tibetan sounds are represented by two groups of symbols: the thirty 'consonants' (usually referred to as the alphabet) and the four vowel markers. All these consonants are thought of as having an in-built *a*-sound, so there is no separate vowel marker for 'a'. The vowel markers are used to indicate only when the vowel sound is other than 'a'. As the transliteration shows, some of the thirty are not consonants at all.

ཀ **kā**	ཁ **khā**	ག **kha̱**	ང **nga̱**
ཅ **cā**	ཆ **chā**	ཇ **cha̱**	ཉ **nya̱**
ཏ **tā**	ཐ **thā**	ད **tha̱**	ན **na̱**
པ **pā**	ཕ **phā**	བ **pha̱**	མ **ma̱**
ཙ **tsā**	ཚ **tshā**	ཛ **tsha̱**	ཝ **wa̱**
ཞ **sha̱**	ཟ **sa̱**	འ **a̱**	ཡ **ya̱**
ར **ra̱**	ལ **la̱**	ཤ **shā**	ས **sā**
ཧ **hā**	ཨ **ā**		

The vowel markers (Audio 1:06)

Any one of the four vowel markers can be added to any of the thirty letters of the alphabet. This addition will change the natural 'a' vowel sound of the letter to the one indicated by the marker. Here is the first letter of the alphabet, with each marker attached.

ཀི **kī**	ཀུ **kū**	ཀེ **kē**	ཀོ **kō**

The marker changes the vowel sound, but not the tone of the letter. There are other vowel sounds in Tibetan, but they don't have separate markers. They are modifications which occur in particular letter combinations, explained in Unit 1.

Rows and columns (helpful patterns)

The first nineteen letters of the alphabet are organised in a grid: a pattern of rows and columns, according to their sounds. It is not necessary to learn the names that describe each row ('Velar', etc.), but they show the main source of the sounds – they trace a general forward movement with each row; starting at the back of the tongue, they move to the palate, teeth, lips, etc. As should be clear from the transliteration, the organisation of the columns shows whether sounds are high or low tone (H or L), and aspirated or non-aspirated (A or NA). Various sound changes which occur in letter combinations depend upon which column letters fall into, so it is a good idea to learn the sounds within this grid.

	Column 1 H/NA	Column 2 H/A	Column 3 L/A	Column 4 L/NA
Row 1 **Velar**	ཀ **kā**	ཁ **khā**	ག **kha̱**	ང **nga̱**
Row 2 **Palatal**	ཅ **cā**	ཆ **chā**	ཇ **cha̱**	ཉ **nya̱**
Row 3 **Dental**	ཏ **tā**	ཐ **thā**	ད **tha̱**	ན **na̱**
Row 4 **Labial**	པ **pā**	ཕ **phā**	བ **pha̱**	མ **ma̱**
Row 5 **Affricate**	ཙ **tsā**	ཚ **tshā**	ཛ **tsha̱**	

Basic punctuation

The most common punctuation symbol in written Tibetan is the dot-like mark, known as a **tshēk** (ཚེག). This is used to separate syllables. So the first four letters of the alphabet would be written:

ཀ་ཁ་ག་ང་

But written Tibetan has no mark to distinguish between words, and does not leave spaces between words. So a sentence will appear as an unbroken string of syllables. For example:

He is a Tibetan. ཁོང་བོད་པ་རེད།

The second most common punctuation mark is the line that appears at the end of the above sentence; it is known as a **shā'** (ཤད།). The function of this mark is to isolate words. It is not equivalent to a full stop (it can also be written at the end of a clause, or after an individual word appearing as a dictionary entry, etc.), but will certainly be used at the end of a Tibetan colloquial sentence, just as a full stop would in English. There is just one technical exception to this. The mark is not written when the last letter in the sentence (dictionary entry, etc.) is ག **kha̱**. More generally, when the last letter is ང **nga̱**, both punctuation marks are written. So most endings will look like this: རེད། but a smaller number like this: འདུག or this: སོང་།

A few words

Now that the alphabet and vowel markers have been covered, it is time to illustrate how simple some Tibetan words can be. A large number of words are made up simply of a letter from the alphabet, or a letter plus a vowel marker.

ཁ། **khā** mouth	ཇ། **cha̱** tea	ར། **ra̱** goat	ས། **sā** ground
ཉ། **nya̱** fish	མི། **mi̱** man	ཆུ། **chū** water	རི། **ri̱** mountain
སོ། **sō** tooth	མེ། **me̱** fire		

Unit One
Syllables, letter combinations and words

In this unit you will learn how to:

- combine letters (single syllables)
- recognise exceptions
- say words of more than one syllable

The opening section dealt with the sound system, as well as the basic script. It also showed that a written Tibetan syllable, or a Tibetan word can be as simple as just one element (a consonant symbol), or two elements (a consonant symbol plus a vowel marker).

Many more Tibetan syllables, however, involve more than just one or two elements, and many words have more than one syllable. This unit focuses upon what sounds are produced when such combinations of elements and syllables occur.

‡ What to expect

Written Tibetan is at the opposite end of the scale from a language like German, where one basically pronounces every letter on the page. Instead, it is closer to French or English.

(a) The fact that a written syllable has multiple elements does not necessarily mean that it is more difficult to pronounce! Just as in English, what looks like a complex combination of letters on the page can still produce a relatively simple sound (e.g. 'tongue', 'borough', 'psycho').

(b) Some consonants are occasionally written, but produce no sound (as in English 'knight', 'subtle').

(c) Many written syllables look quite different from each other, but actually have the same sound (as in English 'bow', 'bough').

Just like in English, discrepancies between the way things are written and spoken are due to historical changes. These discrepancies will initially seem to be more extreme than those in English. But there is perhaps greater consistency; so once one has learnt the rules, it is easier to predict the sound of a word from its spelling.

The transliteration system is obviously there to show how things are pronounced (rather than spelt), so there are no silent letters. Each vowel represents the presence of a distinct syllable. So if there are two vowels within a word/letter combination, such as **y̲ike**, meaning 'letter' (ཡི་གེ), it is to be read as **yi-ke** (i.e. two syllables), and never as a single syllable (as in 'yikes!').

‡ Exercise 1

Here are some words written in a simplified transliteration form; count how many syllables each has:

1 **ming**	4 **shikatse**	7 **yaya**
2 **khyi**	5 **lame**	8 **ṭhaṭik**
3 **eni**	6 **phökä**	

‡ In English, two or more separate consonants can come together to form a sound in which both can still be heard; at the beginning of a word, e.g. *br* in 'bring', *pl* in 'plate', *sk* in 'skill', or at the end, such as *ks* in 'takes', *bls* in 'syllables'. This *never* happens with Tibetan consonants. A syllable can start with one consonant-sound, and may end with one, but that is the limit. Neither **ng** nor **ts** stand for combinations of two different consonant-sounds; they are both individual consonants. So when pronouncing either **ng** and **ts**, try not to make them sound like **t-s** or **n-g**.

‡ Exercise 2

In the two versions of the following words (written in simplified transliteration) the first has all the syllables written together, whilst the second breaks them into their separate syllables. But are all the broken-down versions correct? The section above and the earlier one, on the Sounds of Tibetan Speech, explain what sounds are possible in Tibetan, so provide all the information one needs to answer:

1 **tshongkhang – tshong-khang**
2 **yokpo – yo-kpo**
3 **khongtsho – khong-tsho**
4 **mangpo – ma-ng-po**
5 **kyokpo – kyok-po**
6 **shukchenpo – shu-kchen-po**
7 **ngoshenpa – ngosh-en-pa**
8 **utangwa – ut-an-gwa**
9 **nyungnyung – nyun-gnyung**

Letter combinations

Each syllable has a 'central' letter, a core, or centre-point; sometimes called the 'root letter' or 'radical' of the syllable. This is the one to which the other elements in the syllable are said to be attached. The letter a vowel marker is attached to, for instance, is the central letter of the combination. So in the syllable མི **mi̲**, མ **ma̲** is the central letter.

In dictionaries, words are also listed according to their central letters. Central letters are the main ones determining the tone and aspiration of the syllable. Any of the thirty letters of the alphabet can be a central letter. Combinations can range from two elements, such as in **mi̲**, to seven (the most complex). The most complex syllable is organised as in the diagram below: V represents the vowel marker (of which there can only be one). Each of the other boxes represents a position where another letter can be attached; each of these attached letters (represented by the arrows) is one found in the alphabet. The numbers show the order in which these are explained below ('Position 1', etc.)

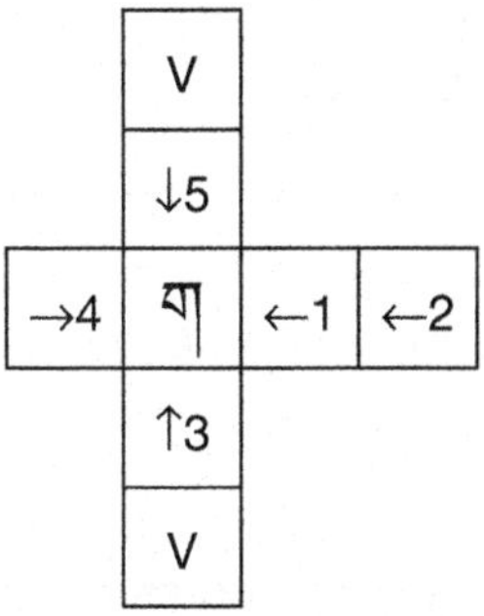

Rules govern which letters can go together (some combinations are not possible). It is not necessary to learn these rules; what follows is how to pronounce combinations which are found in everyday syllables and words.

Position 1 – letters attached after the central letter (suffixes)

Ten of the thirty letters of the alphabet can occupy position 1. These are:

ག ང ད ན བ མ འ ར ལ ས

So combinations like ཀག། ཁང་། ངད། are possible, but ཁཀ། ངཁ ཅཆ are not. The central letter (combined with whatever letters are above and below it) is the beginning of the sound in the syllable, whereas the suffixes are more like the end of that sound. In a simple analogy, in an English word like 'sang', the 'sa' is like the central letter, and the 'ng' is like the suffix. The combination སང་། would come quite close to the English sound.

As this analogy illustrates, the suffix loses its vowel sound, and takes that of the central letter. Generally speaking, only central letters can have vowel markers attached. For example:

ས + ང = སང་། **sāng** སི + ང = སིང་། **sīng** ལ + མ = ལམ། **la̱m**

Exercise 3 **(Audio 1:07)**

Re-write these syllables in transliteration:

(a) ཐམ།
(b) མང་།
(c) ཀིལ།
(d) ཇོམ།
(e) ལུང་།
(f) ཆེམ།
(g) འོང་།

Only some of the suffixes appeared in Exercise 3. Not all of them are so predictable. The way the ten letters act when they are suffixes can be summarised like this:

1 འ། silent; no effect on the syllable's sound
2 ང་བ་མ་ར། articulated (transliterated as **ng**, **p**, **m**, and **r**)

3 ན་ལ། articulated (transliterated as **n** and **l**), they can also change the vowel sound
4 ག articulated (transliterated as **k**)
5 ད་ས། silent, they change the vowel sound, and cause an abrupt glottal stop

More will be said about the articulation of suffixes later in the unit. The vowel changes mentioned are:

a → **ä**
u → **ü**
o → **ö**

So, if a central letter has an **a**, **u**, or **o** vowel sound, attaching any of the suffixes from group 2 or 3 to it will change the sound to **ä**, **ü**, or **ö** respectively (quite similar to the German vowels with an umlaut). There is no change if the vowel sound is **i** or **e**. To illustrate:

ངན། is **ngä̱n**, not **nga̱n**
ཕུན། is **phǖn**, not **phūn**
སུལ། is **sǖl**, not **sūl**
ཁོས། is **khȫ'**, not **khō'**

Exercise 4

From this group of combinations, pick out those in which the vowel sound is changed by the addition of the suffix, and write these in transliteration.

སོམ། ཙུང་། དུབ། པེད། ཏུལ། ཨོན། ཏུང་། ངས། ཁིན།
ཤེང་། ཅུག ཤུབ། རས། སོང་། མུར། ཞོན། ཁལ། ཚོལ།
ཅེང་། དུལ། ཉོབ། ཇུས། ཕོལ། ཡུན། ཚེས།

Position 2 – the letter attached after the suffix (the second suffix; ས།)

Only this letter **sā** can occupy position 2, and follow after one of the ten suffixes described above. As a second suffix, the letter is silent. It does not change the vowel sound or cause a glottal ending, as it does when in position 1. But when following a suffix ག (or sometimes ང) it sometimes affects that suffix; e.g.:

ཐུག **thūk** ཐུགས། **thū:**

That is, it may dampen the sound of the first suffix, and make the vowel sound longer.

Exercise 5

Write these transliterated syllables in Tibetan script:

tāng s̲in kō̄l ngā̲l tha̲ng chī' tsūm chi̲k yül hēp

Can any of them be written in more than one way?

Position 3 – letters attached below the central letter (subscripts)

Four letters can be attached below the central letter: ཝ ཡ ར ལ

It is only in this position that letters can alter their appearance. Taking the first letter of the alphabet as the central letter, each of the four, combined with it, will look like this:

ཀྭ ཀྱ ཀྲ ཀླ

Subscripts can only be attached to certain central letters. To the learner, the sounds the subscripts produce will seem to range from the apparently logical to the baffling. So it is worth going through these combinations in detail.

■ Subscript ཝ

Taking the form of a small triangle on the lower right side of the central letter, this is the easiest subscript. It can be attached to various central letters, but in Tibetan words it is silent and does not affect the sound. For instance, both ཁ and ཁྭ are pronounced **khā**.

The only notable thing about this subscript is that it may be added to a central letter which already has a subscript letter. Even in these unusual situations, the letter remains silent. Such combinations look like this: གྲྭ། ཕྱྭ།

■ Subscript ཡ (Audio 1:08)

This subscript can be attached to seven different central letters, to create these combinations:

ཀྱ **kyā** ཁྱ **khyā** གྱ **khya̱**
པྱ **cā** ཕྱ **chā** བྱ **cha̱** མྱ **nya̱**

So when a subscript **-ya** is attached to any of the first three letters of the alphabet, one hears a combination of the two elements. But perhaps confusingly, attaching **ya** to the set **pā phā pha̱ ma̱** changes them into the same sounds as the second row in the alphabet (ཅ་ཆ་ཇ་ཉ།).

■ Subscript ར

This subscript can be added to twelve central letters (although the three marked in bold hardly ever occur):

ཀྲ **ṭā** ཁྲ **ṭhā** གྲ **ṭha̱**
ཏྲ **ṭā** **ཐྲ** **ṭhā** དྲ **ṭha̱**
པྲ **ṭā** ཕྲ **ṭhā** བྲ **ṭha̱** **མྲ** **ma̱**
སྲ **ṭā** (or sometimes **sā**)
ཧྲ **hrā**

Notice that there are twelve 'spelling' combinations here, but only five (or six) sounds; i.e. different combinations produce the same sounds. The four new sounds are the retroflex ones. To make these sounds, the tip of the tongue is curled back, and touches the roof of the mouth. The **ṭhā** sound comes close to the English 'tra' in 'trance', 'trap', etc. The **ṭha̱** sound is closer to 'dra' in 'drab', 'drag', etc. But no British English sound corresponds to **ṭā**. The difference between the Tibetan **tā** and **ṭā** can be subtle. With **tā**, the tip of the tongue points forward, and touches just behind the top front teeth. With **ṭā** the tip curls backward, touching a point a little further back in the mouth. Retroflex sounds are prominent in languages of the sub-continent (Hindi, Tamil, etc.). The Tibetan ones are less pronounced than in those languages. For the retroflex sounds, including the **hrā**, described in the Sounds of Tibetan Speech section, listen carefully to the audio.

■ Subscript ལ

ཀླ **lā** གླ **lā** བླ **lā** རླ **lā** སླ **lā** ཟླ **ta̱**

The first five combinations all have the same sound; the **la** sound of the alphabet, but with a high tone. The last combination is close to a low tone version of the sound **tā** in the alphabet.

Here, in summary, are the subscript combinations, introduced above:

Subscripts	*(May be attached to) Central letters*	*Appearance*
ཡ།	ཀ། ཁ། ག། པ ཕ བ མ	ཀྱ ཁྱ གྱ པྱ ཕྱ བྱ མྱ
ར།	ཀ། ཁ། ག།	ཀྲ ཁྲ གྲ
	ཏ ཐ ད	ཏྲ ཐྲ དྲ
	པ ཕ བ མ	པྲ ཕྲ བྲ མྲ
	ས ཧ	སྲ ཧྲ
ལ།	ཀ། ག། བ ར ས ཟ	ཀླ གླ བླ རླ སླ ཟླ

These 25 only produce 15 sounds (9 of which are new).

Exercise 6

There are now many combinations which might look completely different, but produce the same sound. These differences are important for spelling. Group together any combinations from the following which have exactly the same sounds as one other:

ལ། ཀླ། ཀྱུ། ཁྱུ། ལང་། གླང་། ཤོ། ཀྱི། སྲུང་། ཚྭ།
དྲོན། ཞུར། སློ། ཛ། ཏྲོ། དོན། ཅ། ཟློན། ལྷ། སྲུང་།
ཟློ། ཀྲབ། ཟླུང་། གྲབ། ཇ། པྲུག ཀྭ། བྲེལ། སྲ། ཚོ།
དྲ། ཕྱ། ཚོད། ཕྱོས། ཕྲུག ཁྲབ། བྱ། ཕྱུར། ཕྱྭ། གྱེལ།

Position 4 – letters attached before the central letter (prefixes) (Audio 1:10)

There are five letters – ག་ད་བ་མ་འ། – which can be attached before the central letter. Letters in position 4 are silent, but when added to any of the following central letters, they will affect its sound.

3rd column	*4th column*
ཁ **kha̱**	ང **nga̱**
ཆ **cha̱**	ཉ **nya̱**
ཐ **tha̱**	ན **na̱**
ཕ **pha̱**	མ **ma̱**
ཚ **tsha̱**	ཡ **ya̱**

The columns here are those in which the alphabet is organised. Other central letters (e.g. those from the 1st or 2nd column) are not affected when a prefix is added. The letter **ya̱** does not belong to either column in the alphabet, but acts like the 4th column letters when a prefix is added.

When a prefix is attached to a central letter from the 3rd column, that letter loses its aspiration. So **kha̱** becomes **ka̱**, and **cha̱** becomes **ca̱**, etc.

When a prefix is attached to a central letter of the 4th column, that letter shifts to a high tone. So **nga̱** becomes **ngā**, and **nya̱** becomes **nyā**, etc.

Exercise 7

Pick out those central letters which would change their sound if a prefix were added to them:

མ།　ས།　ག　ར།　འ།　ང་།　བ།　ལ།

ཕ།　ཀ།　ཤ།　ཞ།　ཇ།　ཚོ།　ད།

In most cases, the central letter will be obvious, because it is the one with a vowel marker, subscribed, or superscribed letter attached to it. Occasionally, a syllable like གཡག occurs. It may not immediately be apparent whether the first letter is a prefix or the central letter. Eventually, when you recognise syllables as words (rather than random letter combinations) you will know how to read them. But whilst learning, it might be necessary to work the sound out based upon the rules. For instance here, the first letter cannot be the central one, because then **ya̱** would have to be a suffix; also, the second **kha̱** would have to be a second suffix; neither of these is possible. So the only possible reading is **yāk** (i.e. the Tibetan animal).

Exercise 8

Prefixes feature in all of the following. Re-write these combinations in transliterated form:

མགོ།། བགྲལ། མགུར། དངོས། གཡུག གསོལ། དགོང་། འཁྲུར། བཀག

Position 5 - letters attached above the central letter (superscripts)

Three letters – ར ལ ས – can be attached above the central letter.

ར། looks different as a superscript; here it is attached to **kā**: རྐ།

These letters act in the same way as the prefixes (position 4 letters); they are silent, and produce the same changes in 3rd and 4th column central letters. The only exception, where one hears the superscript, is when **la̲** is attached above the central letter **hā**: ལྷ This is the heavily aspirated *l* (mentioned earlier); best pronounced by introducing the l-sound having already begun to exhale with a *h*-sound (rather than starting from *l*).

Some central letters have position 4 and 5 letters (both prefixes and superscripts) attached to them. In these cases there is no 'doubling' of the changes; one just reads the combination in the same way as if there were only one of the attached letters.

All the letters in positions have now been explained. A change in sound caused by attaching a letter in one position is *not* cancelled out by attaching another in a different position. Each change can be heard in the final sound. This is most obvious in two combinations: some central letters, as already mentioned, can have letters attached below, which can add a *y*-sound (e.g. གྱ **khya̲**) or create a retroflex (e.g. དྲ **ṭha̲**). These central letters belong to the 3rd column. So they lose their aspiration when a prefix or superscript is attached. Thus if in addition to having a letter attached below, they also have one attached above (or before) them, one can hear both of the additions in the final sound, e.g.: རྒྱ། **kya̲** and སྒྲ། **ṭa̲**.

Exercise 9 **(Audio 1:12)**

Transliterate these combinations, which bring together all of the elements above:

གྲང་། འཐྲང་། ཛ། གསུན། སྒྲུ། འཛོག བཞུ།
ཕྱི། ལྟོགས། རྒྱུན། སྒོང་། བརྐུ། བསླབས།

Exceptions to the rules (in syllables) (Audio 1:13)

There are a couple of letter combinations which do not abide by the above rules:

1 The prefix ད before a central letter བ
Even though the central letter belongs to the 3rd column, in this combination the tone becomes high (as if it were from the 4th column). What is more, there is never any **pha** sound in this combination. The changes are not predictable, so check the transliteration; if combinations such as དབང་། occur (it may be pronounced **wāng** or **āng**).

2 འི (in combinations such as ངའི།, པོའི།, etc.)
Normally, only central letters have vowel markers attached to them. An exception is the letter **a̱**, when it has an 'i' vowel marker added. This is a common grammatical particle. The letter it is attached to (**nga̱** and **pō** in the examples) is the central letter in the combination, and begins the sound. The vowel sound of the combination will depend upon that of the central letter, but will always be long. In the examples the sounds are **ngä:** and **pö:**.

3 Rarities
Two symbols crop up only a couple of times:

ཏ྄; pronounced **ṭā**
པཱ; pronounced **pā** (i.e. the འ is ignored)

Words with more than one syllable: what changes?

Many words have more than one syllable. The pronunciation of some syllables changes only when they form part of such words:

1 Change to the sound of བ
In the alphabet, this letter is pronounced **pha̱**. When it is the first syllable in a word, the same is true. But when it alone is the second, third, etc. syllable in a word, it is always pronounced

wa. As there are so many nouns and verbs which have this letter as a second syllable, almost every time it occurs, it is pronounced **wa**.

2 Invisible suffixes

Sometimes, a suffix-sound can be heard, even though no suffix appears in the spelling. For example, བཅུ་གསུམ། ('13') looks like it should be pronounced **cūsūm**, but instead is **cūksūm**. The prefix **ka** in the second syllable has been 'reawakened' in the combination, and attaches itself to the end of **cū** (this is similar to liaison in French, but in reverse). There are no consistent rules to learn here, and not all cases are as logical as the example. But it only happens in a minority of words (particularly numbers), as the transliteration will demonstrate.

‡ 3 'Toned' and 'weak' syllables

Each letter and letter combination *in isolation* has to be either high or low tone, aspirated or non-aspirated. But the situation can change when the syllables are joined together in words. As explained earlier, the transliteration will indicate (with a mark either above or below the vowel) whether a syllable has a high or low tone. But, for example, in the sentence, 'Is she a student? (**mo̱rang lōpṭhuk re̱'-wä**) we see that not all syllables are marked. A syllable with this marker is 'toned'; the tone is fixed and clear. Whether or not the syllable is aspirated will also be clear. Syllables without tone markers have no fixed tone value; they are 'neutral'. For instance, the high tone ཀ།, and normally low tone བ། come together in ཀ་བ། (meaning 'pillar'). This is pronounced **kāwa**. The pattern here, with the first syllable of the word toned, and the second one neutral, is the most common (although not the only one) followed by Tibetan words. What it means in practice is that **wa**, as the neutral syllable, is not committed to any definite tone; it is 'weak', in the sense that it happily follows the lead set by **kā**. Tibetan words generally don't have dramatic shifts of tone within them; neutral tone syllables often follow the lead of toned ones, creating a smoother sound. Listen carefully to examples of this on the audio.

4 Occasional losses

Linked with the last point, certain other features may get ironed out, to create a smoother sound. 'Uh-oh' is a single expression, but the glottal stop at the end of 'uh' is clear, because someone saying it pauses there. Many letter combinations in Tibetan should produce glottal stops. When such a combination comes at the end of a word, this stop is clearly heard. But the glottal stop may not be detectable if a combination which should produce it comes within a word or expression, because in Tibetan (unlike with uh-oh) one rarely pauses inside these units. Some long vowel sounds can also disappear in a similar way.

Exercise 10 **(Audio 1:14)**

Read these out, checking your pronunciation against that on the audio.

ཕྱོག།	པར།	འོ།	གསེར།	འཚོལ།	སྐད།
བརྡ།	བཞུགས།	སྟོད།	ཟ་བ།	ཕྱིན་པ།	འབྲས།
སློབ་པ།	ཧྲུག	ཞེད་པ།	འགྲོ་བ། ཕྱི།	བསྒྲིགས་པ།	སྦྱུང་།
མངའ་སྡེ།	གཡོན་ཕྱོགས།	སྨོད་པ།	འཛེགས་པ།	སྨུན་པ།	ཚེ་རིང་།
བོད་སྐད།	གནམ་གྲུ།	རྡོ་རྗེ།	ང་གཉིས།	ཆུ་ཚོད།	

‡ A few more points about the transliteration

Full stops and commas are employed, as they are in English. But other punctuation marks, including capital letters, question and exclamation marks, are not. A series of dots within a line of speech (both in the transliteration and the Tibetan script) indicates that the speaker has not completed what he or she was saying (due to interruption, hesitation, or the implication being clear).

Hyphens give some idea of how syllables should be grouped when read. So items linked by hyphens are not one word, but are related, and the way you say them should reflect this; just as in English when you group together the two elements in 'the shop'. It is not necessary to know this at the start, but eventually, the user should be able to see that there are three occasions when a hyphen is being used:

(a) When a particle is attached to a word, e.g. in **khōng-la**; where **la** is a particle.
(b) In certain phrases, such as the greeting, **ṭāshi-tẹle'**.
(c) Linking some auxiliaries to action verbs, e.g. **ṭo̱ki-yi̱n**.

Articulation

The term 'articulated' was used when describing the sounds on the suffix-list; this needs qualification. It is true that the suffix sounds **ng**, **p** and **m** can usually be heard. But the situation with the others (**r**, **n**, **l** and **k**) is more varied. Sometimes **r**, **n** and **l** are heard. Even when they are, the sound is not a strong one; it is just recognisable as that consonant. But at other times, the consonant sound is replaced by a long vowel sound. Similarly, rather than **k**, one often hears just a glottal stop.

r, n, l	→	**:**	(e.g. instead of **phār** one hears **phā:**)
k	→	**'**	(e.g. instead of **lu̱k** one hears **lu'**)

So these suffixes function within a range; at one extreme they are clearly articulated, at the other they transform into long vowels or glottal stops. Because the pronunciation of people and words varies in Central Tibetan, nothing within the range is incorrect. To increase the chances of making themselves understood I would advise learners to lean more towards the extreme of articulation. To support this, the transliteration is rather 'correct' in its treatment of suffixes. In *most* (but not all) cases, the aforementioned suffixes are marked as consonant sounds within the words. Be aware that this represents a starting point. With gradual familiarisation, you can eventually come to a comfortable position within the sound range.

There are other subtleties of sound: tone contours, nasalisation, etc. particularly in relation to suffixes. The ones not noted in the transliteration are mentioned in the Grammar section at the end of the book. The audio also provides clear examples of the range of these sounds.

Unit Two

བཀྲ་ཤིས་བདེ་ལེགས། བདེ་པོ་ཡིན་པས།

ṭāshi-ṭele'. ṭepo yin-pä

Hello. Are you well?

In this unit you will learn how to:

- exchange greetings
- introduce yourself
- make a simple enquiry about health
- construct simple questions about identity

Dialogue 1

Greetings and introductions (Audio 1:15)

Duho is a Korean who speaks Tibetan; he is travelling with his friend, Lisa, who knows just a few sentences. They are meeting Sönam, a Tibetan, who Duho knows from previous visits.

ཏུ་ཧོ།	བསོད་ནམས་ལགས། བཀྲ་ཤིས་བདེ་ལེགས།
བསོད་ནམས།	འོ། ཏུ་ཧོ་ལགས། བཀྲ་ཤིས་བདེ་ལེགས།
ཏུ་ཧོ།	བསོད་ནམས་ལགས། ཁྱེད་རང་བདེ་པོ་ཡིན་པས།
བསོད་ནམས།	ང་བདེ་པོ་ཡིན། ཨེ་ནི་ཁྱེད་རང་་་།
ཏུ་ཧོ།	ང་བདེ་པོ་ཡིན།
	བསོད་ནམས་ལགས། ཁོང་ལི་ས་རེད།
བསོད་ནམས།	ཨ་ལས། ལི་ས་ལགས། བཀྲ་ཤིས་བདེ་ལེགས།
ལི་ས།	བཀྲ་ཤིས་བདེ་ལེགས། བསོད་ནམས་ལགས།

DUHO	sȫnam-la: ṭāshi-te̱le'.
SÖNAM	o̱ tu̱ho-la: ṭāshi-te̱le'.
DUHO	sȫnam-la: khyērang te̱po yi̱n-pä.
SÖNAM	nga̱ te̱po yi̱n. ēni khyērang. . . .
DUHO	nga̱ te̱po yi̱n.
	sȫnam-la:, khōng li̱sa re̱'.
SÖNAM	ālä li̱sa-la: ṭāshi-te̱le'.
LISA	ṭāshi-te̱le'. sȫnam-la:.

DUHO	*Sönam, hello!*
SÖNAM	*Ah, Duho, hello!*
DUHO	*Are you well, Sönam?*
SÖNAM	*Yes, I'm well, and you?*
DUHO	*I'm well.*
	Sönam, this [she] is Lisa.
SÖNAM	*Oh [I see]. Hello Lisa.*
LISA	*Hello, Sönam.*

Vocabulary

བཀྲ་ཤིས་བདེ་ལེགས།	**ṭāshi-te̱le'**	hello/greetings
བསོད་ནམས།	**sȫnam**	(personal name)
ལགས།	**la:/la**	('polite' add-on; see below)
ང་།	**nga̱**	I/me

ཁྱེད་རང་།	**khyērang**	you
ཡིན།	**yi̱n**	am
རེད།	**re̱'**	is/are
འོ།	**o̱**	ah/oh! (exclamation: surprise or pleasure)
བདེ་པོ།	**te̱po**	well
ཨེ་ནི།	**ēni**	and/so
ཨ་ལས།	**ālä**	oh, I see
བོད་པ།	**phö̱pa**	Tibetan (person)
ཕྱི་རྒྱལ་བ།	**chīkyä̱lwa**	foreigner
ཕུན་ཚོགས།	**phǖntshok**	(personal name)
ཐུགས་རྗེ་ཆེ།	**thūce-chē**	'thank you'

Cultural point

Greeting

As well as a greeting, the expression **ṭāshi-te̱le'** can be used as a way of congratulating others, wishing good fortune, etc. As is often the case with the English enquiry, 'How are you?' the Tibetan expression **khyērang te̱po yi̱n-pä** forms part of the process of greeting, rather than an invitation to discuss the actual state of one's health.

Neither speaker uses an equivalent of 'thank you' in the response to that question. The closest Tibetan equivalent of 'thank you' (**thūce-chē**) is usually reserved for expressions of real gratitude, rather than used as a perfunctory expression. There is no direct Tibetan equivalent of 'please', nor a statement which really corresponds to 'pleased to meet you!'

When introduced to someone for the first time **ṭāshi-te̱le'** is often accompanied by a slight bob (rather than a bow) of the head. People in more remote areas may still fold their hands together in a prayer-like ('namaskar') gesture. But more generally, this gesture is common only when meeting religious figures (and of course, in postcard images of Tibetan culture). Men who are acquainted will often clasp, rather than actually shake, one another's hand in greeting.

Cultural point

Names (མིང་། mi̱ng)

The majority of common names used by Central Tibetans are cross-gender. The full name normally consists of two parts, each of two syllables. The character in Dialogue 1, for instance, might be known as **sȫnam phǖntshok**. The literal meanings of a person's names are most commonly positive, with religious associations. Both parts of a person's name are given. Family names are quite rare, unless there were distinguished forebears. As neither part is a family name, one cannot manipulate them, as one might do with the name John Smith, to express either intimacy ('John'), or formality ('Mr Smith').

You can address a person more politely by using the add-on **la:** after his or her name; e.g. **sȫnam-la:**. No English equivalent of **la:** exists. It has various functions, but whenever a speaker uses it, he or she is always showing politeness to the person(s) being addressed. Apart from attaching it to the names of others (as in Dialogue 1), it can also be inserted into responses to questions.

Language points

1 Common personal pronouns

ང་།	**nga̱**	I/me
ཁྱེད་རང་།	**khyērang**	you (polite)
ཁྱོད།	**khyȫ'**	you (non-polite or intimate)
ཁོང་།	**khōng**	he/she (polite)
ཁོ་རང་།	**khōrang**	he (non-polite)
མོ་རང་།	**mo̱rang**	she (non-polite)
ང་ཚོ།	**nga̱n-tsho**	we/us

The syllable **rang** appears in some of the above. You might also hear it added to any of the first syllables (e.g. **nga̱rang** is not uncommon). It has no particular effect upon the meaning. As the last word on the list shows, the plural is formed by simply adding the syllable **tsho** to the end of the pronoun. So 'you' (plural) is **khyērang-tsho**.

khōng is also used as a polite address to a second person, particularly when one does not know that person's name (such as when trying to attract the attention of a stranger).

2 Basic verbs

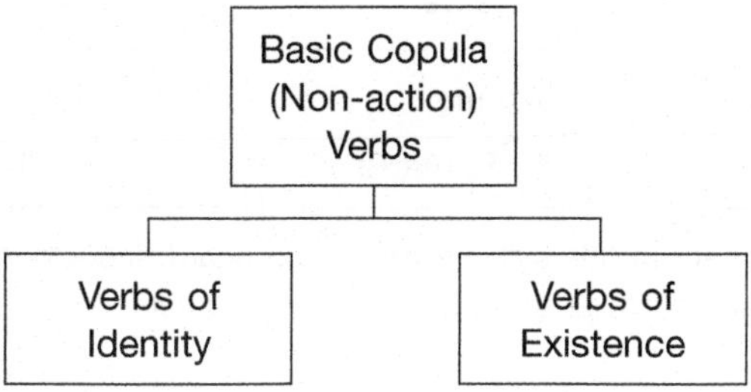

This is a **critical** verb distinction. The terms 'identity' and 'existence' here serve as rough guides to the type of sentences the respective verbs should be used in. Verbs of existence will be dealt with in Unit 4.

■ Verbs of identity

These only partly cover the same territory as the English verb 'to be', and should not be equated with that verb.

In basic statements, where no action verbs appear, **yi̲n** is normally used as the first person verb of identity, and **re̲'** is used for second and third persons.

(I/Tibetan/am)

ང་/བོད་པ་/ཡིན། **nga̲ phö̲pa yi̲n.** I am Tibetan.

(We/Tibetan/are)

ང་ཚོ་/བོད་པ་/ཡིན། **nga̲n-tsho̲ phö̲pa yi̲n.** We are Tibetan.

(You/foreign/are)

ཁྱེད་རང་/ཕྱི་རྒྱལ་བ་/རེད། **khyērang chīkyälwa re̲'.** You are foreign.

Verbs always end the sentence. They have the same form for both singular and plural, so **yi̲n** is used both with 'I' and 'we' in the above sentences. The subject usually begins the sentence, with the property assigned to it following.

(subject/property/verb)

ང་/བོད་པ་/ཡིན། **nga̱ phö̱pa yi̱n.** I am Tibetan.

There is no single negation term like 'not'. Instead, each verb has its own negated form, built around the consonant **m**. This either stands as a separate syllable, or is incorporated into the verb.

Affirmative	*Negative*	
ཡིན། **yi̱n**	མིན། **me̱:***	first person
རེད། **re̱'**	མ་རེད། **ma-re̱'**	second/third person

* The **n** consonant in this syllable cannot be heard. Instead it usually turns into a nasalisation, similar to that in the French article 'un'.

In Tibetan, there are no real equivalents to the English 'yes' or 'no'; verbs, such as the above (or their negated forms), double as responses. So to a question such as, 'Are you Lisa?' the Tibetan response could simply be **yi̱n**, or **me̱:**. A fuller answer to the question would be **yi̱n, nga̱ li̱sa yi̱n**; meaning something like, 'Yes, I am Lisa.' So the same word appears twice, first as an affirmative response, and second as a verb.

Exercise 1

Organise each set of three words to form a sentence and translate the sentences into English.

1	བསོད་ནམས།	**sōnam**	རེད	**re̱'**	བོད་པ	**phö̱pa**
2	(your name)		ཡིན	**yi̱n**	ང	**nga̱**
3	ཁྱེད་རང	**khyērang**	རེད	**re̱'**	ལི་ས	**li̱sa**
4	རེད	**re̱'**	ཕྱི་རྒྱལ་བ	**chīkyälwa**	མོ་རང	**mo̱rang**
5	མ་རེད	**ma-re̱'**	ཁོ་རང	**khōrang**	བསོད་ནམས	**sōnam**

Language point

3 Where to use verbs of identity

Here is a list of the type of things one can talk about using a verb of identity (**yi̱n** or **re̱'**).

- Personal identity (name)
- Nationality/ethnic group
- Gender
- Age
- Religion
- Profession, occupation, or temporary role
- Place of origin

However, unlike the English 'to be', these verbs are *never* used to express location (e.g. 'I am at home.'), temporary states and moods (e.g. 'I am happy', 'he is angry'), or various subjective statements (e.g. see Unit 6) So generally, they are used when describing more fixed features of a person or thing. (Perhaps the only exception to this is the question for 'are you well?' in Dialogue 1, which uses a verb of identity, but is asking about something changeable.) For example:

ཁོང་དགེ་རྒན་རེད།	**khōng ke̱kän re̱'.**	He is a teacher.
ང་ཁ་ཆེ་མིན།	**nga̱ khāche me̱:.**	I am not Muslim.

As explained in Language point 5, there is no equivalent for 'a/an' in these Tibetan sentences.

Vocabulary

བུ།	**phu̱**	boy	སྨན་པ།	**mān̄pa**	doctor
བུ་མོ།	**phu̱mo**	girl	ནང་པ།	**na̱ngpa**	Buddhist
དགེ་རྒན།	**ke̱kän**	teacher	ཁ་ཆེ།	**khāche**	Muslim
སློབ་ཕྲུག	**lōpṯhuk**	student			

Exercise 2

Translate these into Tibetan ((d) has been completed already):

(a) I am Duho.
(b) You are Sönam.
(c) She is Lisa.
(d) Duho is foreign, he's not Tibetan.
ཏུ་ཧོ་ཕྱི་རྒྱལ་བ་རེད། ཁོང་བོད་པ་མ་རེད།
tu̱ho chīkyä̱lwa re̱'. khōng phö̱pa ma-re̱'.

(e) Phuntshok is not a girl, he's a boy.
(f) Sönam is a Buddhist, not a Muslim.

Language points

4 Question forms

There are two basic ways to formulate a question in Tibetan; either:

1 Use a *question word*: these words are easy to identify; apart from the word for 'who' (སུ། **sū**), their first syllable is almost always ག། **kha̱**; e.g. 'what?' (ག་རེ། **kha̱re**), 'when?' (ག་དུས། **kha̱thü'**).
2 Add a *question-particle* straight after the verb, when asking the equivalent of yes/no questions. After **yi̱n**, the particle is pronounced **pä**, and after **re̱'** it is pronounced **wä**. But in both cases it is spelt པས།.

Listen to the examples on the audio to get a clear idea of the intonation used when asking a question. The most important thing is not to inject a foreign tone by rising on the last syllable.

Examples of the two question forms:

ཁོང་སུ་རེད།	**khōng sū re̱'.**	Who is he?
ཁོང་བསོད་ནམས་རེད་པས།	**khōng sō̄nam re̱'-wä.**	Is he Sönam?

The question-particle is also often used together with a negative, as Dialogue 2 will illustrate. The affirmative and negative versions of a question are:

མོ་རང་སློབ་ཕྲུག་རེད་པས།	**mo̱rang lōpṭhuk re̱'-wä.** Is she a student?
མོ་རང་སློབ་ཕྲུག་མ་རེད་པས།	**mo̱rang lōpṭhuk ma-re̱'-wä.** Isn't she a student?

5 Questions – the rule of anticipation

When making statements, the verb **yi̱n** is used for the first person(s), and **re̱'** for second or third person(s). But in Dialogue 1, in the question 'How are you?' **yi̱n** was obviously being addressed to the second person (you). The general rule is that when someone asks a question, the verb they use must be the one that they expect to hear in the answer; it *anticipates* the verb which will be heard in the response. So if I make a statement about you, the verb will be **re̱'**, such as:

ཁྱེད་རང་སློབ་ཕྲུག་རེད། **khyērang lōpṭhuk re̱'.** You are a student.

But when I ask you a question about yourself, I expect you to answer with the verb **yi̱n** (or **me̱:**), so I ask:

ཁྱེད་རང་སློབ་ཕྲུག་ཡིན་པས། **khyērang lōpṭhuk yi̱n-pä.**

Exercise 3

Checking against the English translations, fill in the blanks for the following questions with the correct verbs and question-particles (where necessary).

ཁྱེད་རང་སུ་……།	**khyērang sū . . .**	Who are you?
ཁྱེད་རང་ཉི་མ་……།	**khyērang nyi̱ma** (a personal name) **. . .**	Are you Nyima?
ཁོང་ཚོ་ནང་པ་མ་……།	**khōngtsho na̱ngpa ma . . .**	Aren't they Buddhist?
ཁྱེད་རང་དགེ་རྒན་……།	**khyērang ke̱kän . . .**	Aren't you a teacher?
ང་སློབ་ཕྲུག་……།	**nga̱ lōpṭhuk . . .**	Am I not a student?
བསོད་ནམས་ག་རེ་……།	**sönam kha̱re . . .**	What is Sönam? (e.g. a role)

Dialogue 2

(Audio 1:16)

Duho strikes up a conversation on a bus with an elderly man from a Tibetan village, who is rather inquisitive about various things Duho is carrying.

བོད་པ། དེ་ག་རེ་རེད།

ཏུ་ཧོ། འདི་ཁ་དཔར་རེད།

བོད་པ། པར་ཆས་མ་རེད་པས།
དུ་ཧོ། ཁ་དཔར་རེད། པར་ཆས་ཡང་(ཀྱང་)རེད།
བོད་པ། ཨ་ལས། དེ་ཚོ་ག་རེ་རེད།
དུ་ཧོ། འདི་ཚོ་སྨྱུ་གུ་རེད།
བོད་པ། འདི་ཆུ་རེད་པས།
དུ་ཧོ། མ་རེད། འདི་ཨ་རག་རེད།
བོད་པ། རེད་པས།
དུ་ཧོ། མ་རེད། ཆུ་རེད།

TIBETAN the̱ kha̱re re̱'.
DUHO ti̱ khāpar re̱'.
TIBETAN pārche ma-re̱'-wä.
DUHO khāpar re̱', pārche-yä re̱'.
TIBETAN ālä, the̱n-tsho kha̱re re̱'.
DUHO ti̱n-tsho nyūku re̱'.
TIBETAN ti̱ chū re̱'-wä.
DUHO ma-re̱', ti̱ ārak re̱'.
TIBETAN re̱'-wä.
DUHO ma-re̱', chū re̱'.

TIBETAN *What's that?*
DUHO *This is a [mobile] phone.*
TIBETAN *Isn't it a camera?*
DUHO *It's a camera, as well as a phone.*
TIBETAN *I see. What are those?*
DUHO *These are pens.*
TIBETAN *Is this water?*
DUHO (jokingly) *No, this is alcohol.*
TIBETAN *Is it?*
DUHO *No, it is water.*

Vocabulary

དེ།	**the̱**	that	འདི་ཚོ།	**ti̱n-tsho**	these
འདི།	**ti̱**	this	དེ་ཚོ།	**the̱n-tsho**	those
ག་རེ།	**kha̱re**	what?	སྨྱུ་གུ	**nyūku**	pen
ཁ་པར།	**khāpar**	phone	ཨ་རག	**ārak**	alcoholic spirits
པར་ཆས།	**pārche**	camera	ཆུ།	**chū**	water
ཡང་།*	**yä**	also	དེབ།	**the̱p**	book

* In literary Tibetan, the word for 'also' takes different forms, depending on the suffix of the preceding syllable (see Grammar section). As a compromise, I have used this spelling for 'also' throughout. When the correct literary form differs, it appears immediately afterwards, in brackets.

Language points

6 Single-plural

There are no single or plural forms for a noun. So **the̱p** can be translated as 'book' or 'books', depending on the situation. There is also no real equivalent of the indefinite article 'a/an'. You can of course attach a number to the item, when there is a need to indicate a specific quantity. Apart from that, the only real clue to whether someone is talking about one or many is **tsho**. The pluraliser **tsho** however, can only be added to:

(a) Personal pronouns (e.g. **nga̱n-tsho**)
(b) Demonstratives (e.g. **ti̱n-tsho**)

It should not be attached to nouns.

7 Demonstratives

English makes a two-way distinction, between 'this' and 'that'. In Tibetan, the speaker can actually make a five-fold distinction, when referring to something or someone in relation to him- or herself.

འདི།	**ti̱**	this
དེ།	**the̱**	that
ཕ་གི།	**phāki**	that (over there)
ཡ་གི།	**ya̱ki**	that (up there)
མ་གི།	**ma̱ki**	that (down there)

The last three are obviously linked, and each commonly has **the̱** added to them, to produce **phāki-the̱**, **ya̱ki-the̱**, and **ma̱ki-the̱**. Examples:

ཕ་གི་དེ་མོ་ཊ་རེད།	**phāki-the̱ mo̱ṭa re̱'.**	That (over there) is a car.
མ་གི་དེ་ཁྱི་རེད།	**ma̱ki-the̱ khyī re̱'.**	That (down there) is a dog.

It should be remembered that we are dealing with verbs of identity here. We can use the demonstratives to identify a thing *as* a car, a dog, etc., but not to locate it: we cannot yet say 'there is a dog, over there'.

Exercise 4

(a) Which of the following can the pluraliser **tsho** be directly attached to?

མོ་ཊ། **mo̱ṭa** ཁྱེད་རང་། **khyērang** ཆུ། **chū** དེ། **the̱** ཡིན། **yi̱n**

(b) As discussed in Unit 1, some syllable combinations bring about sound changes which are not reflected in the Tibetan script. One of these occurs when the syllable **tsho** is used. Look at the words in which **tsho** appears in this unit. What change does it bring about?

Exercise 5

Think again about the identity–existence distinction. If you had to translate the following English sentences into Tibetan ones, which of them would use a verb of identity?

1 We are sad.
2 Those (over there) are pens.
3 I am here.
4 Who is that (over there)?
5 The dog is not up there, it is down there.

Exercise 6

Using the new words below, translate these sentences into Tibetan ((a) has already been completed):

(a) This is a door. འདི་སྒོ་རེད། **ti̲ ko̲ re̲'.**
(b) That (up there) is a house.
(c) These are people.
(d) That is the ground.
(e) That (down there) is a bug.

ཁང་པ།	**khāngpa**	house/building
སྒོ།	**ko̲**	door
ས།	**sā**	ground
སྒེའུ་ཁུང་།	**ke̲khung**	window
མི།	**mi̲**	person
འབུ།	**pu̲**	creature/bug

Exercise 7

1 Translate the following statements:

(a) དེ་སྒེའུ་ཁུང་རེད། **the̲ ke̲khung re̲'.**
(b) ཁྱེད་རང་ཕུན་ཚོགས་མ་རེད། **khyērang phūntshok ma-re̲'.**
(c) ཁོང་ཚོ་སྨན་པ་རེད། **khōng-tsho mānpa re̲'.**
(d) ཁྱེད་རང་བོད་པ་རེད། **khyērang phö̲pa re̲'.**

2 Keeping the same subjects, change the statements of (1) into questions.

Unit Three

ཁྱེད་རང་ག་ནས་ཡིན།

khyērang khanä yin

Where are you from?

In this unit you will learn how to:

- seek personal details
- talk about identity (name, place of birth, age)
- express possession
- count
- use question 'tags'
- say the days of the week

Dialogue 1

(Audio 1:20)

Thinking that Duho is Tibetan, someone approaches him, and starts asking about Lisa, who doesn't look Tibetan.

བོད་པ། མོ་རང་ག་ནས་རེད།

ཌུ་ཧོ། མོ་རང་ཨ་རི་ནས་རེད།

བོད་པ། ཨ་ལས། མོ་རང་བོད་རིགས་མ་རེད་པས།

ཌུ་ཧོ། མ་རེད། བོད་རིགས་མ་རེད།

བོད་པ། ཨེ་ན། ཁྱེད་རང་ལུང་པ་ག་ནས་ཡིན།

ཌུ་ཧོ། ང་ཀོ་རི་ཡ་ནས་ཡིན།

བོད་པ།	ཀོ་རི་ཡ། ཨ། ཁྱེད་རང་བོད་པ་མིན་པས།
ཏུ་ཧོ།	མིན། ངོས་གནས་མིན། ང་ཕྱི་རྒྱལ་ནས་ཡིན།

TIBETAN	mo̱rang kha̱nä re̱'.
DUHO	mo̱rang āri-nä re̱'.
TIBETAN	ālä, mo̱rang phö̱rik ma-re̱'-wä.
DUHO	ma-re̱' phö̱rik ma-re̱'.
TIBETAN	ēni, khyērang lu̱ngpa kha̱nä yi̱n.
DUHO	nga̱ kōriya-nä yi̱n.
TIBETAN	kō-ri-ya, ā, khyērang phö̱pa me̱:-pä.
DUHO	me̱:, ngōnä' me̱:. nga̱ chīkyäl-nä yi̱n.

TIBETAN	*Where is she from?*
DUHO	*She's from America.*
TIBETAN	*Oh, she isn't a Tibetan then?*
DUHO	*No, she isn't a Tibetan.*
TIBETAN	*And which area are you from?*
DUHO	*I'm from Korea.*
TIBETAN	*Ko . . . re . . . a . . . What, aren't you Tibetan?*
DUHO	*No, really I'm not. I'm from abroad.*

Vocabulary

ག་ནས།	**khanä**	where from?
ནས།	**nä'**	from
ཨ་རི།	**āri**	America (USA)
རྒྱལ་ཁབ།	**kyälkhap**	country
ཕ་ཡུལ།	**phāyül**	land (see below)
བོད་རིགས།	**phörik**	Tibetan (ethnic group)
རྒྱ་རིགས།	**kyarik**	Han Chinese
དངོས་གནས།	**ngönä'**	really/seriously; real
ཨ།	**ā**	what? (exclamation)
ལུང་པ།	**lungpa**	country/area

Cultural point

Places of origin

khyērang khanä yin is the simplest way to ask where someone is from. If one inserts the word **kyälkhap**, i.e. **khyērang kyälkhap khanä yin**, it becomes an enquiry about which nation/state the person belongs to. When the person being asked is assumed *not* to be Tibetan, the term **lungpa** can substitute **kyälkhap**, without affecting the meaning. To a Tibetan, the question about his or her **lungpa** or **phāyül** (literally, 'father('s)-land') will be understood as an enquiry about the *area* in Tibet he or she hails from. A Tibetan's place of origin has huge cultural significance. It is one of the principal markers of identity, and an enquiry about it usually crops up very early in the conversation.

Tibet (བོད། **phö'**) has traditionally been divided into three major provinces: དབུས་གཙང་། (**ü'-tsang**) 'Central' Tibet (traditionally including Western Tibet), ཁམས། (**khām**), and ཨ་མདོ། (**āmto**); the latter two comprising East Tibet.

Countries bordering Tibet, or those with which it had some historical relations, have proper Tibetan names. Names of the remainder are based upon those used either in English or Chinese. Some of the most commonly encountered are:

རྒྱ་གར།	**kya̱kar**	India	སུད་སི།	**sū̱si**	Switzerland
རྒྱ་ནག	**kya̱nak**	China	དབྱིན་ཡུལ།	**īnyül**	England
བལ་ཡུལ།	**phä̱lyül**	Nepal	དབྱིན་ལན།	**īnlän**	
སོག་ཡུལ།	**sōkyül**	Mongolia			
འབྲུག་ཡུལ།	**ṭu̱kyül**	Bhutan			

When Tibetan (or some foreign) place-names have either a པ། (**pa**) or བ། (pronounced **wa**) attached at the end, they denote someone from that place. Hence a Tibetan is a བོད་པ། (**phö̱pa**). In fewer cases, པོ། (**po**) replaces the last syllable of the country's name to denote the person.

Exercise 1

Try, without the aid of transliterated versions of the names, to identify the following places and peoples. In one case you must use your imagination a bit.

(a) ཨ་མདོ་བ།

(b) ལྷ་ས་བ།

(c) སོག་པོ།

(d) རྒྱ་གར་བ།

(e) འཇར་མན།

(f) འབྲུག་པ།

Dialogue 2

(Audio 1:21)

Duho and Sönam are catching up over tea. Duho still has difficulties with Tibetan polite forms, so he's quite happy to follow Sönam's lead, and speak informally. Sönam returns, after stepping out for a moment.

བསོད་ནམས། ངའི་ཇ་ག་གི་རེད། འདི་རེད་པས།

ཏུ་ཧོ། དེ་ངའི་རེད། ཁྱེད་རང་གི་ཇ་འདི་རེད།

བསོད་ནམས། ཁྱེད་རང་གི་རོགས་པའི་མིང་ལི་ས་རེད་པ།

ཏུ་ཧོ། རེད།

བསོད་ནམས། ལི་ས་ལོ་ག་ཚོད་རེད།

ཏུ་ཧོ། ལི་ས་ལོ་སུམ་ཅུ་སོ་གཅིག་རེད།
བསོད་ནམས། ཁྱེད་རང་ཡང་ལོ་སུམ་ཅུ་སོ་གཅིག་ཡིན་པ།
ཏུ་ཧོ། མིན། ང་ལོ་ཉི་ཤུ་རྩ་དགུ་ཡིན། ད་ལྟ་གཞོན་གཞོན་ཡིན།
བསོད་ནམས། ལི་ས་ཡང་(འང་)ལས་བྱེད་རེད་པས།
ཏུ་ཧོ། མ་རེད། མོ་རང་དགེ་རྒན་རེད།
བསོད་ནམས། ཨ་ལས། ཁྱེད་རང་གཉིས་དགའ་པོ་ཡིན་པས།
ཏུ་ཧོ། མིན། ལི་ས་ངའི་གྲོགས་པོ་རེད། ཡིན་ནའང་ང་གཉིས་དགའ་པོ་མིན།

SÖNAM ngä̱: cha̱ kha̱ki re̱'. ti̱ re̱'-wä.
DUHO the̱ ngä̱: re̱'. khyērang-ki cha̱ ti̱ re̱'.
SÖNAM khyērang-ki ro̱kpä: mi̱ng li̱sa re̱'-wa.
DUHO re̱'.
SÖNAM li̱sa lo̱ kha̱tshȫ' re̱'.
DUHO li̱sa lo̱ sūmcu-socīk re̱'.
SÖNAM khyērang-yä lo̱ sūmcu-socīk yi̱n-pa.
DUHO me̱:, nga̱ lo̱ nyi̱shu-tsaku̱ yi̱n. tha̱nta shö̱nshön yi̱n.
SÖNAM li̱sa-yä lä̱che' re̱'-wa.
DUHO ma-re̱', mo̱rang ke̱kän re̱'.
SÖNAM ālä, khyērang-nyī' ka̱wo yi̱n-pä.
DUHO me̱:, li̱sa ngä̱: ṭho̱kpo re̱'. yi̱nnä: nga̱-nyī' ka̱wo me̱:.

SÖNAM *Which is my tea? Is it this one?*
DUHO *That one is mine. Your tea is this one.*
SÖNAM *Your companion's name is Lisa, isn't it?*
DUHO *Yes.*
SÖNAM *How old is Lisa?*
DUHO *Lisa is thirty-one.*
SÖNAM *You're also thirty-one, aren't you?*
DUHO *No, I am twenty-nine.* (jokingly) *I am still young.*
SÖNAM *Is Lisa also a civil servant?*
DUHO *No, she's a teacher.*
SÖNAM *I see. Are you two partners?*
DUHO *No. Lisa is a friend, but we are not partners.*

Vocabulary

ཇ།	**cha̱**	tea
ག་གི།	**kha̱ki**	which?
ངའི།	**ngä̱:**	my/mine
ལོ།	**lo̱**	year
ཡིན་པ།	**yi̱n-pa**	aren't you?
ཡིན་ནའང་།	**yi̱nnä:**	but
ཁྱེད་རང་གི།	**khyērang-ki**	your/yours
ག་ཚོད།	**kha̱tshō'**	how many/much?
དགའ་པོ།	**ka̱wo**	partner (boyfriend/girlfriend)
ཉི་ཤུ་རྩ་དགུ།	**nyi̱shu-tsaku̱**	twenty-nine
སུམ་ཅུ་སོ་གཅིག	**sūmcu-socīk**	thirty-one
ད་ལྟ།	**tha̱nta**	still/now/at present
གྲོགས་པོ།	**ṭho̱kpo**	friend
རོགས་པ།	**ro̱kpa**	companion/associate
ལས་བྱེད།	**lä̱che'**	civil servant/office worker
གཞོན་གཞོན།	**shö̱nshön**	young
ཁྱེད་རང་གཉིས།	**khyērang-nyī'**	you two
ང་གཉིས།	**nga̱-nyī'**	we (two)

Language point

1 Possessive pronouns

Adding one of two particles (འི། or གི།) to a personal pronoun (I, you, etc.) changes it into a possessive pronoun (my, your, etc.). These particles are discussed further below.

ངའི།	**ngä̱:**	my/mine
ང་ཚོའི།	**nga̱n-tshö:**	our/ours
ཁྱེད་རང་གི།	**khyērang-ki**	your/yours (singular)
ཁྱེད་རང་ཚོའི།	**khyērang-tshö:**	your/yours (plural)

ཁོང་གི།	**khōng-ki**	his/hers
ཁོང་ཚོའི།	**khōng-tshö:**	their/theirs
མོ་རང་གི།	**morang-ki**	her/hers
ཁོ་རང་གི།	**khōrang-ki**	his

Exercise 2

Translate the following into Tibetan (the first one has already been completed):

1 your name ཁྱེད་རང་གི་མིང་། **khyērang-ki ming**
2 our friends
3 her teacher
4 their dog
5 That is your (plural) book.
6 Those are not ours.

Language point

2 Cardinal numbers

		0–9				10–19	
༠	ཀླད་ཀོར།	**lākor**	zero	༡༠	བཅུ།	**cū**	ten
༡	གཅིག།	**cīk**	one	༡༡	བཅུ་གཅིག།	**cūcīk**	eleven
༢	གཉིས།	**nyī'**	two	༡༢	བཅུ་གཉིས།	**cūnyī'**	twelve
༣	གསུམ།	**sūm**	three	༡༣	བཅུ་གསུམ།	**cūksūm**	thirteen
༤	བཞི།	**shi**	four	༡༤	བཅུ་བཞི།	**cūpshi**	fourteen
༥	ལྔ།	**ngā**	five	༡༥	བཅོ་ལྔ།	**cōngā**	fifteen
༦	དྲུག།	**thuk**	six	༡༦	བཅུ་དྲུག།	**cūthuk**	sixteen
༧	བདུན།	**tün**	seven	༡༧	བཅུ་བདུན།	**cūptün**	seventeen
༨	བརྒྱད།	**kyä'**	eight	༡༨	བཅོ་བརྒྱད།	**cōpkyä'**	eighteen
༩	དགུ།	**ku**	nine	༡༩	བཅུ་དགུ།	**cūrku**	nineteen

Apart from 20 (ཉི་ཤུ། **nyishu**), 30, 40, etc. are formed by adding the number ten after the number for three, four, etc. So:

བཅུ་གསུམ། **cūksūm** thirteen

སུམ་ཅུ། **sūmcū** thirty

Fifty is ལྔ་བཅུ། **ngācu** and so forth. The Grammar section has full details of the slight variations in spelling here, as well as the higher numbers.

Each set of ten has its own extra numerical particle:

20 – རྩ། **tsā**	30 – སོ། **sō**	40 – ཞེ། **she̱**	50 – ང་། **nga̱**
60 – རེ། **re̱**	70 – དོན། **thö̱n**	80 – གྱ། **khya̱**	90 – གོ། **kho̱**

One of these must be inserted between the tens and the units to form 21–29, 31–39, etc.:

ཉི་ཤུ + རྩ + གཅིག = 21 (**nyi̱shu-tsacīk**)
བདུན་ཅུ + དོན + དྲུག = 76 (**tüncu-thö̱nṭhuk**)

In numbers beyond 10, there are many 'invisible suffixes' (of the type described in Unit 1). These extra sounds almost always occur when the unit is either 3, 4, 5, 7, or 8. Check the audio for these.

Exercise 3

Write these numbers in Tibetan:

(a) 23
(b) 48
(c) 85
(d) 66
(e) 77
(f) 52
(g) 99

Language point

3 Word order

Look at this sentence: འདི་དེབ་རེད། **ti̱ the̱p re̱'.** ('This is a book.')

In such simple sentences, a demonstrative such as **ti̱** ('this') or **the̱** ('that') is the subject; it is the first word in the sentence. But whenever the demonstrative is attached to a noun (i.e. 'this box', 'that person'), it is placed *after* that noun. The word order is basically the opposite of the English; 'that friend' in Tibetan is གྲོགས་པོ་དེ། **ṭho̱kpo-the̱**.

Adjectives (colours, numbers, etc.) also come after the noun, with the demonstrative last in the order:

'That black book' is དེབ་ནག་པོ་དེ། **thep nakpo the.**

In Tibetan, there is no direct equivalent for 'the'. But **the** will often appear in a Tibetan sentence where one would expect to find 'the' or 'it' in English.

Exercise 4

Translate these into Tibetan:

1 the Lhasan
2 this white (དཀར་པོ། **kārpo**) car
3 these people from Kham
4 pens
5 the clean (གཙང་མ། **tsāngma**) water
6 those countries

Dialogue 3

(Audio 1:22)
Duho shows photos from home to Sönam, who asks about the people and things in them.

བསོད་ནམས། མི་འདི་སུ་རེད།
ཏུ་ཧོ། ངའི་ཕ་ལགས་ཀྱི་ཛོ་ཞེས་པ་རེད།
བསོད་ནམས། ཁྱེད་རང་གི་གྲོགས་པོ་མ་རེད་པ།
ཏུ་ཧོ། མ་རེད། ཡིན་ནའང་ཁོ་རང་གི་བུ་ངའི་གྲོགས་པོ་རེད།
བསོད་ནམས། ཁང་པ་དེ་སུའི་རེད།
ཏུ་ཧོ། མི་དེའི་ནང་རེད།
བསོད་ནམས། ཁོ་རང་རྒྱ་ཕྱུགས་པོ་རེད་པས།
ཏུ་ཧོ། རེད། ཁོ་རང་ཚོང་པ་རེད། མི་སྐད་གྲགས་ཆེན་པོ་རེད།
བསོད་ནམས། ཁོ་རང་ཚོང་ཁང་མང་པོའི་བདག་པོ་རེད་པས།
ཏུ་ཧོ། རེད། ཟ་ཁང་གི་བདག་པོ་ཡང་(འང་)རེད།
བསོད་ནམས། ཟ་ཁང་དེ་ཚོ་ཀོ་རི་ཡའི་ཟ་ཁང་རེད་པས།
ཏུ་ཧོ། མ་རེད། དེ་ཚོ་རྒྱ་མིའི་ཟ་ཁང་རེད།

SÖNAM mi̱ ti̱ sū re̱'.
DUHO ngä̱: pāla:-ki ngo̱shēnpa re̱'.
SÖNAM khyērang-ki ṭho̱kpo ma-re̱'-wa.
DUHO ma-re̱', yi̱nnä: khōrang-ki phu̱ ngä̱: ṭho̱kpo re̱'.
SÖNAM khāngpa-the sǖ: re̱'.
DUHO mi̱ the̱: na̱ng re̱'.
SÖNAM khōrang kyu̱chūkpo re̱'-wä.
DUHO re̱', khōrang tshōngpa re̱'. mi̱ kā̈ṭhak-chēnpo re̱'.
SÖNAM khōrang tshōngkhang ma̱ngpö: ta̱kpo re̱'-wä.
DUHO re̱', sa̱khang-ki ta̱kpo-yä re̱'.
SÖNAM sa̱khang the̱ntsho koriyä: sa̱khang re̱'-wä.
DUHO ma̱-re̱', the̱ntsho kya̱mi:-sa̱khang re̱'.

SÖNAM *Who is this man?*
DUHO *He's an acquaintance of my father.*
SÖNAM *He isn't your friend then?*
DUHO *No, but his son is a friend of mine.*
SÖNAM *Whose is this building?*
DUHO *It is that man's home.*
SÖNAM *Is he wealthy?*
DUHO *Yes, he's a businessman. He's a prominent person.*
SÖNAM *Is he the owner of many shops?*
DUHO *Yes, he's also a restaurant owner.*
SÖNAM *Are they Korean restaurants?*
DUHO *No, they're Chinese restaurants.*

Vocabulary

ངོ་ཤེས་པ།	**ngo̱shēnpa**	acquaintance
པ་ལགས།	**pāla:**	father
བདག་པོ།	**ta̱kpo**	owner
སུའི།	**sǖ:**	whose?
(རྒྱུ་)ཕྱུག་པོ།	**(kyu̱-)chūkpo**	wealthy
མ་རེད་པ།	**ma-re̱'-wa**	(question tag; see below)
རྒྱ་མིའི་ཟ་ཁང་།	**kya̱mi:-sa̱khang**	Chinese restaurant
སྐད་གྲགས་ཆེན་པོ།	**kā̈ṭhak-chēnpo**	famous/prominent

བུ།	**phu̱**	son (preceded by genitive particle; i.e. 'son of . . .')
ཚོང་པ།	**tshōngpa**	trader/business person
ཚོང་ཁང་།	**tshōngkhang**	shop
མང་པོ།	**ma̱ngpo**	many/much
ནང་།	**na̱ng**	home
ཟ་ཁང་།	**sa̱khang**	restaurant

Language point

4 The genitive particle (འབྲེལ་སྒྲ།)

The genitive particle (**te̱lta**) corresponds in function to *-'s* and *of* in English. Like other Tibetan particles, it comes after the word it refers to. In written form, there are four versions of the particle: ཀྱི་གི་གྱི་འི།. The one used will depend upon the suffix-ending of the word it is attached to (for more details, see the Grammar section).

In *spoken* Tibetan however, the first three of these four are not distinguished; they are pronounced uniformly as **ki**. So you only have to decide between two sounds: **ki** and **i**. These sounds were encountered earlier, when changing personal into possessive pronouns.

ki – use this form of the particle when connecting to a word ending with a *consonant* in written Tibetan. It forms a separate syllable from the word to which it is attached:

e.g. ཟ་ཁང་། → ཟ་ཁང་གི – 'the restaurant' → 'the restaurant's'
sa̱khang → **sa̱khang-ki**

i (འི།) – use this form of the particle when connecting to a word which does not end with a consonant. It is incorporated into the last syllable of that word, creating a long vowel sound:

e.g. སུ → སུའི། – 'who' → 'whose?' (*lit.* 'of who?')
sū → **sǖ:**

To sum up: when speaking, there are only two forms of the genitive particle to choose from; a consonant and a vowel. Use the consonant after those words that end with a consonant in their written form, and the vowel after those that end with a vowel.

Exercise 5

Translate the following:

1 བསོད་ནམས་ཀྱི་དགེ་རྒན། **sōnam-ki ke̲kän**
2 ཉི་མའི་དཔར་ཆས། **nyi̲mä: pārche**
3 the boy's house
4 the wealthy man's house
5 this tea's name

Language point

5 Question tags

Dropping the last letter of the question-particle, like this:

རེད་པས། **re̲'-wä** → རེད་པ། **re̲'-wa**

produces a structure frequently used when stressing a point, seeking to confirm information, or simply stating something that is believed to be incontestable. It shares similarities with question tags in English (such as 'isn't it?'), attached to a question such as, 'Today is Thursday, isn't it?' The Tibetan version does not necessarily require a response; the expectation is always that the listener will or should agree with what is being said.

It can be used either in affirmative or negative forms, and incorporated into a sentence, or used as a stand-alone response.

Examples:

ཁྱེད་རང་ཕྱུགས་པོ་ཡིན་པ།	**khyērang chūkpo yi̲n-pa.** You're wealthy, aren't you?
དེ་བདེན་པ་མ་རེད་པ།	**the̲ te̲npa ma-re̲'-wa.** That's not true, is it?
མི་དེ་སྐད་གྲགས་ཆེན་པོ་རེད།	**mi̲-the kǟṭhak-chēnpo re̲'.** That person is famous.
རེད་པ།	**re̲'-wa.** Yes (he is, isn't he?)

This structure, like the real question forms, follows the rule of anticipation (Unit 2).

Exercise 6

Add the missing tag endings:

(a) This water is clean, isn't it?
ཆུ་འདི་གཙང་མ……། **chū ti̱ tsāngma . . .**

(b) She is your daughter, isn't she?
མོ་རང་ཁྱེད་རང་གི་བུ་མོ……། **mo̱rang khyērang-ki phu̱mo . . .**

(c) They are teachers, aren't they?
ཁོང་ཚོ་དགེ་རྒན……། **khōng-tsho ke̱kän . . .**

(d) I'm not Tibetan, am I?
ང་བོད་པ……། **nga̱ phö̱pa . . .**

(e) You are my friend, aren't you?
ཁྱེད་རང་ངའི་གྲོགས་པོ……། **khyērang ngä̱: ṭho̱kpo . . .**

■ Days of the week

གཟའ་ཟླ་བ།	**sa̱-ta̱wa**	Monday
གཟའ་མིག་དམར།	**sa̱-mikmār**	Tuesday
གཟའ་ལྷག་པ།	**sa̱-lhākpa**	Wednesday
གཟའ་ཕུར་བུ།	**sa̱-phūrpu**	Thursday
གཟའ་པ་སངས།	**sa̱-pāsang**	Friday
གཟའ་སྤེན་པ།	**sa̱-pēnpa**	Saturday
གཟའ་ཉི་མ།	**sa̱-nyi̱ma**	Sunday

sa̱ appears in each of the names, paralleling the English word 'day'. But the general term for day, as a time-period (e.g. 'two days') is ཉིན་མ། **nyi̱ma**. བདུན་ཕྲག **tü̱nṭhak** means 'week', although for Tibetans outside Tibet, **hapta** (Persian via Hindi) is prevalent.

Exercise 7 **(Audio 1:30)**

All the numbers you hear recited for Exercise 7 on the audio are from the list below. Try to recognise them. Then take the letters associated with them on the list, and rearrange them, to form the name of a day in the week.

17	8	24	6	30	14	77	41	5	61
ཉ	ཏ	ས	པ	◌ི	ང	ན	◌ུ	ཕ	ད
4	80	74	95	12	0	2	39	44	9
ལ	ཏ	ག	མ	ར	འ	◌ེ	ཟ	ལ	བ

Unit Four

བཀྲ་ཤིས་ག་པར་འདུག

ṭāshi kha̲wa: tu̲'

Where is Tashi?

In this unit you will learn how to:

- ask about locations (of people and places)
- use verbs of existence
- describe where things are
- give directions
- express 'to have'
- use names for family members

Dialogue 1

(Audio 1:31)

Duho is looking for Tashi. He enters the shop of Lhamo and Tenzin (two Tibetan acquaintances), where he finds Lhamo.

ཧུ་ཧོ། བཀྲ་ཤིས་འདིར་འདུག་གས།
ལྷ་མོ། འདིར་མི་འདུག
ཧུ་ཧོ། འོ་ན་ག་པར་འདུག
ལྷ་མོ། ནང་ལ་མི་འདུག་གས།
ཧུ་ཧོ། མི་འདུག ང་ད་གིན་བཀྲ་ཤིས་ཀྱི་ནང་ལ་ཡོད། ཡིན་ནའང་ཁོ་རང་མི་འདུག
ལྷ་མོ། ལས་ཁུངས་ལ་མི་འདུག་གས།
ཧུ་ཧོ། ལས་ཁུངས་ལ་ཡང་(འང་)མི་འདུག
བསྟན་འཛིན། བཀྲ་ཤིས་ད་ལྟ་ཕ་གིའི་ཇ་ཁང་ལ་འདུག
ཧུ་ཧོ། ཁོ་རང་མཉམ་དུ་མི་འདུག་གས།
བསྟན་འཛིན། ཁོ་རང་མཉམ་དུ་མི་ཁ་ཤས་འདུག ཚང་མ་བཀྲ་ཤིས་ཀྱི་ལས་རོགས་རེད།

DUHO	ṭāshi tä̱: tu̱'-kä.
LHAMO	tä̱: mi̱n-tu̱'.
DUHO	o̱na kha̱wa: tu̱'.
LHAMO	na̱ng-la min-tu̱'-kä.
DUHO	min-tu̱'. nga̱ tha̱ncin ṭāshi-ki na̱ng-la yö̱'. yi̱nnä: khōrang min-tu̱'.
LHAMO	lä̱khung-la min-tu̱'-kä.
DUHO	lä̱khung-la-yä: min-tu̱'.
	(*Tenzin arrives, catching the conversation*)
TENZIN	ṭāshi tha̱nta phāki: cha̱khang-la tu̱'.
DUHO	khōrang nyāmtu mi̱ tu̱'-kä.
TENZIN	khōrang nyāmtu mi̱ khāshä' tu̱'. tshāngma ṭāshi-ki lä̱rok re̱'.

DUHO	*Is Tashi here?*
LHAMO	*No, he's not here.*
DUHO	*Well, where is he?*
LHAMO	*Isn't he at home?*
DUHO	*No, I was just at his home, but he wasn't there.*
LHAMO	*Isn't he in the office?*
DUHO	*He isn't in the office either.*
	(Tenzin arrives, catching the conversation)
TENZIN	*Tashi's at the teahouse over there now.*
DUHO	*Is there anyone with him?*
TENZIN	*There are several people together with him. They're all Tashi's work colleagues.*

Vocabulary

བཀྲ་ཤིས།	**ṭāshi**	(personal name)
འདིར།	**tä̱:**	here
ག་པར།	**kha̱wa:**	where?
འོ་ན།	**o̱na**	so/well then
ལ།	**la**	at/in (see below)
མཉམ་དུ།	**nyāmtu**	together/with

འདུག།	**tu̲'**	is/are (verb of existence)
གས།	**kä**	(question-particle for **tu̲'**)
མི།	**min**	(negating particle for **tu̲'**)
ཡོད།	**yö̲'**	am/are (verb of existence)
མེད།	**me̲'**	(negation of **yö̲'**)
བསྟན་འཛིན།	**tā̲ntsin**	(personal name)
ལྷ་མོ།	**lhāmo**	(personal name)
ཇ་ཁང་།	**cha̲khang**	teahouse
ཡང་།	**yä**	neither (with negation)
ནང་།	**na̲ng**	home
ད་གིན།	**tha̲ncin**	just before/just now
ཚང་མ།	**tshāngma**	all; everything
མི།	**mi̲**	someone/anyone
ཁ་ཤས།	**khāshä'**	several
ལས་ཁུངས།	**lä̲khung**	office
ལས་རོགས།	**lä̲rok**	colleague

Language points

1 Verbs of existence

Dialogue 1 introduces verbs of existence. They are used here because the sentences are about *location*. As with the verbs of identity, there are two separate ones; **tu̲'** is used for the second and third person (roughly equivalent to 'is' and 'are'), whereas **yö̲'**, the abbreviated form of **yö̲'pa**, is used for the first (similar to 'am' and 'are').

2 The ལ་དོན། (la̲thön) particle

Sentences showing location also require a particle, known as the **la̲thön**. This particle has multiple functions. Here, it marks out the location in the sentence, and translates roughly as 'at', or 'in'. In the spoken language, the particle will take one of two forms: ལ། or ར།:

- **la** can follow *any* location, as a separate syllable, e.g. **lä̱khung-la** 'at the office'.
- **ra** is used less, and only when the location does not end in a (written) consonant, so that it may be incorporated into the word, e.g. ལྷ་སར། **lhāsar** 'in Lhasa'.

The most important use of this **ra** is when it is incorporated into the demonstratives such as 'this' and 'that', to form 'here', 'there', etc.

འདི།	**ti̱**	'this'	→	འདིར།	**tä̱:**	'here'
དེ།	**the̱**	'that'	→	དེར།	**thä̱:**	'there'

And ཕ་གིར། **phākä:** ཡ་གིར། **ya̱kä:** མ་གིར། **ma̱kä:** are 'over there', 'up there', and 'down there'. It is the same **ra** in the word 'where?' (ག་པར། **kha̱wa:**). But in such words one hears no real **ra**-sound. As the transliteration shows, it often manifests as a long vowel sound. On other occasions (time-words, discussed below) it does not affect the sound.

Exercise 1

Following the example of 1, add the appropriate **la̱thön**-forms to these locations, and translate them:

1 བོད་...། **phö̱' . . .** བོད་ལ། **phö̱'-la . . .** in Tibet
2 རྒྱ་གར་...། **kya̱kar . . .**
3 ཚོང་ཁང་འདི་...། **tshōngkhang ti̱ . . .**
4 ཟ་ཁང་གཉིས་...། **sa̱khang nyī' . . .**
5 ལུང་པ་དེ་...། **lu̱ngpa the̱ . . .**
6 ལྷ་མོའི་ནང་...། **lhāmö:-na̱ng . . .**

Exercise 2

Translate the following into Tibetan:

1 I'm in Nepal.
2 Sönam isn't here.
3 Is Lhamo in the shop?
4 We're not at home.
5 Is he at the teahouse?
6 Are you with friends?

Language point

3 The implied subject

Just as in English, pronouns, similar to 'he', 'she', 'that', etc. are used in Tibetan, to avoid repetition of the subject. However, unlike English, it is *extremely* common in Tibetan to omit the subject altogether, when it is assumed that it is clear from the conversation. For instance in Dialogue 1, Lhamo uses neither a name nor a pronoun to refer to Tashi in her answer to the first question, because it is obvious who she's talking about.

Exercise 3

Return to Dialogue 1, and count how many times the subject is implied, rather than stated.

Language point

4 Copulas in different times

Copula verbs are used in sentences about the present and the past (sentences about the future require certain action verbs, described from Unit 11 onwards). However, copulas do not vary according to time. So **yö̱'** might indicate either that I 'am', or I 'was' in a certain place. Apart from context, the main way to indicate different times is to add a time word or phrase, such as **tha̱nta** and **tha̱ncin** in Dialogue 1, towards the beginning of the sentence. A sentence without such a term is generally assumed to refer to the present.

སྔོན་མར།	**ngā̄nma**	in the past/used to
དེང་སང་།	**the̱ngsang**	these days
དེ་རིང་།	**the̱ring**	today
ཁས་ས།	**khā̄sa**	yesterday
དེ་དུས།	**the̱thü'**	at that time
རྟག་པར།	**tākpa**	always

In written Tibetan, some of these terms require a **lạthön**-particle, whereas others do not. When a preposition (such as 'in' or 'at') is needed in English, a **lạthön** is *usually* required in Tibetan. However, this **lạthön**-particle is already incorporated into the word, as a **ra**, and in the spoken language is silent.

Exercise 4

Translate the following into Tibetan:

1 Where are you?
2 No, we weren't at home yesterday.
3 Is Tashi in the office today?
4 There were five people here just before, now there are (only) four.
5 Where was your friend at that time?

Dialogue 2

(Audio 1:32)
Yeshe is looking for a hotel to stay in. He asks a woman in a shop.

ཡེ་ཤེས། ཨ་ཅག་ལགས། འདི་པར་མགྲོན་ཁང་ཡོད་རེད་པས།

བུད་མེད། ཡོད་རེད། གཞུང་གི་མགྲོན་ཁང་ཡ་གིར་ཡོད་རེད། ཡིན་ནའང་ཏོག་ཙམ་ཐག་རིང་པོ་ཡོད་རེད། གོང་ཆེན་པོ་ཡང་(འང་)རེད།

ཡེ་ཤེས། གཞན་དག་ཡོད་མ་རེད་པས།

བུད་མེད། ཡོད་རེད། གངས་ལྗོངས་མགྲོན་ཁང་ཟེར་མཁན་གཅིག་ཡོད་རེད། དེ་བོད་པའི་མགྲོན་ཁང་རེད། སྲང་ལམ་ཆེན་པོ་ལ་ཡོད་རེད། ཁྲུ་སིམ་པོ་ཡོད་མ་རེད། ཡིན་ནའང་ཐག་ཉེ་པོ་དང་སྐྱབས་བདེ་པོ་ཡོད་རེད།

ཡེ་ཤེས། ལམ་ཁ་ག་གི་རེད།

བུད་མེད། ཕ་གི་ལ་ཁང་པ་དཀར་པོ་ཁ་ཤས་འདུག་ག སྲང་ལམ་ཆེན་པོ་ཁང་པ་དེ་ཚོའི་རྒྱབ་ལོགས་ལ་ཡོད་རེད།

ཡེ་ཤེས། ཨེ་ནི་འདི་ནས་སྐར་མ་ག་ཚོད་ཀྱི་ལམ་ཁ་རེད།

བུད་མེད། གངས་ལྗོངས་མགྲོན་ཁང་འདི་ནས་སྐར་མ་བཅུའི་ལམ་ཁ་རེད། སྲང་ལམ་གྱི་ཚུར་ཕྱོགས་ལ་དེབ་ཚོང་ཁང་ཡོད་རེད། དེའི་རྩ་ལ་ཡོད་རེད།

ཡེ་ཤེས། འོ་ཡ་ཨ་ཅག་ལགས།

བུད་མེད། འོ་ཡ།

YESHE āca-la:, ti̱wa: ṭö̱nkhang yo̱re'-wä.

WOMAN yo̱re'. shu̱ng-ki ṭö̱nkhang ya̱ki: yo̱re'. yi̱nnä: tēts thā-ri̱ngpo yo̱re'. kho̱ngchēnpo-yä re̱'.

YESHE shä̱nthak yo̱ ma-re̱'-wä.

WOMAN yo̱re'. kha̱ngcong ṭö̱nkhang se̱rkhän-cik yo̱re'. the̱ phö̱pä: ṭö̱nkhang re̱'. sānglam chēnpo-la yo̱re'. khūsimpo yo̱ ma-re̱'. yi̱nnä: thā-nye̱po tha̱ng tāpte̱po yo̱re'.

YESHE la̱mkha kha̱ki re̱'.

WOMAN pha̱ki-la khāngpa kārpo khāshä' tu̱'-ka. sānglam chēnpo khāngpa the̱ntshö: kya̱plo-la yo̱re'.

YESHE ēni, ti̱nä kārma kha̱tshȫ-ki la̱mkha re̱'.

WOMAN kha̱ngcong ṭö̱nkhang ti̱nä' kārma cü̱:-la̱mkha re̱'. sānglam-ki tshūrchok-la the̱p-tshōngkhang yo̱re'. the̱: tsā-la yo̱re'.

YESHE o̱ya āca-la:.

WOMAN o̱ya.

YESHE *'Sister', are there any hotels around here?*

WOMAN *Yes. There's a government hotel up there. But it is a bit far away. It's also expensive.*

YESHE *Aren't there any others?*

WOMAN *Yes, there's one called Gangjong Hotel. It's a Tibetan hotel. It's on a main road. It's not quiet, but it is near and convenient.*

YESHE *Which way [road] is it?*

WOMAN *You see there are several white buildings over there? The big road is behind them.*

YESHE *And how far is it from here [*lit. *'how many minutes' way is it']?*

WOMAN *The Gangjong Hotel is ten minutes from here. There's a bookshop on this side of the road. It's next to that.*

YESHE *Okay, sister.*

WOMAN *Okay.*

Vocabulary

བུད་མེད།	**phü̱me'**	woman
ཡེ་ཤེས།	**ye̱shē'**	(personal name)
ཨ་ཅག།	**āca**	elder sister (see below)
འདི་པར།	**ti̱wa:**	around here
མགྲོན་ཁང་།	**ṭö̱nkhang**	hotel/guesthouse
ཡོད་རེད།	**yo̱re'**	is/are (verb of existence)
གཞུང་།	**shu̱ng**	government; authority
ཏོག་ཙམ།	**tēts**	slightly/a bit
སྐར་མ།	**kārma**	minute
ཚུར་ཕྱོགས།	**tshūr-cho'**	this side
ཟེར་མཁན་གཅིག	**se̱rkhän-cik**	one called
སྲང་ལམ།	**sānglam**	street
ཆེན་པོ།	**chēnpo**	large/major
དེའི་རྩ་ལ།	**the̱: tsā-la**	next to that
གོང་ཆེན་པོ།	**kho̱ngchēnpo**	expensive
སྟབས་བདེ་པོ།	**tāpte̱po**	convenient
ཐག་ཉེ་པོ།	**thā-nye̱po**	near
དང་།	**tha̱ng**	'and'
ལམ་ཁ།	**la̱mkha**	road/path
འདི་ནས།	**ti̱nä**	from here
རྒྱབ་ལོགས།	**kya̱plo:**	behind
འོ་ཡ།	**o̱ya**	okay
ཁུ་སིམ་པོ།	**khūsimpo**	quiet
ཐག་རིང་པོ།	**thā-ri̱ngpo**	far
གཞན་དག	**shä̱nthak**	other; another
དཔེ་ཚོང་ཁང་།	**the̱p-tshōngkhang**	bookshop
འདུག་ག	**tu̱'-ka**	(tag form of **tu̱'**)

Language points

5 The འདུག་-ཡོད་རེད། distinction

Aside from their basic function of connecting words within the sentence, copula verbs convey other important information. **tu̱'** (technically known as an 'evidential' verb) can *only* be used when the speaker has *first-hand* experience of what the sentence asserts, or in a question, when the person asking assumes (following the rule of anticipation) that the one answering will do so based upon such experience. In Dialogue 1, Duho quite correctly uses **tu̱'** when asking Lhamo about Tashi; she has been in her shop, and would have seen if he was there. If Duho had rung to ask her, he should have posed the question in the same way. But Duho was less correct to use **tu̱'** in his subsequent question about where Tashi was, because it presumes that Lhamo should have some first-hand knowledge of his whereabouts.

yo̱re' is used in situations where a second or third person copula of existence is required, but a lack of first-hand knowledge means that **tu̱'** is inappropriate. But do not think that **yo̱re'** suggests uncertainty. A speaker can assert plenty of things confidently, without having experienced them, for instance, general facts, such as:

ལྷ་ས་བོད་ལ་ཡོད་རེད། **lhāsa phö̱'-la yo̱re'.** Lhasa is in Tibet.

or very specific situations, such as my assertion 'You are reading these words'.

yo̱re' is also more likely to be used when talking about things which are relatively stable, like the location of the hotel in Dialogue 2, rather than the more fluid location of a person. However, the first-hand experience of a thing usually takes precedence over its stability. So if the speaker has only recently, through first-hand experience, found out where the hotel is, he or she will talk about its location with **tu̱'** rather than **yo̱re'**.

6 Locations: being more specific

ནང་།	**na̱ng**	inside	འོག	**o̱k**	below
ཕྱི་ལོགས།	**chīlo:**	outside	འཁྲིས།	**ṭhī'**	beside/next to
མདུན།	**tü̱n**	front	བར།	**pha̱r**	between
རྒྱབ་ལོགས།	**kya̱plo:**	behind	སྒང་།	**ka̱ng**	on top; above

The **la̲thön**-particle is enough to convey that something is 'at' a location. To be more specific about where it is, one of the above words is used. A **la̲thön** is still required, and is placed after the position-word. In addition to this, a genitive particle is needed, to join the position-words to the place, for instance: 'In front of the post office':

སྦྲག་ཁང་	+	གི་	+	མདུན་	+	ལ།	**ṭa̲khang-ki tü̲n-la**
place (post office)	+	genitive particle (**ṭe̲lṭa**)	+	position-word	+	**la̲thön**	

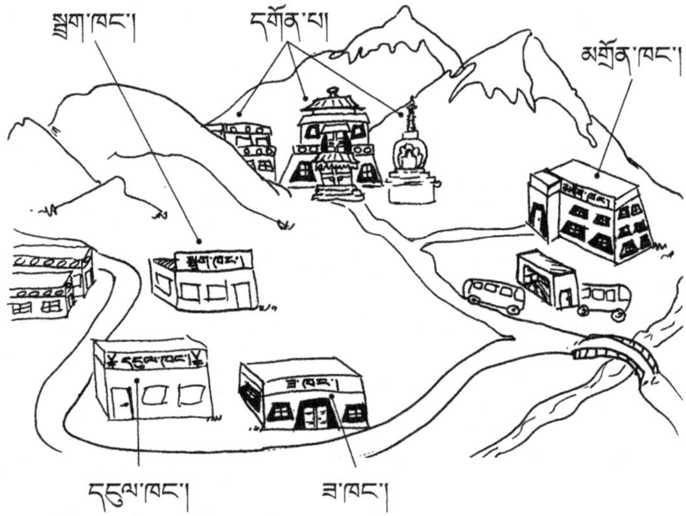

Exercise 5

Imagine that you are looking down upon the settlement in the illustration: With each pairing, describe where A is, in relation to location B (no.1 has been completed already).

1 A. bus (རླངས་འཁོར། **lāngkhor** or སྦ་སི། **pa̲si**)*
  B. road
2 A. post office
  B. bank (དངུལ་ཁང་། **ngǖ̲lkhang**)
3 A. monastery (དགོན་པ། **ko̲mba**)
  B. hill/mountain (རི། **ri̲**)
4 A. restaurant
  B. bank

5 A. bus station (ཀླངས་འཁོར་འབབ་ཚུགས **lāngkhor-paptshuk**)
B. hotel

* **pasi** (for 'bus') and **pasi-ṭīsin** (for 'bus station'), derived from the English, are commonly used outside Tibet.

1 ཀླངས་འཁོར་ལམ་ཁའི་འཁྲིས་ལ་འདུག **lāngkhor lamkha: ṭhī-la tu'.**

■ Practical tip: directions

In Dialogue 2, when the woman wants to point out some buildings to Yeshe, she uses **tu'-ka**, the 'tag' form with **tu'**. This is a way of directing someone's attention to something that both of you are experiencing first-hand (seeing, hearing, etc.). Here, the tag functions similarly to the way in English one might start giving directions by saying 'you see those buildings over there . . . ?'

Exercise 6

You have just had your first look around the place in the illustration. Now you have to give the following instructions/information:

(a) Go to the post office.
(b) Go the bank; it is next to the restaurant.
(c) You see the hotel (over there)? The shop is behind it.
(d) You see the hill over there? His house is up (*lit*. on) there.

To direct someone somewhere, say the location, and then simply add the polite word for 'go!' (ཕེབས། **phēp**)

e.g.: དགོན་པའི་ནང་ལ་ཕེབས། **kombä: nang-la phēp.**
Go inside the monastery!

Dialogue 3

(Audio 1:33)
Falling into conversation with a Tibetan, Duho finds himself, as usual, being quizzed about his family.

བོད་པ། ཁྱེད་རང་ལ་སྤུན་སྐུ་ག་ཚོད་ཡོད།
ཏུ་ཧོ། ང་ལ་སྤུན་སྐུ་གཉིས་ཡོད།

བོད་པ།	གཉིས་ཀ་བུ་རེད་པས།
ཏུ་ཧོ།	མ་རེད། གཉིས་ཀ་བུ་མོ་རེད། ང་ལ་སྤུན་སྐྱ་བུ་མེད། གཅིག་ཨ་ཅག་རེད། གཅིག་འོག་མ་རེད།
བོད་པ།	ཨ་ཅག་ལ་ཕྲུ་གུ་ཡོད་རེད་པས།
ཏུ་ཧོ།	ཡོད་མ་རེད། ང་ལ་ཡང་(འང་)མེད།
བོད་པ།	ཕ་མ་ཡོད་རེད་པས།
ཏུ་ཧོ།	ཡོད་རེད།
བོད་པ།	སྤུན་སྐྱ་དེ་ཚོ་ནང་ལ་ཡོད་རེད་པས།
ཏུ་ཧོ།	ནང་ལ་ཡོད་མ་རེད།
བོད་པ།	ཕ་མ་ལ་རོགས་པ་ཡོད་མ་རེད་པས།
ཏུ་ཧོ།	རོགས་པ་ཡོད་མ་རེད། ཕ་མ་རྐན་འཁོགས་མ་རེད། མ་གཞི་ནས་ཕྱི་རྒྱལ་གྱི་ལུགས་ སྲོལ་དང་བོད་པའི་ལུགས་སྲོལ་ཁག་ཁག་རེད།

TIBETAN	khyērang-la pīnkyak kha̱tshȫ' yö̱'.
DUHO	nga̱-la pīnkyak nyī' yö̱'.
TIBETAN	nyī'ka phu̱ re̱'-wä.
DUHO	ma-re̱', nyī'ka phu̱mo re̱'. nga̱-la pīnkyak phu̱ me̱'. cīk āca re̱'. cīk o̱kma re̱'.
TIBETAN	āca-la phūku yo̱re'-wä.
DUHO	yo̱ ma-re̱'. nga̱-la-yä me̱'.
TIBETAN	phāma yo̱re'-wä.
DUHO	yo̱re'.
TIBETAN	pīnkyak the̱ntsho na̱ng-la yo̱re'-wä.
DUHO	na̱ng-la yo̱ ma-re̱'.
TIBETAN	phāma-la ro̱kpa yo̱ ma-re̱'-wä.
DUHO	ro̱kpa yo̱ ma-re̱'. phāma kä̱nkhōk ma-re̱'. ma-shi̱nä chīkyäl-ki lu̱ksȫl tha̱ng phö̱pä: lu̱ksȫl khākak re̱'.

TIBETAN	*How many siblings do you have?*
DUHO	*I have two siblings.*
TIBETAN	*Are they both boys?*
DUHO	*No, both are girls. I don't have any male siblings.* *One is an elder and the other is a younger sister.*
TIBETAN	*Does your elder sister have children?*
DUHO	*No, neither do I.*

TIBETAN	*Are your parents [there]? [This implies ‘Are your parents still alive?’]*
DUHO	*Yes.*
TIBETAN	*Are the siblings at [your parents’] home?*
DUHO	*No, they’re not at home.*
TIBETAN	*Don’t your parents have any companions?*
DUHO	*No, but they’re not elderly. Anyway, foreign customs and Tibetan customs are different.*

Vocabulary

སྤུན་སྐྱ།	**pīnkyak**	sibling
གཉིས་ཀ།	**nyī’ka**	both
འོག་མ།	**o̱kma**	younger sister
ཕ་མ།	**phāma**	parents
ལུགས་སྲོལ།	**lu̱ksȫl**	customs/traditions
རྒན་འཁོགས།	**kǟ̱nkhōk**	elderly
མ་གཞི་ནས།	**ma-shi̱nä**	anyway
ཕྲུ་གུ།	**phūku**	child
ཁག་ཁག།	**khākak**	different

Language point

7 To have

There is no verb ‘to have’. Instead, as when expressing location, one uses a **la̱thön** in combination with a verb of existence. This time the **la̱thön** marks the person or thing which *has*. The rules determining which verb of existence to use (first-hand experience, etc.) are the same as in sentences of location. So, for example, depending on the situation, ‘Tenzin has some money (**ngǖl**)’ might translate either as:

བསྟན་འཛིན་ལ་དངུལ་འདུག **(tǟntsin-la ngǖl tu̱’.)** or
བསྟན་འཛིན་ལ་དངུལ་ཡོད་རེད། **(tǟntsin-la ngǖl yo̱re’.)**

Exercise 7

In earlier dialogues we learned of things which these people have. Following the pattern of (a), construct sentences expressing who has what:

(a) Unit 2, Dialogue 1 – Duho (2 things)
(b) Unit 2, Dialogue 2 – Duho (3 things)
(c) Unit 3, Dialogue 3 – Duho (1 thing)
(d) Unit 3, Dialogue 3 – the businessman (3 things)

(a) ཏུ་ཧྲོ་ལ་རོགས་པ་/བོད་པའི་གྲོགས་པོ་ཡོད་རེད།
tụho-la rọkpa/phọ̈pä: ṭhọkpo yọre.

■ Members of the family

ཨ་མ།	**āma**			mother
ཨ་ཕ།	**āpha**	པཱ་ལགས།	**pāla:**	father
སྤུན་སྐྱ།	**pīnkyak**			relation/sibling
ཨ་ཅག	**āca**			elder sister
ཅོ་ཅོ།	**cōco**	ཇོ་ལགས།	**chọla:**	elder brother
འོག་མ།	**ọkma**			younger brother or sister
རྨོ་མོ་ལགས།	**mōmola:**	རྨོ་ལགས།	**mōla:**	grandmother
སྤོ་སྤོ་ལགས།	**pōpola:**	སྤོ་ལགས།	**pōla:**	grandfather
ཨ་ཞང་།	**āshang**			uncle (maternal)
ཨ་ཁུ།	**ākhu**			uncle (paternal)
ཨ་ནེ།	**āne**			aunt (paternal)
སྲུ་མོ།	**sūmo**			aunt (maternal)
ཚ་བོ།	**tshāwo**			nephew
ཚ་མོ།	**tshāmo**			niece
ཁྱོ་ག	**khyōka**			husband
སྐྱེ་དམན།	**kyēmän**			wife/woman

These terms are obviously used for an individual's own relations. However, it is also common practice to refer to, or address almost any individual (except religious figures, or people in official positions), including strangers, with these terms. Use of kinship terms can convey both a degree of friendliness and respect. The choice of which is used depends upon your estimate of the age of the person in relation to yourself. A woman or a man who is a little older than yourself is regularly addressed as 'elder sister' or 'elder brother'; elderly persons are either 'grandmother' or 'grandfather', and children are either 'son/boy' or 'daughter/girl'.

Exercise 8

Imagine you are someone of Duho's age. Which kinship terms (if any) could you use when addressing these people?

(a) a taxi-driver, in about his forties
(b) a teenage girl, serving in a restaurant
(c) a female police official, a bit older than you
(d) a monk, probably in his late sixties

Unit Five

མགྲོན་ཁང་ལ་ཡོད་པ།

ṭö̱nkhang-la yö’-pa

At the guesthouse

In this unit you will learn how to:

- book into a hotel room
- make requests and give orders
- say ‘goodbye’
- use adjectives to describe and compare things

Dialogue 1

(Audio 1:38)

Yeshe has found the hotel. At the desk, he speaks to the receptionist.

ཡེ་ཤེས།	བཀྲ་ཤིས་བདེ་ལེགས།
སྒོ་ལེན་པ།	བཀྲ་ཤིས་བདེ་ལེགས། འོ། སྐར་མ་གཅིག་བཞུགས་དང་། ལགས་གསུངས་དང་།
ཡེ་ཤེས།	ཁང་མིག་སྟོང་པ་ཡོད་པས་ལགས།
སྒོ་ལེན་པ།	ད་ལྟ་མི་མང་པོ་འདུག ཡིན་ནའང་ཁང་མིག་སྟོང་པ་གཅིག་གཉིས་ཙམ་ཡོད།
ཡེ་ཤེས།	ཁང་མིག་ག་འདྲ་ཡོད་རེད། ཆུ་ཚ་པོ་ཡོད་རེད་པས།
སྒོ་ལེན་པ།	ཐོག་ག་ལ་ཁང་མིག་ཡག་པོ་གཅིག་ཡོད། དེ་ལ་མཐུན་རྐྱེན་ཆ་ཚང་ཡོད་རེད། ཡིན་ནའང་དེ་ཏོག་ཙམ་གོང་ཆེན་པོ་ཡོད་རེད།
ཡེ་ཤེས།	དེ་ལ་སྒོར་མོ་ག་ཚོད་རེད། གསུངས་དང་།
སྒོ་ལེན་པ།	མཚན་གཅིག་ལ་སྒོར་མོ་སུམ་བརྒྱ་རེད། ཁང་མིག་གཞན་དག་དེ་འོག་ཐོག་རེད། དེ་ལ་ཡང་(འང་)ཆུ་ཚ་པོ་ཡོད་རེད། ཡིན་ནའང་ཚ་སློག་དེ་རྙིང་པ་རེད། དེ་ལ་ཤུགས་ཡོད་མ་རེད།

ཡེ་ཤེས།	གཉིས་ཀ་བསྟན་རོགས་གནང་།
སྡེ་ལེན་པ།	ཡིན་དང་ཡིན། ཕེབས་དང་། ཁྱེད་རང་གི་དོ་པོ་འདིའི་རྒྱབ་ལོགས་ལ་བཞག་གནང་ཨང་།

YESHE	ṭāshi'-te̱le'.
RECEPTIONIST	ṭāshi'-te̱le'. o̱ kārma-cik shu̱-thang. (*she answers a phone call, then returns to Yeshe*) la̱: sūng-thang.
YESHE	khāngmik tōngpa yö̱'-pä la̱:.
RECEPTIONIST	tha̱nta mi̱ ma̱ngpo tu̱'. yi̱nnä: khāngmik tōngpa cīknyī'-ts yö̱'.
YESHE	khāngmik kha̱nṭa yo̱re'. chū tshāpo yo̱re'-wä'.
RECEPTIONIST	thōka-la khāngmik ya̱kpo cīk yö̱'. the̱-la thūnkyen chātshang yo̱re'. yi̱nnä: tēts kho̱ngchēnpo yo̱re'.
YESHE	the̱-la ko̱rmo khātshȫ' re̱'. sūng-thang.
RECEPTIONIST	tshǟn cīk-la ko̱rmo sūmkya re̱'. khāngmik shä̱nthak the̱ o̱ktho' re̱'. the̱-la-yä chū tshāpo yo̱re'. yi̱nnä: tshālok-the nyīngpa re̱'. the̱-la shūk yo̱ ma-re'.
YESHE	nyī'ka tǟn ro-nāng.
RECEPTIONIST	yi̱n-tayi̱n. phēp-thang. khyērang-ki tho̱po tī:-kya̱plo-la sha̱k nāng-a.

YESHE	*Hello.*
RECEPTIONIST	*Hello. Oh, just wait a minute please!* (she answers a phone call, then returns to Yeshe) *Now, tell me [what can I do for you?]*
YESHE	*Do you have rooms available?*
RECEPTIONIST	*Right now there are many people [i.e. guests]. But we do have one or two rooms available.*
YESHE	*What are they like? Is there hot water?*
RECEPTIONIST	*We have one nice room upstairs. That has full facilities. But it's a little expensive.*
YESHE	*Please tell me how much it is.*
RECEPTIONIST	*It's three hundred per night. The other room is a ground floor [room]. It also has hot water, but the heater is old. It doesn't have much power.*
YESHE	*Could you please show me both rooms?*
RECEPTIONIST	*Of course! Please come with me! And leave your luggage behind here!*

Vocabulary

སྣེ་ལེན་པ།	**nēlenpa**	receptionist
ཁང་མིག	**khāngmik**	room
བཞུགས།	**shu̱:**	wait! (*lit.* 'stay!')
སྟོང་པ།	**tōngpa**	available (*lit.* 'empty')
ག་འདྲ།	**kha̱nṭa**	how?
ཚ་པོ།	**tshāpo**	hot
ཡག་པོ།	**ya̱kpo**	good
གཅིག་གཉིས་ཙམ།	**cīknyī'-ts**	one or two
མཐུན་རྐྱེན།	**thūnkyen**	facilities
ཆ་ཚང་།	**chātshang**	all/everything
ཡིན་དང་ཡིན།	**yi̱n-tayi̱n**	of course!
ཕེབས།	**phēp**	come!; go!
གསུངས།	**sūng**	(polite imperative, inviting someone to speak)
དང་།/གནང་ཨང་།/རོགས་གནང་།	**thang/nāng-a/ro-nāng**	(imperative complements: see below)
མཚན།	**tshȫn**	night
སྙིང་པ།	**nyīngpa**	old
གསར་པ།	**sārpa**	new
ཤུགས།	**shūk**	power/strength
སྒོར་མོ།	**ko̱rmo**	denomination (money)
སུམ་བརྒྱ་རེད།	**sūmkya**	three hundred
བསྟན།	**tȫn**	show!
འོག་ཐོག	**o̱ktho'**	ground floor
དོ་པོ།	**tho̱po**	baggage
བཞག	**sha̱k**	put down!
ཐོག་ཀ	**thōka**	upstairs
ཚ་སློག	**tshālok**	heating

Language point

1 Requests and commands

To give a request or command one uses the imperative form of an action verb. The most commonly used ones all have a single syllable. Intonation and the nature of the action will partly determine whether the instruction is understood as a request or an order. More important is whether the polite (honorific) form of the verb is used. (Honorific language is explored in more detail from Unit 11 onwards.) There is no direct equivalent of the word 'please', but an instruction which uses the polite verb form achieves a similar effect. To form the negative, simply add the syllable **ma** before the imperative verb, e.g. མ་གསུངས། **ma-sūng** – 'Please don't say (that)!'

The same polite imperatives are used as ways of communicating welcoming and invitation. Gentle encouragements to come in, sit down, have some food or drink are indispensable for smooth communication in a culture which honours the guest. The most essential of these are:

བཞུགས།	**shu̲:**	Please sit down/please stay!
ཕེབས།	**phēp**	Please come in! (also for invitations related to going, such as 'to follow', 'to lead the way', etc.)
མཆོད།	**chȫ'**	Please eat!/Please drink!
བཞེས།	**she̲'**	Please take! (especially for food or drink)

There is no single word for 'goodbye'. Instead, based upon these invitations:

ཀ་ལེར་བཞུགས།	**kha̲le:-shu̲**	wished by person(s) departing, to those staying
ཀ་ལེར་ཕེབས།	**kha̲le:-phēp**	wished by person(s) staying, to those departing

(ཀ་ལེ། **kha̲le** literally means 'gently', 'leisurely'.)

Single-syllable imperatives can be used to communicate a request, etc. But as Dialogue 1 illustrates, a speaker can *also* choose to attach a variety of single or two-syllable words to the verb. These endings can be added to either polite or non-polite forms. The boundaries between them are not fixed, but they tend to be used in the following situations:

རོགས་བྱེད།	**ro-chi̱'**	Formal requests
རོགས་གནང་།	**ro-nāng**	
ཤོག	**shōk**	Orders
དང་།	**thang**	Neutral: requests, or instructions to intimates
ཨང་།	**a**	Neutral: instruction to an intimate

Exercise 1

(a) Organise these groups of people into matching pairs.

དགེ་རྒན།	**ke̱kän**	རྒན་འཁོགས།	**kä̱nkhōk**	ཕྲུ་གུ།	**phūku**
ཕ་མ།	**phāma**	སློབ་ཕྲུག	**lōpṭhuk**	གཞོན་གཞོན།	**sho̱nshön**

(b) Which imperative endings do you think would be suitable when each one of the pair requests or orders the other? The forms used should reflect the appropriate degree of respect and formality. I (**nga̱**) and my friends (**ngä:-ṭho̱kpo**), for instance, would use intimate forms, such as **thang** or **a**, with each other.

Exercise 2

Translate the following, choosing an ending appropriate to each situation. The object is placed before the imperative, e.g. ཁང་མིག་དེ་བསྟན་རོགས་གནང་། **khāngmik-the tä̱n ro-nāng** 'Please show (me) the room!'

1 Go inside! (formal)
2 Show me the money! (to a friend)
3 Don't go over there! (an order)
4 Sit here! (invitation)
5 Take this! (formal)

Cultural point

Talking about money

Some Tibetans in the PRC may refer to the Chinese currency they use with Tibetanised versions of the Chinese names. But for most

Tibetans the general pattern is to use the generic term **ko̱rmo** to refer to the main unit of a country's currency, instead of using specific denomination names (i.e. rupee, euro, pound, etc.) When it is necessary to distinguish, some version of the country's name might be attached to the word, for instance:

ཨ་རིའི་སྒོར་མོ།   **āri:-ko̱rmo**   (US dollars)

The sub-units are commonly referred to by their actual names (paisa, cents, etc.)

Language point

2 More ལ་དོན། (la̱thön) uses

In Unit 4 the **la̱thön** was introduced as the particle which marks locations and persons who have things. The particle has numerous functions. In Dialogue 1 it appeared in the question about how much the room cost:

(ཁང་མིག་)དེ་ལ་སྒོར་མོ་ག་ཚོད་རེད།
(khāngmik)the̱-la ko̱rmo kha̱tshō̈' re̱'.

This structure will be covered in more detail in Unit 10 (Shopping). On other occasions, the particle is used much like 'for', in sentences such as:

འདི་ང་ལ་རེད། གཞན་དག་དེ་ཁྱེད་རང་ལ་རེད།
ti̱ nga̱-la re̱'. shä̱nthak-the khyērang-la re̱'.
This (one) is for me, the other is for you.

Dialogue 2

(Audio 1:39)
The receptionist shows Yeshe the room downstairs.

སྣེ་ལེན་པ།   འདིར་གཟིགས་དང་།
ཡེ་ཤེས།   ཨ་ལས། ཁང་པ་ཆུང་ཆུང་ཞེ་དྲག་འདུག གྲང་མོ་ཡང་(འང)་འདུག ཙོག་ཙེ་དང་རྐུབ་བཀྱག་ཡང་(ཀྱང་)མི་འདུག་ག ཨེ་ནི་ཆུ་ཁང་གསང་སྤྱོད་''།

སྣེ་ལེན་པ། ཆུ་ཁང་གསང་སྤྱོད་ནང་ལོགས་ལ་ཡོད་མ་རེད། ཕྱི་ལོགས་ལ་ཡོད་རེད། འོ་ན་ཐོག་ག་ལ་ཕེབས། ཁང་མིག་ཆེ་བ་དེ་ལ་གཟིགས།

ཡེ་ཤེས། འདི་ཐད་དེ་ཆེ་བ་འདུག

སྣེ་ལེན་པ། ཁང་མིག་འདི་ལ་ཆུ་ཁང་གསང་སྤྱོད་ཁེ་གཙང་ཡོད་རེད།

ཡེ་ཤེས། གཙང་ང་ཡང་འདུག ཁང་མིག་འདི་ད་གིན་དེ་ལས་དངོས་གནས་ཡག་ག་འདུག

སྣེ་ལེན་པ། ད་གིན་དེ་ལས་གོང་ཆེ་བ་ཡོད་རེད། ཡིན་ནའང་སྐྱིད་བ་ཡོད་རེད།

ཡེ་ཤེས། འདི་ང་ལ་འགྲིག་ས་རེད།

RECEPTIONIST tä̱: si̱-tha̱ng

YESHE ālä, khāngpa chūngchūng she̱ṭhak tu̱'. ṭa̱ngmo-yä tu̱'. cōktse thang kūpkyak-yä min-tu̱'-ka. ēni chūkhang sāngcö'. . . .

RECEPTIONIST chūkhang sāngcö' na̱nglo:-la yo̱ ma-re̱'. chīlo:-la yo̱re'. o̱na thōka-la phēp. khāngmik chē:-the-la si̱'. (*they go upstairs*)

YESHE ti̱ pä̱t chē: tu̱'.

RECEPTIONIST khāngmik-ti̱-la chūkhang sāngcö' khētsang yo̱re'.

YESHE tsāngnga-yä tu̱'. khāngmik-ti̱ tha̱ncin the̱-lä ngō̱nä' ya̱ka tu̱'.

RECEPTIONIST tha̱ncin the̱-lä kho̱ngchē: yo̱re'. yi̱nnä: kyīwa yo̱re'.

YESHE ti̱ nga̱-la ṭi̱k sa-re̱'.

RECEPTIONIST *Here, take a look!*

YESHE *Oh, it's really small. It's also cold, and there are no tables or chairs, are there? And the bathroom and toilet . . . ?*

RECEPTIONIST *There is no bathroom and toilet inside. They're outside. Well, come upstairs then, take a look at the larger room.* (they go upstairs)

YESHE *This is much bigger!*

RECEPTIONIST *This room has an en suite bathroom and toilet.*

YESHE *This one is also cleaner. It really is better than that room just before.*

RECEPTIONIST *It's more expensive than the one just before, but it is more pleasant.*

YESHE *This one should be okay for me.*

Vocabulary

གཟིགས།	**si'**	look! (polite)
ཆུང་ཆུང་།	**chūngchūng**	small
ཀུབ་བཀྱག	**kūpkyak**	chair
གྲང་མོ།	**ṭhangmo**	cold
ཅོག་ཙེ།	**cōktse**	table
ནང་ལོགས།	**nanglo:**	inside
ལས།	**lä**	than (comparative)
ཁེ་གཙང་།	**khētsang**	en suite/separate
འགྲིག་ས་རེད།	**ṭik sa-re'**	should be okay
ཞེ་དྲག	**sheṭhak**	very; a lot
གཙང་ང་།	**tsāngnga**	cleaner
ཆུ་ཁང་།	**chūkhang**	bathroom
གསང་སྤྱོད།	**sāngcö'**	toilet
ཕད་དེ།	**pät**	extremely (emphatic)
ཡག་ག	**yaka**	better
སྐྱིད་པ།	**kyīwa**	more pleasant
ང་ལ།	**nga-la**	for me
ཁ་ལག	**khālak**	food
ཆེ་བ།	**chē:**	bigger

Language point

3 འདུག adjectives and impressions

Unit 4 described how the use of **tu'** indicates the speaker has first-hand experience of the thing that he or she is speaking about, and how it is also often associated with situations that are more changeable and fluid, such as the locations of people (other than oneself) at a particular time.

tu' is also used particularly when giving an *initial impression* of a person or thing. This does not apply to statements of identity, which describe established facts or information, but to sentences where adjectives describing tangible attributes (excluding colours), such as size and shape, as well as those relating to quality, are involved. Such impressions are *subjective*, rather than established fact. In Dialogue 2, for instance, Yeshe is not stating as a fact that the room is cold, just that this is how it strikes *him*.

Exercise 3

Imagine you walk into a restaurant to find:

> *Tashi is there. Tashi is your friend. He has some food.* You order something yourself. *The food smells and tastes good. It is Chinese food.* You order some tea. *It is Tibetan tea. It is hot.* But *there is a bug in the tea.*

Translate the sentences in italics, except those for which **tu'** would not be the appropriate verb. Consult the list below, where necessary.

Adjectives

Basic adjective			*Comparative form*		
ཡག་པོ།	**yakpo**	good	ཡག་ག།	**yaka**	better
ཞིམ་པོ།	**shimpo**	tasty; aromatic	ཞིམ་པ།	**shimpa**	tastier; better smelling
ཆེན་པོ།	**chēnpo**	large; great	ཆེ་བ།	**chē:**	larger; greater
ཆུང་ཆུང་།	**chūngchūng**	small	ཆུང་ང་།	**chūng-nga**	smaller
རིང་པོ།	**ringpo**	long/tall*	རིང་ང་།	**ring-nga**	longer/taller
ཐུང་ཐུང་།	**thūngthūng**	short	ཐུང་ང་།	**thūng-nga**	shorter
མང་པོ།	**mangpo**	much/many	མང་ང་།	**mang-nga**	more
ཉུང་ཉུང་།	**nyungnyung**	few	ཉུང་ང་།	**nyung-nga**	fewer
མཐོ་པོ།	**thōpo**	high	མཐོ་བ།	**thōwa**	higher
དམའ་པོ།	**māpo**	low	དམའ་བ།	**māwa**	lower
གྲང་མོ།	**thangmo**	cold	གྲང་ང་།	**thang-nga**	colder
ཚ་པོ།	**tshāpo**	hot	ཚ་བ།	**tshā:**	hotter
སྙིང་རྗེ་པོ།	**nyīng-cepo**	attractive	སྙིང་རྗེ་བ།	**nyīng-ce:**	more attractive

* For people, 'tall' is གཟུགས་པོ་རིང་པོ། **sukpo-ringpo**, and 'short' is གཟུགས་པོ་ཐུང་ཐུང་། **sukpo-thūngthūng** (**sukpo** refers to the body).

Language point

4 Comparative adjectives

The basic adjectives are turned into the comparative forms in the following ways:

1 For example: མང་པོ། **ma̲ngpo** → མང་ང་། **ma̲ng-nga** – When the first syllable of the basic adjective ends in a ག། **ga** or ང། **nga** sound, the second syllable is replaced in the comparative by an 'echo' of that ending.

2 For example: དམའ་པོ། **māpo** → དམའ་བ། **māwa** – The second syllable པོ། **po** is usually replaced by a པ། **pa** or བ། **wa**.

3 Exceptions – ཆེན་པོ། **chēnpo**, སྙིང་རྗེ་པོ། **nyīng-ce̲po**, and ཚ་པོ། **tshāpo** – The last syllable is dropped, and replaced by a long vowel sound.

When coming across a new adjective, follow whichever of the first two patterns is appropriate, unless it is one of the compound adjectives which incorporate ཆེན་པོ། **chēnpo**, such as 'expensive' གོང་ཆེན་པོ། **kho̲ng-chēnpo** and 'old' (for persons) ལོ་ཆེན་པོ། **lo̲-chēnpo**. In such cases, follow the third pattern.

■ Superlatives

The pattern is always the same: one replaces the final syllable of the basic adjective with ཤོས། **shȫ'**. For example: ཡག་ཤོས།, **ya̲k-shȫ'** ('best'), ཐུང་ཤོས། **thūng-shȫ'** ('shortest').

Exercise 4

Write the comparative and superlative versions for each of these basic adjectives (the first one has already been completed):

1	སྐྱོ་པོ།	**kyōpo**	poor (resources or quality) སྐྱོ་བ། **kyōwa** སྐྱོ་ཤོས། **kyōshȫ'**
2	རྒྱགས་པ།	**kya̲kpa**	stout/fat
3	ལས་སླ་པོ།	**lä̱lāpo**	easy
4	སྐྱིད་པོ།	**kyīpo**	pleasant
5	དྲོ་པོ།	**ṭho̲po**	warm
6	ཤུགས་ཆེན་པོ།	**shūk-chēnpo**	strong/powerful

ལས། **lä** acts similarly to 'than' in the comparative sentence; it is attached to the item one is comparing the other thing *to*. For example:

> དེ་རིང་ཁས་ས་ལས་གྲང་ང་འདུག
> **the̱ring khā̈sa-lä ṭha̱ng-nga tu̱'.**
> Today is colder than yesterday.
>
> ཁང་པ་རྙིང་པ་འདི་ཁང་པ་གསར་པ་དེ་ལས་གོང་ཆེ་བ་འདུག
> **khāngpa nyīngpa-ti̱ khāngpa sārpa the̱-lä kho̱ng-chē: tu̱'.**
> This old house is more expensive than that new one.

Exercise 5

Translate these comparative statements:

༡ བསོད་ནམས་བཀྲ་ཤིས་ལས་ལོ་ཆེ་བ་རེད།
sō̈nam ṭāshi-lä lo̱-chē: re̱'.

༢ མགྲོན་ཁང་དགོན་པ་ལས་ཐག་རིང་ང་ཡོད་རེད།
ṭö̱nkhang ko̱mpa-lä thā-ri̱ng-nga yo̱re'.

༣ མི་ལས་རྐུབ་བརྒྱག་ཉུང་ང་འདུག
mi̱-lä kūpkyak nyu̱ng-nga tu̱'.

༤ རྒྱ་ནག་ལ་ཨ་རི་ལས་མི་མང་ང་ཡོད་རེད།
kya̱nak-la āri-lä mi̱ ma̱ng-nga yo̱re'.

༥ ཁང་པ་དེའི་ཕྱི་ལོགས་ནང་ལོགས་ལས་སྙིང་རྗེ་བ་འདུག
khāngpa-the̱: chīlok na̱nglo-lä nyīng-c̱e: tu̱'.

Exercise 6

Three different verbs were used in Exercise 5 (although this won't show in the English translation). If one replaced the verbs in sentences 1, 2, and 4 with **tu̱'**,

(a) Would any of them be incorrect sentences?
(b) If any are correct, would they convey anything different from the original versions?

Exercise 7

Buchung (བུ་ཆུང་། **phu̱chung**) is seven, his sister, Namgyel (རྣམ་རྒྱལ། **nāmkyäl**) is nine, and their brother, Loṭhö (བློ་གྲོས། **lōṭhö'**) is fifteen.

Make each of the following into a statement in Tibetan (**re̱'** can be used here for the sentences about age, and **tu̱'** for those about height):

(a) Buchung – younger
(b) Namgyel – older
(c) Loṭhö – oldest
(d) Loṭhö – taller
(e) Namgyel – shorter
(f) Buchung – not tall

Unit Six

དགའ་མི་དགའ།

ka̱ mi-ka̱

Likes and dislikes

In this unit you will learn how to:

- talk about likes and dislikes
- express reactions
- communicate degrees (using negation and exclamation)
- make sentences with an equivalent of ‘when’
- say more about things you are experiencing or have experienced

Dialogue 1

(Audio 1:44)

Duho is travelling with Tashi. They have stopped in a spot overlooking a village.

བཀྲ་ཤིས། ས་ཆ་འདི་ག་འདྲ་འདུག
དུ་ཧོ། སྐྱིད་པོ་འདུག རི་ལ་ལྟོས་དང་། ག་འདྲ་རྫིག་པོ་འདུག
བཀྲ་ཤིས། ཡུལ་ལྗོངས་སྐྱིད་པོ་འདུག ཡིན་ནའང་ང་གྲོང་གསེབ་ཁུག་ཀྱུག་ལ་དགའ་པོ་མེད།
དུ་ཧོ། ཁྱེད་རང་ས་ཆ་ག་འདྲ་ལ་དགའ་པོ་ཡོད།
བཀྲ་ཤིས། ང་ཁྲོམ་ས་ལ་དགའ་པོ་ཡོད།
དུ་ཧོ། ངའི་ནང་གྲོང་ཁྱེར་ཆེན་པོ་ལ་ཡོད། འཁྲུག་པོ་ཡོད་རེད། ཡིན་ནའང་སྐྱིད་པོ་ཡོད་མ་རེད།

བཀྲ་ཤིས། ང་ས་ཆ་འཁྲུག་པོ་ལ་དགའ་བ་ཡོད། གྲོང་གསེབ་འདི་ཚོ་ལ་ག་རེ་ཡོད་རེད།
གང་ཡང་ཡོད་མ་རེད།
ཧུ་ཧོ། སེམས་ཀྱི་ཞི་བདེ་ཡོད་རེད།
བཀྲ་ཤིས། སེམས་ཀྱི་ཞི་བདེ་གང་ཤེས། འདི་ལ་ཆང་ཁང་དང་རྩེད་ཁང་མི་འདུག་ག སྐྱིད་པོ་
རྩ་ནས་ཡོད་མ་རེད།

TASHI sācha-ti̲ kha̲nṭa tu̲'.
DUHO kyīpo tu̲'. ri̲-la tȫ'-thang. kha̲nṭa tsi̲kpo tu̲'.
TASHI yu̲lcong kyīpo tu̲'. yi̲nnä: nga̲ ṭho̲ngsep khūkyok-la ka̲po me̲'.
DUHO khyērang sācha kha̲nṭa-la ka̲po yö̲'.
TASHI nga̲ ṭhōmsa-la ka̲po yö̲'.
DUHO ngä̲: na̲ng ṭho̲ngkhyer chēnpo-la yö̲'. ṭhūkpo yo̲re'. yi̲nnä: kyīpo yo̲ ma-re̲'.
TASHI nga̲ sācha ṭhūkpo-la ka̲: yö̲'. ṭho̲ngsep ti̲ntsho-la kha̲re yo̲re'. khä̲: yo̲ ma-re̲'.
DUHO sēm-ki shi̲te yo̲re'.
TASHI sēm-ki shi̲te kha̲ngshē'. ti̲-la chāngkhang thang tsēkhang min-tu̲'-ka. kyīpo tsānä yo̲ ma-re̲'.

TASHI *How is '[how do you find] this place?*
DUHO *It's lovely! Look at the mountains! How majestic they are!*
TASHI *The scenery is pleasant. But I don't like these isolated villages.*
DUHO *What kind of places do you like?*
TASHI *I like the market-place.*
DUHO *Our home is in a large town. It's lively, but it's not pleasant.*
TASHI *I prefer lively places. What is there in these villages? There's nothing!*
DUHO *There is peace of mind.*
TASHI *Peace of mind? I don't know about that! Here there are no bars or gaming centres are there? There's no fun [pleasure] at all!*

Vocabulary

ས་ཆ།	**sācha**	place
རྗིག་པོ།	**tsi̱kpo**	impressive/majestic
ཡུལ་ལྗོངས།	**yu̱lcong**	scenery
གྲོང་གསེབ།	**ṭho̱ngsep**	village
ཁུག་ཀྱོག	**khūkyok**	isolated
དགའ་པོ།	**ka̱po**	to like
ཁྲོམ་ས།	**ṭhōmsa**	market-place
ལྟོས།	**tȫ'**	look!
གང་ཡང་།	**khä̱:**	(negation; see below)
ཙ་ནས།	**tsānä**	(negation; see below)
ལས་ཀ།	**lä̱ka**	work
ག་འདྲ་རྗིག་པོ་འདུག	**kha̱nṭa tsi̱kpo tu̱'**	how impressive it is!
འཁྲུག་པོ།	**ṭhūkpo**	lively/exciting
སེམས།	**sēm**	mind

ཞི་བདེ།	**shi̱te**	peace
ཆང་ཁང་།	**chāngkhang**	pub/drinking place
ཆང་།	**chāng**	beer
རྩེད་ཁང་།	**tsēkhang**	gaming centre
དགའ་བ།	**ka̱:**	prefer
གྲོང་ཁྱེར།	**ṭho̱ngkhyer**	town
གང་ཤེས།	**kha̱ngshē'**	I don't know! (dismissive)
ག་འདྲ་འདུག	**kha̱nṭa tu̱'**	how is it?

Language point

1 Liking and disliking

ka̱po is used to express liking for a person or thing, but only when these likes or dislikes are more deep-rooted, having built up over time. It does not express immediate reactions to things (see below). A **ka̱po** sentence has a verb of existence. It also uses a **la̱thön**, to mark the object that is liked. **ka̱po** is not a verb in the Tibetan system, but as with the verbs explained in Unit 4, you can use it together with a time-word, to show whether your liking relates to the present, past, etc. To say that you do not like something, you use the negative of the copula. Examples:

ང་སེམས་ཅན་ལ་དགའ་པོ་ཡོད། **nga̱ sēmcän-la ka̱po yö̱'.**
I like animals.

ང་གྲོང་ཁྱེར་དེ་ལ་དགའ་པོ་མེད། **nga̱ ṭho̱ngkhyer the̱-la ka̱po me̱'.**
I don't like that town.

The comparative form of **ka̱po** ('to prefer') is **ka̱:**, and the superlative **ka̱shö'** translates as 'favourite'.

It is a slightly tricky point, but when discussing the likes and dislikes of others it is safer to use the copula verb **yo̱re'**, rather than **tu̱'**. For example:

བཀྲ་ཤིས་ཆང་ཁང་ལ་དགའ་པོ་ཡོད་རེད།
ṭāshi chāngkhang-la ka̱po yo̱re'.
Tashi likes pubs.

This is because **tu̱'** indicates that one has first-hand experience of a thing, but it is questionable how much we can actually *experience* the likes of another person.

Exercise 1

Translate the following:

1 I like him.
2 We don't like work.
3 Who do you prefer?
4 Do you prefer the large room?
5 Sönam likes quiet places, Tashi doesn't.
6 Do you like Tibetan tea (བོད་ཇ། **phö̱cha**)?

■ Colours (མཚོན་མདོག **tshȫntok**)

དཀར་པོ།	**kārpo**	white
ནག་པོ།	**na̱kpo**	black
སེར་པོ།	**sērpo**	yellow
དམར་མོ་/པོ།	**mārmo/po**	red
ལྗང་ཁུ།	**ca̱nku**	green
ལི་ཝང་།	**li̱wang**	orange
ཟིང་སྐྱ།	**si̱ngkya**	pink
མུ་མེན།	**mu̱men**	purple
སྔོན་པོ།	**ngȫnpo**	blue (but also the colour of vegetation)

Exercise 2

Translate these questions:

༡ ཁྱེད་རང་མཚོན་མདོག་ག་གི་ལ་དགའ་པ་ཡོད།
khyērang tshȫntok kha̱ki-la ka̱: yö̱'.

༢ ཁྱེད་རང་གི་རྐུབ་བཀྱག་དེའི་མཚོན་མདོག་ག་རེ་རེད།
khyērang-ki kūpkyak the̱: tshȫntok kha̱re re̱'.

༣ དེབ་འདིའི་ནང་ལོགས་ལ་མཚོན་མདོག་ག་ཚོད་འདུག
the̱p ti̱: na̱nglo-la tshȫntok kha̱tshȫ' tu̱'.

Language points

2 Making a negation stronger

Dialogue 1 introduced two new terms sometimes used in negation. Either term may be added just before the copula. **tsānä** can only be used in a sentence where the verb is negated. It is a way of emphasising the negation, similar to adding a phrase such as 'at all'. For instance:

> ང་ཕྲུ་གུའི་རྩེད་མོ་ལ་དགའ་པོ་ཙ་ནས་མེད།
> **nga̱ phūkü: tsēmo-la ka̱po tsānä me̱'.**
> I do not like children's games at all.

Later, used with action verbs, **tsānä** can mean 'never', as in 'I'm never going to do that!'

khä̱: is similar to 'nothing', but only when the verb is in the negative. When the verb is affirmative, **khä̱:** functions like 'any' or 'anything'.

Question: ཁང་མིག་དེ་ལ་གང་ཡང་འདུག་གས།
khāngmik the̱-la khä̱: tu̱'-kä.
Is there anything in that room?

Answer: གང་ཡང་མི་འདུག
khä̱: min-tu̱'.
There's nothing (there).

3 Reactions (using འདུག tu̱')

As explained above, **ka̱po** is used when expressing longer-term likes and dislikes. But when discussing something more immediate, for example that one is *enjoying* a specific thing, as one is experiencing it, one just uses the 'impressions' form described in Unit 5 (adjective + **tu̱'**). The adjectives used most commonly here (those communicating that something is 'good', 'tasty', 'pleasant', or their negations) are strongly subjective; such statements require neither a personal pronoun nor an equivalent for 'like'.

> ཁ་ལག་འདི་ཞིམ་པོ་འདུག **khālak-ti̱ shi̱mpo tu̱'.**
> This food is tasty! (or, 'I'm enjoying this food'.)

Another of these strongly subjective adjectives is **nyǟnpo**, which means ‘pleasant-sounding’ for songs, music and voices, and ‘engrossing’ for written material, particularly stories.

གཞས་འདི་སྙན་པོ་མི་འདུག **shä̱’-ti̱ nyǟnpo min-tu̱’.**
This isn’t a pleasant song. (or, ‘I don’t like this song.’)

To express that one is having fun, one describes the activity, for example, a picnic (**līngka**) as **kyīpo**;

གླིང་ཁ་འདི་སྐྱིད་པོ་འདུག **līngka-ti̱ kyīpo tu̱’.**

Exercise 3

Identify the objects on the left, then indicate (by ticking the box) whether the **ka̱po** or the adjective-**tu̱’** structure would be the better one to use when expressing a liking for them. In some cases (if you can imagine different situations for the same object) both structures might work.

		ka̱po	adjective-**tu̱’**
གཞས་འདི།	**shä̱’-ti̱**	☐	☐
རྒྱ་གར་གྱི་ཁ་ལག	**kya̱kar-ki khālak**	☐	☐
མགྲོན་ཁང་ཆེན་པོ།	**ṭō̱nkhang chēnpo**	☐	☐
དེ་རིང་གི་གླིང་ཁ།	**the̱ring-ki līngka**	☐	☐
དེབ་འདི།	**the̱p-ti̱**	☐	☐
བཀྲ་ཤིས་ཀྱི་ཨ་ནེ།	**ṭāshi-ki āne**	☐	☐

Language point

4 Exclamations

In Dialogue 1 Duho remarks how impressive the mountains are: (**ri̱**) **kha̱nṭa tsi̱kpo tu̱’**. This simple structure:

kha̱nṭa + adjective + **tu̱’**

is a frequently used way of exclaiming surprise, joy, annoyance, etc. The verb (which is most often in the affirmative) must be **tu̱’**, since the speaker is necessarily reporting his or her immediate impression or feeling about the thing in question. For example:

ཙེད་མོ་འདི་ག་འདྲ་སྐྱིད་པོ་འདུག **tsēmo-ti̱ kha̱nṭa kyīpo tu̱'.**
This game is great fun!

Exercise 4

You can now express liking or disliking in two different ways, depending on the situation. You can also express various degrees ('a little', 'a lot', 'not at all'), up to, in more extreme cases, an exclamation. Using the two objects below, construct the sentences indicated on the right. You can make the object more specific, by adding equivalents for 'this', for instance. 'Like' here indicates **ka̱po**:

ཁ་ལག **khālak** – I like/like a little/like a lot/It's delicious!
མི། **mi̱** – I don't like/don't like at all/He's terrible!
(སྡུག་ཅག་ས། **tu̱kcāk**)

■ Summing-up

Unit 4 introduced how verbs of existence are used to talk about location and having. Units 5 and 6 have shown another major function for these verbs: how they are used together with adjectives, when expressing personal impressions.

Dialogue 2

(Audio 1:45)
Tenpa and Norbu, two lay people, pass a monastery. Norbu notices Tenpa looking wistful.

བསྟན་པ། སྔོན་མར་ང་དགོན་པ་དེའི་གྲྭ་པ་ཡིན།
ནོར་བུ། ཨ་ལས། སྔོན་མར་བསྟན་པ་གྲྭ་པ་ཡིན་པས། ཨེ་ནི་ག་འདྲ་ཡོད་རེད།
བསྟན་པ། ང་ཡོད་དུས་དགོན་པ་འདིའི་སྒྲིག་འཛུགས་དམ་པོ་ཡོད་རེད།
ནོར་བུ། ཨེ་ནི་བསྟན་པ་སྒྲིག་འཛུགས་ལ་དགའ་པོ་ཡོད་མ་རེད་པ།
བསྟན་པ། དེ་འདྲ་མ་རེད། ང་གྲྭ་པ་ཡིན་དུས་དངོས་གནས་སྐྱིད་པོ་འདུག ཟ་ཡས་དང་
བསྡད་ས་ཚང་མ་ཡོད། གྲོགས་པོ་ཡག་པོ་ཡང་(འང་)ཡོད།
ནོར་བུ། ཨེ་ནི་དེང་སང་བསྟན་པ་ལ་གྲོགས་པོ་ཡག་པོ་ཡོད་མ་རེད་པ།

བསྟན་པ།	ཨོ། དགོངས་དག་ནོར་བུ། དེང་སང་ཡང་གྲོགས་པོ་ཡག་པོ་ཡོད། ཡིན་ནའང་སྔོན་མར་དགོན་པ་ལ་ཡོད་དུས་སེམས་ཁྲལ་ཉུང་ང་ཡོད་རེད།
ནོར་བུ།	དེ་དུས་ཁྱེད་རང་ཕྲུ་གུ་ཡིན་པ། ཕྲུ་གུ་ལ་སེམས་ཁྲལ་ཡོད་མ་རེད།
བསྟན་པ།	ཡིན་ནའང་སྔོན་མར་ང་གྲྭ་པ་ཡིན་དུས་གཅིག་ཡོད། དེ་དེང་སང་མི་འདུག

TENPA	ngā̃ma nga̱ ko̱mpa-the̱: ṭha̱wa yi̱n.
NORBU	ālä. ngā̃ma tā̃npa ṭha̱wa yi̱n-pä. ēni kha̱nṭa yo̱re’.
TENPA	nga̱ yö̱’-thü’ ko̱mpa-ti̱: ṭi̱ktsu̱k tha̱mpo yo̱re’.
NORBU	ēni tā̃npa ṭi̱ktsu̱k-la ka̱po yo̱ ma-re̱’-wa.
TENPA	the̱nṭä ma-re̱’. nga̱ ṭha̱wa yi̱n-thü’ ngō̃nä kyīpo tu̱’. sa̱yä thang täsa tshāngma yö̱’. ṭho̱kpo ya̱kpo-yä yö̱’.
NORBU	ēni the̱ngsang tā̃npa-la ṭho̱kpo ya̱kpo yo̱ ma-re̱’-wa.
TENPA	o̱, ko̱ng:tha no̱rpu. the̱ngsang-yä ṭho̱kpo ya̱kpo yö̱’. yi̱nnä: ngā̃ma ko̱mpa-la yö̱’-thü’ sēmṭhäl nyu̱ngnga yo̱re’.
NORBU	the̱-thü’ khyērang phūkhu yi̱n-pa. phūkhu-la sēmṭhäl yo̱ ma-re̱’.
TENPA	yi̱nnä: ngā̃ma nga̱ ṭha̱wa yi̱n-thü’ cīk yö̱’. the̱ the̱ngsang min-tu̱’.

TENPA	*I used to be a monk in [of] that monastery.*
NORBU	*Oh! Did you used to be a monk Tenpa? [So] how was it?*
TENPA	*When I was there, the monastery’s rules were strict.*
NORBU	(jokingly) *And Tenpa doesn’t like rules, does he?*
TENPA	*It wasn’t like that. It used to be really pleasant when I was a monk. I had food, a place to stay, everything. And I also had good friends.*
NORBU	*And these days Tenpa doesn’t have [any] good friends, does he?*
TENPA	*Oh, sorry Norbu. These days I also have good friends. But there used to be fewer worries when I was in the monastery.*
NORBU	*You were a child at the time; children don’t have worries.*
TENPA	*But I used to have something when I was a monk. These days it’s no [longer there]. [He suggests that there’s something missing from his life.]*

Vocabulary

བསྟན་པ།	**tãnpa**	(personal name)
ནོར་བུ།	**no̱rpu**	(personal name)
དུས།	**thü'**	when (see below)
གྲྭ་པ།	**ṭha̱wa**	monk
དམ་པོ།	**tha̱mpo**	strict/tight
ཟ་ཡས།	**sa̱yä**	food/foodstuffs
དེ་འདྲ་མ་རེད།	**the̱nṭä ma-re̱'**	it wasn't/isn't like that
བསྡད་ས།	**täsa**	place to stay/sit
དགོངས་དག	**ko̱ng:tha**	sorry!
སེམས་ཁྲལ།	**sēmṭhäl**	worry/concerns
སྒྲིག་འཛུགས།	**ṭi̱ktsu̱k**	rules/regime
གཅིག	**cīk**	something

Language point

5 When

thü̱' (meaning 'at the time that') must be attached to a verb (identity, existence, or action). There are two portions (clauses) in these sentences, and **thü̱'** comes after the verb which ends the first portion. This means that it falls in the middle of the sentence, e.g.:

ང་ཕྲུ་གུ་ཡིན་དུས་ང་ལ་ཁྱི་ཡོད། **nga̱ phūku yi̱n-thü' nga̱-la khyī yö̱'.**
I had a dog when I was a child (*lit.* 'when I was a child, I had a dog').

Again, context or an additional time-word will show whether the sentence with **thü̱'** is set in the past, present, etc.

Tenpa is speaking about himself. So not surprisingly, he combines **thü'** with 'first-person' verbs; in the phrases **yi̱n-thü'** and **yö̱'-thü'**. However, you use the same **yi̱n-thü'** and **yö̱'-thü'** phrases for all three persons. You do not change the verb, e.g.:

ང་/ཁྱེད་རང་/ཁོང་ཕྲུ་གུ་ཡིན་དུས་···།
nga̱/khyērang/khōng phūkhu yi̱n-thü' . . .
When I/you/he/she was a child . . .

The feature of using 'first-person' verbs in this way also occurs in other structures. It is explained in the Grammar section (The rule of the 'essential' verb).

■ Summing-up

None of the verbs introduced so far have different forms indicating different times (i.e. they have no conjugation). Whether talking about identity, existence, having or liking you rely upon context or a time-word to indicate whether the sentence refers to the past or present.

Exercise 5

Translate these sentences:

1 དེང་སང་མི་དེ་གཞུང་གི་ལས་བྱེད་རེད།
the̱ngsang mi̱-the̱ shu̱ng-ki lä̱che' re̱'.
2 ལྷ་མོ་ལ་ཕྲུ་གུ་ག་འདྲ་མང་པོ་འདུག
lhāmo-la phūku kha̱nṭa ma̱ngpo tu̱'.
3 བསྟན་འཛིན་ལོ་ལྔ་ཡིན་དུས་ཁམས་ལ་ཡོད་རེད།
tǟntsin lo̱-ngā yi̱n-thü' khām-la yo̱re'.
4 In the past, we were both at that school.
5 I used not to like Chinese food, but this is really tasty!
6 Nyima used to have an American boyfriend.
7 Weren't you in the bank just now?
8 You see that man over there? He used to be famous.

Dialogue 3

(Audio 1:46)
Nyima has just arrived home after a get-together at the restaurant. She's speaking with her mother.

ཨ་མ། ག་འདྲ་བྱུང་། སྐྱིད་པོ་བྱུང་ངས།
ཉི་མ། སྐྱིད་པོ་བྱུང་།
ཨ་མ། ཁ་ལག་ག་རེ་ག་རེ་འདུག

ཉི་མ། འདྲ་མི་འདྲ་འདུག ཤ་མེད་ཁ་ལག་ཡང་(ཀྱང་)འདུག ཡིན་ནའང་ཤ་མོག་མོག་དཔེ་ཞིམ་པོ་བྱུང་།

ཨ་མ། འོ་རེད། དཔལ་སྒྲོན་ཟ་ཁང་གི་མོག་མོག་དངོས་གནས་ཞིམ་པོ་ཡོད་རེད། ཟ་ཁང་ལ་ཕུན་ཚོགས་འདུག་གས།

ཉི་མ། ཕུན་ཚོགས་མི་འདུག ཨ་མ་ལགས། ཇ་འདུག་གས།

ཨ་མ། ཇ་དམ་ལ་འདུག

ཉི་མ། ཨ་མ་ལགས། འདི་གྲང་མོ་འདུག

ཨ་མ། འོ་ན་ཞིམ་པོ་ཡོད་མ་རེད།

MOTHER khaṉṭa-chuṉg. kyīpo chuṉg-ngä'.

NYIMA kyīpo chuṉg.

MOTHER khālak khaṟe khaṟe tu̱'.

NYIMA ṭa̱-minṭa̱ tu̱'. shāme' khālak-yä tu̱'. yiṉnä: shā-mo̱mo pē: shiṉmpo chuṉg.

MOTHER o̱-re̱', pāṭön sa̱khang-ki mo̱mo ngō̱nä' shiṉmpo yo̱re'. sa̱khang-la phū̱ntshok tu̱'-kä.

NYIMA phū̱ntshok min-tu̱'. āma-la: cha̱ tu̱'-kä.

MOTHER cha̱tham-la tu̱'.

NYIMA āma-la: ti̱ ṭha̱ngmo tu̱'.

MOTHER o̱na shiṉmpo yo̱ ma-re̱'.

MOTHER *How was it? Did you have a good time?*

NYIMA *Yes.*

MOTHER *What food was there?*

NYIMA *There were all sorts. There was also vegetarian food. But the meat momos were really tasty.*

MOTHER *Oh yes, Päḷṭön Restaurant's momos are really good. Was Phuntshok at the restaurant?*

NYIMA *No, Phuntshok wasn't there. Is there any tea, mother?*

MOTHER *Yes, in the thermos.*

NYIMA *Mother, this is cold!*

MOTHER *Well then, it won't be nice.*

Vocabulary

ག་འདྲ་བྱུང་།	**kha̱nṭa-chu̱ng**	how was it?
སྐྱིད་པོ་བྱུང་ངས།	**kyīpo chu̱ng-ngä'**	did you enjoy yourself/have a good time?
འདྲ་མི་འདྲ།	**ṭa̱-minṭa̱**	all sorts
ཤ།	**shā**	meat
ཤ་མེད།	**shāme'**	vegetarian (food)
མོག་མོག	**mo̱mo**	type of food (see Unit 9)
དཔེ།	**pē:**	very/really
ཨོ་རེད།	**o̱-re̱'**	oh yes!
ཇ་དམ།	**cha̱tham**	thermos
ག་རེ་ག་རེ་འདུག	**kha̱re kha̱re tu̱'**	what is/was there? (the question-word is repeated, because the mother expects to hear more than one item in the answer)

Language point

6 Impressions and experiences: past and present

In accordance with what was stated in the last Summing-up, verbs in sentences with adjectives (e.g. **chēnpo** 'large' and **ma̱ngpo** 'many') like the others covered so far, generally don't have conjugation. However, with one group of adjectives there is an exception. These are the very subjective adjectives mentioned above in Language point 3, 'Reactions'. To that list, we can add **khākpo** ('difficult') and **lä̱lāpo** ('easy'). Referring to the present, one still uses **tu̱'**, as already described. For example:

སློབ་ཚན་འདི་ཁག་པོ་འདུག **lōptshän-ti̱ khākpo tu̱'.**
This lesson is difficult/I am finding this lesson difficult.

But to indicate that the sentence is set in the past, **tu̱'** can be replaced by the verb **chu̱ng(-wa)**, e.g.:

ཀྱུག་ས་སྤྱོད་དེ་ལས་སླ་པོ་བྱུང་། **kyu̱kṭö'-the̱ lä̱lāpo chu̱ng.**
The test was easy/I found the test easy.

The question-particle for **chu̱ng** is **ngä**, and the negative form is **ma-chu̱ng**. But **chu̱ng** can only serve as a verb like this when a first person is talking about his or her own experience.

■ Tibetan text

The various ways of talking about the past and present covered in this unit are brought together in the following passage. It just about manages to shift between these times without using action verbs.

Exercise 6

First, try to read the passage out loud; if possible, without looking at the transliteration.

Exercise 7 **(Audio 1:49)**

Using the transliteration if necessary, read the passage again, trying to get the correct emphasis and spacing. The audio will help.

ཁས་ས་གླིང་ཁ་དེ་ཡག་པོ་བྱུང་། ངའི་གྲོགས་པོ་དང་ངོ་ཤེས་པ་མང་པོ་འདུག ཡིན་ནའང་
བཀྲ་ཤིས་མི་འདུག བཀྲ་ཤིས་ངའི་གྲོགས་པོ་ཡག་ཤོས་རེད། བཀྲ་ཤིས་ཡོད་དུས་སྐྱིད་པ་
ཡོད་རེད། ང་གཉིས་ཕྲུ་གུ་ཡིན་དུས་རྟག་པར་མཉམ་དུ་ཡོད། ཡིན་ནའང་དེང་སང་བཀྲ་
ཤིས་ལ་དགའ་པོ་གསར་པ་ཡོད་རེད། དགའ་པོ་དེའི་མིང་སྒྲོལ་མ་རེད། སྔོན་མར་ང་ལ་
དགའ་པོ་གཅིག་ཡོད། ཨེ་ནི། མོ་རང་གི་མིང་…། རེད། སྒྲོལ་མ་རེད། བཀྲ་ཤིས་ཀྱི་དགའ་པོ་
གསར་པ་སྔོན་མར་ངའི་དགའ་པོ་རེད། ཨེ་ནི། ད་ལྟ་སྒྲོལ་མ་ང་ལ་དགའ་པོ་ཡོད་མ་རེད།
ང་བཀྲ་ཤིས་ཀྱི་གྲོགས་པོ་ཡག་ཤོས་ཡིན། ཡིན་ནའང་དེང་སང་ཏོག་ཙམ་ཁག་པོ་ཡོད་རེད།

khǟsa līngka-the̱ ya̱kpo chu̱ng. ngä̱: ṭho̱kpo thang ngo̱shēnpa ma̱ngpo tu̱'. yi̱nnä: ṭāshi' min-tu̱'. ṭāshi' ngä̱: ṭho̱kpo ya̱kshȫ' re̱'. ṭāshi' yö̱'-thü̱' kyīwa yo̱re'. nga̱-nyī phūku yi̱n-thü̱' tākpa nyāmtu yö̱'. yi̱nnä: the̱ngsang ṭāshi'-la ka̱po sārpa yo̱re'. ēni, ka̱po the̱: mi̱ng ṭö̱lma re̱'. ngȫnma nga̱-la ka̱po-cīk yö̱'. ēni, mo̱rang-ki mi̱ng . . . re̱'. ṭö̱lma re̱'. ṭāshi'-ki ka̱po sārpa ngȫnma ngä̱: ka̱po re̱'. ēni tha̱nta ṭö̱lma nga̱-la ka̱po yo̱ ma-re̱'. nga̱ ṭāshi'-ki ṭho̱kpo ya̱kshȫ' yi̱n. yi̱nnä: the̱ngsang tēts khākpo yo̱re'.

Exercise 8

Answer the following questions (in English).

1 Do we learn the name of the speaker?
2 How many other people are mentioned by name?
3 Someone has a problem. What is it?
4 What is the cause of the problem?

Exercise 9

Finally, attempt a translation.

Unit Seven

ཇ་ཁང་ལ་སྐད་ཆ་ཅི་གྲོས་མོལ་གྲོས་ཤོད་པ།

chakhang-la kǟcha cītömöltö’ shǟpa

Banter at the teahouse

In this unit you will learn how to:

- talk to friends informally
- construct sentences with action verbs
- describe what you and others did (intentional actions)
- use the agentive particle

Dialogue 1

(Audio 1:50)
Sönam rings his friend Yeshe.

བསོད་ནམས། ཧེ།
ཡེ་ཤེས། ཧེ། བསོད་ནམས།
བསོད་ནམས། མདང་དགོང་ཁྱེད་རང་ག་པར་ཕྱིན་པ་ཡིན།
ཡེ་ཤེས། ང་ཟླ་བའི་རྩ་ལ་ཕྱིན་པ་ཡིན།
བསོད་ནམས། ངའི་རྩ་ལ་ཡང་(འང་)ག་རེ་བྱས་ནས་ཡོང་མེད།
ཡེ་ཤེས། ང་ཟླ་བའི་རྩ་ལ་ཞེ་དྲག་བསྡད་མེད། ང་ནང་ལ་སྔ་པོར་ལོག་པ་ཡིན།
མདང་དགོང་ང་ཧོག་ཙམ་བདེ་པོ་མ་བྱུང་།
བསོད་ནམས། སྔ་པོར་ཉལ་བ་ཡིན་པས།
ཡེ་ཤེས། ཡིན། ཁྱེད་རང་ནང་ལ་བསྡད་པ་ཡིན་པས།

བསོད་ནམས།	འོང་། བསྡད་པ་ཡིན། ཡེ་ཤེས། རྡུ་ཧོ་ཡོད་པ། ང་ད་ལྟ་ཁོ་རང་མཉམ་དུ་ཡོད། ཨེ་ནི་ཁོ་རང་ལ་རོགས་པ་འདུག ཕྱི་རྒྱལ་གྱི་བུ་མོ་སྙིང་རྗེ་པོ་གཅིག
ཡེ་ཤེས།	ཨེ་ནི་ག་རེ་ཡོད་རེད།
བསོད་ནམས།	ཁྱེད་རང་ཕྱི་རྒྱལ་གྱི་བུ་མོ་ལ་དགའ་པོ་ཡོད་པ།
ཡེ་ཤེས།	ག་པར་ག་པར།
བསོད་ནམས།	རྩེད་མོ་ཡིན། ཡིན་ནའང་ང་ཚོ་ད་ལྟ་ཇ་ཁང་ལ་ཡོད། ཁྱེད་རང་ཤོག་ཨང་།
ཡེ་ཤེས།	ཡ་ཡ།

SÖNAM	we̲.
YESHE	we̲, sȫnam.
SÖNAM	ta̲ngkong khyērang kha̲wa: chīnpa-yi̲n.
YESHE	nga̲ ta̲wä:-tsā-la chīnpa-yi̲n.
SÖNAM	ngä̲: tsā-la-yä kha̲re-chä̲nä yo̲ng-me̲.
YESHE	nga̲ ta̲wä:-tsā-la she̲ṭhak tä̲-me̲. nga̲ ngāpo lo̲kpa-yi̲n. ta̲ngkong nga̲ tēts te̲po ma-chu̲ng.
SÖNAM	ngāpo nyä̲lwa yi̲n-pä.
YESHE	yi̲n. khyērang na̲ng-la tä̲wa yi̲n-pä.
SÖNAM	o̲ng, tä̲wa-yi̲n. ye̲shē, tu̲wo yö̲-pa. nga̲ tha̲nta khōrang nyāmtu yö̲'. ēni khōrang-la ro̲kpa tu̲'. chīkyäl-ki phu̲mo nyīng-ce̲po cīk.
YESHE	ēni kha̲re yo̲re'.
SÖNAM	khyērang chīkyäl-ki phu̲mo-la ka̲po yö̲-pa.
YESHE	kha̲wa:-kha̲wa.
SÖNAM	tsēmo yi̲n. yi̲nnä: nga̲ntsho tha̲nta cha̲khang-la yö̲'. khyērang shōk-a.
YESHE	ya̲:ya.

SÖNAM	*Hey!*
YESHE	*Hey, Sönam!*
SÖNAM	*Where did you go yesterday evening?*
YESHE	*I went to Dawa's place.*
SÖNAM	*Why didn't you come to my place as well?*
YESHE	*I didn't stay long at Dawa's. I went home early. I didn't feel so good last night.*
SÖNAM	*Did you go to bed early?*
YESHE	*Yes. Did you stay at home?*
SÖNAM	*Yes, I stayed at home. Yeshe, you know Duho? I'm with him at the moment. And he has a companion; a pretty foreign girl.*

YESHE	*So what?*
SÖNAM	*You like foreign girls, don't you?*
YESHE	*No way!*
SÖNAM	*I was just joking. But we're at the teahouse now. Come along!*
YESHE	*Okay.*

Vocabulary

ཝེ།	**we̱**	hey! (esp. an informal greeting, on the phone)*
ཡིན་(པ།)	**yi̱n(pa)**	(auxiliary verb)
མེད་(པ།)	**me̱(pa)**	(auxiliary verb: negative)
ཡོང་བ།	**yo̱ngwa**	to come
བསྡད་པ།	**tä̱wa**	stayed
ཕྱིན་པ།	**chīnpa**	went (see below)
ལོག་པ།	**lo̱kpa**	to return/come back
ཉལ་བ།	**nyä̱lwa**	to lie down (implying: to sleep)
བདེ་པོ་མ་བྱུང་།	**te̱po ma-chu̱ng**	didn't feel well
ཟླ་བ།	**ta̱wa**	(personal name)
སྔ་པོར།	**ngāpo**	early
ཤོག	**shōk**	come! (see below)
རྩེད་མོ་ཡིན།	**tsēmo yi̱n**	just joking!
ག་རེ་བྱས་ནས།	**kha̱re-chä̱nä**	why?
ག་རེ་ཡོད་རེད།	**kha̱re yo̱re'**	so what?
འོང་།	**o̱ng**	yes/okay
མདང་དགོང་།	**ta̱ngkong**	last night/yesterday evening
ག་པར་ག་པར།	**kha̱:wa-kha̱wa**	(emphatic denial)
ཡ་ཡ།	**ya̱:ya**	(response indicating agreement)
ཡོད་པ།	**yö̱-pa**	you know . . . (question tag form, used like **tu̱'-ka** in Unit 4)

* As a phone-greeting this rather brusque-sounding term imitates a similar one used in Chinese.

Language points

1 Action verbs

Aside from a small number of purely colloquial verbs (such as the single syllable **re'**), all Tibetan action verbs follow one of two patterns. They are either:

(a) two-syllable verbs
(b) composite verbs (see next unit)

Two-syllable verbs, like ཉལ་བ། **nyālwa**, derive from Old and Classical Tibetan. The second syllable must be either པ། **pa** or བ། **wa**, but this syllable is dispensable, as described below.

As imperatives (see Unit 5), action verbs can be used on their own. In almost all other situations they are fused together with a supporting, or *auxiliary* verb, forming a unit, e.g.:

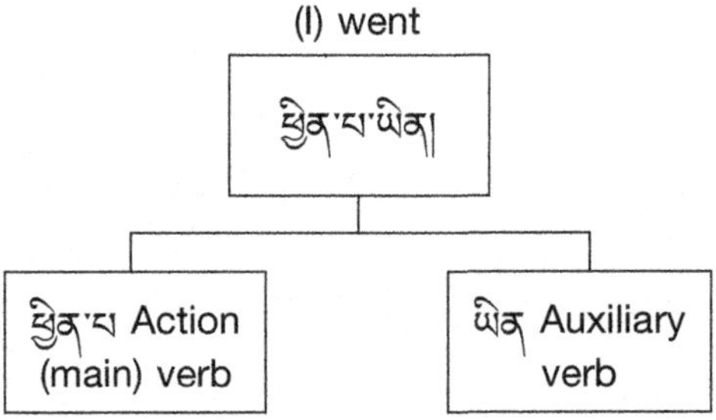

There is little conjugation of action verbs in the spoken language; spoken forms usually don't follow the conjugation found in the written language (watch out for variation between the Tibetan-script and transliterated versions of the dialogues here: the conjugated forms of the written verbs are listed in the Tibetan–English glossary). Main verbs convey the activity itself, but most of the details, such as *when* and *by whom* the action was performed, are provided by the auxiliary (in conjunction with the particle which sometimes stands between the two verbs).

The most important action-verb distinction in colloquial Tibetan is between *intentional* and *non-intentional* verbs. The next few units all deal with the first:

2 Auxiliaries with intentional verbs

Through the previous units, a sort of profile for each of the copula verbs has been built up. They are used with certain persons (first person, second person, etc.), they have their own question-particles, tags and negated forms, and one of them functions as an evidential (showing first-hand experience). All the verbs used as copulas double as auxiliaries for action verbs. Almost all details of their copula-profile also apply when they are auxiliaries.

For instance, in sentences about the past, **yi̱n** is the auxiliary used for first person(s), whereas **re̱'** is used for second and third.

ང་ཇ་ཁང་ལ་ཕྱིན་པ་ཡིན། **nga̱ cha̱khang-la chīnpa-yi̱n.**
I went to the teahouse.

ཁོ་རང་ལྷ་ཁང་ལ་ཕྱིན་པ་རེད། **khōrang lhākhang-la chīnpa-re̱'.**
He went to the temple.

The patterns for negative forms however differ a little:

ང་ཁྲོམ་ལ་ཕྱིན་མེད། **nga̱ ṯhōm-la chīn-me̱.**
I didn't go to the market.*

ཁོ་རང་ནང་ལ་མ་ཕྱིན་པ་རེད། **khōrang na̱ng-la ma-chīnpa-re̱'.**
He didn't go home.

* The Grammar section includes some remarks about the spelling of this negative auxiliary.

Exercise 1

Match the personal pronouns and names of the first group to the appropriate verb-units of the second (more than one combination might be possible). One of the verb-units is *false*, and should be discarded.

1 ང་། ཁྱེད་རང་ཚོ། ཟླ་བ། ང་ཚོ། ཡེ་ཤེས་དང་སྒྲོལ་མ།
nga̱ khyērang-tsho ta̱wa nga̱ntsho ye̱shē' thang ṯö̱lma

2 ཉལ་བ་ཡིན། ཕྱིན་པ་མེད། ཡོང་མེད།
nyä̱lwa-yi̱n chīnpa-me̱ yo̱ng-me̱

བསྡད་པ་རེད། མ་ཡོང་བ་རེད། བསྡད་པ་ཡིན་པས།
tä̱wa-re̱' ma-yo̱ngwa-re̱' tä̱wa-yi̱n-pä

Exercise 2

Translate the following sentences:

1 ང་མགྲོན་ཁང་ལ་བསྡད་པ་ཡིན།
nga̱ ṭö̱nkhang-la tä̱wa-yi̱n.

2 མོ་རང་བོད་ཀྱི་ཟ་ཁང་ལ་ཕྱིན་པ་རེད།
mo̱rang phö̱'-ki sa̱khang-la chīnpa-re̱'.

3 ཁྱེད་རང་སྔ་པོར་ག་རེ་བྱས་ནས་ཡོང་བ་ཡིན།
khyērang ngāpo kha̱re-chä̱nä yo̱ngwa-yi̱n.

4 ས་ལ་མ་བསྡད་ཨང་།
sā-la ma-tä̱'-ā.

5 མདང་དགོང་ག་པར་ཉལ་བ་ཡིན།
ta̱ngkong kha̱wa nyä̱lwa-yi̱n.

Dialogue 2

(Audio 1:51)

Yeshe arrives at the teahouse. Duho, unsure about when to use formal (honorific) language, chooses to speak to Yeshe rather politely, but Yeshe doesn't reciprocate. Yeshe and Sönam address everyone, including the staff, informally.

ཏུ་ཧོ།	འོ་ཡེ་ཤེས་ལགས་ཕེབས་སོང་།
བསོད་ནམས།	ཡེ་ཤེས། ང་ཚོ་འདིར་ཡོད། ཤོག་དང་།
ཏུ་ཧོ།	ཡེ་ཤེས་ལགས། བཞུགས་དང་།
ཡེ་ཤེས།	ཀྱེ། བུ་མོ། ང་ལ་ཇ་སྐྱད་དང་། ཕྱི་རྒྱལ་གྱི་བུ་མོ་དེ་ག་པར་འདུག
བསོད་ནམས།	མོ་རང་མགྲོན་ཁང་ལ་ལོག་ཕྱིན་སོང་།
ཡེ་ཤེས།	ཨ་ཁ། ཨེ་ན་ཏུ་ཧོ། གཅིག་ཤོད་དང་། བུ་མོ་དེ་ཁྱེད་རང་གི་དགའ་པོ་གསར་པ་ རེད་པས། སྐུ་མ་དེ་ལ་ག་རེ་བྱས་སོང་།
ཏུ་ཧོ།	ཨ་ཙི། དེ་འདྲ་མ་གསུངས་དང་། ཁོང་ངའི་དགའ་པོ་མ་རེད།
ཡེ་ཤེས།	ཁྱེད་རང་གཉིས་ཕྱི་རྒྱལ་ནས་ག་དུས་ཡོང་བ་ཡིན།
ཏུ་ཧོ།	ཁས་ས་རང་།
ཡེ་ཤེས།	ཟླ་ཉིན་ཁྱེད་རང་འདིར་ག་རེ་བྱས་ནས་ཡོང་མེད།
ཏུ་ཧོ།	ཟླ་ཉིན་ང་ལ་དངུལ་མང་པོ་མེད། ཡིན་ནའང་ངས་ལས་ཀ་མང་པོ་བྱས་པ་ཡིན།

ཡེ་ཤེས། ད་ལོ་དངུལ་མང་པོ་ཡོད་པས།
ཏུ་ཧོ། ལགས་ཡོད།
ཡེ་ཤེས། འོ་ན་ང་ལ་ཏོག་ཙམ་སྤྲད་དང་།

DUHO o̱ ye̱shē'-la: phēp-sōng.
SÖNAM ye̱shē', nga̱ntsho tä̱: yö̱'. shōk-thang.
DUHO ye̱shē'-la: shu̱:-thang.
YESHE we̱, phu̱mo nga̱-la cha̱ ṭǟ'-thang. chīkyäl-ki phu̱mo-the̱ kha̱wa: tu̱'.
SÖNAM mo̱rang ṭö̱nkhang-la lo̱kchīn-sōng.
YESHE ākha. ēni tu̱ho, cīk shǟ'-thang. phu̱mo-the̱ khyērang-ki ka̱wo sārpa re̱'-wä'. ngāma-the̱-la kha̱re chǟ̱-sōng.
DUHO ātsi. the̱nṭä ma-sūng-thang. khōng ngä:-ka̱wo ma-re̱'.
YESHE khyērang-nyī' chīkyä̱l-nä kha̱thü' yo̱ngwa-yi̱n.
DUHO khǟsa-rang.
YESHE ta̱nyin khyērang tä̱: kha̱re-chǟ̱nä yo̱ng-me̱.
DUHO ta̱nyin nga̱-la ngūl ma̱ngpo me̱'. yi̱nnä: ngä̱' lä̱ka ma̱ngpo chǟ̱wa-yi̱n.
YESHE tha̱lo ngūl: ma̱ngpo yö̱'-pä.
DUHO la̱:-yö̱'.
YESHE o̱na, nga̱-la tēts ṭǟ-thang.

DUHO *Oh, Yeshe has arrived!*
SÖNAM *Yeshe, we're here, come over!*
DUHO *Yeshe, please sit!*
YESHE *Hey* (to the female waitress), *give me a tea! So where is the foreign girl?*
SÖNAM *She went back to the hotel.*
YESHE *What a pity! So Duho, tell us something. Is the girl your new girlfriend? What happened to the last one?*
DUHO (slightly exasperated) *Oh, don't say that! She's not my girlfriend.*
YESHE *When did you [two] come from abroad?*
DUHO *Just yesterday.*
YESHE *Why didn't you come here last year?*
DUHO *Last year I didn't have much money. But I worked a lot.*
YESHE *Have you got much money this year?*
DUHO *Yes, I have.*
YESHE *Well then, give some to me!*

Vocabulary

ཁྱེད་རང་གཉིས།	**khyērang-nyī'**	you (two)
ཕེབས(་པ)།	**phēp(pa)**	went; came (polite)
ག་རེ་བྱས་སོང་།	**khare chä-sōng**	what happened?
རང་།	**rang**	just/really, etc. (emphatic)
སོང་།	**sōng**	auxiliary verb (see below)
ལོག་ཕྱིན་པ།	**lokchīnpa**	went back/returned (for people)
ཨ་ཙི།	**ātsi:**	(exclamation; surprise, dismay, irritation, etc.)
དེ་འདྲ།	**thentä**	like that/that way (in relation to actions)
གཅིག་བཤད་དང་།	**cīk shā-thang**	say/tell (us) something! (བཤད་པ། **shā'pa** to explain/describe)
ངས་ལས་ཀ་མང་པོ་བྱས་པ་ཡིན།	**ngä' läka mangpo chäpa-yin.**	I worked a lot (explained below)
ད་ལོ།	**thalo**	this year
ན་ཉིན།	**tanyin**	last year
ཨ་ཁ།	**ākha**	what a pity!
སྤྲད་དང་།	**ṭā'-thang**	give!
སྔ་མ།	**ngāma**	former

Language point

3 The 'first-hand' auxiliary སོང།

Unit 4 explained how **tu̱'** is used as a copula verb, when the speaker has first-hand knowledge of what she or he is reporting. Such reporting also occurs with actions. A speaker who has first-hand experience of an intentional action performed by someone else will report it using the verb སོང་(བ།) **sōng(wa)** as the auxiliary.

negative form:	མ་སོང། **ma-sōng**
question-particle form:	སོང་ངས། **sōng-ngä'**

This auxiliary is used to report actions done in the past (corresponding to the English simple past, e.g. 'Tenzin stayed'), but sometimes also those which have just occurred (paralleling the present perfect, e.g. 'Tenzin has arrived').

Exercise 3

The following translated text is Dawa's account of Yeshe's visit the previous evening. List the verbs in the passage, then separate them into those for which *first-hand experience* forms – either **sōng(wa)** as the auxiliary, or **tu̱'** as a copula – would be appropriate, and those for which they would not.

> *"Last night I got back home early. Yeshe came to my place at about seven. He also came to my place the night before, but I wasn't there. My neighbour saw him, and told me he'd been there. Last night Yeshe and I drank tea and talked for a while. I asked if he would go to see Sönam later. But he said he was not well. He went home. At least that is where he said he was going . . ."*

Language point

4 Coming and going

The different forms of an action verb (past, imperative, etc.) are generally very similar. The exceptions are the verbs of 'coming' and 'going'.

	Present	*Future*	*Past*	*Imperative*
to go	འགྲོ་བ། **ṭo̱wa**	འགྲོ་བ། **ṭo̱wa**	ཕྱིན་པ། **chīnpa**	རྒྱུགས། **kyu̱k**
to come	ཡོང་བ། **yo̱ngwa**	ཡོང་བ། **yo̱ngwa**	ཡོང་བ། **yo̱ngwa**	ཤོག **shōk**

Here **shōk** is a main verb, not a verb complement, as it was in Unit 5.

These imperative forms are only used in the affirmative. The negatives follow the usual pattern: 'don't go!' is མ་འགྲོ **ma-ṭo̱** and 'don't come!' is མ་ཡོང་། **ma-yo̱ng**. One might expect འགྲོ **ṭo̱** to mean 'go (away)!', but in fact it means, 'let's go!'

A **la̱thön** is used to mark a destination or location, as well as certain activities, that one goes 'on' or 'for', such as 'a holiday' (གུང་སེང་། **ku̱ngseng**), or 'a wander around' (འཁྱམས་འཁྱམས། **khyāmkhyam**):

ང་སྡེ་དགེ་ལ་ཕྱིན་པ་ཡིན། **nga̱ te̱rge-la chīnpa-yi̱n.**
I went to Derge (a Tibetan town).

ང་ཚོ་དགོན་པ་ལ་བསྡད་པ་ཡིན། **nga̱ntsho ko̱mpa-la tä̱wa-yi̱n.**
We stayed at the monastery.

One cannot refer to a person as a location. One does not go to Sönam, or even Sönam's, but always the 'place' where Sönam is (བསོད་ནམས་ཀྱི་རྩ། **sȫnam-ki tsā**).

Exercise 4

Below is a student's completed test. He had to finish some sentences by adding the missing auxiliaries (underlined), and in each case give a reason why the chosen auxiliary was the correct one. He didn't score highly. He got some of the auxiliaries wrong, because his reasoning was faulty or incomplete. For instance, no.1: the subject *does* have first-hand experience, and **sōng** *is* an auxiliary which indicates that. However, he was still wrong, because **sōng** isn't used for first-person, intentional actions.

(a) Identify any of the sentences (apart from no. 1) which are incorrect
(b) Correct the auxiliaries
(c) Supply correct reasons

1 ང་ནང་ལ་ཕྱིན་མ་སོང་།
nga nang-la chīn ma-sōng.
– སོང་།; because the action is experienced first-hand
2 ཁྱེད་རང་ཚོ་རྒྱ་ནག་ལ་ཕྱིན་པ་ཡིན་པས།
khyērang-tsho kyanak-la chīnpa yin-pä.
– ཡིན།; because of the rule of anticipation
3 མི་དེ་སུའི་རྩ་ལ་ཉལ་བ་ཡིན།
mi-the sü:-tsā-la nyälwa-yin.
– ཡིན།; because of the rule of anticipation
4 ཁས་ས་ང་བསྡད་སོང་ང་།
khāsa nga tä' sōng-nga.
– སོང་།; because the action is experienced first-hand
5 ཁྱེད་རང་འཁྱམས་འཁྱམས་ལ་ཕྱིན་སོང་ངས།
khyērang khyāmkhyam-la chīn sōng-ngä.
– སོང་། because it is a second person (you) auxiliary
6 ང་རིའི་སྒང་ལ་ཕྱིན་མེད།
nga ri: kang-la chīn-me.
– མེད། because the first person didn't go

Exercise 5

Translate these sentences:

1 When did you go on holiday?
2 I sat there yesterday, but not today.
3 Don't go inside that old building!
4 The road is not good; we did not go.
5 Tashi slept at his elder sister's.
6 I didn't go to work; it was Saturday.

Language point

5 Question responses

To a question about an action, such as 'Did you sleep/lie on the ground?'

khyērang sā-la nyälwa yin-pä. ཁྱེད་རང་ས་ལ་ཉལ་བ་ཡིན་པས།

one can respond

either with the whole verb-unit: ཉལ་བ་ཡིན།

or the auxiliary verb alone: ཡིན།

Exercise 6

Go through Dialogue 2 again, and answer these questions:

(a) Do any responses not follow either of the aforementioned patterns?
(b) How do Duho's attempts to speak politely manifest in his responses?

Language point

6 The agentive particle

When Duho said 'I worked a lot', towards the end of Dialogue 2, he added ས། **sā** to the word for 'I', to form ངས **ngä̱'**. This is the 'agentive' particle (Tibetan བྱེད་སྒྲ། **che̱ṭa**).

This particle marks the subject (or more properly, the *doer*, or *agent* – the person or thing responsible for the act). However, generally it is only required when the action verb in the sentence is a transitive one. Much more could be said about this particle (further discussion can be found in the Grammar section), but the important point for the learner is to know where and where not to use it. For those unfamiliar with the transitive–intransitive distinction, a starting point (and nothing more than that) could be to follow this rough guide:

> When the action does *not* require the involvement (the movement or re-positioning) of the whole body, *add the particle*. When the action does require such involvement (e.g. the actions of coming, going, sitting, etc.) don't add the particle.

This is sufficient to work with the verbs and situations introduced in the next few units. In the longer term, the Tibetan–English glossary distinguishes between all those action verbs which do, or do not generally require use of the particle.

The forms of the agentive particle are very similar to those of the genitive, except that **sā** always features (for more details, see the Grammar section);

genitive particles – གྱི་གི་ཀྱི་འི།
agentive particles – གྱིས་གིས་ཀྱིས་ས།

Hence the **sā** will either be incorporated into the syllable (agent) where there is no consonant ending, or stand separate from it, where there is. So to indicate that it was Dawa or Tenzin who did a particular action, the particle is added thus:

ཟླ་བ།	**t̲awa**	→	ཟླ་བས།	**t̲awä̲'**
བསྟན་འཛིན།	**tāntsin**	→	བསྟན་འཛིན་གྱིས།	**tāntsin-ki̲'**

If both 'Dawa and Tenzin' performed the action together, usually only the last one mentioned (i.e. Tenzin) has the particle added.

The agentive particle has to be attached to the subject (agent), so it cannot be heard on the frequent occasions when the subject is only implied.

The agentive particle is the only one of the Tibetan particles that is stressed when spoken. In the transliteration, this will be indicated by its having a tone-marker.

Exercise 7

Go back to Dialogues 1 and 2. Identify those verbs which require the use of the agentive particle in each.

Exercise 8

Make the following into agents, by adding the written form of the agentive particle to each:

1 you
2 we
3 our parents
4 the government
5 the car
6 Dawa and Phuntshok

Unit Eight

ཆུ་ཚོད་ག་ཚོད་ལ།

chūtshö' khatshȫ'-la

At what time? (Making arrangements)

In this unit you will learn how to:

- tell the time
- talk about what you or others are doing now
- fix appointments and make plans (speaking about the future)
- have a phone conversation
- use a phrase equivalent to 'because'
- say the calendar dates

Dialogue 1

(Audio 2:01)

Sönam phones Duho. (Translations of this and following dialogues can be found in the glossary.)

བསོད་ནམས། ཧེ། རྡུ་ཧོ། ཁྱེད་རང་ག་རེ་བྱེད་ཀྱི་ཡོད།

རྡུ་ཧོ། ད་ལྟ་ང་དམིགས་བསལ་གང་ཡང་བྱེད་ཀྱི་མེད།

བསོད་ནམས། རྡུ་ཧོ། དོ་དགོང་ཟློས་གར་ཁང་ལ་ལྟད་མོ་ཡོད་རེད། ང་གཉིས་འགྲོ།

རྡུ་ཧོ། ཆུ་ཚོད་ག་ཚོད་ལ།

བསོད་ནམས། ལྟད་མོ་ཆུ་ཚོད་བདུན་པ་ལ་ཡོད་རེད།

རྡུ་ཧོ། ད་ལྟ་ཆུ་ཚོད་ག་ཚོད་རེད།

བསོད་ནམས། ཆུ་ཚོད་ལྔ་པ་ཙམ་རེད། ད་ལྟ་ཁྱེད་རང་ལ་ལས་ཀ་ཡོད་མ་རེད་པ། སྔོན་ལ་ང་ཚོ་ཁྲོམ་ལ་འགྲོ། ཁ་སྒྲིག་བྱེད་ཨང་། ང་ཁྱེད་རང་གི་རྩ་ལ་ཡོང་གི་ཡིན།

ཏུ་ཧོ།	བསོད་ནམས་སྐུག་དང་། ཆུ་ཚོད་དྲུག་པ་ནས་དྲུག་དང་ཕྱེད་ཀའི་བར་ལ་དུས་ཚོད་མེད། འདིར་མི་གཅིག་ཡོང་གི་རེད།
བསོད་ནམས།	ཡིན་ནའང་དེའི་རྗེས་ལ་སྟོང་པ་ཡིན་པས།
ཏུ་ཧོ།	ཡིན།
བསོད་ནམས།	འོ་ན་སྔོན་ལ་ང་ནང་ལ་འགྲོ་གི་ཡིན། ཆུ་ཚོད་དྲུག་དང་ཕྱེད་ཀའི་རྗེས་ལ་ཡོང་གི་ཡིན།

SÖNAM	we̱, tu̱ho, khyērang kha̱re chi̱ki-yö̱'.
DUHO	tha̱nta nga̱ mīksäl khä̱: chi̱ki-me̱'.
SÖNAM	tu̱ho, tho̱kong tö̱karkhāng-la tā̃mo yo̱re'. nga̱-nyī' ṭo̱.
DUHO	chūtshö' kha̱tshȫ'-la.
SÖNAM	tā̃mo chūtshö' tü̱npa-la yo̱re'.
DUHO	tha̱nta chūtshö' kha̱tshȫ' re̱'.
SÖNAM	chūtshö' ngāpa-ts re̱'. tha̱nta khyērang-la lä̱ka yo̱ ma-re̱'-wa. ngā̃n-la nga̱ntsho ṭhōm-la ṭo̱. ṭha̱ṭik chi̱'-ā. nga̱ khyērang-ki tsā-la yo̱ngki-yi̱n.
DUHO	sō̃nam ku̱k-thang. chūtshö' ṭhu̱kpa-nä̱ ṭhu̱k-thang chēkä: pha̱r-la thü̱tshȫ' me̱'. tä̱: mi̱-cīk yo̱ngki-re̱'.
SÖNAM	yi̱nnä: thä̱: ce̱-la tōngpa yi̱n-pä.
DUHO	yi̱n.
SÖNAM	o̱na ngā̃n-la nga̱ nang-la ṭo̱ki-yi̱n. chūtshö' ṭhu̱k-thang chēkä: ce̱-la yo̱ngki-yi̱n.

Vocabulary

བློས་གར་ཁང་།	**tö̱karkhāng**	theatre
ཙམ།	**ts**	around/approximately
དམིགས་བསལ།	**mīksäl**	special/particular
ཕྱེད་ཀ།	**chēka**	half
སྔོན་ལ།	**ngā̃n-la**	before that
དེའི་རྗེས་ལ།	**thä̱: ce̱-la**	after that
ཆུ་ཚོད་དྲུག་པ།	**chūtshö' ṭhu̱kpa**	six o'clock
ཆུ་ཚོད་ག་ཚོད་ལ།	**chūtshö' kha̱tshȫ'-la**	at what time?

ཆུ་ཚོད་ག་ཚོད་རེད།	**chūtshö' kha̱tshȫ' re̱'**	what time is it?
གྲ་སྒྲིག་བྱེད་པ།	**ṭha̱ṭik-che̱pa**	to get ready/make preparations
ཁྱེད་རང་ག་རེ་བྱེད་ཀྱི་ཡོད།	**khyērang kha̱re chi̱ki-yö̱'**	what are you doing?
ལྟད་མོ།	**tǟmo**	spectacle/performance (either live or viewed through various media)
དོ་དགོང་།	**tho̱kong**	this evening
ཁྲོམ།	**ṭhōm**	market
སང་ཉིན།	**sāngnyin**	tomorrow
དུས་ཚོད།	**thü̱tshȫ'**	time
བར་ལ།	**pha̱r-la**	between
སྟོང་པ།	**tōngpa**	free (for time)
སྒུག་པ།	**ku̱kpa**	to wait

Language point

1 Intentional action verbs: standard forms for future and present

To convey that an action is presently being performed, or will, with some certainty, be performed one uses standard verb-units for the present and future, respectively.

In the spoken language, the present and future forms of action verbs sound the same (i.e. they have no conjugation). Instead the whole verb-unit will indicate the time-frame of an action. To form this verb-unit, the last syllable of the main verb's dictionary form is dropped, and replaced by what looks like a linking particle. After this particle, an auxiliary is added, e.g.:

Future	འགྲོ་གི་ཡིན།	**ṭo̱ki-yi̱n**	(I) shall go
Present	འགྲོ་གི་ཡོད།	**ṭo̱ki-yö̱'**	(I) am going

The linking particle follows almost the same pattern as the genitive (Unit 3).

In the spoken language, the sound is a uniform neutral-tone **ki**. In the written sentences it will appear in one of three forms – ཀྱི་གི་གྱི། – (there is no འི། here; it is replaced by གི།).

The main information about when and by whom the action is done is provided by the auxiliary verb. These auxiliaries again take the same form as the copulas of previous units. An auxiliary verb from the identity category (**yi̱n** or **re̱'**) is used to indicate a future action, whereas one of existence (**tu̱'**, **yö̱'**, or **yo̱re'**) shows a present action.

As was explained in Unit 7, the general 'profile' of these auxiliaries (which person they are used for, their question-particles, etc.) is the same as when they acted as copulas.

Examples:

ང་ལས་ཀ་ལ་འགྲོ་གི་མེད།
nga̱ lä̱ka-la ṭo̱ki-me̱:.
I shall not go to work.

ཁྱེད་རང་/ཁོ་རང་སྦྲག་ཁང་ལ་འགྲོ་གི་རེད།
khyērang/khōrang ṭa̱khang-la ṭo̱ki-re̱'.
You/he will go to the post office.

In Unit 7, the **che̱ṭa̱** (agentive particle) was introduced. It features regularly when the sentence is set in the past. In present and future sentences however, it is often omitted. This point is discussed further in the Grammar section.

Exercise 1

Translate:

1 སང་ཉིན་ང་ནང་ལ་བསྡད་ཀྱི་མེད།
sāngnyin nga̱ na̱ng-la tä̱ki-me̱:.
2 ཁྱེད་རང་གི་གྲོགས་པོ་ག་པར་འགྲོ་གི་རེད།
khyērang-ki ṭho̱kpo kha̱wa ṭo̱ki-re̱'.
3 ཁང་མིག་ཆུང་ཤོས་དེ་ལ་སུ་ཉལ་གྱི་འདུག
khāngmik chūngshö' the̱-la sū nyä̱lki-tu̱'.
4 ཁྱེད་རང་ཚོ་ག་དུས་ལོག་གི་ཡིན།
khyērang-tsho kha̱thü' lo̱ki-yi̱n.
5 མི་དེ་དངུལ་སྤྲད་ཀྱི་མ་རེད།
mi̱-the ngǖl ṭǟki ma-re̱'.

Language point

2 Telling the time

An *ordinal number* is formed by adding the syllable **pā** after a *cardinal number* (see Unit 3), e.g.:

གཉིས།	**nyī'**	(two)	→	གཉིས་པ།	**nyī'pa**	(second)
དགུ།	**ku̱**	(nine)	→	དགུ་པ།	**ku̱pa**	(ninth)

The exception to this is 'first', which has a completely different word: དང་པོ། **tha̱ngpo**. **thü̱tshȫ'** is the general word for 'time'. But the word for both 'hour' and 'timepiece' ('clock', 'watch', etc.) is **chūtshö'**, which appears in the question 'what time is it?' (*lit*. 'How many hours?') Ordinal numbers are used to indicate different hours o'clock.

For half hours one switches back to cardinal numbers (except for 1, which remains **tha̱ngpo**), and links the word for 'half' (**chēka**) to the o'clock with **thang** ('and'). For example:

five o'clock	ཆུ་ཚོད་ལྔ་པ།	**chūtshö' ngāpa**
half past five	ཆུ་ཚོད་ལྔ་དང་ཕྱེད་ཀ།	**chūtshö' ngā-thang chēka**

No equivalents for 'quarter' are used. There are two ways of including minutes. The 'shorter' version involves simply adding the minutes (**kārma**) to the hour, like with the half hours (the word for 'hour' is sometimes also omitted).

7.15 (ཆུ་ཚོད་)བདུན་དང་སྐར་མ་བཅོ་ལྔ།
(chūtshö') tṳ̈n-thang kārma cōngā

10.45 (ཆུ་ཚོད་)བཅུ་དང་སྐར་མ་བཞི་བཅུ་ཞེ་ལྔ།
(chūtshö') cū-thang kārma shi̱pcū-shengā

The longer version uses cardinal numbers for the hours, and phrases equivalent to 'past' (**yö̱l-nä**) for times up until the half hour (i.e. minutes 1–29), and 'to' (**si̱npa-la**) for times after the hour (minutes 31–59). The longer versions of 7.15 and 10.45 are:

ཆུ་ཚོད་བདུན་པ་ཡོལ་ནས་སྐར་མ་བཅོ་ལྔ་(རེད)།
chūtshö' tṳ̈npa yö̱l-nä kārma cōngā (re̱')

ཆུ་ཚོད་བཅུ་གཅིག་ཟིན་པ་ལ་སྐར་མ་བཅོ་ལྔ་(འདུག)
chūtshö' cūcik si̱npa-la kārma cōngā (tu̱')

However, Tibetans tend not to be very precise about time. The syllable **-ts** ('around') is used liberally, and rather than in minutes, times are frequently described in terms of being either 'past' (**yö̱l** + auxiliary) or 'coming up to' (**si̱n** + auxiliary) the hour or half hour.

There are no colloquial terms for a.m. or p.m. When clarification is necessary, words for 'day', 'night', or 'evening' (དགོང་དག **ko̱ngthak**) and 'morning' (ཞོགས་པ། **sho̱kpa**) are added.

Exercise 2

Give these times in Tibetan:

(a)

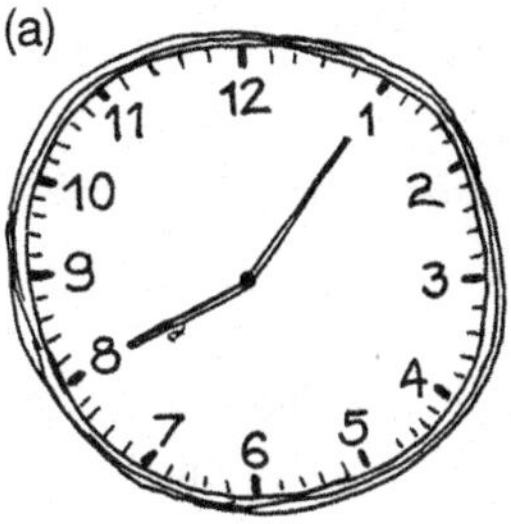

(b)

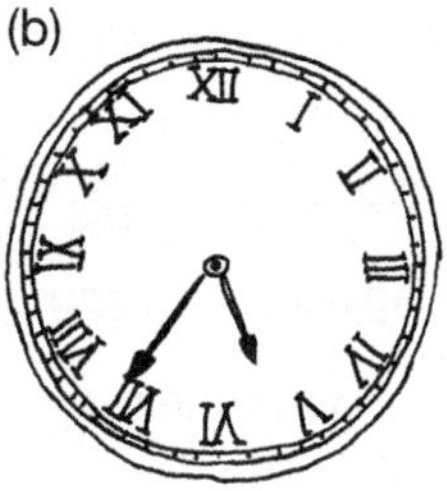

(c)

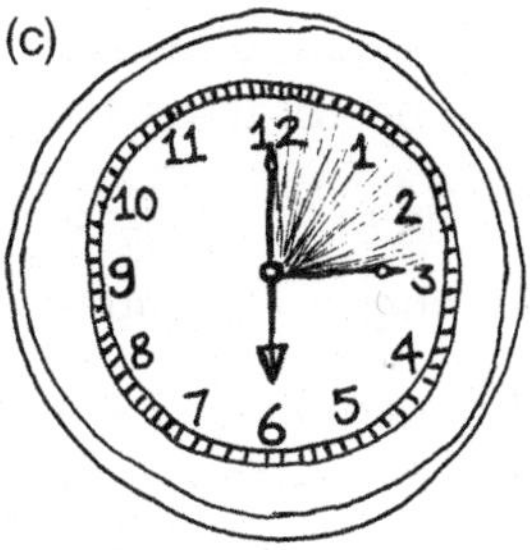

(d)

(e)

Language points

3 Composite verbs and verbalisers

Two-syllable verbs were introduced in Unit 7. Some of those (such as 'eating' and 'drinking') require an object. For example, to say the equivalent of 'I ate', or 'We'll have a drink', one must either mention the type of food or drink (the object), or at the very least, say གཅིག (**cīk**), which is equivalent to 'something'.

Apart from the two-syllable verbs, there are composite verbs. Here a *noun* and *verb* are fused together, to compose a new action verb.

Noun + **Verb**

གྲ་སྒྲིག **thaṯik** (preparation) + བྱེད་པ། **che̱pa** (to do) = གྲ་སྒྲིག་བྱེད་པ། 'to make preparations'

Unlike the example with food and drink, where one can choose a variety of objects (nouns), both the noun and verb parts of the composite verbs are fixed. The second part of the composite (**che̱pa**, in the example) turns the whole thing into a verb. For this reason it is referred to as a 'verbaliser'. Almost all colloquial composite verbs use one of these four verbalisers:

བྱེད་པ།	གཏོང་བ།	བཟོ་བ།	རྒྱག་པ།
che̱pa	**tāngwa**	**so̱wa**	**kya̱pa**

Some of these have meanings in their own right: the first three can be understood as 'to do', 'to send', and 'to make', respectively. But as *verbalisers*, their meaning is more fluid, and varies, depending upon the combination. Here are some illustrations:

ལས་ཀ་བྱེད་པ།	**lä̱ka-che̱pa**	to work
ཉོ་ཆ་རྒྱག་པ།	**nyo̱pcha-kya̱pa**	to shop
མོ་ཊ་གཏོང་བ།	**mo̱ṯa-tāngwa**	to drive
ཚོང་རྒྱག་པ།	**tshōng-kya̱pa**	to trade
སློབ་སྦྱོང་བྱེད་པ།	**lōpcong-che̱pa**	to study
སྐད་གཏོང་བ།	**kä̅'-tāngwa**	to call to; to invite
རོགས་པ་བྱེད་པ།	**ro̱kpa-che̱pa**	to help
ཆང་ས་རྒྱག་པ།	**chāngsa-kya̱pa**	to get married

སྐད་རྒྱག་པ། **kä̅'-kya̱pa** to shout (but **kä̅'** is also 'language', e.g. **phö̱kä̅'** is 'spoken Tibetan', so བོད་སྐད་རྒྱག་པ། **phö̱kä̅'-kya̱pa** is 'to speak Tibetan' – both the act and the ability)

Question-words and adverbs are usually placed in between the noun and verbaliser parts of the composite as in Dialogue 2, Unit 7: **ngä̱' lä̱ka <u>ma̱ngpo</u> chä̱wa-yi̱n.** 'I worked a lot'.

4 The written-spoken divide: verbs

As already stated, spoken Tibetan relies heavily upon auxiliary verbs to indicate time. The sound of the main verb will not necessarily change to reflect different times. But there is verb conjugation (i.e. different forms for the past, present, and future) in written Tibetan. So when writing sentences, one needs to choose the correct form of the main verb. These forms can be found in the glossary. In composite verbs, it is the verbaliser which has conjugation. There is more discussion about these issues in the Grammar section.

Exercise 3

Translate:

1 What is she doing now?
2 They invited me, but I didn't go.
3 What language are they speaking?
4 I shall sit next to you in the car.
5 Tenzin isn't here? Well then, I shall wait.
6 You did the shopping. I shall make food.

Language point

5 Other time-related phrases

Note that the structures used for talking about things in time (Dialogue 1) are similar to those used for talking about things in space (i.e. location, Unit 4). You situate an action or event in time by using a **la̱thön**, which can translate as 'at', 'on' or 'in'. Then to talk about 'after' or 'before' something (i.e. one time in relation to another), you follow the same pattern as the more specific terms for location, linking the time-word to that something with a genitive particle. Examples:

དེའི་སྔོན་ལ།	**the: ngǟn-la**	before that
ང་ཚོའི་རྗེས་ལ།	**nga̱n-tshö: ce̱-la**	after us
ཆུ་ཚོད་གསུམ་གྱི་རིང་ལ།	**chūtshö' sūm-ki ri̱ng-la**	for three hours

Exercise 4

Put these times together with the actions in full Tibetan sentences. Consult the glossary if necessary.

(a) 10.00 – I shall work
(b) 11.30 – you will eat
(c) 17.10 – we were not here
(d) 14.00 – Dawa went to the restaurant
(e) now – will you come here?
(f) 23.00 – go home!

Example:

ཆུ་ཚོད་གསུམ་དང་ཕྱེད་ཀ་ལ་ང་སློབ་སྦྱོང་བྱེད་ཀྱི་ཡིན།
chūtshö' sūm-thang chēka-la nga̱ lōpcong che̱ki-yi̱n.
At half past three, I shall study.

Exercise 5

Marked in bold is the situation. Provide the necessary information in Tibetan, in no more than three sentences each time. Don't forget to use polite verbs when appropriate:

1 **You are making an appointment to see someone.** Inform the person that you will: (a) come to his/her office; (b) come at 14.15; (c) work up until (བར་དུ། **pha̱rthu**) then.
2 **Someone who wants to meet up with you today rings.** Inform this person that: (a) no, you don't have time today; (b) you will be at home tomorrow morning; (c) she could come at 11.00.
3 **You are at a restaurant, and ring a friend.** Inform your friend: (a) where you are; (b) that you are together with an acquaintance; (c) that he/she could come along before 19.00.

Language point

6 ཁང་ཡིན་ཟེར་ན། 'Because'

A straightforward way to express something like 'because' is the phrase **kha̱ngyin-se̱rna**. When written, this is inserted between two sentences, but stands separate from them. The sentence which follows it is always the reason or justification for the previous one.

དེ་རིང་ང་ཇ་ཁང་ལ་ཡོང་གི་མེད། གང་ཡིན་ཟེར་ན། ང་ལ་ལས་ཀ་མང་པོ་ཡོད།
the̱ring nga̱ cha̱khang-la yo̱ngki-me̱: kha̱ngyin-se̱rna nga̱-la lä̱ka ma̱ngpo yö̱'.
I am not coming to the teahouse today, because I have a lot of work.

ཁོ་རང་(གིས་)ང་ལ་རོགས་པ་བྱེད་ཀྱི་རེད། གང་ཡིན་ཟེར་ན། ཁོ་རང་ངའི་གྲོགས་པོ་རེད།
khōrang(-ki̱') nga̱-la ro̱kpa che̱ki-re̱' kha̱ngyin-se̱rna khōrang ngä̱: ṭho̱kpo re̱'.
He will help me, because he's my friend.

Exercise 6

On the left is what you have decided to do, or not do. On the right is the reason. Make these into the five Tibetan sentences suggested, using **kha̱ngyin-se̱rna**:

(a)	Not staying in that big hotel	expense
(b)	Going to your friend's	time
(c)	Going on a picnic	holiday
(d)	Not giving Tenzin that money	not having
(e)	Eating at the Tibetan restaurant	liking

Dialogue 2 (*T*)

(Audio 2:02)

Some exercises from this point on test your understanding of the dialogues and passages. This symbol (*T*) at the start of a dialogue means that you are advised to attempt the related exercises before checking the translation.

Duho has to phone a travel agency. He gets nervous, particularly because he is not confident when using polite language. A female voice answers.

རྡུ་ཧོ། གངས་སེང་འགྲིམ་འགྲུལ་ཁང་རེད་པས་ལགས།
ཚེ་རིང་། ལགས་རེད།
རྡུ་ཧོ། ང་དགའ་སྒྲོ་མགྲོན་ཁང་ནས་ཁ་དཔར་གཏོང་གི་ཡོད། ཁྱེད་རང་ཚེ་རིང་སྒྲོལ་དཀར་ལགས་ཡིན་པས།
ཚེ་རིང་། ལགས་ཡིན།

རྡུ་ཧོ།   བཀྲ་ཤིས་བདེ་ལེགས་ཚེ་རིང་སྒྲོལ་དཀར་ལགས། ངའི་མིང་ལ་རྡུ་ཧོ་ཟེར་གྱི་ཡོད།
ང་བསོད་ནམས་ཀྱི་གྲོགས་པོ་ཡིན།
ཚེ་རིང་།   འོ། བཀྲ་ཤིས་བདེ་ལེགས།
རྡུ་ཧོ།   ཚེ་རིང་སྒྲོལ་དཀར་ལགས། ང་གནངས་ཉིན་ཁ་གནམ་གྲུ་ཐང་ལ་འགྲོ་གི་ཡིན།
ཡིན་ནའང་སྤ་སི་(གླངས་འཁོར)་སྔ་པོར་ཞེ་དྲག་འགྲོ་གི་རེད། བྱས་ན་ང་མོ་ཊ་
འཚོལ་གྱི་ཡོད།
ཚེ་རིང་།   ང་ཚོ་ལ་མོ་ཊ་མེད་ལགས། ཡིན་ནའང་ཁ་ལོ་པ་ངོ་ཤེས་པ་ཁ་ཤས་ཡོད། གནམ་གྲུ་
ཆུ་ཚོད་ག་ཚོད་ལ་འཕུར་གྱི་རེད།
རྡུ་ཧོ།   གནམ་གྲུ་འཕུར་གྱི་མ་རེད། འབབ་ཀྱི་རེད།
ཚེ་རིང་།   ག་འདྲ་ཟེར། ཁྱེད་རང་གནམ་གྲུ་ལ་ཕེབས་ཀྱི་མིན་པས།
རྡུ་ཧོ།   ལགས་མིན། ངའི་གྲོགས་པོ་གནམ་གྲུ་ལ་ཕེབས་ཀྱི་རེད།
ཚེ་རིང་།   ཨ་ལེ་དང་པོ་ཁྱེད་རང་ལས་ཁུངས་འདིར་ཕེབས་དང་།
རྡུ་ཧོ།   ཆུ་ཚོད་དང་པོ་ལ་ཨེ།
ཚེ་རིང་།   མིན། ག་དུས་ཕེབས་ནའང་འགྲིག་གི་རེད།

DUHO   kha̱ngsēng-ṭi̱mṭulkha̱ng re̱'-wä la:.
TSERING   la-re̱'.
DUHO   nga̱ ka̱ṭö ṭö̱nkhang-nä khāpar tāngki-yö̱'. khyērang tshēring ṭö̱lkar-la: yi̱n-pä.
TSERING   la-yi̱n.
DUHO   ṭāshi-te̱le' tshēring ṭö̱lkar-la:. ngä̱: mi̱ng-la tu̱ho se̱rki-yö̱'. nga̱ sȫnam-ki ṭho̱kpo yi̱n.
TSERING   o̱, ṭāshi-te̱le'.
DUHO   tshēring ṭö̱lkar-la:, nga̱ nāngnyinkha nāmṭhuthāng-la ṭo̱ki-yi̱n. yi̱nnä: pa̱si (lāngkhor) ngāpo she̱ṭhak ṭo̱ki-re̱'. chä̱na nga̱ mo̱ṭa tshǟlki-yö̱'.
TSERING   nga̱ntsho-la mo̱ṭa me̱'-la:. yi̱nnä: khālowa ngo̱shēnpa khāshä' yö̱'. nāmṭhu chūtshö' kha̱tshȫ'-la phīrki-re̱'.
DUHO   nāmṭhu phīrki-ma-re̱'. pa̱pki-re̱'.
TSERING   kha̱nṭäs. khyērang nāmṭhu-la phēpki-me̱:-pä.
DUHO   la̱-me̱:. ngä:-ṭho̱kpo nāmṭhu-la phēpki-re̱'.
TSERING   āle-tha̱ngpo khyērang lä̱khung tä̱: phēp-thang.
DUHO   chūtshö' tha̱ngpo-la ē.
TSERING   me̱:. kha̱thü' phēp-nä ṭi̱ki-re̱'.

Vocabulary

ཚེ་རིང་སྒྲོལ་དཀར།	**tshēring tö̱lkar**	(personal name)
གངས་སེང་།	**kha̱ngsēng**	'Snow Lion'
དགའ་སྒྲོ་མགྲོན་ཁང་།	**ka̱ṭö ṭö̱nkhang**	(hotel name)
གནམ་གྲུ་ཐང་།	**nāmṭhuthāng**	airport
འཚོལ་བ།	**tshā̱lwa**	to search/look for
ཨེ།	**ē**	(question-particle: see below)
ག་འདྲ་ཟེར།	**kha̱nṭäs**	how is that? (see below)
ཁ་པར་གཏོང་བ།	**khāpar-tāngwa**	to phone
གནངས་ཉིན་ཁ།	**nāngnyinkha**	day after tomorrow
མིང་ལ་རྡུ་ཧོ་ཟེར་གྱི་ཡོད།	**mi̱ng-la tu̱ho se̱rki-yö̱'**	(I'm) called Duho
ག་དུས་ཕེབས་ནའང་འགྲིག་གི་རེད།	**kha̱thü' phēp-nä ṭi̱ki-re̱'**	come here whenever you like (*lit.* whenever you come, it'll be okay)
གནམ་གྲུ།	**nāmṭhu**	airplane
འབབ་པ།	**pa̱ppa**	to land
(མོ་ཊའི་)ཁ་ལོ་པ།	**(mo̱ṭä:) khālowa**	driver
ཨ་ལེ་དང་པོ།	**āle-tha̱ngpo**	anyway; first
འགྲིམ་འགྲུལ་ཁང་།	**ṭi̱mṭulkha̱ng**	travel agent
འཕུར་བ།	**phīrwa**	to fly
ལ།	**-la**	on/by (for transport)

Exercise 7

Some misunderstandings arose in this conversation. What were they? The answer section has some suggestions about how they might have been avoided.

Cultural point

Phone etiquette - basics

The phone conversation in Unit 7 was between friends. Here, the situation is a little more formal, between people who have not met. In such situations, as a bare minimum, be sure to: (1) adopt a respectful tone, with none of the abrasiveness of playful banter; (2) use the polite request verbs (introduced in Unit 5); (3) liberally sprinkle the conversation with **la:** – if there's no official title you can address the person with, you must add **la:** to their name (there are no direct equivalents for Mr/Mrs).

ṭāshi-te̲le' is not used as a perfunctory opening remark, like 'hello', and is used mainly when one knows the other person (or, as in the dialogue, during introductions). There's no polite way to say goodbye on the phone. If the conversation was between friends, they may exchange the phrase which is also frequently used at the end of a face-to-face meeting, and is similar to 'see you!': མཇལ་ཡོང་། (**cä̲l-yong**). But one is only really sure that the conversation is over when either person says 'I'm putting (the phone/receiver) down': ང་གཞག་གི་ཡིན།. **nga̲ sha̲ki-yi̲n.**

Language point

7 Useful 'checking' questions

When you don't hear or understand what someone has said, you politely prompt them to repeat it with ལགས། **la:** (or impolitely with ཁ་རེ། **kha̲re**, or ཨ། **ā**).

ཁ་འདྲ་ཟེར། **kha̲nṭäs** (or ཁ་འདྲ་སེ།) is a question, used to ask 'how?', in relation to actions, e.g. ཁྱེད་རང་ཁ་འདྲ་སེ་འགྲོ་གི་ཡིན།' **khyērang kha̲nṭäs ṭo̲ki-yi̲n.** 'How will you go?'

But it can also be used as a polite response, when you heard what was said, but didn't understand exactly what someone meant (not dissimilar to 'How is that?).

Another term is useful when you just want to ensure that you have understood correctly what someone has said; it is particularly helpful for checking details, when making practical arrangements, finalising plans for travel, meetings, etc. You simply repeat the piece of information (as you have understood it), then tag ཨེ། **ē** to the end, e.g.:

གཟའ་པ་སངས་ལ་ཨེ།	**sa̱-pāsang-la ē**	On Friday (you said)?

Exercise 8

Over the phone, Sönam has just given some details about where and when you should meet him. Using the new structure, check that you have understood him correctly; you think he said that you should meet (a) tonight at 7.30, and (b) at the bus station. You also want to check whether you should meet (c) in front of (as opposed to inside) the station.

Cultural point

Dates

Instead of referring to individual months by names ('January', 'February', etc.), you use ordinal numbers, to call them the equivalent of 'first month', 'second month'. There are two principal calendars: the general or 'foreign' (i.e. Gregorian) one of everyday affairs, and the Tibetan lunar calendar, used mainly to mark religious dates. So for dates, rather than using the general word for month (ཟླ་བ། **ta̱wa**), you need to specify:

ཕྱི་ཟླ།	**cīnta**	(month of the general calendar)
བོད་ཟླ།	**phö̱nta**	(month of the Tibetan calendar)

For example:

ཕྱི་ཟླ་དང་པོ།	**cīnta tha̱ngpo**	January
བོད་ཟླ་དྲུག་པ།	**phö̱nta ṭhu̱kpa**	the sixth Tibetan month

The pattern for dates is similar to months.

ཚེས་པ། **tshēpa** is the general word for 'date', but one normally specifies, either:
ཕྱི་ཚེས། **chītshe'** (general date)
བོད་ཚེས། **phö̱tshe'** (Tibetan date)

In the subcontinent and amongst the diaspora communities however, it is more common to hear ཏ་རིག **tārik**, a loanword from Hindi (etc.), for dates of the foreign calendar, e.g.

ཏ་རིག་དགུ **tārik-ku̱**, instead of ཕྱི་ཚེས་དགུ **chītshe'-ku̱**, for 'the 9th'

When a month and date are put together, one only needs to specify either 'general', or 'Tibetan' once:

ཕྱི་ཟླ་གསུམ་པའི་ཚེས་པ་བཅུ་གཅིག	**cīnta sūmpä: tshēpa cūcik** 11th of March
བོད་ཟླ་བརྒྱད་པའི་ཚེས་པ་ཉི་ཤུ།	**phȫ̱nta kye̱pä: tshēpa nyi̱shu** 20th of the eighth Tibetan month

Unit Nine

ཁ་ལག་དང་ཟ་ཁང་གི་སྐོར།

khālak thang sa̱khang-ki kōr

Food and restaurants

In this unit you will learn how to:

- order in a restaurant
- identify some Tibetan foods and dishes
- ask about and express wants and needs
- understand food and drink culture
- make sentences which have more than one action verb

Dialogue 1

(Audio 2:07)

Two young women, Lhadzom and Dekyi, together with Lhadzom's son, have taken a break in their journey to eat in a simple restaurant. They address the staff, and each other, informally.

ལྷ་འཛོམས། ག་རེ་བཟའ་གི་ཡིན། ང་ཐུག་པ་བཏུང་གི་ཡིན།

བདེ་སྐྱིད། གནམ་གཤིས་གྲང་མོ་འདུག་ག ང་ཡང་(འང)་ཐུག་པ་བཏུང་གི་ཡིན། བུ་བསྟན་འཛིན་ཁྱོད་ལ་ག་རེ་དགོས།

བསྟན་འཛིན། ང་ལ་མོག་མོག་དགོས།

ལྷ་འཛོམས། ཕྲུ་གུ་འདི་ཡིན་ན། རྟག་པར་གོང་ཆེ་ཤོས་དེ་ཟ་གི་ཡོད་རེད། བདེ་སྐྱིད། ཕ་གི་བུ་དེ་སྐད་བཏང་ནས་ཁ་ལག་མངག་དང་། ང་ཆུ་ཁང་བཙལ་གར་འགྲོ་གི་ཡིན།

བདེ་སྐྱིད།	བུ། ང་ཚོ་ལ་ཐུག་པ་གཉིས་སྟོད་དང་། ཨེ་ནི་མོག་མོག་འདུག་གས།
ལས་མི།	ད་ལྟ་མོག་མོག་བཟོ་གི་འདུག སྐར་མ་བཅོ་ལྔ་ཙམ་འགོར་གྱི་རེད།
བདེ་སྐྱིད།	སྐར་མ་བཅོ་ལྔ་ཙམ་ཨེ། འོ་ན་ཐུག་པ་ཏོག་ཙམ་འཁྱེར་མི་དགོས། མོག་མོག་བཟོས་ཚར་ནས་ཚང་མ་མཉམ་དུ་ཁྱེར་ཤོག
ལས་མི།	ལགས་སོ། འཐུང་ཡས།
བདེ་སྐྱིད།	ཇ་གཉིས། བུ་བསྟན་འཛིན། འཐུང་ཡས་དགོས་པས།
བསྟན་འཛིན།	འཐུང་ཡས་གང་ཡང་མི་དགོས། ཨ་མས་གཅིག་ལབ་ཀྱི་རེད།

LHADZOM	khare saki-yin. nga thūkpa thūngki-yin.
DEKYI	nāmshi' thangmo tu'-ka. nga-yä thūkpa thūngki-yin. phu-tāntsin khyō'-la khare kö'.
TENZIN	nga-la momo kö'.
LHADZOM	phūku ti yin-na. tākpa khong-chēshö'-the saki-yore'. tekyi, phāki phu-the kātang-nä khālak ngāk-thang. nga chūkhang tshāl-ka toki-yin. (*she leaves*)
DEKYI	phu, ngantsho-la thūkpa nyī' tā-thang. ēni momo tu'-kä.
WORKER	thanta momo soki-tu'. kārma cōnga-ts korki-re'.
DEKYI	kārma cōnga-ts ē. ona thūkpa tēts khyēr mo-kö'. momo sö' tshār-nä tshāngma nyāmtu khyēr-shok.
WORKER	la:so. thūngyä.
DEKYI	cha nyī'. phu-tāntsin, thūngyä kö'-pä.
TENZIN	thūngye khä: mo-kö'. āmē' cīk lapki-re'.

Vocabulary

གནམ་གཤིས།	**nāmshi'**	weather
མོག་མོག	**momo**	Tibetan dish (see below)
དགོས།	**kö'**	to want (see below)
ལབ་པ།	**lapa**	to tell/say
མངག་པ།	**ngākpa**	to order (food, etc.)
ནས།	**nä**	(linking-word: see below)
གར།	**ka**	(linking-syllable: see below)
བཟའ་བ། future of ཟ་བ།	**sawa**	to eat
བཏུང་བ། future of འཐུང་བ།	**thūngwa**	to drink

བཙལ་བ། future of འཚོལ་བ།	**tshǟlwa**	to search for
བཟོས་པ།	**sö̱'pa** past of **so̱wa**	to make
འགོར་གྱི་རེད།	**ko̱rki-re̱'**	will take (a certain amount of time)
ཕྲུ་གུ་འདི་ཡིན་ན།	**phūku ti̱ yi̱n-na**	this child! (phrase, expressing exasperation)
ལྷ་འཛོམས།/བདེ་སྐྱིད།/བུ་བསྟན་འཛིན།	**lhātsom/te̱kyi'/phu̱ tǟntsin**	(personal names)
ཐུག་པ།	**thūkpa**	Tibetan food (see below)
ལས་མི།	**lä̱mi**	worker
ལགས་སོ།	**la̱:so**	(expression of assent/agreement)
འཐུང་ཡས།	**thūngyä**	a drink
འཁྱེར་བ།	**khyērwa**	to carry/to take
ཚར་བ།	**tshārwa**	to finish

Cultural point

Eating habits

The term **sa̱khang** (translated here as 'restaurant') encompasses various eateries, ranging (in the Tibetan context) from relatively plush eating-places in hotels, to the far more widespread, extremely humble type of establishment. Eating in the latter is an ordinary, informal and relatively inexpensive social activity. Beyond a standard repertoire, menu variation is not great. Because of their modest scale, these places frequently run out of dishes. It is therefore often sensible to ask what is available, rather than trusting the menu.

Vegetarianism amongst Tibetans was almost unheard of until modern times. The traditional diet was grain and meat-heavy; fruit and vegetables featured little. In more recent times, Chinese and subcontinent influences have altered this to some extent.

Tibetans eat with spoons ཐུར་མ། (**thūrma**), hands ལག་པ། (**la̱kpa**), or chopsticks ཀོ་ཙེ། (**kōtse**).

Language point

1 Expressing wishes, using དགོས།

Tibetan action and modal verbs (see also the Grammar section) generally require auxiliaries; **kö̱'** (dictionary form **kö̱'pa**) is an exception. You use it to ask about or express preferences, wants and needs (mainly related to physical objects and practical matters). This structure is only for first-person statements and second-person questions. A **la̱thön** follows the personal pronoun.

ང་ལ་གྲི་དགོས། **nga̱-la ṭhi̱ kö̱'.** I need a knife.

As Dialogue 1 shows, the negative particle (usually pronounced **mo**) goes directly before the **kö̱'**, and the question-particle (**pä**) goes straight after it.

This form should only be used with intimates, or those you would not usually address with polite speech (such as children). It would be rude to address someone who would normally be shown respect (including strangers) with phrases such as:

ཁྱོད་/ཁྱེད་རང་ལ་ག་རེ་དགོས། **khyȫ'/khyērang-la kha̱re kö̱.**
What do you want?

Exercise 1

Translate these as though they were spoken amongst intimates:

1 Do you want a chair?
2 I want the cheaper one.
3 Don't you want some of this (food)? It's tasty.
4 ཁྱེད་རང་ལ་རོགས་པ་དགོས་པས། **khyērang-la ro̱kpa kö̱'-pä.**
5 ང་ལ་ཁང་པ་ཁེ་གཙང་མི་དགོས། **nga̱-la khāngpa khētsang mo-kö̱'.**

Cultural point

Ordering food

Addressing restaurant workers in very polite terms (the polite instructions of Unit 5, etc.) is permissible. But it is more common to use less formal request forms, particularly verb complements, such as **thang**. There are no phrases corresponding to 'I would like', or 'please' here. The simplest request is to name the item required, preceded by the equivalent of 'for me' (i.e. **nga̲-la**).

Language point

2 Measure words

Simple requests for individual cups or bowls of things can be made by attaching a number to the item in question; e.g. **cha̲-cīk**, ('one (cup of) tea'), or **thūkpa nyī'** ('two (bowls) of thukpa'). གང་། **kha̲ng** and དོ། **tho̲** are terms sometimes used instead of 'one' and 'two', respectively.

Certain words of English origin are standard amongst Tibetans outside Tibet, e.g. པ་ལེ་ཏ། **pāleta** ('plate'), གླ་ལ་སི། **kha̲lasi** ('glass').

In Tibet, one is more likely to encounter Tibetan terms, such as:

ཕོར་པ། **phōrpa** ('bowl'), དཀར་ཡོལ། **kāryöl** ('porcelain cup'), and སྡེར་ཚེ། **tērtse** ('plate').

རྐང་། **kāng** followed by a number can be used to refer to many items (food or other) which are countable. Three 'apples' (ཀུ་ཤུ། **kūshu**), for instance, is ཀུ་ཤུ་རྐང་གསུམ། **kūshu kāng-sūm**.

■ Meals and foodstuffs

ཐུག་པ། **thūkpa** – (1) noodles and noodle dishes, (2) soups and broths

རྒྱ་ཐུག། **kya̲thuk** – Chinese-style long noodles, and soups with these noodles

འཐེན་ཐུག། **thēnthuk** – soup with flattened noodles

མོག་མོག། **mo̲mo** – parcels of dough, encasing meat or other stuffing, which are steamed or fried

ཤ་བག་ལེབ། **shāpha̲klep** – fried, meat-filled flattened 'breads'

(སྔོ་)ཚལ། **(ngō-)tshā̲l** – vegetables

བག་ལེབ། **pha̲klep** – bread

འབྲས། **ṭä̲'** – rice

ཤ་འབྲས། **shānṭä'** – meat and rice dish

ཤ་སྦྲེག། **shāpṭak** – fried meat and chilli dish

ཕིང་ཤ། **phīngsha** – dish with glass noodles and meat

འབྲས་བཛོས། **ṭängö̈'** – fried rice

གྲང་ཚལ། **ṭhangtshäl** – salad

གྲིན་མོག། **ṭīmo** – steamed bread

མར། **mar** – butter

སྒོ་ང་། **konga** – eggs

ཞོ། **sho** – yoghurt

འོ་མ། **oma** – milk

གུང་ལ་ཕུག། **khunglaphūk** – carrots

ཕག་ཤ། **phāksha** – pork, གླང་ཤ། **lāngshā** – beef

བྱ་ཤ། **chashā** – chicken

ཕྱུར་བ། **chūra** – cheese (the Tibetan form of which is often rock-hard)

རྩམ་པ། **tsāmpa** – (roasted) barley-grain flour; the Tibetan staple food

ཤ་མེད་(པའི་)ཁ་ལག། **shāme' (pä:) khālak** – vegetarian (i.e. meatless) food

མངར་མོ། **ngārmo** – (1) sweet (taste), (2) sweet dishes (desserts, etc.)

ཞོགས་ཇ། **shokcha** – 'morning tea' (the closest word to 'breakfast', in normal conversation, but used with the verb 'to drink', not 'to eat')

ཉིན་གུང་ཁ་ལག། **nyinkung-khālak** – lunch

དགོང་དྲོའི་ཁ་ལག། **kongṭhö:-khālak** – evening meal

Exercise 2

Imagine that you are in a restaurant with a friend. Do the following in Tibetan:

(a) Ask your friend what she wants.

(b) Ask the restaurant worker whether fried rice, yoghurt and tea are available.

(c) Order rice and yoghurt for yourself.

Language point

3 More than one action verb

So far sentences have been limited to single action verbs. Equivalents of 'but' and 'because' (conjunctions) have been explained, but these are stand-alone phrases; they don't affect the order of the words around them. The following two structures are embedded in the sentences. They allow you to add more action verbs, to make more complex sentences. Note that in both, you remove the auxiliary from the first verb-unit:

(a) གར།

When someone comes or goes somewhere, to do a particular action, the two verbs (one showing motion and the other showing the intended action) can be included in one sentence with the syllable **ka**; it functions like '(in order) to'.

The verb-unit expressing motion is the primary one here (so the personal pronoun has no agentive particle); it ends the sentence, and varies according to time (past, present, etc.). The verb expressing the intended action stands in the first part of the sentence. That first verb has no auxiliary, and its (disposable) last syllable is replaced with the **ka**. Whatever time the sentence is set in, that first verb, showing the intended act, always takes the future form.

ང་ཁ་ལག་བཟོ་གར་འགྲོ་གི་ཡིན།	**nga̱ khālak so̱ka ṯoki-yi̱n.** I shall go (in order) to make food.
ང་ཁ་ལག་བཟོ་གར་ཕྱིན་པ་ཡིན།	**nga̱ khālak so̱ka chīnpa-yi̱n.** I went (in order) to make food.

(b) ནས།

If there were two separate actions, with one following after the other, instead of expressing these in two separate sentences, **nä** allows you to combine them in one. The action in the first part of the sentence is the one done first, and the one in the second part follows it. The one who performs the actions is frequently (although not always) the same person: i.e. 'having done A, she did B'. The pattern for the second verb-unit is the same as with **ka**. That for the first verb is also very similar (with **nä** replacing **ka**), except that the first verb takes the *past* form.

In these examples, very literal translations are given, to help demonstrate the order:

ང་ཟ་ཁང་ལ་ཕྱིན་ནས་ཁ་ལག་བཟས་པ་ཡིན།
nga sakhang-la chīn-nä khālak säwa-yin.
Having gone to the restaurant, I ate.

ངས་བཀྲ་ཤིས་ལ་ཁ་པར་བཏང་ནས་སྐད་ཆ་བཤད་པ་ཡིན།
ngä' ṭashi-la khāpar tāng-nä kăcha shăpa-yin.
Having phoned Tashi, I spoke (with him).

If the first verb is in the negative, the negating particle (**ma**) goes just before the last syllable of that verb.

ཁོ་རང་ཚོས་གྲ་སྒྲིག་མ་བྱས་ནས་འགྲོ་གི་འདུག
khōrang-tshö' ṭhaṭik ma-chä-nä ṭoki-tu'.
Having not made preparations, they are going.

Exercise 3

Perhaps someone (let's say Duho) was once learning the structures just described. He wrote different portions of sentences on flash-cards, and practised creating sentences by neatly arranging the cards in various orders on a table. When he briefly left the room, *let's suppose* a Tibetan friend thought that it would be 'amusing' if he switched certain verbs and negations in these sentences, creating chaos. Please restore some order.

(c) གནམ་གྲུ་དེ་རིང་འཕུར་ནས་ཁས་ས་བབ་པ་རེད།
nāmṭhu thering phīr-nä khăsa phap-wa-re'.

(a) ང་ཡོང་གར་རོགས་པ་བྱེད་གི་ཡིན།
nga yong-ka rokpa cheki-yin.

(b) ཁོ་རང་གིས་བཟས་ནས་ཁ་ལག་མངགས་སོང་།
khōrang-ki' sä'-nä khālak ngāk-sōng.

(e) ངས་དངུལ་ཕྱིན་མ་ནས་ཟློས་གར་ཁང་(གི་)ནང་ལོགས་ལ་སྤྲད་པ་ཡིན།
ngä' ngül chīn ma nä tökarkhāng-ki nanglo-la ṭāpa-yin.

(d) ང་མ་ནས་ཉལ་འགྲོ་གི་ཡིན།
nga ma-nä nyäl ṭoki-yin.

Exercise 4

The sentences below are formulated in a variety of ways in English. But they all fit comfortably in the aforementioned two structures. Translate them:

1 He went without saying anything.
2 We sat and talked in the restaurant.
3 I shall go and search for a hotel.
4 I don't want food. I ate something before coming here.
5 Having ordered two noodle-soups, Nyima gave one of them to me.

One of Dekyi's sentences in Dialogue 1 uses the standard present form introduced in Unit 8. But she is commenting on her son's eating habits. So obviously this form is not just for describing what someone is doing right now, but also talking in more general terms about the present. This point will be explored more in Unit 10. But bear it in mind when doing the next exercise.

Exercise 5

According to your current understanding of Tibetan culture, judge which of these generalisations are likely to be true, and which are likely to be false.

༡ བོད་པ་ཤ་ལ་དགའ་པོ་ཡོད་མ་རེད།
phö̱pa shā-la ka̱po yo̱ ma-re̱'.
༢ བོད་པ་འོ་མ་ལས་ཇ་ལ་དགའ་པ་ཡོད་རེད།
phö̱pa o̱ma-lä cha̱-la ka̱: yo̱re'.
༣ བོད་པས་ནང་ལ་ཆང་བཟོ་གི་ཡོད་རེད།
phö̱pä̱' na̱ng-la chāng so̱ki-yo̱re'.
༤ བོད་པ་ལག་པས་རྩ་ནས་ཟ་གི་ཡོད་མ་རེད།
phö̱pa la̱kpä̱' tsā-nä sa̱ki-yo̱ ma-re̱'.
༥ བོད་པས་ཟ་ཡས་མངར་མོ་ཞེ་དྲག་ཟ་གི་ཡོད་མ་རེད།
phö̱pä̱' sa̱yä ngārmo she̱ṭhak sa̱ki-yo̱ ma-re̱'.
༦ རྒྱ་རིགས་ལས་བོད་པས་ཞོ་མང་ང་འཐུང་གི་ཡོད་རེད།
kya̱rik-lä phö̱pä̱' sho̱ ma̱ng-nga thūngki-yo̱re'.

Dialogue 2

(Audio 2:08)

Yeshe's mother has invited Duho to the family home for a meal. Yeshe and Duho talk to each other using informal terms, whereas Yeshe's mother addresses Duho as befits a guest.

ཨ་མ།	ཁོང་། འདིར་བཞུགས་དང་། ཨ་ལེ་དང་པོ་གསོལ་ཇ་གང་མཆོད། ང་མོག་མོག་ལེན་གར་འགྲོ་གི་ཡིན། ང་ཚོ་འདིར་ཞལ་ལག་ཡག་པོ་མེད། ཡིན་ནའང་མཉེས་པོ་མཆོད་རོགས་ཨང་།
ཡེ་ཤེས།	ཏུ་ཧོ། མོག་མོག་ཟ་དུས་གཟབ་གཟབ་བྱེད་ཨང་། ཚ་པོ་འདུག
ཨ་མ།	གསོལ་ཇ་བཞེས། མོག་མོག་ག་འདྲ་འདུག་ལགས།
ཏུ་ཧོ།	ལགས། ཞིམ་པོ་ཞེ་དྲག་འདུག
ཨ་མ།	གྲང་ཆལ་ཡང་མཆོད། ཐབ་ཚང་ལ་མོག་མོག་མང་པོ་ཡོད། གསོལ་ཇ་མཆོད། གྲང་མོ་མི་འདུག་གས།
ཏུ་ཧོ།	ང་ལ་གསོལ་ཇ་མིན་ཨ་ཅག་ལགས། ཡེ་ཤེས། ཁྱེད་རང་གི་ཨ་མས་ང་ལ་ཇ་ག་འདྲ་མང་པོ་བླུག་གི་འདུག ང་ལ་དགོས་གནས་མི་དགོས། ཡིན་ནའང་ཉན་གྱི་མི་འདུག ང་ལ་རོགས་པ་བྱེད་དང་།
ཡེ་ཤེས།	གང་ཡང་ཡོད་མ་རེད། ལུགས་སྲོལ་རེད།
ཨ་མ།	འདིར། མོག་མོག་ཚ་པོ་མཆོད།
ཏུ་ཧོ།	ཨ་ཅག་ལགས། ངར་དགོས་གནས་འགྲིགས་སོང་།
ཨ་མ།	རྐང་ཁ་ཤས་བཞེས་དང་།
ཡེ་ཤེས།	ཏུ་ཧོ། ཁྱེད་རང་(གིས)་བོད་སྐད་བོད་པ་ནང་བཞིན་རྒྱག་གི་ཡོད་པ། ད་མོག་མོག་བོད་པ་ནང་བཞིན་ཟ་ཨང་། མཛངས་མ་བྱེད་དང་། མང་ཙམ་ཟ་ཨང་།
ཏུ་ཧོ།	ང་མཛངས་བྱེད་ཀྱི་མེད། ཨ་ར། ངའི་གྲོད་ཁོག
ཡེ་ཤེས།	སྙིང་རྗེ། ཕྱི་རྒྱལ་(གྱི་)མི་དེ་ཚོ་…།

MOTHER	khōng, tä: shu:-thang. āle-thangpo sölcha khang chö'. nga momo lenka toki-yin. (*she returns*) ngantsho tä: shälak yakpo me', yinnä nyēpo chö'-ro-a.
YESHE	tuho, momo sa-thü' sapsap chi-a, tshāpo tu'.
MOTHER	sölcha she'. momo khanța tu'-la:.
DUHO	la: shimpo shețhak tu'.

MOTHER ṭha̱ngtshäl-yä chȫ’. thāptsang-la mo̱mo ma̱ngpo yö̱’. sȫlcha chȫ’. ṭha̱ngmo min-tu̱’-kä.

DUHO nga̱-la sȫlcha me̱: āca-la: (*she leaves the room*) ye̱shē’, khyērang-ki āmǟ’ nga̱-la cha̱ kha̱nṭa ma̱ngpo lūki-tu̱’. nga̱-la ngȫnä’ mo-kö̱. yi̱nnä: nyä̱nki min-tu̱’. nga̱-la ro̱kpa chi̱’-thang.

YESHE khä̱: yo̱ ma-re̱’. lu̱ksȫl re̱’. (*she returns*)

MOTHER tä̱: mo̱mo tshāpo chȫ’.

DUHO āca-la: nga̱: ngȫnä’ ṭi̱k-song.

MOTHER kāng khāshä’ she̱’-thang.

YESHE tu̱ho, khyērang phö̱kǟ’ phö̱pa na̱ngshin kya̱ki-yö̱’-pa. tha̱ mo̱mo phö̱pa na̱ngshin sa̱-a. tsa̱ng ma-chi̱’-thang. ma̱ngtsa sa̱-a.

DUHO nga̱ tsa̱ng chi̱ki-me̱’. āra, ngä̱: ṭho̱khok.

YESHE nyīngce̱:, chīkyäl-mi̱ the̱ntsho . . .

Vocabulary

གསོལ་ཇ།	**sōlcha**	tea (polite/honorific)
ལེན་པ།	**le̱npa**	to take/collect/get (intentional)
ཞལ་ལག	**shä̱lak**	food (polite/honorific)
ཐབ་ཚང་།	**thāptsang**	kitchen
ཟ་དུས།	**sa̱-thü'**	when eating
གཟབ་གཟབ་བྱེད་པ།	**sa̱psap-che̱pa**	to be careful
ང་ལ་གསོལ་ཇ་མིན།	**nga̱-la sōlcha me̱:**	no tea for me! (polite)
གང་ཡང་ཡོད་མ་རེད།	**khä̱: yo̱ ma-re̱'**	it doesn't matter/it's okay!
(ངར་)འགྲིགས་སོང་།	**(nga̱:) ṯi̱k-song**	that's enough (for me)!
སྙིང་རྗེ།	**nyīngce̱:**	(exclamation of sympathy; meant mockingly here, like 'oh, poor you!')
མཛངས་བྱེད་པ།	**tsa̱ng-che̱pa**	to hold back/to act with restraint (out of politeness)
གྲོད་ཁོག	**ṯho̱khok**	stomach
བླུག་པ།	**lūkpa**	to pour/put (in)
ཉན་པ།	**nyä̱npa**	to listen
ནང་བཞིན།	**na̱ngshin**	the same as
མང་ཙམ།	**ma̱ngtsa**	some more
ད།	**tha̱**	so/now
ཨ་ར།	**āra**	ow!
ཞལ་ལག་མཉེས་པོ་མཆོད། or ཞལ་ལག་མཉེས་པོ་གནང་གོ།	**shä̱lak nyēpo chȫ'/ shä̱lak nyēpo nāng-ko**	enjoy the food!

Cultural point

Eating etiquette; host and guest roles

The Tibetan host abhors an empty vessel; such a vessel verges on being something of ill-portent. Hence the host's most essential role is to ensure that the guest's bowl, cup, etc. are constantly replenished. This is accompanied with unremitting encouragement to 'eat!' and 'drink!' These are delivered in the form of polite imperatives. Note also that certain polite nouns are required (explained further in Unit 15). Protests from overwhelmed guests are treated as part of the performance (and are generally ignored). A guest showing frustration at the host's apparent disregard of his/her protests would obviously be offensive. The seasoned guest paces him/herself (taking, for instance, just small sips of tea, when invited, so that the cup is only topped-up by a small amount each time).

The idea of 'going Dutch' after eating or drinking out with someone is a rather alien one. Indeed, showing eagerness to foot the whole bill is almost expected. It is not uncommon to see two parties physically restraining one another, in their desperate attempts to be the one to pay!

Because of the association between appetite and health, an observation that someone is eating well (i.e. 'a lot') is a positive thing to say, rather than a criticism. Similarly, to say 'you have put on weight!' is a compliment, akin to 'you look well!'

Exercise 6

The snippets of speech below are possible statements and responses.

མི་དགོས།	**mo-kö̲'**	མཉེས་པོ་མཆོད་ཡང་།	**nyēpo chȫ-a**
ལགས་མིན།	**la-me̲:**	འདི་ཞིམ་པོ་མི་འདུག	**ti̲ shi̲mpo min-tu̲'**
འགྲིགས་སོང་།	**t̲i̲k-song**	འོ་ཡ།	**o̲ya**
ང་བཟའ་གི་མིན།	**nga̲ sa̲ki-me̲:**	ཐུགས་རྗེ་ཆེ།	**thūce-chē**
ཡག་པོ་ཟ་ཡང་།	**ya̲kpo sa̲-a**	ང་(X)་ལ་དཀའ་པོ་མེད།	**nga̲ (X)-la ka̲po me̲'**
འགྲིགས་སོང་ལགས།	**t̲i̲k-sōng-la:**		

Choose which one(s) would be appropriate if you found yourself in each of these social situations (sometimes it is stipulated whether the situation is formal or informal):

1 You need to respond to someone who has just invited you for a drink, but who you don't particularly like.
2 You've invited someone for a meal; the food's on the table, ready to be eaten (formal).
3 Someone's attempting to put more food on your plate, but you aren't sure if you can eat more (formal).
4 Someone's attempting to put more of some dish on your plate, which you didn't like the taste of.
5 Your friend has just poured you some more beer (informal).
6 The restaurant worker brings your food and drink.

Exercise 7 (Audio 2:12)

Two elderly Tibetans sit, with their tea, in a restaurant, sharing thoughts. They eventually notice two other customers, and their conversation turns in a new direction.

ཁོ་ཚོས་ག་རེ་ཟ་གི་འདུག དེ་ལ་གྲང་ཚལ་ཟེར་གྱི་རེད། གྲང་ཚལ་ཨེ། རེད། ཕྱི་རྒྱལ་གྱི་མིས་ཚལ་སྔོན་པོ་མང་པོ་ཟ་གི་ཡོད་རེད། ཨ་ལས། ང་ཚོ་བོད་པ་ལ་ཞིམ་པོ་ཡོད་མ་རེད་པ། ཡོད་མ་རེད། ང་ཚོའི་ལུང་པ་ལ་ཚལ་དེ་ཚོ་སེམས་ཅན་ལ་སྤྲོད་ཀྱི་ཡོད། ཨེ་ནི་ཁོ་ཚོས་ག་རེ་འཐུང་གི་འདུག དེ་ཆུ་མངར་མོ་རེད། ཁོ་རང་ཚོས་ཕྲུ་གུའི་འཐུང་ཡས་ག་རེ་བྱས་ནས་འཐུང་གི་ཡོད་རེད། གང་ཤེས།

khōtshō̄' khare saki-tu'. the-la ṭhangtshäl serki-re'. ṭhangtshäl-ē. re', chīkyäl-ki mi' tshā̄l ngō̄npo mangpo saki-yore'. ālä, ngantsho phöpa-la shimpo yo ma-re'-wa. yo ma-re'. ngantshö: lungpa-la tshā̄l thentsho sēmcän-la ṭā̄ki-yō̄'. ēni, khōtshō̄' khare thūngki-tu'. the chū ngārmo re'. khōrang-tshō̄' phūkü: thūngye khare-chänä thūngki-yore'. khang-she'.

1 Who else is in the restaurant?
2 Organise the text into portions, for speaker A and speaker B.
3 How many different uses are made of the standard present here?

Unit Ten

ཉོ་ཆ་རྒྱག་པ།

nyo̲pcha-kya̲pa

Shopping

In this unit you will learn how to:

- make purchases and bargain for prices
- personalise statements
- use volunteering structures (similar to 'I'll do it!')
- describe actions done regularly or repeatedly
- use phrases equivalent to 'only', 'whether or not', 'too', etc.

Dialogue 1

(Audio 2:13)

Whilst shopping in Kathmandu, Penpa addresses a female shopkeeper.

སྤེན་པ།	ཨ་ཅག་ལགས། ཁ་བཏགས་ཡོད་པས།
ཚོང་མཁན།	ལགས་ཡོད།
སྤེན་པ།	བསྟན་རོགས་བྱེད། དེ་ཚོ་ལ་ག་ཚོད་རེད།
ཚོང་མཁན།	འདི་ཚོ་སྤུས་ཀ་ཡག་ག་ཡོད་རེད། རེ་རེ་ལ་སྒོར་མོ་ལྔ་བཅུ་ལྔ་བཅུ་ཡིན། གཟིགས་ཀྱི་ཡིན་པས།
སྤེན་པ།	ཏོག་ཙམ་གཅིག་ཡས་འདུག་གས།
ཚོང་མཁན།	གཉིས་གཟིགས་དང་། ངས་སྒོར་མོ་དགུ་བཅུ་ལ་འཚོང་དགོས།
སྤེན་པ།	ཡོང་ང་། ངས་གཉིས་ཉོ་དགོས། རྩམ་པ་ཡང་(འང་)ཡོད་པས།

ཚོང་མཁན།	རྩམ་པ་ཡོད་ལགས།
སྤེན་པ།	ཀི་ལོ་ལ་ག་ཚོད་བྱེད་ཀྱི་ཡོད་རེད།
ཚོང་མཁན།	ཀི་ལོ་ལ་སྐོར་མོ་བརྒྱད་ཅུ་རེད།
སྤེན་པ།	སྐོར་མོ་བརྒྱད་ཅུ། ཟླ་ཉིན་ངས་སྐོར་མོ་དྲུག་ཅུ་ལ་ཉོས་པ་ཡིན།
ཚོང་མཁན།	ད་དེང་སང་ཚང་མ་ཡར་འཕར་གྱི་ཡོད་རེད། ཚོང་པ་ལ་ཡང་(འང་)དཀའ་ལས་ཁག་པོ་འདུག སྔོན་མར་ས་ཆ་འདི་ལ་བོད་པའི་ཚོང་ཁང་མང་པོ་ཡོད་རེད། ཡིན་ནའང་དེང་སང་ང་གཅིག་པོ་ཡིན། བོད་རིགས་ལ་རྩམ་པ་དམིགས་བསལ་གྱི་གལ་ཆེན་པོ་རེད། འདིས་བྱས་ནས་འཚོང་གི་ཡོད། ཁེ་བཟང་ཞེ་དྲག་ཡོད་མ་རེད།
སྤེན་པ།	དེ་ག་རང་རེད། ཨ་ཅག་ལགས། རྩམ་པ་དངོས་གནས་གལ་ཆེན་པོ་རེད།

PENPA	āca-la: khāta yö̱'-pä.
SHOPKEEPER	la-yö̱'.
PENPA	tā̈n ro-chi̱'. the̱ntsho-la kha̱tshō̈' re̱'.
SHOPKEEPER	ti̱ntsho pṻka ya̱ka yo̱re'. re̱re-la ko̱rmo ngāpcu ngāpcu yi̱n. si̱ki-yi̱n-pä'.
PENPA	tēts cāk-yä tu̱'-kä.
SHOPKEEPER	nyī' si̱k-thang, ngä̱' ko̱rmo ku̱pcu-la tshōng-ko̱.
PENPA	yo̱ngnga, ngä̱' nyī' nyo̱-ko̱. tsāmpa-yä yö̱'-pä.
SHOPKEEPER	tsāmpa yö̱'-la:.
PENPA	kīlo-la kha̱tshō̈' che̱ki-yo̱re'.
SHOPKEEPER	kīlo-la ko̱rmo kyä̱cu re̱'.
PENPA	ko̱rmo kyä̱cu. ta̱nyin ngä̱' ko̱rmo ṭhu̱kcū-la nyö̱wa-yi̱n.
SHOPKEEPER	tha̱ thēngsang tshāngma ya̱r-phārki-yo̱re'. tshōngpa-la-yä kāle-khākpo tu̱'. ngā̈nma sācha tä̱: phö̱pä: tshōngkhang ma̱ngpo yo̱re'. yi̱nnä: the̱ngsang nga̱ cīkpo yi̱n. phö̱rik-la tsāmpa mīksäl-ki khä̱l-chēnpo re̱'. ti̱: chä̱-nä tshōngki-yö̱'. khēpsang she̱ṭhak yo̱ ma-re̱'.
PENPA	tha̱ka-rang re̱' āca-la:. tsāmpa ngō̈nä khä̱l-chēnpo re̱'.

Vocabulary

སྤེན་པ།	**pēnpa**	(personal name)
ཚོང་མཁན།	**tshōngkhā̃n**	shopkeeper/seller
སྤུས་ཀ་ཡག་ག།	**pū̃ka ya̱ka**	better quality
རེ་རེ།	**re̱re**	each (see below)
ཉོ་བ།	**nyo̱wa**	to buy
གཟིགས་པ།	**si̱kpa**	to buy (honorific)
འཚོང་པ།	**tshōngpa**	to sell
ཡོང་ང།	**yo̱ngnga**	okay!
དེ་ག་རང་རེད།	**tha̱ka-rang re̱'**	(you are) quite right!
ཅ་ལག	**cālak**	thing (manmade, mainly small items)

དེ་ཚོ་ལ་ག་ཚོད་རེད།	**the̱ntsho-la kha̱tshȭ' re̱'**	how much are they?
གཅག་ཡས་འདུག་གས།	**cāk-yä tu̱'-kä**	any chance of a reduction?
ག་ཚོད་བྱེད་ཀྱི་ཡོད་རེད།	**kha̱tshȭ' che̱ki-yo̱re'**	how much? (see below)
དམིགས་བསལ(་གྱི)།	**mīksäl(-ki)**	especially
ཡར་འཕར་བ།	**ya̱r-phārwa**	increasing
དཀའ་ལས་ཁག་པོ།	**kāle-khākpo**	difficult
ཁེ་བཟང་།	**khēpsang**	profit/gain
གལ་ཆེན་པོ།	**khä̱l-chēnpo**	important
གཡར་བ།	**yārwa**	to borrow; to lend
ཡིན།	**yi̱n**	(personalised verb; see below)
ད།	**tha̱:**	(speech-filler)
ཁ་བཏགས།	**khāta**	Tibetan silk 'scarf', usually white, signifying auspiciousness; presented in various religious and social situations (when greeting, parting, congratulating, etc.)

Language point

1 Talking about prices

nyo̱pcha-kya̱pa is usually shopping for essentials, rather than as a pastime. There is no separate verb for 'pay'; instead equivalents for 'give' are used. Whether talking about buying, selling, or indeed borrowing, prices and rates are always attached to items by a **la̱thön** – the closest English equivalent here would be 'for' (as in, 'how much for this?') This use of **la̱thön** is illustrated in Dialogue 1, in both questions about prices:

> **the̱ntsho-la kha̱tshȭ' re̱'.** (How much do they cost?), and
> **kīlo-la kha̱tshȭ' cheki-yo̱re'.** (How much is it per kilo?)

The first question is accompanied by a verb of identity, whereas the second – used more when asking about rates of things – may have either one of existence, or identity. The word **re̱re** (for 'each') here is necessarily referring to a number of uniformly priced items, so as in the example, the price is repeated (**re̱re-la ko̱rmo ngāpcu-ngāpcu yi̱n**).

Exercise 1

Translate the following. The first sentence has already been done.

1 How much is a (cup of) tea?
ཇ་གཅིག་ལ་ག་ཚོད་རེད། **cha̱-cīk-la kha̱tshȫ' re̱'.**
2 A (cup of) tea costs 5 rupees.
3 No, I don't want (to buy) that one. How much is the green one?
4 Please sell this to us.
5 I paid 14 Yuan for these noodles.
6 How much will you sell that table for?
7 We borrowed his car for two days.

Cultural point

Shopping and bargaining

For someone learning a language, regular engagement with native speakers is usually guaranteed when shopping for essentials (in supermarkets, grocers, etc.) However, due to prevailing economic, social and political conditions, Tibetans are not active in a huge range of commercial spheres. Perhaps the most likely interactions are with Tibetans who are owners of small shops and stalls, selling cultural and religious artefacts, souvenir items and trinkets.

Not all prices are open to negotiation. You can establish whether the price is fixed or negotiable (and gain an idea of the range for negotiation) by asking whether there is any possibility of a reduction (as in Dialogue 1). This is preferable to 'suggesting' an alternative price at the outset.

Some points on currency variations were discussed in Unit 5. Tibetans outside Tibet usually adopt the weights and measures of the society they live in, so things are frequently purchased in ཀེ་ལོ།

(**kīlo** 'kilograms'). More common in Tibet is the རྒྱ་མ། (**kyama** – 500g, or about 1.1 pounds).

Language point

2 Personalisation

In previous units, **yin** and **yö'** (verbs of identity and existence, respectively) were used only for the first person; that is, sentences with 'I' or 'we' as their subject. But the boundaries of these verbs can be extended. So instead of using them only to refer to him- or herself, a speaker may choose to use them when the subject is a second or third person, possession, place or institution *in order to indicate that the speaker has a close or personal relationship* with the person or thing in question. Saying 'he is my friend' using the verb **re'** is obviously still correct, e.g.:

ཁོ་རང་ངའི་གྲོགས་པོ་རེད། **khōrang ngä: ṭhokpo re'.**
because 'he' is a third person.

But a greater sense of intimacy or personalisation would be conveyed by instead saying:

ཁོ་རང་ངའི་གྲོགས་པོ་ཡིན། **khōrang ngä: ṭhokpo yin.**

The shopkeeper in Dialogue 1 uses this type of personalisation in relation to her goods, when she tells Penpa the price of her **khāta** (**rere-la kormo ngāpcu ngāpcu yin**).

For another example, a wife might say:

ངའི་ཁྱོ་ག་ནང་ལ་ཡོད། **ngä: khyōka nang-la yö'.**
My husband is at home.

Although the subject (her husband) is a third person, the wife chooses to personalise what she says, by using **yö'**, instead of another verb of existence.

Exercise 2

The following are statements about purchases. Each has a reason why the purchase goes ahead or not. Add the missing words, then translate the sentences into English.

1 ང་ཐུག་པ་ཉོ་གི་______། གང་ཡིན་ཟེར་ན། ང་ཚོའི་ནང་ལ་ཐུག་པ་______འདུག
nga̱ thūkpa nyo̱ki ______ kha̱ngyin-se̱rna, nga̱ntshö: na̱ng-la thu̱kpa ______tu̱'.

2 ང་ད་ལྟ་དེ་ཉོ་______འགྲོ་གི་མིན། གང་ཡིན་ཟེར་ན། ང་ལ་______ཀ་ཡོད།
nga̱ tha̱nta the̱ nyo̱______ ṭo̱ki me̱: kha̱ngyin-se̱rna, nga̱-la ______ka yö̱'.

3 ངས་སྔོན་པོ་ཉོས་མེད། གང་ཡིན་ཟེར་ན། ང་______ ______ལ་དགའ་པོ་མེད།
ང་དམར་མོ་ལ་དགའ་བ་______།
ngä̱ ngȫnpo nyö̱' me̱ kha̱ngyin-se̱rna, nga̱ ______ ______ la ka̱po me̱'. nga̱ mārmo-la ka̱: ______.

4 ང་ཁོ་ཚོ་ལ་ཞ་བག་ལེབ་ཉོ་གི་______། གང་ཡིན་ཟེར་ན། ཁོ་ཚོས་______ཟ་གི་
ཡོད་མ་རེད།
nga̱ khōtsho-la shāpha̱klep nyo̱ki-______ kha̱ngyin-se̱rna, khōtshȫ ______sa̱ki yo̱ ma-re̱'.

5 ང་མི་དེའི་རྩ་______ཉོ་གི་ཡིན། གང་ཡིན་ཟེར་ན། ཁོ་རང་གི་ཅ་ལག་གོང་
______ ______ཡོད་རེད།
nga̱ mi̱ the̱: tsā ______ nyo̱ki-yi̱n kha̱ngyin-se̱rna, khōrang-ki cālak kho̱ng______ ______ yo̱re.

Exercise 3 (Audio 2:17)

We have been employing **la̱thön** in a variety of ways. Pay special attention to these, as you:

(a) Translate the following passage.
(b) Make a list of the different ways in which **la̱thön** is used here.

དེ་རིང་ང་ཁྲོམ་ལ་ཉོ་ཆ་རྒྱག་གར་ཕྱིན་པ་ཡིན། ངས་བཀྲ་ཤིས་ལ་ཕག་ཤ་ཉོས་པ་ཡིན། གང་ཡིན་ཟེར་ན། བཀྲ་ཤིས་ཕག་ཤ་ལ་དམིགས་བསལ་དགའ་པོ་ཡོད་རེད། ཚལ་ཡག་པོ་ཡང་(འང་)ཉོས་པ་ཡིན། ངས་གུང་ལ་ཞུག་ལ་སྒོར་མོ་དྲུག་སྤྲད་པ་ཡིན། ཉོ་ཆ་བརྒྱབ་ནས་ང་ལྟད་མོ་གཡར་གར་ཕྱིན་པ་ཡིན། ཁོ་རང་ཚོས་ཉིན་མ་གཅིག་ལ་ལྟད་མོ་རེ་རེ་ལ་སྒོར་མོ་བདུན་བདུན་ལེན་གྱི་ཡོད་རེད། ཡིན་ནའང་ང་འགྲོ་དུས་ཁོ་ཚོ་ལ་ལྟད་མོ་ཡག་པོ་མི་འདུག ངས་གང་ཡང་གཡར་མེད།

the̱ring nga̱ ṭhōm-la nyo̱pcha-kya̱pka chi̱npa-yi̱n. ngä̱' ṭāshi'-la phāksha nyö̱wa-yi̱n. kha̱ngyin-se̱rna, ṭāshi' phāksha-la mīksäl ka̱po yo̱re'. tshä̱l ya̱kpo-yä nyö̱wa-yi̱n.

ngä̱' khu̱nglaphūk-la ko̱rmo ṭhu̱k ṭä̱wa-yi̱n. nyo̱pcha kya̱p-nä nga̱ tǟmo yārka chīnpa-yi̱n. khōrangtshȫ' nyi̱ma-cīk-la tǟmo re̱re-la ko̱rmo tü̱n-tü̱n le̱nki-yo̱re'. yi̱nnä: nga̱ ṭo̱-thü̱' khōtsho-la tǟmo ya̱kpo min-tu̱'. ngä̱' khä̱: yār-me̱.

Language point

3 The 'volunteering' form

The standard future form (Unit 8) is used to express an intention to perform an action, e.g. **nga̱ khālak so̱ki-yi̱n.** ('I shall make food.') But another first-person structure can be used to show willingness to do an action, similar to what 'let me . . . !', or 'I'll do it!' convey in English. This would usually be chosen, for example, when expressing a wish to help. But equally, the situation might be as in Dialogue 1, where the trader expresses her preparedness (rather than enthusiasm) to reduce her price. Or, it might be uttered in exasperation, when someone else seems unwilling or incapable of doing a particular action (a mother, for instance, talking to her child).

Example: ངས་བྱེད་དགོས། **ngä̱' che̱' ko̱.** I'll do it!

The structure might appear curious: 'I' has the **che̱ṭa**-particle attached to it. In Unit 7, as the 'agentive' marker, this particle only accompanied certain verbs. But with this volunteering form, whatever intentional action verb is used, the first-person form is always **ngä̱'**. One can use the present forms of action verbs in this structure (although some prefer other forms). Note also that unlike in Unit 9, དགོས། is pronounced **ko̱**.

Like English sentences with 'let me . . . !', Tibetan volunteering sentences tend to be quite brief. When negotiating over a price, both the potential seller and buyer would regularly use this structure, as they indicate their preparedness to sell for, or pay a certain price, e.g.

Buyer ངས་སྐོར་མོ་ཉི་ཤུ་སྤྲོད་དགོས།
ngä̱' ko̱rmo nyi̱shu ṭǟ-ko̱.
I'll give you twenty Yuan for it!

Seller ངས་སྐོར་མོ་ཉི་ཤུ་རྩ་ལྔ་ལ་འཚོང་དགོས།
ngä̱' ko̱rmo nyi̱shu-tsengā-la tshōng-ko̱.
I'll sell it for twenty-five Yuan!

Exercise 4

Translate the following:

(a) ངས་ཕུན་ཚོགས་ལ་ལབ་དགོས། **ngä̱' phǖntshok-la la̱p-ko̱.**
(b) ངས་ཆུ་ཚོད་བདུན་པ་ལ་སྡོད་དགོས། **ngä̱' chūtshö' tü̱npa-la ṭǟ̱'-ko̱.**
(c) ངས་ཁོ་ཚོ་ལ་ཁ་པར་གཏོང་དགོས། **ngä̱' khōtsho-la khāpar tāng-ko̱.**
(d) ངས་རོགས་པ་བྱེད་དགོས། **ngä̱' ro̱kpa-che̱'-ko̱.**
(e) དེ་རིང་དུས་ཚོད་མེད། ངས་སང་ཉིན་འགྲོ་དགོས། **the̱ring thü̱tsȫ' me̱'. ngä̱' sāngnyin ṭo̱-ko̱.**

Exercise 5

Create a Tibetan sentence for each of the following situations, expressing the decision that you have made. You must choose whether the volunteering structure, or some other, is more appropriate for each one.

1 Eating with friends, you decide to return home.
2 You decide to pour some tea for your companion.
3 In the marketplace, you decide not to buy the item the trader wants to sell you.
4 You decide to leave work early; you tell your colleague.
5 Your friends are encouraging you to stay for another drink; you decide to do so.

■ More useful shopping phrases and vocabulary **(Audio 2:15)**

གོང་ཁེ་པོ། **kho̱ng-khēpo** – cheap
གོང་ཚད། **kho̱ngtshä'** – price
བསིལ་མ། **sīlma** – change (i.e. coins)
གྱོང་། **khyo̱ng** – loss (financial)
གོང་སྒྲིག་པ། **kho̱ng-ṭi̱kpa** – to bargain/negotiate a price
གཅོག་རོགས་གནང་། **cāk ro-nāng** – (Please) reduce the price.
ག་ཚོད་ཆགས་སོང་། **kha̱tshȫ' chāk-sōng** – How much does that come to?
རྒྱ་མ་བརྒྱབ་དང་། **kya̱ma kya̱k-thang** – Weigh that (for me).
རྩིས་རྒྱབ་རོགས་བྱེད། **tsī' kya̱p ro-che̱'.** – Please make up the bill/ How much do I owe you?

Dialogue 2

(Audio 2:14)

Duho is out with Tashi. He sees a shirt outside a Chinese shop, and asks Tashi about it.

ཏུ་ཧོ། ད་གིན་ཚོང་ཁང་གཞན་དག་དེ་ལ་སྟོད་ཐུང་འདི་འདྲ་པོ་གཅིག་འདུག ཡིན་ནའང་དེ་གོང་ཆེ་བ་འདུག

བཀྲ་ཤིས། འདྲ་པོ་འདུག ཡིན་ནའང་གཅིག་པ་མ་རེད།

ཏུ་ཧོ། ཁྱད་པར་ག་རེ་འདུག

བཀྲ་ཤིས། ད་གིན་དེའི་རྒྱུ་ཆ་ཡག་ག་འདུག ཡིན་ནའང་གྱོན་དང་། ཁྱེད་རང་ལ་ལན་པོ་འདུག་མི་འདུག་ངས་ལྟ་དགོས། ཤོང་གི་འདུག་གས། དམ་དྲགས་མི་འདུག་གས།

ཏུ་ཧོ། དམ་དྲགས་མི་འདུག ག་འདྲ་འདུག

བཀྲ་ཤིས། ཁྱེད་རང་ལ་ལན་པོ་འདུག ཏུ་ཧོ། མཚམས་མཚམས་ལ་ཕྱུ་པ་གྱོན་གྱི་ཡོད་པས།

ཏུ་ཧོ། ཕྱུ་པ་ཨེ། ང་གྱོན་གྱི་མེད། འོ། ལག་ཤུབས་འདི་ཡང('འང)་ཡག་པོ་འདུག་ག ཡིན་ནའང་ཆ་མི་འདུག ཡ་གཅིག་ག་པར་འདུག ང་ཚོང་པ་དེ་ལ་སྐད་ཆ་དྲི་གི་ཡིན།

བཀྲ་ཤིས། ག་འདྲ་ཟེར། ཁོ་རང་བོད་སྐད་ག་པར་རྒྱུག་གི་རེད། ཚོང་པ་འདི་ཚོ་རྒྱ་སྐད་མ་གཏོགས་རྒྱུག་གི་ཡོད་མ་རེད། ཁྱེད་རང་བསྡད་ཨང་། ངས་འདྲི་དགོས།

ཏུ་ཧོ། ཁོ་རང་གིས་ག་རེ་ལབ་སོང་།

བཀྲ་ཤིས། ཡ་གཅིག་མ་གཏོགས་མི་འདུག་ལབ་ཀྱི་འདུག

ཏུ་ཧོ། ལག་ཤུབས་ཡ་གཅིག་སུས་ཉོ་གི་རེད།

བཀྲ་ཤིས། མི་ཁ་ཤས་ལ་ལག་པ་གཅིག་མ་གཏོགས་ཡོད་མ་རེད་པ།

ཏུ་ཧོ། ཚོ་ག་རེ་ཡོད་རེད།

DUHO tha̲ncin tshōngkhang shä̲nthak the̲-la tȫthung ti̲ ṭa̲po cīk tu̲'. yi̲nnä: the̲ khōng-chē: tu̲'.

TASHI ṭa̲po tu̲'. yi̲nnä: cīkpa ma-re̲'.

DUHO khyēpar kha̲re tu̲'.

TASHI tha̲ncin the̲: kyu̲pcha ya̲ka tu̲'. yi̲nnä: khö̲n-thang. khyērang-la lä̲npo tu̲' min-tu̲' ngä̲' tā-ko̲. shōngki-tu̲'-kä'. tha̲m-ṭhak min-tu̲'-kä.

DUHO tha̲m-ṭhak min-tu̲'. kha̲nṭa tu̲'.

TASHI khyērang-la lä̲npo tu̲'. tu̲ho, tshāmtsham-la chūpa khö̲nki-yö̲'-pä.

DUHO	chūpa-ē. nga̱ khö̱nki-me̱'. o̱, la̱kshup ti̱-yä ya̱kpo tu̱'-ka. yi̱nnä: cha̱ min-tu̱'. ya̱-cīk kha̱wa: tu̱'. nga̱ tshōngpa the̱-la kā̈cha ṭi̱ki-yi̱n.
TASHI	kha̱nṭäs, khōrang phö̱kā̈' kha̱wa: kya̱pki-re̱'. tshōngpa ti̱ntsho kya̱kā̈' matōk kya̱pki yo̱ ma-re̱'. khyērang tä̱-a: ngä̱' ṭi̱-ko. (*he goes, then returns*)
DUHO	khōrang-kī' kha̱re la̱p-song.
TASHI	ya̱-cīk matōk min-tu̱' la̱pki-tu̱'.
DUHO	la̱kshup ya̱-cīk sṻ' nyo̱ki-re̱'.
TASHI	mi̱ khāshä-la la̱kpa cīk matōk yo̱ ma-re̱'-wa.
DUHO	chō kha̱re yo̱re'.

Vocabulary

སྟོད་ཐུང་།	**tȫthung**	shirt/blouse
འདྲ་པོ།	**ṭa̱po**	similar (see below)
གཅིག་པ།	**cīkpa**	the same
ཁྱད་པར།	**khyēpar**	difference
རྒྱུ་ཆ།	**kyu̱pcha**	material(s)
གྱོན་པ།	**khö̱npa**	to wear
ལན་པོ།	**lä̱npo**	becoming
མཚམས་མཚམས་(ལ)།	**tshāmtsham**	sometimes
འདུག་མི་འདུག	**tu̱' min-tu̱'**	'is or isn't' (see below)
ཕྱུ་པ།	**chūpa**	traditional Tibetan dress (with both male and female versions)
ཚོ་ག་རེ་ཡོད་རེད།	**chō kha̱re yo̱re'**	(*lit.* 'what is the point?' This rhetorical question is used to scorn what someone has said or done)
ག་པར།	**kha̱wa:**	(*lit.* 'where?'. This term is used either to deny or call into doubt an assertion – in this case, that the shopkeeper will be able to speak Tibetan – a similar phrase appeared in Unit 7, Dialogue 1)

དྲགས།	**ṭhak**	too (see below)
ཤོང་བ།	**shōngwa**	to fit
ལག་ཤུབས།	**la̱kshup**	gloves
ཆ།	**chā**	pair
ཡ་གཅིག	**ya̱-cīk**	one of a pair
སྐད་ཆ་འདྲི་བ།	**kǟcha-ṯi̱wa**	to ask
ངས་ལྟ་དགོས།	**ngä̱' tā-ko̱**	I'll take a look!
མ་གཏོགས།	**matōk**	only (see below)
ལྟ་བ།	**tāwa**	to look

Language points

4 Likeness, similarity and difference

Dialogue 2 has examples of each of these, in the discussion about the shirts. Note that when talking about things or people being the 'same' (**cīkpa**), or 'different' (**khāka**), verbs of identity are used:

> གོས་ཐུང་འདི་གཉིས་གཅིག་པ་རེད་པས།
> **khö̱thung ṯi̱-nyī' cīkpa re̱'-wä.**
> Are these two (pairs of) trousers the same?

Things referred to as 'pairs' are those made up of two separable items (shoes, gloves, etc.), not trousers, glasses and so forth.

Things or people are described as 'similar' or 'alike' (**ṯa̱po**) mainly using a verb of existence. The word **khyēpar** allows one to talk about specific differences.

> ཅ་ལག་འདི་གཉིས་ལ་ཁྱད་པར་ག་རེ་འདུག
> **cālak ṯi̱-nyī'-la khyēpar kha̱re tu̱'.**
> What difference is there between these two items?

> ཁྱད་པར་ཆེ་ཤོས་དེ་སྤུས་ཀ་རེད།
> **khyēpar chēshö' the pǖka re̱'.**
> The principal (biggest) difference is the quality.

5 Too

As shown in Unit 5, **she̱ṭhak** is used in sentences such as:

མི་མང་པོ་ཞེ་དྲག་འདུག **mi̱ ma̱ngpo she̱ṭhak tu̱'.**
(There are/were *very* many people.)

In this sentence, **she̱ṭhak** might be understood as an emphatic, like 'so', suggesting that there were too many people. This would depend upon the situation; in certain circumstances the same statement might be an expression of pleasant surprise.

A less ambiguous way of saying something like 'too' appears in Dialogue 2. The last syllable of an adjective (such as those introduced in Unit 5) is simply replaced with **ṭhak**. Examples:

མང་པོ། **ma̱ngpo** many → མང་དྲགས **ma̱ng-ṭhak** too many
ཆུང་ཆུང་། **chūngchūng** small → ཆུང་དྲགས **chūng-ṭhak** too small

With the small number of 'exceptions' noted in Unit 5, **ṭhak** is added to the comparative form of the adjective:

ཆེན་པོ། **chēnpo** large → ཆེ་དྲག **chē-ṭhak** too large

Exercise 6

Translate these sentences:

1 Who did you buy that for?
2 The shopkeeper hasn't got change. Have you?
3 This thing is cheaper than the others.
4 How much are they selling it for?
5 I didn't buy the book, it was too expensive.
6 All these bowls are similar.
7 Which of these Tibetan dresses will you buy?

Language point

6 Talking about actions done regularly

Unit 8 introduced a standard form of the present, as one used to express ongoing actions (those with *-ing* endings in English, often described as 'present continuous' or 'present progressive'). But as mentioned in Unit 9, exactly the same form is used for more general statements. In Dialogue 2 of this unit, for instance, Duho is asked about an item of clothing; not about whether he's wearing one right now, but whether he *ever* wears one. So what was first introduced as the standard present form is also used to say things like 'goes', 'eats', 'drinks', or in this case, 'wears' (i.e. like the English simple present); actions which are repeated or usual. For example:

ང་དུག་སློག་ནག་པོ་གྱོན་གྱི་ཡོད།
nga̱ thu̱klōk (clothes) **na̱kpo khö̱nki-yö̱'.**

Depending on the situation, this sentence might mean either 'I am wearing black clothes.' or, 'I wear black clothes'. To help distinguish, one can, of course, add certain time-words, such as ནམ་རྒྱུན། **na̱mkyun** ('usually/normally').

Exercise 7

Select which time-word in column B goes together with which group of words in column A. Then construct each sentence in Tibetan. The first one has been completed below:

	A	B
1	I/study/Tibetan	never
2	Duho/wear/Tibetan traditional dress	sometimes
3	Penpa/buy/tsampa	now
4	Duho/live/Korea	usually + negation
5	Duho/buy/clothes/from market	sometimes
6	Chinese traders/speak/Tibetan	normally

1 ད་ལྟ་ང་བོད་སྐད་སྦྱོང་གི་ཡོད། **tha̱nta nga̱ phö̱kǟ' ca̱ngki-yö̱'.**

Language point

7 Helpful phrases which use negations

Dialogue 2 introduces two new expressions equivalent to ‘only’ and ‘whether’.

The most common way to say something like ‘only’ is by adding the word **matōk** after the thing in question. But this *only* works when you negate the verb (the copula or the auxiliary) standing at the end of the sentence. For example:

> ང་ལ་སྐོར་མོ་གསུམ་**མ་གཏོགས་མེད**།
> **nga̲-la ko̲rmo sūm matōk me̲’.**
> I only have three units of money (Yuan, Rupees, etc.)

> ཁང་པ་དེ་ལ་མི་གཅིག་**མ་གཏོགས་**སྡོད་ཀྱི་**ཡོད་མ་རེད**།
> **khāngpa the̲-la mi̲-cīk matōk tä̲ki yo̲ ma-re̲’.**
> There is only one person living in that house.

> ཁྱེད་རང་གིས་འདི་**མ་གཏོགས་**ཉོས་**མེད་**པས།
> **khyērang(-kī’) ti̲ matōk nyö̲’ me̲-pä.**
> Did you only buy this one? (or, ‘Is this all you bought?’)

There is no word directly equivalent to ‘whether’, but a similar effect is produced in another way. For instance, you have an affirmative statement, such as:

> ཞྭ་མོ་དེ་ཁྱེད་རང་ལ་ལན་པོ་འདུག
> **sha̲mo-the khyērang-la lä̲npo tu̲’.**
> That hat suits you.

You take the negated form of the verb, and affix it to the affirmative form already in the sentence (so here, **tu̲’** becomes **tu̲’ min-tu̲’**).

> ཞྭ་མོ་དེ་ཁྱེད་རང་ལ་ལན་པོ་འདུག་མི་འདུག
> **sha̲mo-the khyērang-la lä̲npo tu̲’ min-tu̲’.**

With this ‘is or isn’t’ ending, the meaning is similar to ‘whether or not the hat suits you’ (or, ‘if the hat suits you’). Comments such as ‘I don’t know’, etc., can be added straight after this ending, e.g.:

ཞྭ་མོ་དེ་ཁྱེད་རང་ལ་ལན་པོ་འདུག་མི་འདུག ངས་ལབ་དགོས།
shamo-the khyērang-la länpo tu' min-tu' ngä' lap-ko.
I'll tell you whether or not the hat suits you.

The verbs which such endings are normally created with are **tu'**, **yin**, and **yö'**. Unit 13 has more examples.

Exercise 8

Yesterday you made a list (in English) of the things you needed to do in or near the market. Today, because you feel unwell, your friend has offered to go for you.

(a) Translate (into informal Tibetan) the list of instructions for your friend. Start with the Tibetan equivalent of 'first' for no.1. Begin each subsequent instruction with the term དེ་ནས། **the-nä**, meaning something like 'then', or 'next'.

1 Go to Dölma's, give 90 Yuan
2 Buy bread (for five people)
3 Buy 1kg apples
4 Buy 2kg rice
5 See whether there's any good meat
6 Collect my shirt from the tailor's (ཚེམ་(བུ་)ཁང་། **tshēm(pu)-khāng)**

(b) Two other phrases or structures apart from **the-nä'** could be employed here, to show one thing following after another – one was introduced in Unit 8, the other in Unit 9. What are they, and how would they work here?

Unit Eleven

བདེ་པོ་མི་འདུག་གས།

t̲epo min-tu̲'-kä

Aren't you well?

In this unit you will learn how to:

- talk to the doctor about ailments
- use non-intentional verbs
- name parts of the body
- use honorific terms
- describe physical sensations
- express 'must', 'should', etc.

Dialogue 1

(Audio 2:18)

Tashi, who's not feeling well, enters the local doctor's surgery.

ཨེམ་ཆི། བཞུགས་དང་། ཁྱེད་རང་བདེ་པོ་མི་འདུག་གས།

བཀྲ་ཤིས། ཨེམ་ཆི་ལགས། ང་ཚ་བ་འབར་གྱི་འདུག མགོ་ཡང་(འང་)ན་གི་འདུག

ཨེམ་ཆི། གཞན་དག་གང་ཡང་མི་འདུག་གས།

བཀྲ་ཤིས། ཞོགས་པར་ཡར་ལང་དུས་སློ་ཞེ་དྲག་རྒྱག་གི་འདུག

ཨེམ་ཆི། སློ་རྒྱག་དུས་ག་རེ་བྱེད་ཀྱི་འདུག

བཀྲ་ཤིས། མིད་པ་ཚ་གི་འདུག ཨེ་ནི་མགོ་ཡུ་འཁོར་གྱི་འདུག་ལགས།

ཨེམ་ཆི། ཆམ་པ་ཡིན་ས་རེད། དེང་སང་མི་མང་པོ་ཆམ་པ་རྒྱག་གི་འདུག

བཀྲ་ཤིས། ཨེམ་ཆི་ལགས་བསྐྱུངས་མ་སོང་ངས།

ཨེམ་ཆི། ཨེམ་ཆི་ཆམ་པ་རྒྱག་གི་ཡོད་མ་རེད། འདི་སྨན་པའི་སྒྲིག་ཁྲིམས་རེད། མ་རེད། ང་རྩེད་མོ་རྩེ་གི་ཡོད། ཡིན་ནའང་འདི་དངོས་གནས་རེད། ང་ཚོ་ལ་ན་ཚ་ཞེ་དྲག་འགོ་གི་ཡོད་མ་རེད།
བཀྲ་ཤིས། ཨེམ་ཆི་ལགས་བསོད་བདེ་ཆེན་པོ་རེད།
ཨེམ་ཆི། འཕྲོད་བསྟེན་དང་གཙང་སྦྲ་ལ་ཡང་(འང་)རག་ལས་ཀྱི་རེད།
བཀྲ་ཤིས། རེད་ལགས།
ཨེམ་ཆི། ང་འདིར་སྨན་གཉིས་ཀྱི་མིང་འབྲི་གི་ཡོད། འདི་ཚོས་ཏོག་ཙམ་ཕན་གྱི་རེད།

DOCTOR shu̱:-thang. khyērang te̱po min-tu̱'-kä.
TASHI ēmchi-la: nga̱ tshāwa pa̱rki-tu̱'. ko̱-yä na̱ki-tu̱'.
DOCTOR shä̱nthak khä̱: min-tu̱'-kä.
TASHI sho̱kpa ya̱r-la̱ng-thü' lō she̱ṭhak kya̱pki-tu̱'.
DOCTOR lō kya̱p-thü' kha̱re che̱ki-tu̱'.
TASHI mi̱pa tshāki-tu̱'. ēni ko̱yu khōrki-tu̱'-la:.
DOCTOR chāmpa yi̱n-sa-re̱'. the̱nsang mi̱ ma̱ngpo chāmpa kya̱pki-tu̱'.
TASHI ēmchi-la: nyūng ma-sōng-ngä.
DOCTOR ēmchi chāmpa kya̱pki yo̱ ma-re̱'. ti̱ mä̱npä: ṯikṭhim re̱'. ma-re̱'. nga̱ tsēmo tsēki-yö̱'. yi̱nnä: ti̱ ngö̱nä' re̱. nga̱ntsho-la na̱tsha she̱ṭhak khö̱ki yo̱ ma-re̱'.
TASHI ēmchi-la: sōte-chēnpo re̱.
DOCTOR ṭhö̱ten thang tsāngṭa-la-yä ra̱klä̱ki-re̱'.
TASHI re̱'-la:.
DOCTOR nga̱ tä̱: mä̱n nyī'-ki mi̱ng ṯiki-yö̱'. mä̱n ti̱ntshö̱ tēts phä̱nki-re̱'.

Vocabulary

ཨེམ་ཆི།	**ēmchi**	doctor
ན་བ།	**na̱wa**	to be ill (non-honorific)
ན་ཚ།	**na̱tsha**	illness
མགོ་ན་བ།	**ko̱-na̱wa**	headache
གཞན་དག	**shä̱nthak**	other than that
སློ་རྒྱག་པ།	**lō-kya̱pa**	to cough
ཆམ་པ།	**chāmpa**	a cold

ཆམ་པ་རྒྱག་པ།	**chāmpa-kya̱pa**	to have a cold
རྩེད་མོ་རྩེ་བ།	**tsēmo-tsēwa**	to joke; to play
འཕྲོད་བསྟེན་དང་གཙང་སྦྲ།	**ṭhȭten-thang tsāngṭa**	health and hygiene
ཚ་བ་འབར་བ།	**tshāwa-pa̱rwa**	to have a fever
མིད་པ་ཚ་བ།	**mi̱pa-tshāwa**	to have a sore throat
མགོ་ཡུ་འཁོར་བ།	**ko̱yu-khōrwa**	to feel dizzy
ཡར་ལང་དུས།	**ya̱r-la̱ng-thü'**	when (I) arise/get up
····དུས་ག་རེ་བྱེད་ཀྱི་འདུག	**. . . thü' kha̱re che̱ki-tu̱'**	what happens when you . . . ?
ཡིན་ས་རེད།	**yi̱n-sa-re̱'**	I should think it is . . . (see Unit 12)
བསོད་བདེ་ཆེན་པོ།	**sōte-chēnpo**	to be fortunate (usually attributed to a person's virtuous actions)
སྙུང་བ།	**nyūngwa**	to be ill (honorific)
སྒྲིག་ཁྲིམས།	**ṯikṭhim**	rule(s)
འབྲི་བ།	**ṯiwa**	to write
སྨན།	**mā̱n**	medicine
ནད་པ།	**nā̱pa**	patient/sick person
འགོ་བ།	**khȫ̱pa**	to contract (an illness)
ཕན་པ།	**phā̱npa**	to be helpful/beneficial
རག་ལས་པ།	**ra̱klā̱pa**	to depend

Language point

1 Non-intentional verbs

The most important verb division was mentioned in Unit 7: the units since then have concentrated on intentional action verbs. But Dialogue 1 here contains some non-intentional verbs. These verbs indicate things which (especially in this unit) happen *to* people, rather than actions that they consciously perform or have control over.

In Dialogue 1, for instance, **na̱wa** expresses that someone is 'ill'. The Tibetan equivalent of 'I am ill' is not a statement of identity; **na̱wa** is a non-intentional *action verb*. The same is true not only of all other physical complaints (having a cold, headache, etc.), but most other transient physical and emotional states which we experience. In English we communicate these with adjectives, and verbs of 'being' (e.g. we *are* angry, happy, bored, etc.), or 'having'.

An action verb generally has to be either intentional or non-intentional. Non-intentional verbs, like intentional ones, require auxiliaries, but the first-person auxiliaries particularly differ from those used with intentional verbs. The intentional action of eating, for example, requires the auxiliary **yö̲'**:

ང་ཁ་ལག་ཟ་གི་ཡོད།	**nga̲ khālak sa̲ki-yö̲'.** I am eating (intentional; present).

Contrast this with a non-intentional action, such as:

ང་སྐྱུག་པ་སྐྱུག་གི་འདུག	**nga̲ kyūkpa kyūki-tu̲'.** I am vomiting (non-intentional; present).

The first person uses **tu̲'** to refer to his or her own *non-intentional* actions. In fact **tu̲'** is used for all three persons (as long as the speaker observes the action). This is, at least partly, because with a non-intentional action (like vomiting), the first person is more of an observer than its conscious performer.

Other sentences using non-intentional verbs:

ང་གཉིད་ཁུག་གི་འདུག	**nga̲ nyī' khūki-tu̲'.** I am falling asleep.
ང་ཟ་ཕྲུག་ལང་གི་འདུག	**nga̲ sa̲pt̲huk la̲ngki-tu̲'.** I am itching.

The auxiliaries for the first person in the past and future are generally the same as those already in use for intentional actions performed by second and third persons. So whether it is mine, yours, or some-one else's non-intentional action, such as falling over (**ri̲lwa**), the verbs are the same:

ང་/ཁྱེད་རང་/ཁོ་རང་རིལ་གྱི་རེད།	**nga̲/khyērang/khōrang ri̲lki-re̲'.** I/you/he/she will fall over.
ང་/ཁྱེད་རང་/ཁོ་རང་རིལ་སོང་།	**nga̲/khyērang/khōrang ri̲l-sōng.*** I/you/he/she fell.

* In the Lhasa dialect the auxiliary བྱུང་། (**chu̲ng**) would be used here, rather than སོང་།.

In summary, a non-intentional action verb must be combined with a non-intentional auxiliary. The auxiliaries **yi̱n** and **yö'** are generally associated with intentional actions. The sentence ང་རིལ་གི་ཡིན། **nga̱ ri̱lki-yi̱n**, for example, is wrong, because it uses an intentional auxiliary.

In previous units **tu̱'**, **re̱'**, and **sōng** were used only for other people. But from now on (with non-intentional actions) they will be used for all persons. The only one which should not be used for the first person (singular) is **yo̱re'**.

Exercise 1

Each sentence introduces a new action verb. Consider whether the action is intentional or non-intentional before completing the sentence, using the correct auxiliary.

1 You will recover (**ṭha̱kpa**).
ཁྱེད་རང་དྲག་_______ **khyērang ṭha̱k** _______

2 I forgot (**ce̱pa**) it.
ངས་དེ་བརྗེད་_______ **ngä̱' the̱ ce̱'** _______

3 I shall consult (**tēnpa**) a doctor.
ང་ཨེམ་ཆི་བསྟེན་_______ **nga̱ ēmchi tēn** _______

4 We heard (**kho̱wa**) something.
ང་ཚོས་གཅིག་གོ་_______ **nga̱ntshȫ' cīk kho̱**_______

5 I shall catch (**si̱mpa**) the thief (**kūma**).
ང་རྐུན་མ་དེ་གཟུང་_______ **nga̱ kūma-the si̱m** _______

6 She is reading (**lōkpa**) my book.
མོ་རང་ངའི་དེབ་ཀློག_______ **mo̱rang ngä̱: the̱p lōk** _______

7 We didn't find (**nyēpa**) the road.
ང་ཚོ་ལམ་ཁ་དེ་རྙེད་_______ **nga̱ntsho la̱mkha-the̱ nyē'** _______

8 I received (**ra̱kpa**) two letters today.
དེ་རིང་ང་ལ་ཡི་གེ་གཉིས་རག་_______
the̱ring nga̱-la yi̱ke nyī' ra̱k_______

Non-intentional verbs are roughly divided into three types, those related to:

- **reception** – with a **la̱thön** marking the person or thing which receives
- **perception** – with a **che̱ṭa** (agentive) particle marking the one who perceives, etc.
- **occurrence** – with no particle marking the subject

Exercise 2

So far, twenty-one non-intentional verbs have appeared in this unit. Locate them, and organise them into the three groups given above.

Exercise 3

Running horizontally are the six common auxiliary verbs. Based upon what has been explained so far, put either a tick or a cross, depending on whether or not they can go together with the categories on the left. The first has been completed: **re̲'** is generally not used as an auxiliary with a first person, where the action is an intentional one.

		རེད།	ཡིན།	འདུག	ཡོད།	ཡོད་རེད།	སོང་།
I	Int.	✗					
	Non-int.						
You	Int.						
	Non-int.						
He/she	Int.						
	Non-int.						

Cultural point

Honorific words

In certain European languages you show politeness by addressing a person with plural forms of personal pronouns and verbs. In Tibetan there is a far broader scheme. Terms described in previous units as 'polite' actually form part of a formalised system of respectful language, which has whole sets of alternative vocabulary, specially reserved for polite communication. The following classes of words have honorific equivalents:

1 personal pronouns
2 nouns
3 action verbs
4 adjectives and adverbs

The more polite versions of personal pronouns were introduced in Unit 2, and there are only a small number of honorific adjectives and adverbs. So the main challenge is with nouns and action verbs; all of those related to the individual have honorific and ordinary (i.e. non-honorific) alternatives. As we have seen from the dialogues so far, in conversations between friends, relations, and so forth, honorific forms can have a limited role. But in more formal situations they become important.

Language point

2 Honorific nouns

One of the best illustrators of the two sets of vocabulary (i.e. ordinary and honorific) is names for parts of the body. The following list gives the ordinary term, and then the honorific alternative (in brackets). It shows that these equivalents can be very different from one another, but that sometimes (as in the terms for 'body', 'finger', etc.) the honorific version differs from the ordinary one by a single syllable.

■ Parts of the body

གཟུགས་པོ།	(སྐུ་གཟུགས།)	**s̱ukpo (kūsuk)**	body
ལག་པ།	(ཕྱག)	**ḻakpa (chāk)**	arm/hand
རྐང་པ།	(ཞབས།)	**kāngpa (sha̱p)**	foot/leg
མཛུབ་མོ།	(ཕྱག་མཛུབ།)	**tsu̱ku (chāktsuk)**	finger
ཨ་མཆོག	(སྙན་མཆོག)	**āmcok (nyēncok)**	ear
མགོ།	(དབུ།)	**ko̱ (ū)**	head
གདོང་པ།	(ཞལ་རས།)	**to̱ngpa (shǟ̱lrä')**	face
སྐྲ།	(དབུ་སྐྲ།)	**ṭā (ūṭa)**	hair
མིག	(སྤྱན།)	**mīk (cǟn)**	eye
ཁ།	(ཞལ།)	**khā (shǟ̱l)**	mouth
སོ།	(ཚེམས།)	**sō (tshēm)**	tooth
ལྕེ་ལེ།	(ལྗགས།)	**cēle (ca̱k)**	tongue
སྣ་ཁུང་།	(ཤངས།)	**nāku (shāng)**	nose
གྲོད་ཁོག	(གསོལ་གྲོད།)	**ṭho̱khok (sȫlṭhö')**	stomach
སྒལ་པ།	(སྐུ་སྟོད།)	**kǟ̱lpa (kūtȫ')**	back

Rules for honorific language usage are discussed in the following units. For now, the basic rule is: use honorific terms for others, and ordinary terms for oneself!

Duho is more familiar with ordinary Tibetan than honorific. He's particularly anxious about accidentally referring to himself using honorific terms. The danger of this blunder is illustrated in the medical situation. Questioning you about an ailment, a doctor or nurse might show respect to you by using honorific language. But in response, because you are talking about yourself, you must use ordinary terms. For example:

Question: ཁྱེད་རང་དབུ་སྙུང་གི་འདུག་གས།
khyērang ū nyūngki-tu̲'-kä.
Do you have a bad head?

Answer: ང་མགོ་ན་གི་འདུག
nga̲ ko̲ na̲ki-tu̲'.
(Yes,) I have a bad head.

Exercise 4

Duho practises with this format. First, imagining himself as the doctor, using honorific terms, he asks whether there is something wrong with some part of the body. Second, as the patient, he answers with non-honorific terms. Follow his example in the sequence below. Use only the two verbs in the example (**na̱wa** and **nyūngwa**):

(a)	Q. bad arm?	A. Yes, . . .
(b)	Q. ,, eyes?	A. Yes, . . .
(c)	Q. ,, leg?	A. Yes, . . .
(d)	Q. ,, head and back?	A. No, . . .
(e)	Q. ,, head, yesterday?	A. No, . . .

Language points

3 Describing physical sensations

Exercise 4 demonstrates the general pattern for expressing pain: after the part of the body, you add the non-intentional verb which conveys what you feel. For example:

ང་རྐང་པ་ན་གི་འདུག **nga̱ kāngpa na̱ki-tu̱'** My foot/leg hurts.

Note: there is no genitive particle linking the person with the part of the body (i.e. it is not **ngä̱: kāngpa**, 'my foot').

na̱wa or **nyūngwa** can both be used to communicate either that something is not right with the part of the body, or that it hurts. There are some other, more specific verbs:

ཚ་བ།	**tshāwa**	for stinging and burning sensations
ཟུག་རྒྱག་པ།	**su̱k-kya̱pa**	for aching
སྦྲིད་པ།	**pi̱:wa**	for a lack of sensation and numbness

Other verbs describing physical sensations generally incorporate the name for the part of the body they are experienced in, e.g.

གྲོད་ཁོག་ལྟོགས་པ།	**ṭho̱khok-tōkpa**	to be hungry
གྲོད་ཁོག་རྒྱགས་པ།	**ṭho̱khok-kya̱kpa**	to be full (stomach)
ཁ་སྐོམ་པ།	**khā-kōmpa**	to be thirsty

So the way to express illness and sensation is *noun + non-intentional verb*. Do not try to replicate the patterns of English.

4 Verbs of thought and perception

Some verbs describing perception are intentional, others are non-intentional. Intentional verbs are used to describe situations where you actively control the process, and/or direct your attention to a thing. If, on the other hand, the verb is describing the experience of sensations (sights, sounds, and so forth) that come *to* you, and are experienced in a more passive or accidental way, non-intentional verbs are employed. Both sets of verbs require use of the agentive particle.

Intentional action			*Non-intentional action*		
ཉན་པ།	**nyä̲npa**	to listen	གོ་བ།	**kho̲wa**	to hear
ལྟ་བ།	**tā̆wa**	to watch/look at	མཐོང་བ།	**thōngwa**	to see
སྣོམ་པ།	**nūmpa**	to smell	ཁ་བ།	**khāwa**	to smell
(to intentionally sniff something)			(to get a whiff of something)		

For example:

ངས་མེ་ཏོག་གི་དྲི་མ་བསྣམས་པ་ཡིན།
ngä̲' me̲tok-ki ṭhi̲ma nūmpa-yi̲n.
I smelt/sniffed the scent (of those) flowers.

སྨན་གྱི་དྲི་མ་ཁ་སོང་།
mā̆n-ki ṭhi̲ma khā song.
(I) caught a whiff of a medicinal smell ('the smell of medicine').

The same distinction of intentional and non-intentional action is made with respect to thought:

བསམ་བློ་གཏོང་བ། **sāmlo-tāngwa**	སེམས་པ། **sāmpa**
to think	to think
(when you reflect upon something, or think it over)	(when something – an impression, assumption, thought, or idea – comes to mind)

Usually, intentional verbs of thought or perception are linked to their objects by **la̱thön**, whereas non-intentional ones are not.

■ Language tip – Forget about it!

Instructions such as 'go to sleep!' or 'forget about it!' make perfect sense in English. But non-intentional actions are, by definition, not in your control. So when giving someone an instruction to do something, or volunteering to do an action yourself, avoid using non-intentional actions, because most of the time such sentences will make no sense in Tibetan!

Exercise 5

How do you say these in Tibetan? The first sentence has been completed already.

1 I have toothache. ང་སོ་ན་གི་འདུག **nga̱ sō na̱ki-tu̱'.**
2 It stings!
3 Don't your ears hurt?
4 I'm thirsty; let's go to drink something!
5 Because we didn't eat lunch today we are all very hungry.
6 My tongue goes (is) numb when I eat Szechuan pepper (གཡེར་མ། **ērma**).
7 Many children had diarrhoea (གྲོད་ཁོག་བཤལ་བ། **ṭho̱khok-shā̆lwa**) yesterday.

Dialogue 2

(Audio 2:19)

Lhamo returns home to her husband Tenzin.

ལྷ་མོ།	བསྟན་འཛིན། ངས་ད་གིན་ཁྱེད་རང་ལ་ཁ་དཔར་བཏང་བ་ཡིན། གོ་མ་སོང་ངས།
བསྟན་འཛིན།	ངས་གོ་མ་སོང་། ང་ད་གིན་སྨན་ཚོང་ས་ལ་ཡོད།
ལྷ་མོ།	ངའི་སྨན་དེ་ཉོས་པ་ཡིན་པས།
བསྟན་འཛིན།	ཉོས་པ་ཡིན།
ལྷ་མོ།	ཡག་བྱུང་། རིལ་བུ་ག་ཚོད་ཟ་དགོས་རེད།

བསྟན་འཛིན། ངས་ཉོས་དུས་མི་དེས་ལབ་སོང་། དེ་ནས་ངས་ལམ་སེང་ཤོག་བུའི་སྒང་ལ་བྲིས་པ་ཡིན། ཡིན་ནའང་...།

ལྷ་མོ། ད་ག་རེ་བྱས་སོང་།

བསྟན་འཛིན། བསྡད་ཨང་། ང་བསམ་བློ་གཏོང་གི་ཡོད། རིལ་བུ་གསུམ་རེད་དྲན་སོང་། ཞོགས་ཀས་གཉིས་དང་དགོང་དག་གཅིག

ལྷ་མོ། གཏན་གཏན་ཡིན་པས། གཞན་ཉེན་ཁ་ཡོད་རེད། སྨན་འདི་ཤུགས་ཆེན་པོ་ཡོད་རེད།

བསྟན་འཛིན། ད་དྲན་གྱི་མི་འདུག

ལྷ་མོ། མ་གཞི་ནས་ཤོག་བུ་དེ་ག་པར་འདུག ང་ལ་བསྟན་དང་། ད་ག་པར་འགྲོ་གི་ཡིན།

བསྟན་འཛིན། ང་འགོ་ནས་སྨན་ཚོང་ས་ལ་སྐད་ཆ་འདྲི་གར་འགྲོ་དགོས་ཀྱི་འདུག

ལྷ་མོ། ཨེ་ནི་ཤོག་བུ་དེ།

བསྟན་འཛིན། ཤོག་བུ་དེ་སྨན་ཚོང་ས་ལ་ལུས་སོང་།

ལྷ་མོ། ཨ་ཡོ། དེ་འདྲ་མི་གཅིག་འདུག

LHAMO tā̃ntsin, ngä̱' tha̱ncin khyērang-la khāpa tāngwa-yi̱n. kho̱ ma-sōng-ngä.

TENZIN ngä̱' kho̱ ma-sōng. nga̱ tha̱ncin mā̃n-tshōngsa-la yö̱'.

LHAMO ngä̱: mā̃n-the nyö̱wa-yi̱n-pä.

TENZIN nyö̱wa-yi̱n.

LHAMO ya̱kchung. ri̱lpu kha̱tshȫ' sa̱-kö'-re̱'.

TENZIN ngä̱' nyö̱-thü' mi̱-the̱' la̱p-song. the̱nä ngä̱' la̱msāng shūkü: ka̱ng-la ṭhi̱wa-yi̱n. yi̱nnä: . . .

LHAMO tha̱ kha̱re chä̱-sōng.

TENZIN tä̱'-a, nga̱ sāmlo tāngki-yö̱'. ri̱lpu sūm re̱' ṭhä̱n-song. sho̱kä nyī' thang ko̱ngthak cīk.

LHAMO tā̃ntän yi̱n-pä. shä̱n: nye̱nkha yo̱re'. mā̃n-ti̱ shūk-chēnpo yo̱re'.

TENZIN tha̱ ṭhä̱nki-min-tu̱'.

LHAMO ma-shi̱nä shūku-the kha̱wa tu̱'. nga̱-la tā̃n-thang. tha̱ kha̱wa ṭo̱ki-yi̱n.

TENZIN nga̱ ko̱nä mā̃n-tshōngsa-la kā̃cha-ṭi̱ka ṭo̱-kö'-ki tu̱'.

LHAMO ēni shūku-the . . .

TENZIN shūku-the mā̃n-tshōngsa-la lä̱'-song.

LHAMO āyo, the̱nṭä: mi̱-cik tu̱'.

Vocabulary

རིལ་བུ།	**ri̲lpu**	pill
ལམ་སེང་།	**la̲msāng**	immediately
ཤོག་བུ།	**shūku**	paper
བྲིས་པ།	**ṭhi̲wa**	wrote
བསྡད་ཨང་།	**tä̲'-a**	hold on!
ལུས་པ།	**lä̲wa**	to leave something (accidentally)
སྨན་ཚོང་ས།	**mǟ̲n-tshōngsa**	chemist/pharmacy
ཨ་ཡོ།	**āyo**	(expression of weariness or discontent)
དྲན་པ།	**ṭhä̲npa**	to remember
གཞན།	**shä̲n**	otherwise
འགོ་ནས།	**ko̲nä**	again
ཉེན་ཁ།	**nye̲nkha**	danger/risk
དྲན་སོང་།	**ṭhä̲n-song**	(I) thought . . .
ཁྲལ།	**ṭhǟ̲l**	tax/duty
གཏན་གཏན་ཡིན་པས།	**tǟ̲ntän yi̲n-pä**	are you sure?
ཞོགས་ཀས།	**sho̲kä**	morning (alternative for **sho̲kpa**)
ཡག་ཆུང་།	**ya̲kchung**	(expression, somewhere between 'that's good!' and 'thanks!')
དེ་འདྲ་མི་གཅིག་འདུག	**the̲nṭä: mi̲-cik tu̲'**	(expression uttered when irritated with someone, stronger in tone than the literal meaning: 'such a person/individual!')

Language point

5 Need to, should, must (དགོས་པ།)

In Unit 9 **kö̲'** was used alone, as a main verb. Here it is attached to an action verb, to express necessity, etc. (that is, **kö̲'** is a modal verb). Usually, auxiliaries such as **re̲'** and **tu̲'** give information about time, person, etc. But when combined with **kö̲'** they work differently, conveying various types of necessity, like you do in English, with 'need', 'should', and so forth. However, as the table shows, the distinctions do not match the English ones exactly.

ང་འགྲོ་གི་ཡིན།		going (simple statement of intent)	'shall'/'will'
ང་འགྲོ་**དགོས་རེད།**	**kö' re̱'**	going because I am compelled to by some outside force (duty, responsibility, an order, or pressing circumstances)	'must'/'need to'
ང་འགྲོ་**དགོས་ཀྱི་འདུག**	**kö'-ki tu̱'**	going because my presence (somewhere) will be useful or necessary	'should'/'need to'
ང་འགྲོ་**དགོས་ཡོད།**	**kö' yö̱'**	going because of an urge or personal choice	'should'/'wish to'

In these sentences, neither **kö'** nor the action verb varies, to indicate different times: any of the above could mean either 'I have to go' or 'I had to go'. When clarification is necessary, a time-word can be used.

kö' yö̱' is only for first-person sentences; the others may be said by or about anyone.

Exercise 6

In English, the phrase 'I have to' might refer to a whole range of necessities or wishes. There is no such single phrase in Tibetan; you must be more specific, by choosing the **kö̱'** ending most appropriate to the situation.

Complete the sentences in Tibetan adding the correct **kö̱'** ending (following the example of no. 1). Even if you can imagine more than one possible scenario for some of them, try to select the most obvious one.

1 we – pay taxes ང་ཚོ་ཁྲལ་སྤྲོད་དགོས་རེད། **nga̱ntsho ṭhā̈l ṭā̈'-kö' re̱'.**
2 I – eat (I'm hungry)
3 you – take medicine (i.e. instructing someone with a serious illness, like TB)
4 I – go to (i.e. walk towards) the toilet
5 I – help an ill friend
6 I – go on holiday
7 you – go to bed/sleep (e.g. parents telling their children)

Exercise 7

A new computer program can translate from English to Tibetan! But the differences between the languages mean that it has problems distinguishing between intentional and non-intentional verbs. The mistakes in the passage are all due to this problem.

(a) Locate where verbs have been translated incorrectly.
(b) Replace these mistaken verbs with the correct ones.
(c) Translate the passage; you should end up with a reconstruction of the original, with all the English verbs which confused the programme in place.

ངའི་ཨ་མ་ལ་ཆམ་པ་རག་སོང་། ང་ཆམ་པའི་སྨན་ཉོ་གར་ཕྱིན་པ་ཡིན། ཡིན་ནའང་ང་ལ་
རག་མ་སོང་། གང་ཡིན་ཟེར་ན། གྲོང་གསེབ་འདི་ལ་མི་མང་པོ་ལ་ཆམ་པ་རག་གི་ཡོད་རེད།
ཨེ་ནི་ཁོ་རང་ཚོས་སྨན་ཚང་མ་ཉོ་གི་འདུག ཁས་ས་ང་གྲོང་གསེབ་གཞན་དག་ལ་སྨན་རྙེད་
གར་ཕྱིན་པ་ཡིན། དེ་ལ་ཆམ་པའི་སྨན་འདུག ང་ལ་སྨན་ལེན་པ་ཡིན། ཡིན་ནའང་ད་ལྟ་ང་
ཡང་(འང་)གློ་རྒྱག་གི་ཡོད། ང་ལ་ཆམ་པ་བཟུང་སོང་།

ngä̱: āma-la chāmpa ra̱k-song. nga̱ chāmpä: mā̈n nyo̱-ka chīnpa-yi̱n. yi̱nnä nga̱-la ra̱k ma-sōng. kha̱ngyin-se̱rna ṭho̱ngsep ti̱-la mi̱ ma̱ngpo-la chāmpa ra̱k-ki yo̱re'. ēni khōrang-tshȫ' mā̈n tshāngma nyo̱ki-tu̱'. khā̈sa nga̱ ṭho̱ngsep shā̱̈nthak-la mā̈n nyē'-ka chīnpa-yi̱n. the̱-la chāmpä:-mā̈n tu̱'. nga̱-la mā̈n le̱npa-yi̱n. yi̱nnä: tha̱nta nga̱-yä lō kya̱pki-yȫ̱'. nga̱-la chāmpa si̱m-song.

Exercise 8

Some Tibetan sentences below don't match the translations: identify and correct them. The only mistakes are in the verbs (action or auxiliary).

1 ཨ་ཁུ་ན་གི་ཡོད་རེད།
ākhu na̱ki-yo̱re'.
Uncle (paternal) is ill.

2 ང་དེ་རིང་ཁྲོམ་ལ་ཕྱིན་སོང་།
nga̱ the̱ring ṭhōm-la chīn-song.
I went to the market today.

3 ཁྱེད་རང་ག་པར་ན་གི་འདུག
khyērang kha̱wa na̱ki-tu̱'.
Where does it hurt?

4 ཞོགས་པར་ང་སྨན་ཁང་ལ་མེད། ཡིན་ནའང་ཡེ་ཤེས་འདུག
sho̱kpa nga̱ mā̆nkhang-la me̱'. yi̱nnä: ye̱shē tu̱'.
This morning I wasn't at the hospital, but Yeshe was.

5 ཁྱེད་རང་ཨེམ་ཆི་བསྟེན་སོང་ངས།
khyērang ēmchi tēn sōng-ngä.
Did you consult the doctor?

6 ང་རིའི་སྒང་ལ་འགྲོ་དུས་མགོ་ཡུ་འཁོར་སོང་།
nga̱ ri̱: ka̱ng-la ṭo̱-thü' ko̱yu khōr-song.
I get dizzy when I go in (*lit.* on) the mountains.

Unit Twelve

འགྲུལ་སྐྱོད་ཀྱི་སྐོར།

ṭü̱lkyö’-ki kōr

Travel

In this unit you will learn how to:

- discuss travel arrangements
- talk about the weather
- express a lack of certainty
- say ‘able to’/‘can’
- describe how actions are done
- construct sentences with ‘if’ in them
- communicate feelings and reactions to events

Dialogue 1

(Audio 2:23)

Duho and Sönam want to visit Gyantse. Last night, they arranged for a jeep-driver to collect them early this morning. But another driver has turned up at the meeting-place, and is signalling to them. Duho makes various comments to Sönam (out of the driver’s earshot).

ཁ་ལོ་བ།	ཕེབས་ཤོག
དུ་ཧོ།	དེ་ཁས་སའི་མི་ཡིན་ས་མ་རེད།
བསོད་ནམས།	ཁས་ས་ང་ཚོས་ཁ་ལོ་བ་གཞན་དག་མཉམ་དུ་སྐད་ཆ་བྱས་པ་ཡིན།
ཁ་ལོ་བ།	ཁོ་ངའི་རོགས་པ་རེད། ཡིན་ནའང་དེ་རིང་ཁོ་རང་རྒྱལ་རྩེ་ལ་འགྲོ་ཐུབ་ཀྱི་མ་རེད། ཁོ་རང་གི་ཚབ་ལ་ང་བཏང་སོང་།

ཏུ་ཧོ། ང་ཚོ་གཟབ་གཟབ་བྱེད་དགོས་ཀྱི་འདུག མི་དེས་ང་ཚོ་ལ་མགོ་སྐོར་གཏང་ས་རེད།

བསོད་ནམས། ཏུ་ཧོ་སེམས་ཁྲལ་མ་བྱེད། ངས་སྐད་ཆ་བཤད་དགོས། ཁས་ས་ཁྱེད་རང་གི་རོགས་པ་མཉམ་དུ་གོང་བསྒྲིགས་ཚར་བ་ཡིན།

ཁ་ལོ་པ། འདི་ངས་ཧ་གོ་གི་མེད། ཁས་ས་ང་མེད། ཡིན་ནའང་ངས་སྒོར་མོ་སུམ་བརྒྱ་ལ་སྐྱེལ་དགོས།

བསོད་ནམས། ལམ་ཁ་རྒྱུས་ཡོད་པ། ཆུ་ཚོད་ག་ཚོད་འགོར་གྱི་རེད།

ཁ་ལོ་པ། ཆུ་ཚོད་བཞི་ཙམ་འགོར་གྱི་རེད།

བསོད་ནམས། སྒོར་མོ་ཉིས་བརྒྱ་ལྔ་བཅུ་ལ་སྐྱེལ་དང་།

ཁ་ལོ་པ། དེ་ཉུང་དྲགས་ཀྱི་རེད་ལགས། ང་སྒོར་མོ་སུམ་བརྒྱ་ལ་བསྐྱལ་གྱི་ཡིན། ད་ལྟ་ཁྱེད་རང་ཚོ་ལ་མོ་ཊ་གཞན་དག་རག་གི་མ་རེད།

བསོད་ནམས། ཏུ་ཧོ་དེ་དངོས་གནས་ཡིན་ས་རེད། ང་ཚོ་ལ་མོ་ཊ་གཞན་དག་རག་ས་མ་རེད། ཁོ་རང་མཉམ་དུ་འགྲོ།

DRIVER phēp-shōk.

DUHO the̱ khā̈sä: mi̱ yi̱n-sa ma-re̱'.

SÖNAM (*to the driver*) khā̈sa nga̱ntshȫ' khālowa shä̱nthak nyāmtu kā̈cha-chä̱pa-yi̱n.

DRIVER khō ngä̱: ro̱kpa re̱'. yi̱nnä: the̱ring khōrang kya̱ntse-la ṭo̱ thūp-ki ma-re̱'. khōrang-ki tshāp-la nga̱ tāng-song.

DUHO nga̱ntsho sa̱psap che̱' ko'-ki tu̱'. mi̱-the nga̱ntsho-la ko̱kor tāng-sa re̱'.

SÖNAM tu̱ho, sēmṭhäl ma-chi̱'. ngä̱' kā̈cha shā̈'-ko̱.
(*to the driver*) khā̈sä: khyērang-ki ro̱kpa nyāmtu kho̱ng ṭi̱k-tshārwa-yi̱n.

DRIVER ti̱ ngä̱' hāko̱ki-me̱'. khā̈sa nga̱ me̱'. yi̱nnä: ngä̱' ko̱rmo sūmkya-la kyā̈l-ko̱.

SÖNAM la̱mkha kyü̱' yö̱'-pa. chūtshö' kha̱tshȫ' ko̱rki-re̱'.

DRIVER chūtshö' shi̱-ts ko̱rki-re̱'.

SÖNAM ko̱rmo nyi̱kya-ngāpcu-la kyā̈l-thang.

DRIVER the̱ nyu̱ng-ṭhaki-re̱'-la:. nga̱ ko̱rmo sūmkya-la kyā̈lki-yi̱n. tha̱nta khyērang-tsho-la mo̱ṭa shä̱nthak ra̱ki-ma-re̱'.

SÖNAM tu̱ho, the̱ ngȫnä' yi̱n-sa re̱'. nga̱ntsho-la mo̱ṭa shä̱nthak ra̱k-sa ma-re̱'. khōrang nyāmtu-ṭo̱.

Vocabulary

ཚབ།	**tshāp**	replacement/instead of
སེམས་ཁྲལ་མ་བྱེད།	**sēmṭhäl ma-chi̱'**	don't worry!
མགོ་སྐོར་གཏོང་བ།	**ko̱kor-tāngwa**	to deceive
སླེབ་པ།	**lēpa**	to arrive (non-intentional)
ཉིས་བརྒྱ་ལྔ་བཅུ།	**nyi̱kya-ngāpcu**	two hundred and fifty
སྐད་ཆ་བྱེད་པ།	**kā̈cha-che̱pa**	to negotiate/discuss a plan
སྐྱེལ་བ།	**kyā̈lwa**	to transport/carry (past form: བསྐྱལ་བ།)
ཧ་གོ་གི་མེད།	**hāko̱ki-me̱'**	I don't know anything about that
ཁས་སའི་མི་ཡིན་ས་མ་རེད།	**khā̈sä: mi̱ yi̱n-sa ma-re̱'**	doesn't seem like the man from yesterday
ཐུབ་པ།	**thūpa**	able to (see below)
ཚར་བ།	**tshārwa**	already/finished
གླ་བ།	**lāwa**	to hire (past: གླས་པ། **lā̈wa**)
སྒོ་རྒྱག་པ།	**ko̱-kya̱pa**	to close the door

རྒྱུས།	**kyü̲'**	familiar with
རྒྱལ་རྩེ།	**kya̲ntse**	a Tibetan town
སུམ་བརྒྱ།	**sūmkya**	three hundred
ཊི་ཀེ་ཊེ་གཏོག་པ།	**ṭīkate-tōkpa**	to book something (*lit.* 'to get a ticket'; an expression used by Tibetans outside Tibet: **ṭīkate** is derived from 'ticket'.)

Cultural point

Travel in Tibet

With only a small number of airports and one train line, public transport options in Tibet are limited. Travel by bus is popular; but vast distances, poor roads, and rather basic facilities can make it a gruelling experience. The main alternative is hiring private jeeps or minivans. These are readily available, popular with both Tibetans and visitors, and usually quite reasonably priced. Negotiation is an integral part of this travel experience. Having located the point where these vehicles congregate, one attempts to work out a deal with drivers and/or other passengers.

There are particular problems in Tibet at the time of writing; these are causing major disruption to travel by visitors.

Language point

1 A note of uncertainty . . .

In English, to communicate that you are not totally sure of a thing, you add words such as 'probably' or 'maybe' (adverbs). But in Tibetan, you show a lack of certainty by modifying the verb (copula/auxiliary). This book will not cover the many variations of this in Tibetan. Instead it will focus upon one widely used structure, which involves adding the particle **sā**. Duho especially favours this most versatile structure.

The translation 'I should think that . . .' will often be used. But sometimes another phrase, such as 'seems' or 'more than likely' might better capture **sā**. This will depend upon the situation. There can be no fixed English equivalents for such structures as **sā**, because Tibetan recognises more degrees of uncertainty than English. Whichever way **sā** is translated though, it always suggests that there is greater certainty than doubt about what is being asserted; i.e. it is closer to saying 'probably' than 'might be'.

As in one example below, **sā** is also used in questions, anticipating that the answer a person will give is unlikely to be one that he or she is completely sure of.

sā can be used to show that a statement, etc. is an *assumption* which one has grounds for believing is correct. The verb forms change here, as follows:

	Certain			*Reasonable assumption*	
Identity	རེད།	**re̱'**	→	ཡིན་ས་རེད།	**yi̱n-sa re̱'**
Existence	ཡོད་རེད།	**yo̱re'**	→	ཡོད་ས་རེད།	**yö̱'-sa re̱'**

Question: ཁོ་རང་བོད་པ་ཡིན་ས་རེད་པས།
khōrang phö̱pa yi̱n-sa re̱'-wä.
Do you think he's Tibetan?

Answer: ཡིན་ས་མ་རེད།
yi̱n-sa ma-re̱'.
I shouldn't think so.

རྡོ་རྗེ་ཚོང་ཁང་ལ་ཡོད་ས་མ་རེད།
to̱ce tshōngkhang-la yö̱'-sa ma-re̱'.
I shouldn't think that Dorje (a personal name) is at the shop.

Only **re̱'** and **yore'** can be modified to accommodate the use of **sā**. The verbs **yi̱n**, **yö̱'**, **tu̱'**, and **sōng** cannot; they are used when talking about yourself or things you have witnessed, so they always convey some certainty.

This structure can also be used in a *predictive* sense, with both intentional and non-intentional action verbs. As the example shows, all you have to do is to replace the linking particle with **sā**:

Certain: དེ་རིང་བསོད་ནམས་དང་ཏུ་ཧོ་འགྲོ་གི་རེད།
the̱ring sȫnam thang tu̱ho ṭo̱ki-re̱'.
Sönam and Duho will go today.

Less certain: དེ་རིང་བསོད་ནམས་དང་རྡུ་ཧོ་འགྲོ་ས་རེད།
the̱ring sȫnam thang tu̱ho ṭo̱-sa re̱'.
I should think Sönam and Duho will go today.

In English, one can say 'probably' about one's own actions; such as 'I shall probably go . . .'. **sā** cannot be used for the first person in that way (i.e. with intentional verbs). The only situation where a first person can use it is when predicting that something will happen *to* him or her (i.e. using a non-intentional verb):

ང་ན་ས་རེད། **nga̱ na̱-sa re̱'.**
There is a good chance I will fall ill . . .

Exercise 1

Different English phrases have been used in the following sentences to express a lack of certainty. But in Tibetan, they can all be expressed with the **sā** structure. Translate them, remembering to choose the right ending according to the identity–existence divide:

1 The car/jeep seems to be new.
2 I doubt this restaurant has vegetarian food.
3 The airport is more than likely far from here.
4 I shouldn't think we'll arrive by (at) 10 o'clock.
5 There are probably many people in that car.
6 I shouldn't think the bus will go there.
7 Do you think that our driver is drinking spirits?

Language point

2 Weather གནམ་གཤིས། (nāmshi')

When non-intentional verbs were introduced in Unit 11, the focus was upon things which happen to people. But non-intentional verbs are also used to describe events, occurrences, etc. unrelated to people, such as weather conditions (which are obviously very relevant to travel). Weather-related words are almost all composite verbs (see Unit 8). For example, **chārpa** is 'rain': when the verbaliser **kya̱pa** is added, it produces 'to rain':

ཆར་པ་རྒྱག་པ། or ཆར་པ་གཏོང་བ།	**chārpa-kya̱pa/tāngwa**	to rain
གངས་རྒྱག་པ། or གངས་གཏོང་བ།	**kha̱ng-kya̱pa/tāngwa**	to snow
ཉི་མ་སྟོན་པ།	**nyi̱ma-tā̃npa**	to be sunny
ལྷགས་པ་རྒྱག་པ།	**lhākpa-kya̱pa**	to be windy
སེར་བ་རྒྱག་པ།	**sēra-kya̱pa**	to hail
སྨུག་པ་འཁོར་བ།	**mūkpa-khōrwa**	to be misty/foggy

There is no equivalent of 'it'; one just adds the appropriate (non-intentional) auxiliary to one of the above. For instance:

ལྷགས་པ་རྒྱག་གི་འདུག **lhākpa kya̱pki-tu̱'.** It is windy.

Exercise 2

Translate:

1 དེ་རིང་ཆར་པ་གཏང་གི་རེད། **the̱ring chārpa tāngki-re̱'.**
2 དགོང་དག་ཆར་པ་གཏང་ས་རེད། **ko̱ngthak chārpa tāng-sa re̱'.**
3 ཞོགས་ཀས་ཉི་མ་བསྟན་ས་མ་རེད། **sho̱kä nyi̱ma tā̃n-sa ma-re̱'.**
4 Is it raining?
5 It was cold yesterday, but it didn't snow.
6 It hailed when we were going to Lhasa.
7 It seems to be snowing up there.

Language point

3 ཐུབ་པ། 'can'/'to be able'

thūpa is a modal verb (see Grammar section). Usually, sentences with modal verbs (such as **kö̱'**) have time-words, showing when the action occurs. But with **thūpa**, time is indicated by auxiliary verbs, like normal sentences with action verbs.

thūp slots in after the action verb:

ཁོ་རང་འགྲོ་ཐུབ་ཀྱི་རེད། **khōrang ṯo thūpki-ṟe'.**
He will be able to go.

ཁྱེད་རང་འཁྱེར་ཐུབ་ཀྱི་མི་འདུག **khyērang khyēr thūpki min-ṯu'.**
You cannot carry it.

thūpa is generally attached to intentional, rather than non-intentional action verbs. In this respect it is like 'am able to'; one is able to 'go', 'eat', etc., but not to 'get ill'. Despite this, one attaches **thūp** to talk about the *ability* to do the action, rather than the action itself, and this ability is seen as *non-intentional*. So sentences with **thūp** (and other modal verbs) use non-intentional auxiliaries.

A sentence like ང་འགྲོ་ཐུབ་ཀྱི་ཡིན། is impossible.

With **thūpa**, the same auxiliaries can be used for all three people:

ང་/ཁྱེད་རང་/ཁོ་རང་ལབ་ཐུབ་ཀྱི་མི་འདུག
nga̱/khyērang/khōrang la̱p thūpki min-ṯu'.
I am/you are/he is not able to say.

sā can also be added, straight after **thūp**, indicating that one is not completely certain, e.g.

ང་འགྲོ་ཐུབ་ས་རེད། **nga̱ ṯo thūp-sa ṟe'.**
I should think I'll be able to go.

Exercise 3

Complete the sentences according to what appears in brackets (in the affirmative, unless otherwise indicated).

1 ང་ཚོ་ཆུ་ཚོད་དང་པོ་ལ་ཡོང་ཐུབ་________ །
nga̱ chūtshö' tha̱ngpo-la yo̱ng-thūp ________ (future-definite)

2 ང་མོ་ཊ་ཆེན་པོ་འདི་གཏང་ཐུབ་________ །
nga̱ mo̱ṭä chēnpo ti̱ tāng-thūp________ (future-predictive)

3 ཁོ་རང་མི་གསུམ་བསྐྱལ་ཐུབ་________ །
khōrang mi̱ sūm kyǟl-thūp________ (past)

4 ང་ཚང་མ་བཏུངས་ཐུབ་________ །
nga̱ tshāngma thūng-thūp________ (past-negative)

5 སྒོ་རྒྱག་ཐུབ་________ །
ko̱ kya̱p-thūp________ (present-negative)

6 ཅ་ལག་འདི་ཚོ་འཁྱེར་ཐུབ་_______ །
cālak ti̱ntsho khyēr-thūp_______ (future-predictive-question)

7 ཁོ་རང་ཚོ་མོ་ཊའི་མདུན་ལ་བསྡད་ཐུབ་_______།
khōrang-tsho mo̱ṭä: tü̱n-la tä̱'-thūp_______ (future-definite)

Dialogue 2

(Audio 2:24)

Things have not gone well. There has been a mishap with the vehicle as Duho and Sönam were travelling on a mountain pass. There is no mobile signal, so now they must just wait.

ཧུ་ཧོ། མི་དེས་མོ་ཊ་ཡག་པོ་བཏང་མ་སོང་ང་། ང་དང་པོ་ནས་ཁོ་ལ་དོགས་པ་ཟ་སོང་།
བསོད་ནམས། ཁ་ལོ་པའི་ནོར་འཁྲུལ་མ་རེད།
ཧུ་ཧོ། འོ་ན་སུའི་སྐྱོན་རེད། མོ་ཊ་གཞན་དག་མ་ཡོང་ན་ང་ཚོ་ག་རེ་བྱེད་དགོས་རེད།
བསོད་ནམས། སེམས་ཁྲལ་མ་བྱེད། མོ་ཊ་གཞན་དག་ཡོང་གི་རེད།
ཧུ་ཧོ། ཡིན་ནའང་མགྱོགས་པོར་ཡོང་ས་མ་རེད། ཨེ་ནི་གངས་བརྒྱབ་ན་….།
བསོད་ནམས། གངས་བརྒྱབ་ན་ག་རེ་ཡོད་རེད། གངས་(ཀྱི་)དཀྱིལ་ལ་མོ་ཊ་འགྲོ་ཐུབ་ཀྱི་རེད།
ཧུ་ཧོ། ཡིན་ནའང་ང་ཚོ་ལ་ཟ་ཡས་མང་པོ་མེད། ཨེ་ནི་ས་ཆ་མཛེ་པོ་འདུག ང་ དབུགས་ཡག་པོ་གཏོང་ཐུབ་ཀྱི་མི་འདུག
བསོད་ནམས། ཧུ་ཧོ། ང་ཚོ་ལ་བྱེད་ཡས་གང་ཡང་མི་འདུག འདིར་བསྒུགས་ནས་བསྡད་དགོས་རེད། ཨེ་ནི་ང་ཚོ་འཁྱགས་ནས་ཤི་ས་མ་རེད། ལ་དུག་བརྒྱབ་ནས་ཤི་ས་མ་རེད། ཡིན་ནའང་སྐད་ཆ་འདི་འདྲ་མང་པོ་བཤད་ན་ཕན་གྱི་མ་རེད། གཏན་གཏན་སྒུག་སྒུབ་དོག་པོ་བཟོ་གི་རེད། བསམ་བློ་ཞེ་དྲག་མ་གཏོང་། སྟོད་སྟོད་བྱས་ནས་སྡོད།

DUHO mi̱ the̱' mo̱ṭa ya̱kpo tāng ma-sōng-nga. nga tha̱ngpo-nä khō-la tho̱kpa sa̱-song.
SÖNAM khālowa no̱rṭhül ma-re̱'.
DUHO o̱na sū: kyȫn re̱'. mo̱ṭa shä̱nthak ma-yo̱ng-na nga̱ntsho kha̱re che̱-kö' re̱'.
SÖNAM sēmṭhäl ma-chi̱'. mo̱ṭa shä̱nthak yo̱ngki-re̱'.
DUHO yi̱nnä: kyo̱kpo yo̱ng-sa ma-re̱'. ēni kha̱ng kya̱p-na . . .
SÖNAM khang kya̱p-na kha̱re-yo̱re'. kha̱ng kyīl-la mo̱ṭa ṭo̱ thūpki-re̱'.

DUHO	yi̱nnä: nga̱ntsho-la sa̱yä ma̱ngpo me̱'. ēni sācha thōpo tu̱'. nga̱ ūk ya̱kpo tāng-thūpki min-tu̱'.
SÖNAM	tu̱ho, nga̱ntsho-la che̱yä khä̱: min-tu̱'. tä̱: ku̱k-nä tä̱'-kö'-re̱'. ēni nga̱ntsho khyāk-nä shī-sa ma-re̱'. la̱thuk-kya̱p-nä shī-sa ma-re̱'. yi̱nnä: kǟcha ti̱nṭä ma̱ngpo shǟ-na phǟnki ma-re̱'. tǟntän bu̱ksup-tho̱kpo so̱ki-re̱'. sāmlo she̱ṭhak ma-tāng. lhȫlhö'-chä̱nä tä̱'.

Vocabulary

དང་པོ་ནས།	**tha̱ngpo-nä**	(right) from the start
ནོར་འཁྲུལ།	**no̱rṭhül**	mistake/error
དཀྱིལ་(ལ)།	**kyīl**	in the centre of/amidst
འཁྱགས་པ།	**khyākpa**	to feel cold
འདི་འདྲ།	**ti̱nṭä**	like this/in this way
དོགས་པ་ཟ་བ།	**tho̱kpa-sa̱wa**	to have doubts
ལ་དུག་རྒྱག་པ།	**la̱thuk-kya̱pa**	to have altitude sickness
……ག་རེ་ཡོད་རེད།	**kha̱re-yo̱re'**	so what (if) . . . ?/what does that matter?
ང་ཚོ་ག་རེ་བྱེད་དགོས་རེད།	**nga̱ntsho kha̱re che̱-kö' re̱'**	what are we to do?
སྦུག་སུབ་དོག་པོ་བཟོ་བ།	**bu̱ksup-tho̱kpo so̱wa**	to make a situation tense/ more stressful
ཀློད་ཀློད་བྱས་ནས་སྡོད།	**lhȫlhö'-chä̱nä tä̱'**	stay calm!
བྱེད་ཡས་གང་ཡང་མི་འདུག	**che̱yä khä̱: min-tu̱'**	there's nothing we can do/nothing to be done
སྐྱོན།	**kyȫn**	fault/defect; harm
མགྱོགས་པོ།	**kyo̱kpo**	quickly/soon
དབུགས་གཏོང་བ།	**ūk-tāngwa**	to breathe
ཤི་བ།	**shīwa**	to die
གཏན་གཏན།	**tǟntän**	definitely

Language point

4 Describing how actions are done

Many words such as **yākpo** ('good') can also be used to describe how an action is done (i.e. adjectives also function as adverbs): they go immediately before the action they describe, e.g.:

མི་དེས་ལམ་ཁ་ཡག་པོར་བསྟན་སོང་།
mi̲ the̲' la̲mkha ya̲kpo tǟn-sōng.
That man showed us the route well (i.e. did a good job of showing us the route).

As illustrated, these words may have **la̲thön** incorporated into them (as **ra**) in written form. But this is not heard in spoken Tibetan.

In the case of composite verbs, these words go in between the two parts (i.e. just before the verbaliser).

ཁོས་མོ་ཊ་མགྱོགས་པོར་གཏོང་གི་འདུག
khȫ' mo̲ṭa kyo̲kpo tāngki-tu'.
He is driving quickly.

The term **chä̲nä** can also be used when describing actions. It can be tagged onto the end of the words like **yākpo** (instead of **ra**), with the same meaning as above. It can also modify the end of some action verbs, changing them into descriptions of how the action is performed, e.g.

ཡག་པོ་བྱས་ནས། **ya̲kpo-chä̲nä**
(to do, drive, etc.) well

མགྱོགས་པོ་བྱས་ནས། **kyo̲kpo-chä̲nä**
(to do) quickly/hurriedly

གཟབ་གཟབ་བྱས་ནས། **sa̲psap-chä̲nä**
(to do) carefully

Exercise 4

Following the example, join each description phrase (adverb) with its accompanying verb, and translate the combination. The same phrase may translate in different ways, according to which action it describes.

	Description phrase		Action	
(a)	ཤུགས་ཆེན་པོ།	**shūk-chēnpo**	སྐད་ཆ་བཤད་པ།	**kā̆cha-shā̆pa**
(b)	ཤུགས་ཆེན་པོ་བྱས་ནས།	**shūk-chēnpo-chä̱nä**	བསྡད་པ།	**tä̱wa**
(c)	དྲོ་པོ་བྱས་ནས།	**ṭho̱po-chä̱nä**	གྱོན་པ།	**khö̱npa**
(d)	སྐྱིད་པོ་བྱས་ནས།	**kyīpo-chä̱nä**	ལྟད་མོ་ལྟ་བ།	**tēmo-tāwa**
(e)	སྐྱིད་པོ་བྱས་ནས།	**kyīpo-chä̱nä**	ཉལ་བ།	**nyä̱lwa**
(f)	ལས་སླ་པོ།	**läläpo**	འགོ་བ།	**ko̱wa**
(g)	ལྷོད་ལྷོད་བྱས་ནས།	**lhȫlhö’-chä̱nä**	ཁ་ལག་ཟ་བ།	**khālak sa̱wa**

(a) སྐད་ཆ་ཤུགས་ཆེན་པོར་བཤད་པ། **kā̆cha shūk-chēnpo shā̆pa** (to speak forcefully/powerfully)

Language point

5 What happens if . . . ? ན།

‘If’ is expressed with the particle **na**. As Dialogue 2 shows, **na** is inserted at the end of the clause with the if (‘the conditional clause’), unlike in English, where it goes at the beginning. **na** can combine with the verb(s) in a variety of ways. Here we shall use a very common variation, where **na** simply replaces the auxiliary and linking-particle. The second (‘the main’) clause takes the same form as a sentence in the future. This is similar to the English use of ‘will/won’t’, as in the examples below.

མོ་ཊ་གཞན་དག་ཡོང་ན་ང་ཚོ་འགྲོ་ཐུབ་ཀྱི་རེད།
mo̱ṭa shä̱nthak yo̱ng-na nga̱ntsho ṭo̱-thūpki re̱’.
If another car comes, we will be able to go. (Or, ‘We’ll be able to go if another car comes.’)

When the if-clause is negative, the negating particle goes before the action verb:

མོ་ཊ་གཞན་དག་མ་ཡོང་ན་ང་ཚོ་འགྲོ་ཐུབ་ཀྱི་མ་རེད།
mo̱ṭa shä̱nthak ma-yo̱ng-na nga̱ntsho ṭo̱-thūpki ma-re̱’.
If no other cars come, we won’t be able to go. (Or, ‘We won’t be able to go unless another car comes.’)

The action verb to which **na̱** is attached will often have the past form (both when written and spoken). This indicates nothing about time; whether the action verb is in the past or the present/future forms, the meaning is the same.

ཁྱེད་རང་ཚོ་རྒྱལ་རྩེ་ལ་འགྲོ་ན་......
khyērang-tsho kya̱ntse-la ṭo̱-na . . .
If you go to Gyantse . . .

ཁྱེད་རང་ཚོ་རྒྱལ་རྩེ་ལ་ཕྱིན་ན་......
khyērang-tsho kya̱ntse-la chīn-na . . .
If you go to Gyantse . . .

Exercise 5

Duho has nothing to do except ponder various potential outcomes of the present situation. He imagines a range of 'what if . . .' scenarios, all of which are unfortunately bad! The sentences below are split into their separate clauses, to help clarify the structure. **sā** cannot be used in the if-clause, but it can appear in the second (indicated by 'might') to express a strong likelihood, rather than a definite occurrence. Follow Duho through his increasing panic as you translate these sentences (vocabulary below):

(a)	If no other cars come . . .	We can't go to Gyantse.
(b)	If no other cars come . . .	We can't go/return to the guesthouse.
(c)	If no other cars come . . .	We must go to search for help.
(d)	If we go searching for help . . .	We might get bitten by a mastiff.
(e)	If robbers come . . .	What are we to do?
(f)	If we don't get water . . .	We'll become (i.e. be) thirsty.
(g)	If we don't get any food . . .	We'll get hungry.
(h)	And, if we don't get water . . .	We might die!
(i)	And, if we don't get any food . . .	WE MIGHT DIE!

Vocabulary

ཇག་པ།	**cha̱kpa**	robber/bandit
ཡོང་བ།	**yo̱ngwa**	to happen
གྲ་མ་སྒྲིག	**ṭha̱:-maṭi̱k**	unfortunate events/mishaps
བཏོན་པ།	**tȫnpa**	(past of འདོན་པ། **tö̱npa**) to extract
འདོགས་ཁྱི།	**to̱kkhyi**	Tibetan Mastiff (large, ferocious type of dog, used to guard herds, monasteries, villages, etc.)
སྐྱོན་བཙུགས་པ།	**kyȫn-tsūkpa**	(past of སྐྱོན་འཛུགས་པ།) to blame/criticise someone
སོ་རྒྱག་པ།	**sō-kya̱pa**	to bite
འཛུལ་བ།	**tsü̱lwa**	to enter
ས་ཀོང་།	**sākong**	rut

Two views of the situation (*T*) (Audio 2:26)

Here is Duho's account of the mishap and its aftermath. Read the passage, with the help of the additional vocabulary above and in the list on p. 178:

ལམ་ཁ་དེ་དངོས་གནས་ཡག་པོ་མི་འདུག ཡིན་ནའང་ང་ཚོའི་ཁ་ལོ་པ་དེས་མོ་ཊ་གཟབ་གཟབ་བྱས་ནས་བཏང་མ་སོང་། ལམ་ཁ་ལ་ས་ཀོང་གཅིག་འདུག ཡིན་ནའང་ཁོ་རང་གིས་སྐད་ཆ་མང་པོ་བཤད་ནས་དེ་མ་མཐོང་བ་རེད། ཨེ་ནི་ང་ཚོའི་མོ་ཊ་དེའི་ནང་ལ་འཛུལ་སོང་། ང་ཚོ་ལ་གང་ཡང་བྱས་མ་སོང་། མོ་ཊ་ལའང་སྐྱོན་མི་འདུག ཡིན་ནའང་ང་ཚོས་ས་ཀོང་ནས་མོ་ཊ་བཏོན་ཐུབ་མ་སོང་། ང་ཚོ་ལ་རོགས་པ་དགོས་ཀྱི་འདུག མོ་ཊ་ལ་ཡང་(འང་)སྐྱོན་མི་འདུག་ཡོང་ན་རོགས་པ་རག་གི་རེད། ཡིན་ནའང་མོ་ཊ་གཞན་དག་ཡོང་གི་མི་འདུག ང་ཁ་ལོ་པ་དེ་ལ་ཚིག་པ་ཟ་གི་འདུག ཨེ་ནི་བསོད་ནམས་ཀྱིས་ང་ལ་སྐད་ཆ་ཞེ་དྲག་བཤད་ཀྱི་མི་འདུག ཧོབ་ཀྱི་འདུག

la̱mkha-the ngȫne' ya̱kpo min-tu̱'. yi̱nnä nga̱ntshö: khālowa the̱' mo̱ṭa sa̱psap-chä̱nä tāng ma-sōng. la̱mkha-la sākong-cīk tu̱'. yi̱nnä khōrang-kī' kǟcha ma̱ngpo shǟ-nä the̱ ma-thōngwa-re̱'. ēni nga̱ntshö: mo̱ṭa thä: na̱ng-la tsü̱l-sōng.

nga̱ntsho-la khä̱: chä̱’ ma-sōng. mo̱ṭa-la-yä kyȫn min-tu̱’. yi̱nnä nga̱ntshȫ’ sākong-nä’ mo̱ṭa tȫn thūp ma-sōng. nga̱ntsho-la ro̱kpa kö̱’-ki tu̱’. mo̱ṭa shä̱nthak yo̱ng-na ro̱kpa ra̱ki-re̱’. yi̱nnä mo̱ṭa shä̱nthak yo̱ngki min-tu̱’. nga̱ khālowa the̱-la tshīkpa sa̱ki-tu̱’. ēni sȫnam-kī’ nga̱-la kǟcha she̱ṭhak shǟki min-tu̱’. nyo̱pki-tu̱’.

Exercise 6 (Audio 2:27)

Translate the passage. But first gauge how well you have understood it by trying to answer these questions (in English).

According to Duho’s account;

1 Was it only the driver who was to blame for the accident?
2 Is there any suggestion that the driver might have been drinking?
3 What have the three travellers been unable to do?
4 Do we hear anything about the driver’s reaction to the mishap?
5 What frustrates Duho about the situation?

Sönam’s thoughts on the situation are summed up in a few words:

ཕྱི་རྒྱལ་(གྱི་)མི་མང་པོས་ཏུ་ཧོ་ནང་བཞིན་བྱེད་ཀྱི་ཡོད་རེད། ཕྱི་རྒྱལ་གྱི་ལུགས་སྲོལ་ཡིན་ས་རེད། མཚམས་མཚམས་ལ་གྲ་མ་སྒྲིག་ཡོང་གི་ཡོད། ཡིན་ནའང་ལམ་སེང་རོགས་པ་ལ་སྐྱོན་བཙུགས་ན་ག་རེ་ཕན་གྱི་ཡོད་རེད། སྐྱིད་པོ་ཡོད་མ་རེད།

chīkyäl(-ki) mi̱ ma̱ngpō’ tu̱ho na̱ngshin che̱ki-yo̱re’. chi̱kyäl-ki lu̱ksȫl yi̱n-sa re̱’. tshāmtsham-la ṭha̱:-mati̱k yo̱ngki-re̱’. yi̱nnä: la̱msang ro̱kpa-la kyȫn tsūk-na kha̱re phǟnki-yo̱re’. kyīpo yo̱ ma-re̱’.

Exercise 7

Based upon what Sönam says here (and doesn’t say), answer these questions (in English):

1 Who does Sönam blame for the accident?
2 What does he find least pleasant about the situation?
3 Are his private thoughts (expressed here) different from what he communicated to Duho in Dialogue 2?

4 He refers to customs; what do you think he means?
5 What differences in attitude do Duho’s and Sönam’s reactions to the situation seem to suggest?
6 What qualities and types of behaviour do these thoughts suggest Sönam prizes?

Language point

6 Feelings and reactions

····(ལ་)ཚིག་པ་ཟ་བ།	**tshīkpa-sa̱wa**	to be angry/annoyed
····(ལ་)དོགས་པ་ཟ་བ།	**tho̱kpa-sa̱wa**	to be suspicious/ have doubts
····(ལ་)ཞེད་པ།	**she̱pa**	to be scared
····(ལ་)ཧ་ལས་པ།	**hāläwa**	to be surprised/ shocked
དངངས་སྐྲག་བྱེད་པ།	**ngāmṭak-che̱pa**	to be anxious
ཉོབ་པ།	**nyo̱pa**	to be bored/listless
ཐང་ཆད་པ།	**thāng-chä̱pa**	to be tired

These are non-intentional actions. We know when we feel these things, so can use the auxiliaries **tu̱’** and **sōng** to report them. We can be less certain about other people: **sā** can be added when talking about them, to show that we are only inferring that this is what they feel.

Exercise 8

Emotions are running quite high. Sönam, Duho, and perhaps the driver have reacted to the situation in different ways. Link these private thoughts with the individuals you think they belong to.

1 ཁོ་ལ་ཚིག་པ་ག་རེ་བྱས་ནས་ཟ་གི་ཡོད་རེད།
khō-la tshīkpa kha̱re-chä̱nä sa̱ki-yo̱re’
2 ཁོ་ཉོབ་ཀྱི་ཡོད་ས་རེད།
khō nyo̱pki yö̱’-sa re̱’
3 མོ་ཏ་ལ་སྐྱོན་མི་འདུག
mo̱ṭa-la kyȫn min-tu̱’

4 ཞེད་ཀྱི་ཡོད་ས་རེད།
she̲ki yö̲' sa re̲'

5 ཁོ་ལ་ཧ་ལས་ཀྱི་འདུག
khō-la hāläki-tu̲'

6 ང་ལ་ཚིག་པ་ཟ་གི་ཡོད་ས་རེད།
nga̲-la tshīkpa sa̲ki yö̲-sa re̲'

7 ཁོ་གཉིས་ག་རེ་བྱས་ནས་ཉོབ་ཀྱི་ཡོད་མ་རེད།
khō-nyī' kha̲re-chä̲nä nyo̲pki yo̲ ma-re̲'

8 ང་ལ་ཚིག་པ་ག་རེ་བྱས་ནས་ཟ་གི་ཡོད་རེད།
nga̲-la tshīkpa kha̲re-chä̲nä sa̲ki-yo̲re'

9 ཁོ་གཉིས་སྐད་ཆ་ག་རེ་བྱས་ནས་བཤད་ཀྱི་ཡོད་མ་རེད།
khō-nyī' kǟcha kha̲re-chä̲nä shǟki yo̲ ma-re̲'

Unit Thirteen

ཁ་རེ་ཟེར།

khare-sa

What did he say?

In this unit you will learn how to:

- pass on messages and report what someone said
- deal with direct and indirect speech
- use a structure similar to 'the one who . . .'
- describe two types of past action
- talk about knowing and understanding
- express the content of thought and speech
- ask questions related to names, meaning, etc.

Dialogue 1

(Audio 2:28)

As Duho passes through the marketplace, someone recognises him as a friend of Tashi's.

ཚེ་ནོར། ཁོང་། ཁྱེད་རང་བཀྲ་ཤིས་ཀྱི་གྲོགས་པོ་ཡིན་པ། དེ་རིང་བཀྲ་ཤིས་ཐུག་ས་རེད་པས།

ཏུ་ཧོ། ང་ད་ལྟ་བཀྲ་ཤིས་ཀྱི་རྩ་ལ་འགྲོ་གི་ཡིན།

ཚེ་ནོར། འོ་ཏག་ཏག་ཐེམས་སོང་། བཀྲ་ཤིས་ལ་ལན་སྐྱེལ་ཐུབ་ས་རེད་པས།

ཏུ་ཧོ། ངས་ལན་སྐྱེལ་དགོས། ཇོ་ལགས། ཁྱེད་རང་(གི་)མཚན་ལ་ག་རེ་ཞུ་གི་ཡོད།

ཚེ་ནོར། ངའི་མིང་ལ་ཚེ་དབང་ནོར་བུ་ཟེར་གྱི་ཡོད། བཀྲ་ཤིས་ལ་འདི་འདྲ་གསུངས་དང་། ང་སང་ཉིན་བཀྲ་ཤིས་ཀྱི་ཅ་ལག་དེ་ཚོ་རྒྱལ་ས་ལ་འཁྱེར་གྱི་ཡིན་ཟེར་ལབ་པ་

ཡིན། ཡིན་ནའང་ནང་ལ་གནས་ཚུལ་ཞིག་ཐོན་ནས་ང་སང་ཉིན་འགྲོ་ཐུབ་ས་མ་
རེད། ཡིན་ནའང་ཨ་ཁུ་ཐུབ་བསྟན་སང་ཉིན་འགྲོ་མཁན་རེད། ཅ་ལག་དེ་ཚོ་
འཁྱེར་དགོས་ཟེར་གྱི་འདུག ཨེ་ནི། དེ་ཚོ་ཁོ་རང་གི་རྩ་ལ་མགྱོགས་པོར་སྐྱེལ་
དགོས་ཀྱི་འདུག གང་ཡིན་ཟེར་ན། ཁོ་རང་སང་ཉིན་སྔ་པོར་འགྲོ་མཁན་ཡིན་
ཟེར་གྱི་འདུག འདི་བཀྲ་ཤིས་ལ་གསུངས་ཨང་།

ཏྲུ་ཧོ། ཏོག་ཙམ་བཞུགས་ཨང་། ཇོ་ལགས་ཀྱིས་མང་པོ་གསུངས་སོང་། ང་ཚང་མ་མགོ་
འཚོས་མ་སོང་། ཅ་ལག་དེ་ཚོ་ག་རེ་རེད།

ཚེ་ནོར། འདི་གལ་ཆེན་པོ་མ་རེད། བཀྲ་ཤིས་ཧ་གོ་གི་རེད།

ཏྲུ་ཧོ། ཨོ་ན། ཅ་ལག་འཁྱེར་གྱི་ཡིན་ཟེར་ལབ་མཁན་དེ་སུ་རེད། ཇོ་ལགས་རེད་པས།
ཡང་མིན་ན་ཨ་ཁུ་ཐུབ་བསྟན་རེད།

ཚེ་ནོར། དང་པོར་ང་འཁྱེར་གྱི་ཡིན་ཟེར་ལབ་པ་ཡིན། ཡིན་ནའང་ད་ལྟ་ཨ་ཁུ་ཐུབ་བསྟན་
གྱིས་འཁྱེར་དགོས་ཟེར་ལབ་ཀྱི་འདུག

ཏྲུ་ཧོ། ཨེ་ནི། བཀྲ་ཤིས་འགྲོ་དགོས་ཀྱི་མི་འདུག་ག

ཚེ་ནོར། ད་ཡག་པོར་གསན་ཨང་། ཨ་ཁུ་ཐུབ་བསྟན་རྒྱལ་ས་ལ་འགྲོ་མཁན་རེད། བཀྲ་
ཤིས་འགྲོ་མཁན་མ་རེད། ཡིན་ནའང་བཀྲ་ཤིས་ཀྱིས་ཅ་ལག་དེ་ཚོ་ཨ་ཁུ་ཐུབ་
བསྟན་གྱི་རྩ་ལ་སྐྱེལ་དགོས་ཀྱི་འདུག མ་བསྐྱལ་ན་ཨ་ཁུ་ཐུབ་བསྟན་གྱིས་སང་
ཉིན་འཁྱེར་ཐུབ་ཀྱི་མ་རེད་པ།

ཏྲུ་ཧོ། ད་མགོ་འཚོས་སོང་། ངས་བཀྲ་ཤིས་ལ་ལན་ཏག་ཏག་སྐྱེལ་དགོས།

ཚེ་ནོར། ·····ད་ག་འདྲ་ཡིན་ན།

TSHENOR khōng. khyērang ṭāshi-ki ṭho̱kpo yi̱n-pa. the̱ring ṭāshi thūk-sa re̱'-wä.

DUHO nga̱ tha̱nta ṭāshi-ki tsā-la ṭo̱ki-yi̱n.

TSHENOR o̱ tākāk chä̱-song. ṭāshi-la lä̱n kyǟl thūp-sa re̱'-wä.

DUHO ngä̱' lä̱n kyǟl-ko̱. cho̱-la: khyērang(-ki) tshǟn-la kha̱re shu̱ki-yö'.

TSHENOR ngä: mi̱ng-la tshēwang no̱rpu se̱rki-yö̱'. ṭāshi-la ti̱nṭä sūng-thang. nga̱ sāngnyin ṭāshi-ki cālak the̱ntsho kyä̱lsa-la khyērki-yi̱n-s la̱pa-yi̱n. yi̱nnä: na̱ng-la nǟtshül-shik thö̱n-nä nga̱ sāngnyin ṭo̱ thūp-sa ma-re̱'. yi̱nnä: ākhu thūptän sāngnyin ṭo̱-nyän re̱'. cālak the̱ntsho khyēr-ko̱ se̱rki-tu̱'. ēni the̱ntsho khōrang-ki tsā-la kyo̱kpo kyǟl kö'-ki tu̱'. kha̱ngyin-se̱rna khōrang sāngnyin ngāpo ṭo̱-nyän yi̱n se̱rki-tu̱'. ti̱ ṭāshi-la sūng-a.

DUHO tēts shu̱-a. cho̱-la-kī’ ma̱ngpo sūng-sōng. nga̱ tshāngma ko̱-tshȫ’ ma-sōng. cālak the̱ntsho kha̱re re̱’.

TSHENOR ti̱ khä̱l-che̱npo ma-re̱’. ṭāshi hākho̱ki-re̱’.

DUHO o̱na cālak the̱ntsho khyērki-yi̱n-s la̱p-nyän the̱ sū re̱’. cho̱-la: re̱’-wä ya̱ng-me̱:na ākhu thūptän re̱’.

TSHENOR tha̱ngpo nga̱ khyērki-yi̱n-s la̱pa-yi̱n. yi̱nnä: tha̱nta ākhu thūptän-kī’ khyēr-ko̱-s la̱pki-tu̱’.

DUHO ēni ṭāshi ṭo̱ kö̱’-ki min-tu̱’-ka.

TSHENOR tha̱ ya̱kpo sä̅n-a. ākhu thūptän kyä̱lsa-la ṭo̱-nyän re̱’. ṭāshi ṭo̱-nyän ma-re̱’. yi̱nnä: ṭāshi-kī’ cālak the̱ntsho ākhu thūptän-ki-tsā-la kyä̅l kö̱’-ki tu̱’. ma-kyä̅l-na ākhu thūptän-kī’ sāngnyin kyä̅l-thūpki ma-re̱’-wa.

DUHO tha̱ ko̱-tshȫ-song. ngä̱’ ṭāshi-la lä̱n tākāk-kyä̅l-ko̱.

TSHENOR (*as Duho walks away*) tha̱ kha̱nṭa yi̱n-na.

Vocabulary

ཐུག་པ།	**thūkpa**	to meet (non-intentional)
མཁན།	**nyän/khän**	the one who . . . (see below)
གསན་པ།	**sä̅npa**	to listen (honorific)
རྒྱལ་ས།	**kyä̱lsa**	capital city
ལན་སྐྱེལ་བ།	**lä̱n-kyä̅lwa**	to deliver a message

ཟེར་ལབ་པ་ཡིན།	**-s l̲apa-yi̲n**	I said (see below)
ཨ་ཁུ་ཐུབ་བསྟན།	**ākhu thūptän**	(personal name)
ད་ག་འདྲ་ཡིན་ན།	**tha̲ kha̲nṭa yi̲n-na**	I wonder . . .
ཧ་གོ་གི་རེད།	**hākho̲ki-re̲'**	(he) will know
མགོ་འཚོས་མ་སོང་།	**ko̲ tshō̃' ma-sōng**	(I) haven't got it/understood
ཚེ་ནོར།	**tshēno̲r**	(abbreviation of the name ཚེ་དབང་ནོར་བུ། **tshēwang no̲rbu**)
ཁྱེད་རང་(གི་)མཚན་ལ་ག་རེ་ཞུ་གི་ཡོད།	**khyērang(-ki) tshā̃n-la kha̲re shu̲ki-yö'**	what's your name? (honorific)
ངའི་མིང་ལ་X་ཟེར་གྱི་ཡོད།	**ngä: mi̲ng-la X se̲rki-yö̲'**	my name is. . . .
གནས་ཚུལ་ཐོན་པ།	**nā̃tshül thö̲npa**	a situation has cropped up
ཏག་ཏག་བྱས་སོང་།	**tākāk chä̲'-song**	that's perfect! (i.e. 'that's really convenient for me')
ཟེར་གྱི་འདུག	**se̲rki-tu̲'**	(he) says
ཏག་ཏག	**tākāk**	exactly/precisely
ཞིག	**shi̲k**	a (used only occasionally)
ཡང་མིན་ན།	**ya̲ng-me̲:na**	or/alternatively

Cultural point

An oral culture

Tibetan may verge on the monosyllabic, but Tibetans certainly do not! Indeed taciturnity generally creates discomfort. Banter is highly appreciated, and people relish opportunities to gather together, and engage in long, raucous sessions of conversation involving joking, repartee, and the telling (as well as the frequent re-telling) of events and stories. Tibetans also often speak very fast! The distinction between knowing the language and knowing *some* of the language is one lost upon many Tibetans; getting people to make allowances for learners can be a struggle. Negotiating situations such as Duho's in Dialogue 1 is therefore an experience familiar to many.

Language point

1 Describing what someone says

Spoken Tibetan doesn't recognise a divide between direct (quoted) speech and indirect speech (which reports the content, without directly quoting). Instead there is a standard form, indicating that something should be understood as 'said'. This form combines features of both direct speech and indirect speech (or what count as such from the English perspective). The most frequently used verbs indicating that someone has said something are:

ལབ་པ། **la̱pa** – to say/tell བཤད་པ། **shā̃pa** – to say/explain
ཟེར་བ། **se̱rwa** – say གསུང་བ། **sūngwa** – to say/tell (honorific)

se̱ (written like the verb above) acts like a verbal speech-mark. It signifies the end of the speech content. For instance, 'he said that Tashi is not over there.':

(ཁོ་རང་གིས་)བཀྲ་ཤིས་ཕ་གིར་མི་འདུག་ཟེར་ལབ་སོང་།
(khōrang-kī') ṭāshi phākä mi-tu̱k-s la̱p-song.

As the transliteration shows, this speech-marker is tagged to the end of the speech content without a pause, sounding similar to a short hiss, or the way that the plural 's' is tagged, for example, onto 'dogs'.

The speech-marker indicates where the speech-content part of the sentence ends. But speech-content is *not* considered a verbatim quotation. It sets out to capture the gist of what is said, rather than the actual words (i.e. like indirect speech in English, it's a paraphrase).

The auxiliary verb in English direct speech is the one which the person being quoted actually said (e.g. "He said 'I <u>am</u> going'.", instead of "He said that he is going.") The same is true in Tibetan:

X འགྲོ་གི་ཡིན་ཟེར་ལབ་སོང་། X **ṭo̱ki-yi̱n-s la̱p-song.**

However, personal pronouns are not used as they are in English. Firstly, Tibetan never repeats the personal pronoun, as in the English '<u>he</u> said that <u>he</u> is going'. (The agentive particle is often omitted; a single personal pronoun is understood as subject for both the sentence and the quotation.) And when the personal pronoun is used, the voice is that of the person reporting, *not* the original speaker. The sentence above, with the personal pronoun included, would be:

ཁོ་རང་འགྲོ་གི་ཡིན་ཟེར་ལབ་སོང་། **khōrang ṭo̱ki-yi̱n-s la̱p-song.**

This sentence has no equivalent for 'I' in it, and because there is no differentiation between direct and indirect speech, it can be translated either as 'he said "I am going"' or 'he said that he is going.'

Exercise 1

The English sentences report things various people have said: the Tibetan snippets are supposed to match what should appear at the end of the 'quote' in their Tibetan equivalents. Indicate with a tick or a cross whether the snippet matches the English sentence.

(a) I said, 'they won't look.'	བལྟ་གི་མིན་ཟེར་…	**tāki-me̱:-s**	✗
(b) He says he likes you.	དགའ་པོ་ཡོད་ཟེར་…	**ka̱po-yö̱'-s**	
(c) You told me he didn't stay.	བསྡད་མེད་ཟེར་…	**tä̱-me̱'-s**	
(d) We said 'we don't have any money'.	དངུལ་མེད་ཟེར་…	**ngūl me̱'-s**	
(e) They say they don't have any money.	དངུལ་མེད་ཟེར་…	**ngūl me̱'-s**	
(f) He told me you'd go to sleep.	ཉལ་གྱི་རེད་ཟེར་…	**nyä̱lki-re̱'-s**	
(g) 'I've got it!' she shouted.	རག་སོང་ཟེར་…	**ra̱k-sōng-s**	
(h) I'll ask her whether she'll wear it.	གྱོན་གྱི་ཡིན་པས་ཟེར་…	**khö̱nki-yi̱n-pä-s**	

■ Speech: abbreviated

The personal pronoun is dropped when it is clear from the context whose speech is being reported. Similarly, it is not repeated when a whole series of things said by a single individual are being reported, one after another. A further abbreviation is also common in these situations: the speech-marker and verb of speech, which are normally separate, are collapsed into the single syllable **sa**. So the *whole* sentence ('he said he is going'), in this highly abbreviated version would be:

འགྲོ་གི་ཡིན་ཟེར། **ṭo̱ki-yi̱n-sa̱.**

This final syllable may be heard either as the 'hiss' mentioned earlier, or, as shown in the transliteration, as a distinct syllable **sa̱**.

Exercise 2

Translate these into English, following the example.

1 ངས་རྗེས་ལ་ཁ་པར་གཏང་གི་ཡིན་ཟེར་ལབ་པ་ཡིན།
ngä̱' ce̱-la khāpar tāngki-yi̱n-s la̱pa-yi̱n. I said I'd ring later.

2 ཁོ་རང་(གིས་)བྱས་མེད་ཟེར་ལབ་ཀྱི་རེད།
khōrang(-ki̱') chä̱-me̱'-s la̱pki-re̱'.

3 གནམ་གྲུ་ལ་འགྲོ་གི་ཡིན་ཟེར་ལབ་ཀྱི་འདུག
nāmṭhu-la ṭo̱ki-yi̱n-s la̱pki-tu̱'.

4 ཐུབ་བསྟན་དགོང་དག་ཁྱེད་རང་གི་རྩ་ལ་ཡོང་གི་ཡིན་ཟེར།
thūptän ko̱ngthak khyērang-ki tsā-la yo̱ngki-yi̱n-sa̱.

5 ཁོ་གཉིས་གྲོགས་པོ་མ་རེད་ཟེར་སུས་ལབ་ཀྱི་འདུག
khō-nyī' ṭho̱kpo ma-re̱'-s sǖ' la̱pki-tu̱'.

6 བསོད་ནམས་མ་བསྡད་ན་སྒྲོལ་མ་ཡང་(འང་)བསྡད་ཀྱི་མིན་ཟེར་ལབ་སོང་།
sȫnam ma-tä̱-na ṭö̱lma-yä tä̱ki-me̱:-s la̱p-song.

7 ཕ་གི་ལ་གནམ་གཤིས་ཡག་པོ་འདུག་ཟེར།
phāki-la nāmshi' ya̱kpo tu̱k-sa̱.

8 རྗེས་ལ་བཤད་དགོས་ཟེར།
ce̱-la shǟ̱'-ko̱-s.

9 ད་ལྟ་ལས་ཀ་ཡོད་ཟེར། ཆུ་ཚོད་བཞི་པ་ལ་ཤོག་ཟེར།
tha̱nta lä̱ka yö̱'-s. chūtshö' shi̱pa-la shōk-sa̱.

Language point

2 མཁན།

This word is pronounced either **nyän** or **khän**. It replaces the final syllable of a verb (either action or copula), and is roughly equivalent to saying 'the one who . . .'. That is, it indicates that the person (or physical object, etc.) is somehow associated with the action or state shown by the verb. Placed after an intentional verb, for example, it refers to the doer of the action:

ལན་སྐྱེལ་མཁན། **lä̱n kyǟl-nyän** the one who delivers the message

The action verb here generally remains in the present form whether or not the action has been performed. So, depending on the situation, the above might translate in various ways:

the one who delivers/delivered the message/the one who will deliver the message/the messenger (etc.)

Attached to a non-intentional verb, it denotes the one(s) who experience(s) the action/state shown by the verb, e.g.:

ན་མཁན། **na̱-nyän** the one/those who are ill

It can also be attached to either of the 'essential' verbs (see Grammar section) of identity or existence, primarily for purposes of description:

གྲྭ་པ་ཡིན་མཁན། **ṭha̱pa yi̱n-khän** the one(s) who are/were monks
སྐྲ་རིང་པོ་ཡོད་མཁན། **ṭā-ri̱ngpo yö̱'-khän** the one/ones with long hair

Negations within **nyän**-phrases are also common. Here essential verbs are negated in the usual way (i.e. either **me̱:** or **me̱'**), whereas **ma** is added before action verbs (both intentional and non-intentional). Other words relating to gender and number can be added after **nyän** when clarification is necessary, e.g.:

ལྷ་ས་ལ་འགྲོ་མཁན་བུ་མོ་དེ། **lhāsa-la ṭo̱-nyän phu̱mo-the**
the girl who is going to Lhasa

Exercise 3

Formulate these in Tibetan, using **nyän**, as in the example:

1 The one who's reading Tibetan
2 The one who's drinking beer
3 The ones talking outside
4 The ones who didn't return home
5 The one who wears white clothes
6 The boy who has no parents
7 Those who've got long legs
8 The children who don't study

1 བོད་ཡིག་ཀློག་མཁན་དེ། **phö̱'yik lōk-khän-the**

■ Language tip – description vs. naming

Learning something's name might seem like the logical first step to being able to talk about it. But in Tibetan, the tendency to describe people and things in terms of their functions, actions, or appearance rather than their names is stronger than in English. So add **nyän** generously! The closest comparable English structures are the 'relative pronouns' (*who, whom, whose, that, which*, such as in: 'the man who called me', etc.), but their frequent use in normal conversation would sound impersonal. However, **nyän** sounds completely natural in Tibetan. When trying to unravel what has been said in accounts or messages, presented in long blocks of speech, it often helps to break things down, using **nyän** questions, to work out the various roles of the people involved (something Duho attempts in Dialogue 1).

Exercise 4

Each of these dialogues has a character that can be described using the accompanying **nyän**-phrase; identify each character by name (U = Unit, D = Dialogue):

1 U5–D1 – ཁང་མིག་འཚོལ་མཁན། **khāngmik tshā̃l-nyän**
2 U6–D2 – སྔོན་མར་དགོན་པ་ལ་སྟོད་མཁན། **ngā̃nma ko̱mpa-la tā̃-khän**
3 U7–D1 – ཁ་དཔར་གཏོང་མཁན། **khāpar tāng-nyän**
4 U9–D1 – ཁ་ལག་གོང་ཆེན་པོ་ལ་དགའ་མཁན། **khālak kho̱ng-chēnpo-la ka̱-nyän**
5 U10–D2 – ཚོང་པ་ལ་སྐད་ཆ་འདྲི་མཁན། **tshōngpa-la kā̃cha ti̱-nyän**
6 U11–D2 – སྨན་ཚོང་ས་ལ་མ་འགྲོ་མཁན། **mā̃n-tshōngsa-la ma to̱-khän**
7 U12–D2 – སེམས་ཁྲལ་བྱེད་མཁན། **sēmṭhäl che̱-khän**

Language point

3 Two types of past action

The structures introduced so far to describe past actions (for example, **chīnpa-yin, chīn-song**) refer to actions which occurred or were performed a single, or a limited number of times. In similar situations in English, one would use the simple past, e.g. 'I went', 'you went'. These structures can be categorised as 'Type 1', to distinguish them from what follows.

Spoken Tibetan distinguishes Type 1 actions from those which occurred or were performed continuously, or repetitively, and are described in terms of some flow of time. These will be referred to as Type 2 actions. English uses structures like 'used to go', or 'was going' to express these situations.

You express Type 2 actions in Tibetan by using the following set of verb-units:

main verb (present form) + linking particle + verb of existence
འགྲོ་གི་ཡོད/འདུག/ཡོད་རེད། **ṭo̲ki-yö̲'/tu̲'/yo̲re'**

This set of verb-units is multi-functional; it is already used for actions done in the present, expressing things like 'I am going', and 'I go' (explained in Units 8–10). But time-words or context will indicate whether a particular verb-unit refers to the present or the past, e.g.

སྔོན་མར་ང་སློབ་སྦྱོང་བྱེད་ཀྱི་ཡོད།
ngǟnma nga̲ lōpcōng che̲ki-yö̲'.
I used to study.

དེ་དུས་ཕྲུ་གུ་དེ་ཚོ་སློབ་གྲྭ་ལ་འགྲོ་ཐུབ་ཀྱི་ཡོད་མ་རེད།
the̲thü' phūku the̲ntsho lōpṭa-la ṭo̲-thūpki yo̲ ma-re̲'.
The children weren't able to go to school then.

Exercise 5

If you had to translate the following sentences into Tibetan, would you choose Type 1 or Type 2 structures? Mark the appropriate column with a tick, as in the example. Consider the nature of the actions; some verbs imply activity spread over time (i.e. Type 2 actions), even if this isn't reflected in the English sentence structure:

		Type 1	Type 2
1	I **stayed** at home yesterday.	✓	
2	He used to **talk** to me every Monday.		
3	I got **angry** with him.		
4	She **lived** in Beijing.		
5	Did your father **speak** Lhasa dialect?		
6	Our dog **died** yesterday.		
7	I constantly **read** when I was young.		
8	But were you **ill** during that time?		
9	He **sold** cheap things in his shop.		
10	They would **wear** attractive clothes.		

Dialogue 2

(Audio 2:29)

Lhakpa enters a café where he finds his friend Tshering, who seems to be concentrating on something.

ལྷག་པ། ཀྱེ་ཚེ་རིང་། ག་རེའི་ཐོག་ལ་བསམ་བློ་གཏོང་གི་ཡོད།

ཚེ་རིང་། བསམ་བློ་གཏོང་གི་མེད། ང་ཚོའི་རྒྱབ་ལོགས་ལ་མི་གཉིས་འདུག་ག ཕོ་གཉིས་ཀྱི་སྐད་ཆ་དེ་ཉན་གྱི་ཡོད།

ལྷག་པ། ཕོ་གཉིས་སྐད་ག་རེའི་ཐོག་ལ་སྐད་ཆ་བཤད་ཀྱི་འདུག

ཚེ་རིང་། ཏ་གོ་གི་མི་འདུག ང་དང་པོར་དེ་རྒྱ་སྐད་རེད་བསམས་སོང་། ཡིན་ནའང་བརྟད་ཨང་། ཕལ་ཆེར་ཉེ་རོང་གི་སྐད་ཡིན་ས་རེད།

ལྷག་པ། ཕོ་གཉིས་ག་རེའི་སྐོར་ལ་བཤད་ཀྱི་ཡོད་ས་རེད།

ཚེ་རིང་། གང་ཤེས། ཉེ་རོང་གི་སྐད་ཤེས་ཀྱི་མེད། འོ། ང་གཉིས་ལ་ལྟ་གི་འདུག

ཞྭོ་འཆམ་པ། ཏ་ཤི་དེ་རེ།

ལྷག་པ། ཨ། ག་རེ་ཟེར། ག་རེ་ལབ་སོང་།

ཚེ་རིང་། སྐུགས་པ། ང་གཉིས་ལ་བཀྲ་ཤིས་བདེ་ལེགས་ལབ་ཀྱི་འདུག་ག ཕོ་ཚོ་ལ་བཀྲ་ཤིས་བདེ་ལེགས་ལབ།

ལྷག་པ། བཀྲ་ཤིས་བདེ་ལེགས། ཁྱེད་རང་ག་ནས་ཡིན།

ཚེ་རིང་། ཨ་ཙི། ཕོ་གཉིས་ཕྱི་རྒྱལ་གྱི་མི་རེད། བོད་སྐད་ག་པར་ཤེས་ཀྱི་རེད།

ལྷག་པ། མ་རེད། ཁོ་རང་ཚོའི་སྐད་དང་ང་ཚོའི་སྐད་ཏོག་ཙམ་འདྲ་པོ་ཡོད་རེད། སྐལ་བཟང་གིས་ང་ལ་ལབ་སོང་། ཐང་ཀ་རྒྱག་སྟངས་ལ་ཁྱད་པར་ཞེ་དྲག་ཡོད་མ་རེད་ཟེར།
ཚེ་རིང་། འོ་ཏག་ཏག་རེད། ཁྱོད་ཁོ་གཉིས་མཉམ་དུ་ཐང་ཀ་བརྒྱབ་ནས་བལྟད་ཨང་།
ལྷག་པ། སྙད་མ་གཙེས་དང་།

LHAKPA we̱ tshēring, kha̱re:-thōk-la sāmlo tāngki-yö̱'.
TSHERING sāmlo tāngki-me̱'. nga̱ntshö: kya̱plo-la mi̱-nyī' tu̱'-ka. khō-nyī'-ki kăcha-the nyä̱nki-yö̱'.
LHAKPA khō-nyī' kä̆' kha̱re:-thōk-la kăcha shä̆ki-tu̱'.
TSHERING hākho̱ki min-tu̱'. nga̱ tha̱ngpo the̱ kya̱kä̆' re̱' sām-song. yi̱nnä tä̱-a.
(*he listens again*) phä̆lcher nyi̱hong-ki-kä̆' yi̱n-sa re̱'.
LHAKPA khō-nyī kha̱re:-kōr-la shä̆ki yo̱ sa-re̱'.
TSHERING kha̱ngshē', nyi̱hong-ki-kä̆' shīnki-me̱'. o̱ nga̱-nyī'-la tāki-tu̱'.
TOURIST tāsi-there̱.
LHAKPA ā, kha̱re-sa̱, kha̱re la̱p-sōng.
TSHERING kūkpa, nga̱-nyī'-la ṭāshi-te̱le' la̱pki-tu̱'-ka. khōtsho-la ṭāshi-te̱le' la̱p.
LHAKPA ṭāshi-te̱le', khyērang kha̱nä yi̱n.
TSHERING ātsi:, khō-nyī' chīkyäl-ki-mi̱ re̱'. phö̱kä̆' kha̱wa: shīnki-re̱'.
LHAKPA ma-re̱', khōrang-tshö:-kä̆' thang nga̱ntshö:-kä̆' tēts ṭa̱po yo̱re'. kä̆lsang-kī' nga̱-la la̱p-sōng. ṭha̱ngka kya̱ptāng-la khyēpar she̱ṭhak yo̱ ma-re̱'-sa̱.
TSHERING o̱ tāktāk re̱'. khyö̆' khō-nyī' nyāmtu ṭha̱ngka kya̱p-nä tä̱-a.
LHAKPA nyä̆' ma-tsē-thang.

Vocabulary

ཤེས་པ།	**shēpa**	to understand/know
ཧ་གོ་བ།	**hākho̱wa**	to understand/know
ལྐུགས་པ།	**kūkpa**	fool/idiot (*lit.* mute)
ཉི་ཧོང་གི་སྐད།	**nyi̱hong-ki-kä̆'**	Japanese (language)
སྟངས།	**tāng**	the way/style (of doing something)

ག་རེ་ཟེར།	**kha̱re-sa̱**	what did (he) say? (see below)
···རེད་བསམས་སོང་།	**re̱ sām-song**	(I) thought it was . . .
ཏག་ཏག་རེད།	**tāktāk re̱'**	that's right! (meant here sarcastically)
སྤྲོ་འཆམ་པ།	**ṭōchāmpa**	tourist
ཕལ་ཆེར།	**phā̈lcher**	probably
སྐལ་བཟང་།	**kā̈lsang**	(personal name)
གྲངས་ཀ་རྒྱག་པ།	**ṭha̱ngka-kya̱pa**	to count
ཐོག	**thōk**	in (i.e. a language); about
སྙད་གཙོ་བ།	**nyā̈'-tsēwa**	to ridicule
སྐོར།	**kōr**	about

Language points

4 Knowing and understanding

Two key verbs are **hākhowa** and **shēpa**. English has no exact comparison for the distinction between them: but for *skills* and learnt knowledge – e.g. knowing a language, how to drive or to communicate well – **shēpa** is generally used. Verbs about knowing and understanding are non-intentional. For certain reasons (not explored here) **yö̱'**, rather than the normal non-intentional auxiliary, is used for first-person statements and questions to second persons about skills. Note that when this verb is followed by the linking-particle **ki**, its sound changes to **shīn**.

For things one can be 'aware' of – facts, bits of information, short-term or changeable situations (e.g. the time, or where Tshering is at present) – **hākho̱wa** is used more.

In the area of comprehending things however, there is cross-over between them. For example, having explained something to someone, you might check whether he has understood it by asking either: **shē' sōng-ngä**, or **hākho sōng-ngä**.

Another useful verb is **ko̱-tshȫpa** (Dialogue 1), which relates specifically to comprehending something that has been explained, read, etc. And for knowing in the sense of recognising (people, and sometimes places), the verb used is ངོ་ཤེས་པ། **ngo̱-shēpa**.

5 Said X, thought Y . . . Linking content to verbs of thought and speech:

■ A. ཐོག། **thōk** and སྐོར། **kōr**

As Dialogue 2 shows, these terms can convey something like 'about', either for thought or speech. They are attached to their topic by a genitive, and followed by a **la̱thön**, e.g.

ནང་མིའི་ཐོག་ལ་གཅིག་ཤོད་དང་།
na̱ngmi: thōk-la cīk shā̱-thang.
Tell me something about (your) family.

■ B. As explained above, the speech-marker **s/sa̱** stands directly between the verb and the content of speech. Occasionally, in a similar fashion, it links a verb of thought with its content. But Dialogue 2 illustrates the more common approach with thought (in the sentence **the kya̱kā̱' re̱ sām-song**), where the verb for thought is added directly after the content.

■ C. ཡིན་མིན། **yi̱n-mä** etc.

A and B work when thought has a single object. But sometimes you represent what you are thinking as two alternatives. Here you use the copula/auxiliary verb together with its negative form, at the end of the content (as in 'whether': Unit 10). Compare, for example:

ཁོང་ཉི་ཧོང་གི་མི་རེད་བསམས་སོང་།
khōng nyi̱hong-ki mi̱ re̱' sām-song.
I thought that he was Japanese.

ཁོང་ཉི་ཧོང་གི་མི་ཡིན་མིན་ངས་ཧ་གོ་མ་སོང་།
khōng nyi̱hong-ki mi̱ yi̱n-mä ngä̱ hākho ma-sōng.
I didn't know whether (or not) he was Japanese.

As hinted in Unit 10, **tu̱' min-tu̱'** is likely to be used when referring to something changeable or immediate. But apart from that, the essential verbs are the most common.

མོས་སྐད་ཆ་དྲང་པོ་བཤད་ཀྱི་ཡོད་མེད་ངས་ཧ་གོ་གི་མེད།
mö̱ kā̱cha ṭha̱ngpo shā̱ki yö̱'-me' ngä̱ hākho̱ki-me̱'.
I don't know whether she speaks honestly/truthfully.

Exercise 6

Translate into Tibetan:

1 We need to talk about Kelsang.
2 I thought you were at work.
3 I don't know whether Tashi is here today.
4 She didn't ask about the money.
5 Do you know if the doctor understands Tibetan?
6 I thought you were my friend.
7 Do you recognise that man?
8 Did you think I wouldn't go?
9 Do you know what time the jeep will come here?

■ How do I say. . . .? – asking about names, meaning, etc. **(Audio 2:30)**

དེ་ལ་ག་རེ་ཟེར་གྱི་ཡོད་རེད། **the̱-la kha̱re se̱rki-yo̱re.** What is that called?

འདིའི་མིང་ལ་ག་རེ་ལབ་གྱི་རེད། **ti̱: mi̱ng-la kha̱re la̱pki-re̱'.** What is this called?

X་ཟེར་ན་ག་རེ་རེད། **X se̱r-na kha̱re re̱'.** What does x (i.e. a word) mean?

དྲི་བ་གཏོང་བ། **ṭhi̱wa-ta̱ngwa** to ask a question

ལན་རྒྱག་པ། **lä̱n-kya̱pa** to answer

ག་རེ་ལབ་དགོས་རེད། **kha̱re la̱p-kö' re̱'.** (1) What can I say? (2) (a speech-filler)

ག་འདྲ་ཟེར་ལབ་དགོས་རེད། **kha̱nṭäs la̱p-kö' re̱'.** How should I put this? (rhetorical question)

X་ག་འདྲ་ཟེར་ལབ་དགོས་རེད། **X kha̱nṭäs la̱p-kö' re̱'.** How do I say x? (e.g. when asking about a word, expression etc.; how to pronounce it, phrase it, or say it in another language)

ག་རེ་ཟེར། **kha̱re-sa̱** (multiple uses) What is he (etc.) saying?; What are you talking about? (challenging or mocking); What does it (e.g. something written) say?; (also perhaps the most common speech-filler, used particularly when trying to recall names, etc.)

Exercise 7

Here are a series of answers, related to names and meaning. Which Tibetan questions might have prompted each of them?

A1 ངའི་མིང་ལ་པ་སངས་ཟེར་གྱི་ཡོད།
ngä̱: mi̱ng-la pāsang se̱rki-yö̱'.

A2 ངས་གང་ཡང་ལབ་མེད།
ngä̱ khä̱: la̱p me̱.

A3 བོད་སྐད་(ཀྱི་)ཐོག་ལ་དེ་ལ་མིང་ཡོད་མ་རེད།
phö̱kǟ'(-ki) thōk-la the̱-la mi̱ng yo̱ ma-re̱'.

A4 དབྱིན་(ཇིའི་)སྐད་ལ་student ཟེར་གྱི་ཡོད་རེད།
īn(chi:) kǟ'-la student **se̱rki-yo̱re'.**

A5 རྒྱ་སེ་ཨེ། དེ་མེ་ཏོག་གཅིག་ལ་ལབ་ཀྱི་ཡོད་རེད།
kya̱se-ē, the̱ me̱tok cīk-la la̱pki-yo̱re'.

A6 བོད་སྐད་(ཀྱི་)ཐོག་ལ་དེ་ལ་སྐུགས་པ་ཟེར་གྱི་རེད།
phö̱kǟ'(-ki) thōk-la the̱-la kūkpa se̱rki-re̱'.

Exercise 8 **(Audio 2:32)**

Duho eventually reaches Tashi's place. This is what he tells him:

ང་འདིར་ཡོང་དུས་ཁྱེད་རང་གི་ངོ་ཤེས་པ་གཅིག་ཐུག་སོང་། ཁོ་རང་གི་མིང་ལ་ཚེ་རིང་ནོར་བུ་ཟེར་གྱི་རེད། བཀྲ་ཤིས་ལ་ལན་འདི་བརྒྱལ་རོགས་བྱེད་ཟེར་ལབ་སོང་། ཁོ་རང་སང་ཉིན་རྒྱལ་ས་ལ་འགྲོ་མཁན་མིན་ཟེར། ཡིན་ནའང་ཨ་ཁུ་ཐུབ་བསྟན་འགྲོ་མཁན་རེད་ཟེར། ཨེ་ནི་བཀྲ་ཤིས་ཀྱི་ཅ་ལག་དེ་ཚོ་ཨ་ཁུ་ཐུབ་བསྟན་གྱིས་བརྒྱལ་གྱི་ཡིན་ཟེར་ལབ་ཀྱི་འདུག་ཟེར། ཨེ་ནི་ག་རེ་ཟེར། ཅ་ལག་དེ་ཚོ་ཕལ་ཆེར་ཚེ་རིང་ནོར་བུ། ཡང་མིན་ན་ཨ་ཁུ་ཐུབ་བསྟན་ལེན་གར་ཡོང་གི་རེད། གང་ཡིན་ཟེར་ན། ཚེ་རིང་ནོར་བུས་བཀྲ་ཤིས་འགྲོ་དགོས་ཀྱི་མི་འདུག་ལབ་སོང་།

nga̱ tä̱: yo̱ng-thü̱' khyērang-ki ngo̱shēnpa-cīk thūk-song. khōrang-ki mi̱ng-la tshēring no̱rpu se̱rki-re̱'. ṭāshi-la lä̱n-ti̱ kyǟl-ro-che̱-s la̱p-song. khōrang sāngnyin kyä̱lsa-la ṭo̱-nyän me̱:-s. yi̱nnä ākhu thūptän ṭo̱-nyän re̱'-s. ēni ṭāshi-ki cālak the̱ntsho ākhu thūptän-kī' kyǟlki-yi̱n-s la̱pki-tu̱k-s. ēni kha̱re-sa̱. cālak-the̱ntsho phǟlcher tshēring no̱rpu yang-me̱:na ākhu thūptän lä̱nka yo̱ngki-re̱'. kha̱ngyin-se̱rna tshēring no̱rpü̱ ṭāshi ṭo̱-kö'-ki min-tu̱' la̱p-song.

Duho tried to decipher the message by working out who said, and who did what, but . . .

(a) Does Duho mention the same number of people referred to in the original message?
(b) Duho doesn't say what the 'things' are; will that matter?
(c) Does Duho seem confident or unsure that he has understood the message?
(d) Does Duho leave anything unclear, or make mistakes; and if he does, what are they?
(e) Regardless of mistakes, will what Duho said be sufficient to get the message across?

Finally, translate the passage.

Unit Fourteen

གུས་ཞབས་ཐོག

khushap thōk

Respectfully

In this unit you will learn how to:

- engage in polite conversation with religious and other figures
- recognise when and with whom to use honorific language
- work with some of the levels of speech and divisions within honorific language
- deal with quotes in honorific speech
- use essential honorific verbs
- say 'Is it all right if . . . ?'
- make use of **yä**-combinations
- use time-related structures: 'before', 'since', etc.

Dialogue 1 (T)

(Audio 2:33)
A middle-aged layman (Dönthup) has invited the abbot of a monastery to his home to perform a blessing ceremony. The day before the visit, Dönthup finalises details with the monastery manager (in the monastery office).

གཉེར་པ། མོ་ཏའི་གྲ་སྒྲིག་དོན་གྲུབ་ལགས་གནང་གི་ཡིན་པས།

དོན་གྲུབ། དེ་སོས་ཡིན་སྐུ་ཞབས་གཉེར་པ་ལགས། འདི་ང་ཚོའི་ལས་འགན་རེད། དེའི་ཐོག་ལ་ཐུགས་ཁྲལ་མ་གནང་དང་། གསན་ཨང་། མཁན་རིན་པོ་ཆེས་ཚོགས་གྲོལ་ནས་ལམ་སེང་པར་ཆིབས་བསྒྱུར་གནང་གི་ཡིན་ཟེར་གསུངས་པ་རེད་པ་ལགས། དེ་འདྲ་ཡིན་ན་ང་ཞོགས་ ཀས་སྔ་པོ་ནས་མོ་ཏ་དེ་ཁྲིད་ནས་འདིར་བསྒུག་གི་ཡིན། ཨེ་ནི་མོ་ཏ་དེ་རྒྱལ་སྒོའི་འགྲམ་ལ་བཞག་ན་འགྲིག་གི་རེད་པས་ལགས།

གཉེར་པ།	འགྲིག་གི་རེད་ལགས།
དོན་གྲུབ།	ལགས་སོ། ཨེ་ནི་མཁན་རིན་པོ་ཆེས་ཚུར་ཕྱག་མཚོད་ཁ་མཚོད་ལ་ཆིབས་བསྐྱུར་གནང་གི་ཡིན་གསུང་གི་འདུག
གཉེར་པ།	འདི་ངས་ཧ་གོ་མ་སོང་ལགས། དོན་གྲུབ་ལགས། མཁན་རིན་པོ་ཆེའི་གསོལ་དཔོན་ངོ་མཁྱེན་གྱི་ཡོད་པས།
དོན་གྲུབ།	ངོ་ཤེས་ཀྱི་ཡོད་ལགས།
གཉེར་པ།	གསོལ་དཔོན་ལགས་ལ་བཀའ་འདྲི་གཅིག་གནང་དང་། གཞན་སང་ཉིན་མོ་ཊའི་གྲ་སྒྲིག་དོན་གྲུབ་ལགས་ཀྱིས་གནང་མ་ཐུབ་ན་གང་ཡང་གནང་གི་མ་རེད། ང་ཚོས་དགོན་པའི་མོ་ཊ་དེ་གཏང་ཚོག་གི་རེད་ལགས།
དོན་གྲུབ།	དེ་འདྲ་མ་གསུང་དང་སྐུ་ཞབས་གཉེར་པ་ལགས། མོ་ཊའི་ཐོག་ལ་ཐུགས་ཁྲལ་རྩ་ནས་མ་གནང་ཨང་། སང་ཉིན་ངའི་སྤུན་སྐྱ་དེས་ཇུས་གཏོགས་གང་ཡང་བྱེད་ཀྱི་མ་རེད། མི་བརྟན་པོ་ཁྱོན་ནས་ཡོད་མ་རེད། སྔོན་མར་ཁོ་རང་གིས་ནང་མི་ཚང་མ་ངོ་ཚ་པོ་བཟོས་སོང་། ད་ལན་ཡག་པོ་མ་བྱུང་ན་…།

MANAGER	mo̲ṭä: ṭha̲ṭhik thö̲nṭup-la: nāngki-yi̲n-pä.
DÖNDUP	the̲ lö̲' yi̲n kūsho' nyērpa-la:. ti̲ nga̲ntshö: lä̲nkän re̲'. the̲: thōk-la thūkṭhäl ma-nāng-thang. sǟn-a. khǟn-ri̲npochē tshōk ṭhö̲l-nä la̲msang phār chīpkyur nāngki-yi̲n-s sūngpa re̲'-wa-la:. the̲nṭä-yi̲n-na nga̲ sho̲kä ngāpo-nä mo̲ṭa-the ṭhī-nä tä: ku̲ki-yi̲n. ēni mo̲ṭa-the kyä̲lkö-ṭa̲m-la sha̲k-na ṭi̲kki-re̲'-wä-la:
MANAGER	ṭi̲kki-re̲'-la:
DÖNDUP	la̲:so. ēni khǟn-ri̲npochē' tshūr chāktshö' kha̲tshȫ'-la chīpkyur nāngki-yi̲n-s sūngki-tu̲'.
MANAGER	ti̲ ngä̲' hākho̲ ma-sōng-la:. thö̲nṭup-la: khǟn-ri̲npochē: sȫlpön ngo̲khyīnki-yö̲'-pä.
DÖNDUP	ngo̲shīnki-yö̲'-la:.
MANAGER	sȫlpön-la:-la kānṭi-cīk nāng-thang. shä̲n sāngnyin mo̲ṭä: ṭha̲ṭhik thö̲nṭup-la:-kī nāng ma-thūp-na khä̲: nāngki-ma-re̲'. nga̲ntshȫ' ko̲mpä: mo̲ṭa-the tāng chōki-re̲'-la:.
DÖNDUP	the̲nṭä ma-sūng-thang kūsho' nyērpa-la. mo̲ṭä:-thōk-la thūkṭhäl tsā-nä ma-nāng-a. sāngnyin ngǟ: pīnkyak-the̲' chu̲tōk khä̲: che̲ki ma-re̲'. mi-tǟnpo khyȫnnä yo̲ ma-re̲'. ngǟnma khōrang-kī' na̲ngmi tshāngma ngo̲-tshāpo sö̲'-song. tha̲län ya̲kpo ma-chu̲ng na. . . .

Vocabulary

གཉེར་པ།	**nyērpa**	(monastery) 'manager'
གནང་བ།	**nāngwa**	to do (honorific)
སྐུ་ཞབས།	**kūsho'**	(polite address: see below)
མཁན་རིན་པོ་ཆེ།	**khā̃n-ri̱npochē**	abbot
ཚོགས།	**tshōk**	prayer assembly (for monks or nuns)
གྲོལ་བ།	**ṭhō̱lwa**	to end (for gatherings; non-intentional)
ཕར།	**phār**	away from here
ཚུར།	**tshūr**	back here
ལས་འགན།	**lã̱nkän**	responsibility
ཕྱག་ཚོད།	**chāktshö'**	o'clock (honorific)
རྒྱལ་སྒོ།	**kyä̱lkö**	gate
བརྟན་པོ།	**tā̃npo**	reliable

གསོལ་དཔོན།	**sōlpön**	main attendant
ཁྲིད་པ། (past of འཁྲིད་པ།	**ṭhīwa**)	to bring/take
དེ་འདྲ་ཡིན་ན།	**thentä-yin-na**	if that's the case . . .
ངོ་ཚ་པོ་བཟོ་བ།	**ngotshāpo-sowa**	to embarrass/shame
ངོ་མཁྱེན་པ།	**ngokhyēnpa**	to know someone (honorific)
འགྲིག་གི་རེད་པས།	**ṭikki-re'-wä**	is it okay if. . . . ? (see below)
ཆིབས་བསྐྱུར་གནང་བ།	**chīpkyur-nāngwa**	to come/go (high honorific)
ཐུགས་ཁྲལ་གནང་བ།	**thūkṭhäl-nāngwa**	to worry/concern oneself (honorific)
དེ་ལོས་ཡིན།	**the lö' yin**	of course/that goes without saying
བཀའ་འདྲི་གནང་བ།	**kānṭi-nāngwa**	to ask (honorific)
ཇུས་གཏོགས་བྱེད་པ།	**chutōk-chepa**	to interfere/be involved
གང་ཡང་གནང་གི་མ་རེད།	**khä: nāngki-ma-re'**	it doesn't matter (honorific)
ད་ལན་ཡག་པོ་མ་བྱུང་ན་་་་།	**thalän yakpo ma-chung na . . .**	if it doesn't work out this time . . .
ཆོག་གི་རེད།	**chōki-re'**	it will be all right/we can (especially when offering to do something)
ཁྱོན་ནས།	**khyōnnä**	(emphatic; for negation)
སྔ་པོ་ནས།	**ngāpo-nä**	early on
ངོ་ཚ་བ།	**ngotshāwa**	shame
འགྲམ།	**ṭam**	near

Cultural point

Honorific language (ཞེ་ས།) - when to use it

Unit 11 introduced the classes of honorific words. It is best to think that the spoken language has two distinct registers or levels; the Ordinary level (i.e. the non-honorific), and the Honorific level. Two principal rules of usage are:

1 A speaker must use the ordinary (never the honorific) level to talk about him/herself.
2 The honorific level must be used for 'special individuals' – widely respected or high-status figures – associated with culture, religion, or holding positions of authority.

Outside these two, there is considerable variation. Honorific language is often associated with formality. So in official situations, or at first-time meetings, and even when addressing strangers, it is advisable to use the honorific level (or as much of it as you know). Because of this association with formality, many speakers prefer to drop the honorific in favour of the ordinary level when communicating with friends and intimates (as many dialogues illustrate). But the ordinary level is also sometimes used to show a *lack* of respect, so caution is necessary when making this shift.

The main factor determining the use of honorific language is the *speaker's* background; honorifics are used widely in Central Tibetan dialect, but with varying degrees of density. People from certain areas (particularly Lhasa and its surroundings) communicate on the honorific level a great deal. Honorific language is also associated with higher status and sophistication, so those of certain family backgrounds rely on it more than others.

The best tip is to 'play it by ear': use honorific language in the situations already mentioned, but more generally, follow the lead of others; don't insist upon using it if others involved in the conversation seem more comfortable using the ordinary level.

Language point

1 General honorifics

Honorific language is about showing respect; using speech to elevate some 'other' (referred to here as 'A'). A can be the person you are speaking to (i.e. 'you'), someone you are speaking about (she, he, Sönam, etc.), or even institutions. An obvious way to show respect is to elevate the actions (eating, talking, etc.) that A performs and the various states (hunger, understanding, etc.) that A experiences, by describing them in honorific terms. These terms are 'general honorifics'.

These are primarily verbs and nouns. The polite or honorific terms already introduced all fall into this category.

Honorific language doesn't necessarily signify differences in social status. If a person addresses A with honorific language, it does not mean that the person is 'lower ranking' than A. Dialogue 1 illustrates the norm for polite conversation; both speakers address each other with general honorifics. One speaker is a monk and the other is a lay person, but they communicate, more or less, as polite equals. They use one 'high honorific', but only in reference to one of those special individuals. High honorifics are not a separate level of honorific language; they are a relatively small group of terms (reserved mainly for such individuals) sometimes inserted into general honorific-level conversation, e.g.: **chīpkyur-nāngwa** (Dialogue 1) and དགོངས་པ་རྫོགས་པ། **ko̱ngpa-tso̱kpa** ('to die').

■ General honorific – key verbs

གནང་བ། **nāngwa** (verbaliser; replacing བྱེད་པ། **che̱pa**)
སྐྱོན་པ། **kyȫnpa** (verbaliser; replacing རྒྱག་པ། **kya̱pa**)
གཏོང་གནང་བ། **tāng-nāngwa**/གནང་བ། **nāngwa** (verbalisers; replacing གཏོང་བ། **tāngwa**)
གནང་བ། **nāngwa** to give
བཞེངས་པ། **sha̱ngwa** to rise (e.g. in morning); to stand up
གཟིགས་པ། **si̱kpa** to look; to see; to buy
མཁྱེན་པ། **khyēnpa** to know/to understand

Exercise 1

From this jumble, pick out those combinations (persons and verbs) which never go together in sentences. Also, pick out the one word which doesn't belong here.

འགྲོ་བ།	**to̱wa**	ཁྱེད་རང་།	**khyērang**	ཕེབས་པ།	**phēpa**
སྣོམ་པ།	**nūmpa**	ཁོ་ཚོ།	**khōtsho**	ལོག་པ།	**lo̱kpa**
མཆོད་པ།	**chȫpa**	ཀློག་པ།	**lōkpa**	ཁ་སྐོམ་པ།	**khā-kōmpa**
special individual		རོགས་གནང་།	**ro-nāng**	བཞེས་པ།	**she̱pa**
ཕུན་ཚོགས།	**phǖntshok**	སྙུང་བ།	**nyūngwa**	ང་།	**nga̱**

Cultural point

Interaction with religious figures

Robed figures are generally treated with some respect. But aside from polite addresses, no special language or communication rules apply when interacting with most of these people. Ordained and lay communities intermingle quite freely and informally in most Tibetan areas. Far more respect, however, is shown when the person is deemed a 'special individual'; a more aloof group, made up of recognised 'reincarnates', monastery officials, religious scholars, and others highly regarded for their religious practice. Both body language and speech are utilised to show respect to such persons.

Special individuals are always addressed by titles. Using equivalents of 'you' is not respectful. To a lesser extent this is also true of more minor religious figures.

■ Addresses for religious figures

Form of address	*Title/Description*
རིན་པོ་ཆེ། **r̲inpochē**	སྤྲུལ་སྐུ། **ṭūlku** recognised 'incarnate'
	བླ་མ། **lāma** lama (often synonymous with **ṭūlku**)
མཁན་རིན་པོ་ཆེ། **khǟn-r̲inpochē**	མཁན་པོ། **khǟnpo** abbot
རྒན་ལགས། **kä̲n-la:***	གྲྭ་བ་རྒན་པ། **ṭha̲wa kä̲npa** elder monk
སྐུ་ཞབས་ལགས། **kūsho'-la:**	གྲྭ་བ། **ṭha̲wa** monks (of all ages)
ཨ་ནེ་ལགས། **āne-la:**	ཨ་ནེ། **āne** nun
ཆོས་ལགས། **chȫ'-la:** (slightly more polite than **āne-la:**)	
རྒན་ལགས། **kä̲n-la:**	དགེ་བཤེས། **ke̲shē'** (person with specific monastic degree)

* **kä̲n-la:** is also the address for any teacher (male or female)

Exercise 2

Which choice of language level do you think appropriate in each situation, as one person addresses the other? (a) ordinary, (b) general honorific, (c) general honorific with some high honorifics, (d) a matter of choice:

1. Female student to male teacher
2. Male student to female teacher
3. One special individual to another
4. Child to parent
5. Middle-aged lay person to young monk or nun
6. Government official to his/her former schoolteacher
7. You to shopkeeper

Language point

2 Honorifics in quotations

To report, in respectful terms, what someone else said, you make two modifications to the pattern explained in Unit 13. First, you use an honorific verb for 'said', e.g. **sūngwa**

ཟེར་ལབ་སོང་། **-s lap-song** → ཟེར་གསུངས་སོང་། **-s sūng-song**

Second, you translate the *content* part into honorific terms. Thus, 'he said he'll stay.'

བསྡད་ཀྱི་ཡིན་ཟེར་ལབ་སོང་། **täki-yin-s lap-song** becomes:
བཞུགས་ཀྱི་ཡིན་ཟེར་གསུངས་སོང་། **shuki-yin-s sūng-song**

Again, you aim to capture the gist of what the person said, not their actual words: there is no situation in which anyone would use the honorific **shu:** for him/herself.

Exercise 3

Translate: use honorifics when translating into Tibetan, following the pattern shown above.

(a) ཁོང་དབུ་སྙུང་གི་འདུག་ཟེར་གསུངས་སོང་།
khōng ū nyūngki-tuk-s sūng-song.

(b) ཀྲན་ལགས་ཕེབས་ཀྱི་ཡིན་ཟེར་གསུང་གི་འདུག་གས།
ka̱n-la: phēpki-yi̱n-s sūngki-tu̱'-kä.

(c) མཁྱེན་གྱི་མེད་ཟེར་གསུང་གི་མ་རེད།
khyīn-ki-me̱'-s sūngki-ma-re̱'.

(d) གཟིགས་གར་ཕེབས་ཀྱི་མིན་གསུངས་སོང་།
si̱ka phēpki-me̱-s sūng-sōng.

(e) She says she'll do it.

(f) They said they won't come here tomorrow.

(g) Did she say that she would phone us?

(h) Tshering says he's ill, but he has a good appetite (*lit.* is eating well).

(i) Why did he say he won't stay with us?

Language point

3 Making requests and seeking consent

English sentences beginning with 'is it all right if . . . ?' or 'is it okay if . . . ?' use 'if' (like conditional sentences), but are questions, for checking whether another person minds us (or someone we speak on behalf of) doing a particular action. Such questions can be phrased in other ways ('can I . . . ?', 'may I . . . ?' etc.) In Tibetan an 'if' structure (what might be called a 'quasi-conditional') is always required, as long as the point of the question is asking whether some action may be done; this structure isn't for asking someone else to do something.

The 'is it all right . . . ?' part (**ṭi̱kki-re̱'-wä**) is a standard phrase. It is added after the **na**, in what otherwise looks like a normal if-sentence.

ང་ནང་ལ་ཡོང་ན་འགྲིག་གི་རེད་པས།
nga̱ na̱ng-la yo̱ng-na ṭi̱kki-re̱'-wä.
Is it all right if I come inside?

ང་ཚོ་འདིར་བསྡད་ན་འགྲིག་གི་རེད་པས།
nga̱ntsho tä̱: tä̱'-na ṭi̱kki-re̱'-wä.
Is it all right if we sit here?

You will notice numerous other cases where a quasi-conditional form is used, such as the various uses of **se̱rna** ('because', and 'what does X mean?')

Exercise 4

Translate all of the following which work with the structure just described.

1 Is it okay if I tell you that later?
2 Would you mind carrying this chair?
3 Is it okay if my friends come around tonight?
4 They say they have no money now. Is it all right if they pay you tomorrow?
5 I'm looking for the bridge (ཟམ་པ། **sampa**). Can you take me to the bridge?
6 May I take this salt (ཚྭ། **tshā**)?

Dialogue 2 (*T*)

(Audio 2:34)

Tenpa (who featured in Unit 6, Dialogue 2) was once a monk, but he left the monastery. Now, years later, he's plucked up the courage to revisit. He interacts with occupants of the monastery in the same style as he did in years past.

བསྟན་པ། རྒན་ལགས། ང་བཅར་ན་འགྲིག་གི་རེད་པས། རྒན་ལགས། ང་ངོ་མཁྱེན་མ་
སོང་ངས། ང་བསྟན་པ་ཡིན། སྔོན་མར་རྒན་དབང་འདུས་ལགས་ཀྱི་དགེ་ཕྲུག···

རྒན་པ་སངས། བསྟན་པ་ཨེ། འོ་ཡ་ཡ། ང་གཉིས་མ་ཐུག་ནས་ལོ་ག་འདྲ་མང་པོ་འགྲོ་སོང་།
ད་ཁྱོད་ཐོག་རྒྱུག་སླེབས་ནས···། འདི་ག་རེ་རེད།

བསྟན་པ། འདི་རྒན་ལགས་ལ་དབུལ་ཡས་ཡིན།

རྒན་པ་སངས། ང་ལ་སྤྲད་ཡས་ཡིན་པས། ཡ་ཡ།

བསྟན་པ། ང་དགོན་པ་ལ་མ་ཡོང་ནས་ལོ་བཅུ་ཙམ་འགྲོ་ཚར་རེད་རྒན་ལགས།

རྒན་པ་སངས། སྔོན་མར་ག་རེ་བྱས་པ་རེད། ཁྱོད་ནང་ལ་ཕྱིན་ནས་ཚུར་མ་ཡོང་བ་དེ་ག་རེ་རེད།

བསྟན་པ། དེ་དུས་ང་ཚོའི་ནང་གི་གནས་སྟངས་དེ་དཀའ་ལས་ཁག་པོ་ཡོད་རེད་ལགས།
ཨ་མ་རྒན་འཁོགས་རེད། དངོས་གནས་བྱས་ན་ཨ་མ་ལ་རོགས་པ་དགོས་ཀྱི་
ཡོད་རེད། ཨེ་ནི་ནང་ལ་སྤུན་སྐྱ་གཞན་དག་ཡོད་མ་རེད། དགོན་པ་ནས་མ་
ཐོན་གོང་ལ་ང་རྒན་དབང་འདུས་ལ་གནས་ཚུལ་དེ་ཞུ་དགོས་ཀྱི་ཡོད་རེད།
ཡིན་ནའང་རྒན་དབང་འདུས་ལགས་ཀྱིས་དགོངས་པ་གནང་གི་མ་རེད་
བསམས་ནས་ངས་ཞུས་མེད། ངས་ཨ་མ་ལ་རོགས་པ་བྱས་ནས་ལོ་གཉིས་

བསྡད་པ་ཡིན། དེ་ནས་ཨ་མ་ལགས་གྲོངས་སོང་། ང་དགོན་པ་ལ་ཚུར་ཡོང་ན་ཚུད་ཀྱི་མ་རེད་བསམས་སོང་། ང་རྒན་དབང་འདུས་ལགས་མཇལ་གར་བཅར་དགོས་ཀྱི་ཡོད་རེད། ཡིན་ནའང་ང་ངོ་ཚ་སོང་། ད་ཁྲི་དྲགས་སོང་། ང་འགྱོད་པ་ཞེ་དྲག་སྐྱེ་གི་འདུག

རྒན་པ་སངས། ད་དེ་འདས་པའི་གནས་ཚུལ་རེད། ད་ལྟ་བྱེད་ཡས་གང་ཡང་ཡོད་མ་རེད། དེང་སང་ཁྱོད་ག་རེ་བྱེད་ཀྱི་ཡོད། སྐྱེ་དམན་ཡོད་པས།

བསྟན་པ། ཚོང་ཏོག་ཙམ་རྒྱག་གི་ཡོད་ལགས། ང་ཆང་ས་བརྒྱག་ནས་ལོ་བཞི་ཕྱིན་ཚར་སོང་། ཨེ་ནི་ང་ཚོ་ལ་བུ་མོ་གཅིག་ཡོད་ལགས།

རྒན་པ་སངས། དུས་ཚོད་འདི་ཡག་པོ་ཡོད་མ་རེད། ཡིན་ནའང་བསྟན་པ། སེམས་པ་བཟང་པོ་བྱེད། ཕྲུ་གུ་དང་སྐྱེ་དམན་ལ་ཡག་པོ་བྱེད། ཚོང་རྒྱག་དུས་དྲང་པོ་བྱེད་ཨང་། དུས་ཚོད་ཡོད་དུས་མཆོད་འབུལ་ཞུ།

TENPA kā̲n-la: nga̲ ca̲r-na ṭi̲kki-re̲'-wä. kā̲n-la: nga̲ ngo̲khyēn ma-sōng-ngä. nga̲ tā̲npa yi̲n. ngā̲nma kā̲n wāngthü-la:-ki ke̲ṭhuk . . .

GEN PASANG tā̲npa-e, o̲-ya̲:ya, nga̲-nyī' ma-thūk-nä lo̲ kha̲nṭa ma̲ngpo ṭo̲-sōng. tha̲ khyō̲' thōkyap lēp-nä . . . ti̲ kha̲re re̲'. (*Tenpa offers something*)

TENPA ti̲ kā̲n-la:-la phū̲l-yä yi̲n.

GEN PASANG nga̲-la ṭā̲'-yä yi̲n-pä. ya̲:ya.

TENPA nga̲ ko̲mpa-la ma-yo̲ng-nä lo̲ cū-ts ṭo̲-tshār re̲' kā̲n-la:.

GEN PASANG ngā̲ma kha̲re chā̲wa-re̲'. khyō̲' na̲ng-la chīn-nä tshūr ma-yo̲ngwa-the kha̲re re̲'.

TENPA the̲thü' nga̲ntshö: na̲ng-ki nā̲tang-the kālekhākpo yo̲re'-la:. āma kā̲nkhōk re̲'. ngō̲nä-chā̲na āma-la ro̲kpa kö̲'-ki yo̲re'. ēni na̲ng-la pīnkyak shā̲nthak yo̲ ma-re̲'. ko̲mpa-nä ma-thō̲n kho̲ng-la nga̲ kā̲n wāngthü'-la nā̲tshül-the shu̲-kö̲'-ki yo̲re'. yi̲nnä kā̲n wāngthü'-la:-kī' ko̲ngpa nāngki ma-re̲' sām-nä ngä̲' shu̲' me̲. ngä̲' āma-la ro̲kpa chā̲nä lo̲-nyī' tā̲wa-yi̲n. the̲nä āma-la: ṭho̲ng-song. nga̲ ko̲mpa-la tshūr yo̲ng-na tshū̲ki ma-re̲' sām-song. nga̲ kā̲n wāngthü'-la: cā̲lka cār-kö̲'-ki yo̲re'. yi̲nnä nga̲ ngo̲-tshā-song. tha̲ chīṭhak sōng. nga̲ kyö̲pa shā̲ṭhak kyēki-tu̲'. (*visibly upset*)

GEN PASANG tha the̲ tā̲wä:-nā̲tshül re̲'. tha̲nta che̲-yä khä̲: yo̲ ma-re̲'. the̲ngsang khyō̲' kha̲re che̲ki-yö̲'. kyēmän yö̲'-pä.

TENPA	tshōng tēts kya̱pki-yö̱'-la:. nga̱ chāngsa kya̱p-nä lo̱-shi̱ chīn-tshār re̱'. ēni nga̱ntsho-la phu̱mo-cīk yö̱'-la:.
GEN PASANG	thü̱tshȫ'-ti̱ ya̱kpo yo̱ ma-re̱'. yi̱nnä tā̃npa sēmpa-sa̱ngpo chi̱'. phūku thang kyēmän-la ya̱kpo chi̱'. tshōngkya̱p-thü' ṭha̱ngpo chi̱'-a. thü̱tshȫ' yö̱'-thü' chȫnpu̱l-shu̱.

Vocabulary

ཀུན་པ་སངས།/ ཀུན་དབང་འདུས།	**kä̱n pāsang/ kä̱n wāngthü'**	(personal names)
དངོས་གནས་བྱས་ན།	**ngȫnä-chä̱na**	actually
ཡ་ཡ།	**ya̱:ya**	(response; indicating acceptance)
ཕྱི་དྲགས་སོང་།	**chīṭhak song**	it's too late
དྲང་པོ་བྱེད་པ།	**ṭha̱ngpo-che̱pa**	to act honestly
ཚུད་པ།	**tshǖpa**	to be (re-)admitted (non-intentional)
སེམས་པ་བཟང་པོ་བྱེད་པ།	**sēmpa-sa̱ngpo che̱pa**	to act kindly
འདས་པའི་གནས་ཚུལ་རེད།	**tä̱wä:-nā̃tshül re̱'**	that's in the past
དགོངས་པ་གནང་བ།	**ko̱ngpa-nāngwa**	to grant permission (honorific)
གྲོངས་པ།	**ṭho̱ngwa**	died (past of འགྲོངས་པ།: general honorific)
མཇལ་གར་བཅར་བ།	**cä̱lka-cārwa**	to go to meet (honorific: see below)
བྱེད་ཡས་གང་ཡང་ཡོད་མ་རེད།	**che̱-yä khä̱: yo̱ ma-re̱'**	there's nothing one can do about it
མ་ཡོང་ནས་ལོ་བཅུ་འགྲོ་ཚར་རེད།	**ma-yo̱ng-nä lo̱ cū ṭo̱-tshār re̱'**	haven't been here for ten years
མ་...གོང་ལ།	**ma . . . kho̱ng-la**	before (see below)
མཆོད་འབུལ་ཞུ་བ།	**chȫnpü̱l shu̱wa**	to make religious offerings (lighting lamps, etc.: at monasteries and temples, particularly by lay people)

དབུལ་ཡས།/སྤྲད་ཡས།	**phūl-yä/ṭā'-yä**	for offering/giving (see below)
····དེ་ག་རེ་རེད།	**... the khare re'**	why? (following an action verb; here 'not coming', hence 'why didn't you return?')
གནས་སྟངས།/གནས་ཚུལ།	**nātang/nātshul**	situation
ཞུ་བ།	**shuwa**	to tell (honorific: see below)
ཡག་པོ་བྱེད་པ།	**yakpo-chepa**	to treat well
ཐོག་རྒྱག	**thōkyap**	all of a sudden
ཐོན་པ།	**thōnpa**	to leave
འགྱོད་པ་སྐྱེ་བ།	**kyöpa-kyēwa**	to regret
དགེ་ཕྲུག	**kethuk**	disciple

Language point

4 Honorific language: actions done 'humbly'

Earlier we saw that a speaker shows respect to A by describing A's actions in general honorific terms. It's an imperfect analogy, but in English one might choose to say that someone 'bestows', rather than 'gives', or that someone 'graciously' or 'kindly' did something. Such descriptions are similar in function to general honorifics; they elevate the performer of the action, and cannot be used for oneself.

There is a second step in showing deference. Again, by analogy, instead of saying that something was 'given' to A, we might say that it was 'humbly offered' (the analogy can only be pushed so far; English, of course, has no comparable honorific system). The action was not done by A, but directed towards A. Still, the description managed to show respect to A. This is *not* a separate form of honorific; it is used within the framework of general honorific. You describe A's actions of going, eating, sleeping, etc. as before. But when person B (me, you, he/she) performs an action focused upon A (*doing something to, for, or accepting something from A*), B's action is described in these terms. For example, I would normally use ordinary-level language to report that I said something:

ངས་ལབ་པ་ཡིན། **ngä̱' la̱pa-yi̱n.**

But if what I said was directed to the respected A, I would instead describe my action thus:

ངས་ཞུས་པ་ཡིན། **ngä̱' shu̱wa-yi̱n.**

You must switch the action verb. The most commonly occurring verbs are shown in the list below. Ideally, you also switch the nouns (more of this in Unit 15). Even though it was my action, described with an honorific term, the respect it conveyed wasn't directed towards me.

In summary: there is another party (B) who does an action directed towards A. But the action is described in such a way that it shows respect to A, and not B.

■ Situations

Dialogue 2 illustrates a common situation. Tenpa uses general honorifics when addressing or speaking about his teachers: when describing his own actions directed towards them, he speaks 'humbly'. But the teacher addresses Tenpa with ordinary-level speech: the teacher–student relationship is not an equal one; something reflected in the language.

But conversations between polite equals also require the use of humble language. No such language appeared in Dialogue 1 only because neither speaker mentioned any of his actions directed towards the other. If either Dhöndup or the manager had said 'I gave you', for instance, he would have described this giving as something performed humbly.

■ Humbly performed actions – key verbs

འབུལ་བ། **phǖlwa** to offer

བཅར་བ། **cārwa** to approach (used for visiting, in the sense of 'entering the presence of . . .')

མཇལ་བ། **cä̱lwa** to meet

ཞུ་བ། **shu̱wa** (past ཞུས་པ། **shü̱wa** – verbaliser; replacing བྱེད་པ། **che̱pa**; also used for to listen, take/accept, speak, tell, request, and offer [help])

Exercise 5

Each situation involves a special individual (Rinpoche) and I. Judge whether the verb accompanying each is the correct one to describe the action.

1 Rinpoche talks to me. གསུང་བ། **sūngwa**
2 I talk to Rinpoche. ལབ་པ། **la̱pa**
3 I met Rinpoche. མཇལ་བ། **cä̱lwa**
4 Rinpoche gives me something. འབུལ་བ། **phǖlwa**
5 Rinpoche recognises me. ངོ་མཁྱེན་པ། **ngo̱khyēnpa**
6 I phone Rinpoche. ཁ་པར་གཏོང་བ། **khāpar-tāngwa**

Language point

5 ཡས (yä)

yä has many functions, so no single translation is possible. But it is always attached to the end of an action verb (or a modal verb referring to that action verb), and communicates something related to the action. This purely colloquial particle appears with a variety of spellings, each representing an approximation of how it sounds in the spoken language (ཡ། ཡག། ཡས།).

In Dialogue 2 an object passes from one speaker to the other. It is not named. But both speakers create a term to refer to it, by adding **yä** to an action verb. Through their choice of action verb, the speakers describe the object in terms of what it is intended for; it is something 'for giving'. **yä** can be added to various intentional verbs, creating terms to describe objects, etc. according to what the plan or intention for them is, or how they function (i.e. what they're 'for').

འདི་ཁོ་རང་ལ་ལབ་ཡས་རེད།
ti̱ khōrang-la la̱p-yä re̱'.
This is (something which is) to be told to him.

དངུལ་དེ་མོ་རང་གི་རྩ་ནས་ལེན་ཡས་རེད།
ngǖl the̱ mo̱rang-ki tsā-nä le̱n-yä re̱'.
That money is to be collected from her.

Only single (literal) translations are provided here, but a **yä**-combination can be interpreted in different ways, depending on the situation. Anyway in these sentences, they are describing the things in the subject position ('this' and 'the money'). Once it is clear what the thing being defined by the action is, the **yä**-combination can occupy that subject position. For example:

<u>ལབ་ཡས</u>་དེ་གལ་ཆེན་པོ་རེད། **la̱p-yä the̱ khä̱l-chēnpo re̱'.**
That thing (which is to be said) is important.

Sometimes, the action so comes to define a thing, that the **yä**-combination becomes that thing's actual name. As introduced in Unit 9, for instance, the word for 'food' is **sa̱-yä** ('that which is to be/for eating'), and for 'drink', **thūng-yä**.

■ Practical tip – working without names

yä, like the earlier **nyän/khan**, demonstrates the Tibetan habit of describing things (and people) in terms of their functions and actions. Learners should exploit this habit: the fact that a physical object (or even a concept) has no Tibetan name, or has a name that one is unaware of, need not prevent its being discussed.

Exercise 6

Each statement refers to a different thing by its function (using a **yä**-combination), rather than its name. What are the Tibetan names of these things?

༡ འདི་ལག་པ་ལ་གྱོན་ཡས་རེད། **ti̱ la̱kpa-la khö̱n-yä re̱'.**
༢ འདི་ཁ་ཆེའི་ཟ་ཡས་མ་རེད། **ti̱ khāchä: sa̱-yä ma-re̱'.**
༣ འདིས་ཅ་ལག་ཉོ་ཡས་ཡོད་རེད། **ti̱' cālak nyo̱-yä yo̱re'.**
༤ ན་དུས་མི་འདི་བསྟེན་ཡས་རེད། **na̱-thü' mi̱-ti tā̈n-yä re̱'.**

Language point

6 Time-related structures

■ 'Before'

Unit 8 had an equivalent for 'before that/this'. But to express the time before a specific action (e.g. 'before eating', 'before speaking') the pattern is different. One puts **ma** (the negating-particle) in front of the action verb (present form), and **kho̱ng-la** after it; e.g.

མ་འགྲོ་གོང་ལ་་་། **ma-ṭo̱ kho̱ng-la** before going

With compound verbs, **ma** comes in front of the verbaliser:

སྐད་ཆ་མ་བཤད་གོང་ལ་་་། **kǟcha ma-shǟ' kho̱ng-la**
before speaking

■ Since/for

In English, you can answer 'how long have you been here?' by giving a specific time (e.g. 'since 3 o'clock', 'since last Friday'), or in terms of the number of hours, days, years, etc. that have passed (e.g. 'I've been here for two weeks'). The choice is similar in Tibetan. The structure for the first is easy, and has appeared in earlier units.

ང་ཚོ་འདིར་ཆུ་ཚོད་གསུམ་པ་ལ་ཡོང་བ་ཡིན།
nga̱ntsho tä̱: chūtshö' sūmpa-la yo̱ngwa-yi̱n.
We have been here since 3 o'clock./We got here at 3 o'clock.

The second response (equivalent to using 'for') has quite a different structure. As Dialogue 2 shows, the passage of time is described in terms of years, days, etc. having 'gone' (**ṭo̱wa/chīnpa**). But before this, you must state the action which was done, marking the beginning of the time period referred to (a bit like saying, for instance, 'having arrived, two weeks have passed').

ང་ཚོ་འདིར་སླེབས་ནས་བདུན་ཕྲག་གཉིས་ཕྱིན་སོང་།
nga̱ntsho tä̱: lēp-nä tü̱nṭhak nyī' chīn-song.
We have been here for two weeks.

In Tibetan, the preference is very definitely for this second structure, but not just for saying when someone arrived. It is the usual way to express how long someone has been doing something for (where English uses has/have + 'for' + a time period). For example, 'I have lived here for . . .', 'we have studied Tibetan for . . .', 'he has been ill for . . .'. As in these examples, the activity or state must be ongoing.

You use the same structure to say how long you haven't done something for, by putting **ma** before the action verb.

The affirmative structure is not used if the period referred to has now ceased (e.g. 'I studied Tibetan for two years'); for this, one instead simply attaches a **la̱thön** to the time. Compare these structures in the following examples:

ང་འདིར་བསྡད་ནས་ལོ་གཅིག་ཕྱིན་སོང་།
nga̱ tä̱: tä̱'-nä lo̱-cīk chīn-song.
I have been/lived here for a year.

ང་ལྷ་ས་ལ་མ་བསྡད་ནས་ལོ་དྲུག་ཕྱིན་སོང་།
nga̱ lhāsa-la ma-tä-nä lo̱-ṭhu̱k chīn-song.
I haven't lived in Lhasa for six years.

ང་ལྷ་ས་ལ་ལོ་བརྒྱད་བསྡད་པ་ཡིན།
nga̱ lhāsa-la lo̱-kyä̱' täwa-yi̱n.
I lived in Lhasa for eight years.

Exercise 7

Translate these:

1 I have been here for six months.
2 Think carefully before writing!
3 This book? I haven't read it for years.
4 That is a high altitude place. One must prepare well before going there.
5 How long have you been studying Chinese for?
6 Q. When was this car made? A. A long time ago.
7 Nyima says she hasn't seen her elder brother for three days.

Exercise 8

Certain events led to the conversations in Dialogues 1 and 2. Read the dialogues again; try to get some idea of what these events might have been. Answer the questions in English.

■ Dialogue 1

1 Who needs reassuring, and about what?
2 If the previous event had gone well, what was supposed to have happened?
3 What do you think actually happened?
4 Did anyone feel let down?

■ Dialogue 2

1 How is the visitor received?
2 Why did he stay away for so long?
3 Why is it too late?
4 Has anyone been let down?

Choose a verb from the list, and then put it together with a character or object mentioned in the dialogue, so that it sums up what happened at the earlier event (one for each dialogue).

Second, choose one word (from those below or elsewhere) which expresses some strong feeling which seems to underlie each dialogue.

མ་བཞུགས་པ།	**ma-shu̱kpa**	བརྗེད་པ།	**ce̱pa**
གྲོངས་པ།	**ṭho̱ngwa**	འགྲོ་བ།	**ṭo̱wa**
ཕེབས་པ།	**phēpa**	མ་བསྡད་པ།	**ma-te̱wa**
མ་སྤྲད་པ།	**ma-ṭā̄wa**	ཤི་བ།	**shīwa**
ངོ་ཚ་བ།	**ngo̱tshāwa**	དགོངས་པ་རྫོགས་པ།	**ko̱npa-tso̱kpa**
རྐུན་མ།	**kūma**	སྐྱོན།	**kyȫn**
ཡོང་བ།	**yo̱ngwa**	མ་ཞུས་པ།	**ma-shu̱wa**
མ་གནང་བ།	**ma-nāngwa**	ཆིབས་བསྐྱུར་གནང་བ།	**chīpkyur-nāngwa**
མ་ཡོང་བ།	**ma-yo̱ngwa**	གསུངས་པ།	**sūngwa**
མ་གསུངས་པ།	**ma-sūngwa**		

Unit Fifteen

ཕྱོགས་གཞན་དག་ནས་བལྟས་ན་…།

chōk shä̲nthak-nä tā̈'-na . . .

From another perspective . . .

In this unit you will learn how to:

- deal with nuances in honorific usage
- avoid common mistakes with honorific language
- observe the basics of gesture and body language
- use phrases with fixed auxiliaries
- make use of abbreviated question-forms
- use another form of 'if'
- employ direction words
- make verbs into nouns
- express views and opinions

Dialogue 1

(Audio 2:35)

A senior monk – teacher of many young monks at the monastery – is being visited by a distinguished lay woman.

ཀུན་བཟོད་པ།	ཨུམ་སྐུ་ཞབས་ལགས། གསུངས་དང་། གཞུང་གི་ལས་བྱེད་དེ…། ལྷེ་ཁྲོད་གཉིས་ཚོག་གེར་སྡོད།
ཨུམ་སྐུ་ཞབས།	ངོ། སྐུ་ཞབས་གསར་པ…། ཁོང་ག་ནས་ཕེབས་པ་རེད་ལགས། སྐུ་ཞབས་ལགས། མཚན་ལ་ག་རེ་ཞུ་གི་ཡོད།
ཐུབ་བསྟན།	ངའི་མཚན…ངའི་མིང་ལ་ཐུབ་བསྟན་ཞུ་གི་ཡོད།
སྤྲིན་པ།	ཧ་ཧ་ཧ། ཕྲུ་གུ་འདིས་གད་མོ་སློང་གི་འདུག

ཀུན་བཟོད་པ། ཁ་ཁ་སྡོད། འདི་ཁྱོད་ཀྱིས་བསླབས་པ་ཡིན་ས་རེད། སྙིང་རྗེ། ཁོ་རང་ཚོའི་ལུང་པའི་སྐད་ལ་ཞེ་ས་ཡོད་མ་རེད་ལགས། ཁོ་རང་ཀྱག་ཤེས་ཀྱི་མི་འདུག ཨེ་ནི་ཨིན་ཇུང་གཞན་དག་དེ་ཚོ་ཁོ་ལ་འཕྱ་ལད་རྒྱུག་གི་ཡོད་རེད། ཁོ་ལ་རྐང་བཙུགས་ནས་ཞེ་ས་ནོར་ཀྱོག་སློབ་ཀྱི་ཡོད་ས་རེད། སྦྱིན་པ། ཁྱོད་ཁོ་ལ་འདི་བསླབས་པས།

སྦྱིན་པ། བསླབས་མེད་ཀུན་ལགས། ངས་འདི་འདྲ་ལབ་པ་ཡིན། མི་ཀུན་པས་སྐད་ཆ་བཤད་དུས་ཡག་པོར་ཉན། ཨེ་ནི་ལད་ཟློས་བྱེད་ཟེར་ལབ་པ་ཡིན། དེ་འདྲ་མ་རེད་པས་ཀུན་ལགས།

ཀུན་བཟོད་པ། ཁ་བདེ་པོ་མ་ཤོད། སྦྱིན་པ་ཁྱོད་ཁྲིམ་ལ་ལས་ཀ་ཡོད་པ། དེ་བྱེད་གར་རྒྱུགས། ཕ་གིའི་ཅོག་ཙེའི་སྟེང་ལ་ཙ་ལག་ཁ་ཤས་འདུག དེ་ཚོ་ཕར་ཨ་ཞང་པད་མའི་རྩ་ལ་བསྐྱལ་ཡས་རེད། ཨེ་ནི་ཁོ་རང་གི་རྩ་ནས་ཡི་གེ་ལེན་ཡས་ཡོད་རེད། ད་རྒྱུགས།

སྦྱིན་པ། ཀུན་ལགས། འཁྱེར་ཡས་མང་པོ་འདུག་ག ང་ལ་རོགས་གཅིག་དགོས་ས་རེད། ང་ཁོ་འཁྲིད་ཆོག་གི་རེད་པས། ཀུན་ལགས་སྐུ་མཁྱེན།

ཀུན་བཟོད་པ། ཁོ་ཨེ། ཁོ་འཁྲིད་ཀྱི་ཡིན་ན་དགེ་སྐོས་ལགས་ལ་དགོངས་པ་ཞུ་དགོས་རེད། ཨེ་ནི་ལམ་སེང་ཚུར་ཤོག་ཨང་། འགྱངས་མ་འགྲོ།

སྦྱིན་པ། ལོས། ཀུན་ལགས། སྐུ་ཞབས་ཐུབ་བསྟན་ལགས། ང་ལ་ཕྱག་རོགས་གནང་གར་ཕེབས་གས།

ཐུབ་བསྟན། ང་ཕྱག་རོགས་་་། ང་་་ཕེབས་་། ང་་་་*འགྲོ་རྒྱུ་ཡིན*།

ཀུན་བཟོད་པ། ཕ་ཡུལ་སྐད་མ་རྒྱུག མིས་གོ་གི་མ་རེད། སྦྱིན་པ། ཁོ་ལ་སྐད་ཡག་པོ་བྱས་ནས་སློབ།

GEN SÖPA cām kūsho', sūng-thang. shu̱ng-ki lä̱che the̱ . . . (*two young monks burst in*) we̱, khyȫ'-nyī' tsūke-tä̱'.

LADY o̱, kūsho' sārpa . . . khōng kha̱nä phēpa-re̱'-la:. kūsho'-la:, tshä̃n-la kha̱re shu̱ki-yo̱'.

THUPTEN ngä̱: tshä̃n . . . ngä̱: mi̱ng-la thūptän shu̱ki-yo̱'.

JINPA hahaha phūku-ti̱ khä̱mo lāngki-tu̱'.

GEN SÖPA khāka-tä̱'. ti̱ khyȫ'-kī' lāpa yi̱n-sa-re̱'. (*to the woman*) nyīngce̱, khōrang-tshȫ: lu̱ngpä kä̃'-la she̱sa yo̱ ma-re̱'. khōrang kya̱k shīnki-min-tu̱'. ēni ēnchung shä̱nthak the̱ntshȫ' khōrang-la chālä kya̱pki-yo̱re'. khō-la kāngtsuk-nä she̱sa no̱rkyok lāpki-yo̱re'. ci̱npa, khyȫ' khō-la ti̱ lāp-pä.

JINPA	lāp-me̱ kä̱n-la:. ngä̱ thi̱nṭä la̱pa-yi̱n. mi̱ kä̱npā̈' kā̈cha shā̈-thü' ya̱kpo nyä̱n, ēni lä̱ntö' chi̱-s la̱pa-yin. the̱nṭä ma-re̱'-wä kä̱n-la:.
GEN SÖPA	khā-te̱po ma-shā̈'. ci̱npa khyȫ' ṭhōm-la lä̱ka yö̱'-pa. the̱ che̱ka-kyu̱k. phāki: cōktsä: ka̱ng-la cālak khāshä tu̱'. the̱ntsho phār āshang pā̈mä:-tsā-la kyā̈l-yä re̱'. ēni khōrang-ki tsā-nä yi̱ke lä̱n-yä yo̱re'. tha̱ kyu̱k.
JINPA	kä̱n-la:. khyīr-yä ma̱ngpo tu̱'-ka. nga̱-la ro̱kpa-cīk kö̱' sa re̱'. nga̱ khō ṭhī' chōki re̱'-wä. kä̱n-la: kūkyi.
GEN SÖPA	khō-ē. khō ṭhīki-yi̱n-na ke̱kȫ'-la:-la ko̱ngpa shu̱-kö' re̱'. ēni la̱msang tshūr-shōk-a. khyām ma-ṭo̱.
JINPA	lo̱:s kä̱n-la:. kūsho thūptän-la: nga̱-la chākrok nāngka-phēp-kä.
THUPTEN	nga̱ chākrok . . . nga̱ . . . phēp nga̱ . . . *kyo̱-kyu̱ yā̈.*
GEN SÖPA	phāyül-kā̈ ma-kya̱p. mi̱' kho̱ki ma-re̱'. ci̱npa, khō-la kā̈' ya̱kpo-chä̱nä lāp.

Vocabulary

ཧ་ཧ་ཧ།	**hahaha**	(sound of laughter)
བསླབས་པ།	**lāpa**	taught (past of སློབ་པ། to teach)
ཆོག་པ།	**chōkpa**	to be allowed (modal verb)
དགེ་སྐོས།	**ke̱kȫ'**	monastery disciplinarian
ཁ་བདེ་པོ་མ་ཤོད།	**khā-te̱po ma-shā̈'**	don't be cheeky!
དགོངས་པ་ཞུ་བ།	**ko̱ngpa-shu̱wa**	to request permission
ཀང་བཙུགས་ནས།	**kāngtsūk-nä**	on purpose
འཁྱམས་མ་འགྲོ།	**khyām ma-ṭo̱**	don't go roaming about!
ཁ་ཁ་སྡོད།	**khākha-te̱'**	be quiet!
ཨེན་ཆུང་།	**ēnchung**	young monks
ཕ་ཡུལ་སྐད།	**phāyül-kā̈**	regional dialect
འཕྱ་ལད་རྒྱག་པ།	**chālä-kya̱pa**	to mock
ནོར་གྱོག།	**no̱rkyok**	mistaken
ཚུར་ཤོག།	**tshūr-shōk**	come back!

ལད་ཟློས་བྱེད་པ།	**lāntö'-chepa**	to imitate
མི་རྒན་པ།	**mi-kānpa**	elders
…ཀྱི་ཡིན་ན།	**. . . ki yin-na**	if (see below)
ཕྱག་རོགས་གནང་བ།	**chākrok-nāngwa**	to help (honorific)
ལྕམ་སྐུ་ཞབས།	**cām kūsho'**	(address for women of aristocratic origin)
བསླབས་པས།	**lāp-pä:**	did you teach? (abbreviated question-form)
གད་མོ་སློང་བ།	**khāmo-lāngwa**	to amuse (*lit.* to raise laughter)
འགྲོ་རྒྱུ་ཡིན།	**co-cu**	I am going (spoken in an Eastern Tibetan dialect)
སྐུ་མཁྱེན།	**kūkyi**	'please!' (usually when pleading: an expression popular with children)
རྒན་བཟོད་པ།/སྦྱིན་པ།/ཐུབ་བསྟན།/ཨ་ཞང་པད་མ།	**kān sōpa/cinpa/ thūptän/ āshang pāma**	(personal names)
ལོས།	**lo:s***	(polite expression of agreement)
ཚོག་གེར་སྡོད།	**tsūke-tä'**	behave!

* This word has no proper written form; this is an approximation of the way it sounds.

Language points

1 Honorific . . . a more nuanced picture

As explained in Unit 14, certain regional and social backgrounds make some Tibetans more conversant with honorific language than others. Fluent users often assert that unless you speak 'purely' (i.e. use full-blown) honorifics, your language isn't really honorific language at all. In reality, many Central Dialect speakers fail to meet these exacting standards, but still manage to use honorifics very effectively to convey respect.

Learners should certainly focus upon the basics of honorific conversation – using polite personal pronouns, the **la:**-syllable, polite invitations (Unit 5). Everyone speaking some Central Tibetan (probably even Thupten in Dialogue 1) will be familiar with these. But beyond that, honorific usage can be patchy and inconsistent (particularly amongst Tibetans outside Tibet).

Even those who function comfortably on the honorific level (probably Jinpa) may tone down the honorifics in certain situations and company: Lhasa dialect (with its pure honorifics), so often advertised as the most prestigious form of spoken Tibetan, is derided by many as pretentious. Certain non-native speakers detect a mocking tone. Some (e.g. Jinpa) manipulate it, for that very purpose.

There is, anyway, more to conveying respect than using honorific language: correct body language and gestures are also essential. Choosing the right topics of conversation – knowing what subjects to avoid, for instance, because they are culturally sensitive – is also important.

2 Honorific – Where one might trip up . . .

Failing to address someone in honorific language might cause offence, but most Tibetans are quite forgiving if they believe that it was due to ignorance rather than rudeness. The mistake Tibetans can't resist poking fun at is when a speaker uses an honorific term for him- or herself.

A major source of this mistake is the humbly performed actions. A correct exchange, when person 1 offers person 2 some tea, would be:

P1	གསོལ་ཇ་མཆོད་ཀྱི་ཡིན་པས།	**sōlcha chōki-yi̱n-pä.** (*lit.* 'Will you drink tea?')
P2	ལགས། གསོལ་ཇ་ཞུ་གི་ཡིན།	**la: sōlcha shu̱ki-yi̱n.** (*lit.* 'I shall accept tea.')

Person 1 'respects' person 2 with the general honorific verb **chōpa**. But in response, person 2 is describing his or her own humbly performed action, so must use the verb **shu̱wa**.

Person 2 *expects* to follow Person 1's lead – not only because of the rule of anticipation, but because Person 2 is trying to match Person 1 in politeness. So unless careful, Person 2 might just repeat the verb in the original question (here **chȫpa**). A bit like saying 'I *kindly* accept.' Surprisingly, even Tibetans who are familiar with the system trip up sometimes.

For learners, nouns also sometimes cause problems here. The divide between ordinary and honorific level is generally clear; for instance, you refer to your own hand as **l̲akpa**, but refer politely, to the hand of another as **chāk**. In the exchange above, the division between the verbs **chȫpa** and **shu̲wa** is also clear. However, both question and answer use the same honorific term (**sȫlcha**) for the tea.

Here are some other examples where the noun has a single honorific form, but the verbs differ, depending on whether the action is a general honorific or a humbly performed one:

བཀའ་སློབ།
advice
→ གནང་བ། **kālop-nāngwa** to bestow
→ ཞུ་བ། **kālop-shu̲wa** to request/accept

དགོངས་པ།
permission
→ གནང་བ། **ko̲ngpa-nāngwa** to grant
→ ཞུ་བ། **ko̲ngpa-shu̲wa** to request/accept

This occurs only when the item in question can pass from one party to another; be it food, a service, or whatever, it is something that can be offered and accepted (or refused). The verb **phǖlwa** is used for offering physical items, and **shu̲wa** for services, or more abstract things.

Exercise 1

These are honorific Tibetan nouns of the above kind. The accompanying English sentences present various situations for their use. Following the example of no.1, add the appropriate verb. The (slightly artificial) English terms indicate the type of situation.

1 ཕྱག་རོགས། **chākrok:** help –
Can I (humbly) help you? ཞུ་བ། **shu̲wa**
2 ཕྱག་དངུལ། **chākngül** money –
She (graciously) bestowed this money.
3 ཞལ་ལག། **shǟlak** food –
We shall (humbly) offer them some food.

4 ཞལ་ལག། **shä̱lak** –
I (humbly) accepted the food.
5 བཀའ་མོལ། **kāmöl** speech –
They (kindly) spoke to them.
6 བཀའ་འདྲི། **kānṭi** question –
I (humbly) asked Rinpoche.
7 ཞལ་དཔར། **shä̱lpar** a phone call –
You should (humbly) phone her.

Cultural point

Basics of gesture and body language

■ General

People are quick to smile and laugh broadly. But aside from friends grasping hands, the culture is not particularly tactile; adults do not publicly hug or kiss, either in greeting or general affection, although members of the same family or those with some religious connection may touch foreheads, when departing one another's company.

■ Respectful

Overt signs of humility are used to indicate respect or welcoming. The main instrument here is the upper body. This is inclined forward, as it, the head, and the shoulders are dipped. This posture of incline and lowering is held permanently in the company of special individuals (particularly religious figures). A sort of open-palmed 'ushering' posture is regularly adopted; both arms, slightly bent, are directed forward. One hand may lead, depending on whether the person is offering, accepting, or showing the way. Gesticulating limbs, fully outstretched hands, and bolt upright stances are rather foreign. Positive Tibetan body language tends more towards curvature than angularity.

■ Disrespectful

It is offensive to sit (whether on a chair, cushion, or bed) with legs outstretched pointing at another person or at religious symbols. As

Tibetans prefer to sit cross-legged, this is not a problem for them. Pointing with a finger is considered rude, or even threatening.

■ Gesturing

One does not nod or shake the head vigorously to indicate 'yes' or 'no', although slight nods or dips of the head can indicate agreement or compliance. The ushering gesture may be used to point to something or someone, but another, perhaps unique gesture is common (Gen Söpa probably employed it, when pointing to the things on the table, in Dialogue 1). This gesture involves pointing with the lips. Held in a sort of kissing position (often to the alarm of the uninitiated), the lips are projected in the direction of the indicated object.

Language point

3 Abbreviating questions

Dialogue 1 illustrates how to shorten questions, by dropping the auxiliary. This only works with questions directed to a second person. Also, these questions must be about things the person did, or intends to do (i.e. intentional actions, past and future); questions about the present can't be abbreviated. Here are more examples:

ཁྱེད་རང་ག་དུས་བལྟ་གས།	**khyērang kh̲athü' tā-kä.** When will you look at it?
ཞལ་ལག་མ་མཆོད་པས།	**shä̱lak ma-chȫ'-pä.** Didn't you eat?

These abbreviations are normal both on the ordinary and honorific levels; they do not sound casual, or slang-like. The auxiliary is dropped, and a question-particle is added straight after the action verb. In questions about the future, the particle is **kä**; in those about the past, **pä**.

འགྲོ་གི་ཡིན་པས།	**ṭo̱-ki yi̱n-pä**	→	འགྲོ་གས།	**ṭo̱-kä**	Will you go?
ཕྱིན་པ་ཡིན་པས།	**chīn-pa yi̱n-pä**	→	ཕྱིན་པས།	**chīn-pä.**	Did you go?

Questions about the future are only shortened if they are *affirmative* (e.g. 'will you . . . ?'). Those about the past can be either affirmative or negative. Sentences with modal verbs can't be abbreviated in this way. When the question includes a question-word, ས is often dropped from the particle.

Exercise 2

The number beside each dialogue shows how many sentences it has which can be abbreviated. Locate the sentences, and then re-write them with the shorter endings, as just described.

(a) Unit 7, Dialogue 2 – 2
(b) Unit 9, Dialogue 1 – 1
(c) Unit 10, Dialogue 1 – 1
(d) Unit 11, Dialogue 2 – 2
(e) Unit 14, Dialogue 1 – 1

Exercise 3

There are now a number of structures which don't use auxiliary verbs; this is a revision exercise made up of them. One of these sentences is not a correct structure. Identify it, and translate the others.

(a) ང་གཉིས་འགྲོ། **nga̱-nyī' ṭo̱.**
(b) ཆང་བཟོ་གས། **chāng so̱-kä.**
(c) གཟབ་གཟབ་བྱེད། **sa̱psap-chi̱'.**
(d) ངས་ལབ་དགོས། **ngä̱ la̱p ko̱.**
(e) སྐད་ཆ་མ་བཤད་པས། **kǟcha ma-shǟ'-pä.**
(f) མགྱོགས་པོར་རྒྱུགས། **kyo̱kpo kyu̱k.**
(g) ཡི་གེ་གཏང་གས། **yi̱ke tāng-kä.**
(h) ཉི་མ་མཐོང་བས། **nyi̱ma thōng-wä.**
(i) ཚལ་དགོས་པས། **tshǟl kö̱'-pä.**

Language point

4 Another form of 'if'

The 'if'-structure in Dialogue 1 is almost the same as that in Unit 12. But the earlier one didn't use a whole verb-unit in the if-clause; this one does. So instead of: ཁོ་འཁྲིད་ན་.... **khō ṭhī'-na**, it says; ཁོ་འཁྲིད་ཀྱི་ཡིན་ན་ ... **khō ṭhīki yi̱n-na**.

Either of these ways can be used to talk about situations set in the future or the present. Situations set in the past require other forms, not covered in this book.

The auxiliary in this longer form is usually one of the essential verbs, but **tu'** is also sometimes heard. This longer form is used in many situations where the shorter one is, although rarely to express generalisations, or when talking in the first person. The example in Dialogue 1 is typical; it is one in which a proposed plan of action is being considered. Other examples:

ལས་ཁུངས་དེ་ལ་ཕྱག་ལས་གནང་གི་ཡིན་ན་ཞེ་ས་ཏོག་ཙམ་སྦྱོང་དགོས་ཀྱི་འདུག
lä̱khūng-the̱-la chāklä' nāngki-yi̱n-na she̱sa tēts ca̱ng kö̱'-ki tu̱'.
If you are going to work (honorific) in that office, you should learn more honorific language.

དགེ་སྐོས་ལགས་ཀྱིས་དགོངས་པ་གནང་གི་མེད་ན་འགྲོ་ཆོག་གི་མ་རེད།
ke̱kȫ' la:-kī' ko̱ngpa nāngki-me̱-na ṭo̱ chōki-ma-re̱'.
If the disciplinarian won't grant you permission, you aren't allowed to go.

ཆར་པ་གཏོང་གི་འདུག་ན་ཉི་གདུགས་འདི་འཁྱེར།
chārpa tāngki-tu̱k-na nyi̱tuk-ti̱ khyīr.
If it's raining, take this umbrella.

Dialogue 2 (T)

(Audio 2:36)
Duho is in a reflective mood. He arrived with Lisa, but the two of them chose to spend their time (in the Tibetan community) in different ways. They met up again. However, differences in their views emerged. Things came to a head, in a heated conversation. Duho sits dejectedly, reporting what happened to Yeshe, who seems apathetic (and perhaps slightly drunk).

ཡེ་ཤེས། ཨ་ལས། ཁྱོད་གཉིས་(ཀྱིས་)རྒྱབ་འདྲེ་བརྒྱག་པས།

ཏུ་ཧོ། ངས་ཕར་རྒྱབ་འདྲེ་རྒྱབ་མེད། རྒྱབ་འདྲེ་རྒྱག་མཁན་ལི་ས་རེད། ང་ཁས་ས་ཕྱི་རྒྱལ་མི་གཅིག་ཐུག་སོང་། ཁོ་རང་འདིར་བོད་ཀྱི་ཅ་ལག་རྙིང་པ་ཉོས་ནས་དེ་ཚོ་ཕྱི་རྒྱལ་ལ་འཚོང་གི་ཡོད་ཟེར། ཁོས་བོད་སྐད་ཤེས་ཀྱི་མི་འདུག ཨེ་ནི་ཁོ་རང་གིས་ཅ་ལག་ཉོ་དུས་ངས་རོགས་པ་བྱས་པ་ཡིན། ཡིན་ནའང་ངས་འདི་ལི་ས་ལ་ལབ་དུས་མོ་རང་རླུང་ལངས་ནས་ཚུར་སྐད་ཆ་རྩུབ་པོ་བཤད་སོང་།

ཡེ་ཤེས། ག་རེ་བཤད་སོང་།

ཏུ་ཧོ། མང་པོ་བཤད་སོང་། དཔེར་ན་མི་དེ་ཚོས་བོད་པ་སྐྱོ་པོ་ལ་མགོ་སྐོར་གཏོང་གི་ཡོད་
རེད་ཟེར། ཁོ་ཚོ་ལ་རོགས་པ་བྱས་ན་བོད་ཀྱི་རིག་གཞུང་ལ་གནོད་ཀྱི་ཡོད་རེད་ཟེར།
ཨེ་ནི་བོད་སྐད་ཤེས་ན་ཡག་པོ་བྱས་ནས་བེད་སྤྱོད་གཏོང་དགོས་ཀྱི་ཡོད་རེད་ཟེར།
ཡེ་ཤེས། ངས་ཁོ་ལ་རོགས་པ་བྱས་པ་ཡིན། དེ་མི་ལ་ཕན་ཐོགས་ཀྱི་རེད་པ།

ཡེ་ཤེས། དེ་ག་རེ་བྱས་ནས་ལབ་ཀྱི་ཡོད།

ཏུ་ཧོ། ང་སྐྱིད་པོ་གཏོང་ཡས་ལ་དགའ་པོ་ཡོད། རོགས་པ་མཉམ་དུ་དུས་ཚོད་སྐྱེལ་ཡས་ལ་
དགའ་པོ་ཡོད། ཡིན་ནའང་ལི་ས་ཟེར་ན་ང་དུས་ཚོད་ཚང་མ་འཕྲོ་བརླག་གཏོང་གི་
ཡོད་རེད་ཟེར། ཡེ་ཤེས། ཁྱེད་རང་ཟེར་ན་ང་མི་ག་འདྲ་ཡོད་རེད།

ཡེ་ཤེས། ངས་ཟེར་ན་ཁྱོད་མི་སྣང་བ་སྐྱིད་པོ་རེད།

ཏུ་ཧོ། ལི་ས་བོད་ཀྱི་ཆོས་དང་རིག་གཞུང་སྦྱོང་འདོད་ཡོད་རེད། ཡིན་ནའང་ང་…… ཡེ་ཤེས།
རོགས་པ་མཉམ་དུ་ཆང་འཐུང་ཡས་དང་། སྐད་ཆ་བཤད་ཡས་དེ་ཚོ་ཡང་(འང་)
བོད་པའི་རིག་གཞུང་མ་རེད་པས།

ཡེ་ཤེས། ལུགས་སྲོལ་རེད།

ཏུ་ཧོ། མོ་རང་གིས་འདི་འདྲ་ལབ་སོང་། སྐད་ཤེས་ན་ཆོས་དང་རིག་གཞུང་སྦྱང་ཡས་དེ་
ལས་འགན་རེད་ཟེར། ཡེ་ཤེས། འདིའི་ཐོག་ལ་བསམ་ཚུལ་ག་རེ་ཡོད།

ཡེ་ཤེས། དེའི་ཐོག་ལ་བསམ་ཚུལ་གང་ཡང་མེད། ངའི་བསམ་པ་ལ་སྐད་ཆ་དེ་འདྲ་མང་པོ་
བཤད་ན་ཆང་ལ་བྲོ་བ་མི་འདུག

ཏུ་ཧོ། ཕྱི་ལོགས་ནས་གཅིག་གོ་གི་འདུག སྐད་རྒྱག་གི་འདུག་ག གཅིག་དུ་གི་ཡོད་ས་རེད།

ཡེ་ཤེས། ཡ་མེད་གཏོང་། ང་ཚོ་གང་ཡང་བྱེད་ཐུབ་ཀྱི་མ་རེད། མར་བསྡད། ཆང་འཐུང་།

YESHE ālä khyȫ'-nyī'-(kī') kya̱mṭe kya̱p-pä.

DUHO ngä̱ phār kya̱mṭe kya̱p-me̱. kya̱mṭe kya̱p-khän li̱sa re̱'. nga̱ khǟ̱sa chīkyäl mi̱-cīk thūk-song. khōrang tä̱: phö̱ki cālak nyīngpa nyö̱-nä the̱ntsho chīkyäl-la tshōngki-yö̱'-s. khȫ' phö̱kǟ̱' shīngki-min-tu̱'. ēni khōrang-kī' cālak nyo̱-thü' ngä̱' ro̱kpa chä̱pa-yi̱n. yi̱nnä ngä̱ ti̱ li̱sa-la la̱p-thü' mo̱rang lūng la̱ng-nä tshūr kä̱cha tsūpo shǟ̱'-song.

YESHE kha̱re shǟ̱'-song.

DUHO ma̱ngpo shǟ̱'-song. pērna mi̱ the̱ntshȫ' phö̱pa kyōpo-la ko̱kor tāngki-yo̱re'-s. khōtsho-la ro̱kpa chä̱'-na phö̱'-ki ri̱kshung-la nöki-yo̱re'-s. ēni phö̱kǟ̱' shē'-na ya̱kpo-chä̱nä phe̱cö' tāng kö̱'-ki yo̱re'-s. ye̱shē' ngä̱' khō-la ro̱kpa chä̱pa-yi̱n. the̱ mi̱-la phǟ̱nthöki-re̱'-wä.

YESHE the̱ kha̱re-chä̱nä la̱pki-yö̱'.

DUHO nga̱ kyīpo tāng-yä-la ka̱po yö̱'. ro̱kpa nyāmtu thü̱tshȫ' kyǟl-yä-la ka̱po yö̱'. yi̱nnä li̱sa se̱r-na nga̱ thü̱tshȫ' tshāngma ṭhōlak tāngki-yo̱re'-s. ye̱shē' khyērang se̱r-na nga̱ mi̱ kha̱nṭa yo̱re'.

YESHE ngä̱ se̱r-na khyȫ' mi̱ nāngwa-kyīpo re̱'.

DUHO li̱sa phö̱-ki chȫ' thang ri̱kshung ca̱ng-tö̱' yo̱re'. yi̱nnä nga̱ . . . ye̱shē ro̱kpa nyāmtu chāng thūng-yä thang kǟcha shǟ'-yä the̱ntsho-yä phö̱'-ki ri̱kshung ma-re̱'-wä.

YESHE lu̱ksöl re̱'.

DUHO mo̱rang-ki̱' ti̱nṭä la̱p-song. kǟ' shē'-na chȫ' thang ri̱kshung ca̱ng-yä-the̱ lä̱nkän re̱'. ye̱shē ti̱: thōk-la sāmtshul kha̱re yö̱'.

YESHE the̱: thōk-la sāmtshul khä̱: me̱'. ngä̱ sāmpa-la kǟcha ti̱nṭä māngpo shǟ'-na chāng-la ṭho̱wa min-tu̱'.

DUHO chīlo-nä cīk kho̱ki-tu̱'. kǟ' kya̱pki-tu̱'-ka. cīk ngu̱ki yö̱'-sa re̱'.

YESHE ya̱me'-tāng. nga̱ntsho khä̱: chi̱'-thūpki ma-re̱'. ma̱r-tä̱' chāng thūng.

Vocabulary

སྐྱིད་པོ་གཏོང་བ།	**kyīpo-tāngwa**	to have a good time (intentional)
གནོད་པ།	**nȫ'pa**	to harm/damage (non-intentional)
བེད་སྤྱོད་གཏོང་བ།	**phecȫ-tāngwa**	to use (int.)
དུས་ཚོད་སྐྱེལ་བ།	**thütshȫ'-kyā̈lwa**	to spend time
སྣང་བ་སྐྱིད་པོ།	**nāngwa-kyīpo**	happy-go-lucky
འཕྲོ་བརླག་གཏོང་བ།	**ṭhōlak-tāngwa**	to waste (int.)
ཡ་མེད་གཏོང་བ།	**yame'-tāngwa**	to ignore (int.)
རླུང་ལང་བ།	**lūng-langwa**	to lose one's temper (non-int.)
འདོད་(་པ)།	**tö'(-pa)**	to wish/want (modal verb)
ཁྱེད་རང་ཟེར་ན།	**khyērang serna**	according to you
ཕན་ཐོགས་པ།	**phā̈nthōkpa**	to be helpful
ཚུར།	**tshūr**	to me (see below)
རྩུབ་པོ།	**tsūpo**	rough; harsh
རིག་གཞུང་།	**rikshung**	culture
བསམ་ཚུལ།	**sāmtshul**	opinion
བྲོ་བ།	**ṭhowa**	taste (food or drink)
ངུ་བ།	**nguwa**	to cry (int.)
མར་བསྡད།	**mar-tä'**	sit down!
དཔེར་ན།	**pērna**	for example
ཡས།	**yä**	(see below)
རྒྱབ་འདྲེ་རྒྱག་པ།	**kyamṭe-kyapa**	to quarrel
ངའི་བསམ་པ་ལ།	**ngä sāmpa-la**	I think that . . .

Language point

5 Direction words

Many actions are spoken of as though they follow a direction: the four 'directionals' ('up', 'down', 'there', 'back') which express this are attached to the front of the verb. These combine with various verbs to express movement. Demonstratives, introduced in Unit 4, related to these (ཕ་གིར། ཡ་གིར། མ་གིར།), are used more when talking about fixed locations, as in: 'Tashi is up there.'

■ ཡར། **ya̱r** (up), མར། **ma̱r** (down)

These two are often used literally. When, for example, travelling by foot or bus involves going upwards, instead of just **ṭowa**, it is more usual to say: ཡར་འགྲོ་བ། **ya̱r-ṭo̱wa**. But as in English, one can also go 'up' or 'down' a street, when no actual ascent or descent is involved.

Plenty of other action verbs also incorporate **ya̱r** and **ma̱r**, as with English 'up' and 'down'. In many cases, they simply describe the direction of the physical movement, e.g.:

ཡར་ལེན་པ།	**ya̱r-le̱npa**	to pick up
མར་བཞག་པ།	**ma̱r-sha̱kpa**	to put down

Sometimes usage is more figurative (e.g. Unit 10: ཡར་འཕར་བ། **ya̱r-phārwa** 'increasing'). Occasionally, the 'direction' is not immediately obvious (e.g. ཡར་ཕེབས། **ya̱r-phēp** 'come in!') They also have a role in expressing respect; the direction of offerings and requests, made to authorities, religious figures, etc. is always up (e.g. ཡར་འབུལ་བ། **ya̱r-phǖlwa**).

■ ཕར། **phār** (there/away), ཚུར། **tshūr** (back/to)

In their literal sense (see Unit 14), **phār** and **tshūr** are used respectively, to describe moving in the direction *away from*, and *back towards* a particular place. Often they might refer to the two stages of a return journey.

In Dialogue 2 however, they refer to a conversation. Two parties are involved; **phār** is used to show something that comes *from* the side of the speaker (in this case Duho), and **tshūr** refers to what comes *to* the speaker (here, Lisa's words). Other actions (giving, receiving, etc.) are described in this way. There must always be one party, from whose perspective the back (**tshūr**) and forth (**phār**) directions are described. When it is clear who the two parties involved are, **phār** and **tshūr** will often be used in place of the names or personal pronouns.

Exercise 4

Directionals are usually optional; most of these sentences originally appeared in the dialogues without them. Add the correct directionals in the spaces indicated. Sentences marked X should have their personal pronouns removed and replaced by directionals.

1 འདི་བཀྲ་ཤིས་ལ་________གསུངས་ཨང་།
ti̱ ṭāshi-la ________sūng-a.

2 ངས་རྒྱལ་རྩེ་ལ་________ སྐྱེལ་དགོས།
ngä̱' kya̱ntse-la ________kyǟ̱l-ko̱.

3 མི་དེས་ང་ཚོ་ལ་________མགོ་སྐོར་གཏོང་ས་རེད།
mi̱-the̱' nga̱ntsho-la ________ko̱kor tāng-sa re̱'. X

4 ང་གཉིས་ལ་________བཀྲ་ཤིས་བདེ་ལེགས་ལབ་ཀྱི་འདུག་ག ཁོ་ཚོ་ལ་________
བཀྲ་ཤིས་བདེ་ལགས་ལབ།
nga̱-nyī'-la ________ṭāshi-te̱le' la̱pki tu̱'-ka. khōtsho-la ________ṭāshi-te̱le' la̱p. X

5 སྒོ་________རྒྱག་ཐུབ་ཀྱི་མི་འདུག
ko̱ ________kya̱p thūpki-min-tu̱'.

Exercise 5

Translate the sentences. Again, in those marked with X, use a directional instead of a pronoun.

1 The plane is landing (descending).
2 Stand up and ask your question!
3 Don't phone them. They can phone you. **X**
4 One bus is going to Lhasa and one is coming from Lhasa. Which is this one?
5 If one speaks honorific to others, they'll speak it in response. **X**
6 I lent you money last year; now give it back to me.

Language point

6 Making verbs into nouns

In Dialogue 2, when Duho adds **yä** (introduced in Unit 14) to various action verbs, he is making them into nouns ('nominalising' them).

So instead of using the verb **chāng thūngwa** to say that he or someone else is drinking, he uses **chāng thūng-yä**, as a way of talking about the activity of 'drinking' itself (e.g. 'drinking is fun' or 'a social obligation'). One can do this with all types of action verbs, including non-intentional ones. For instance, changing **ya̲r-phārwa** ('increasing') into **ya̲r-phār-yä** allows one to talk about 'the increase'.

Here **yä** refers to activities. In Unit 14 it referred to objects (food, etc.). Both structures basically sound the same. Context, familiarity with standard combinations, and sometimes auxiliaries will help you to distinguish.

Exercise 6

Some of these **yä**-combinations refer to things, others to activities. Various 'clues' make some of them more likely to refer to one or the other.

(a) Translate them, deciding which refer to things, and which refer to activities
(b) Identify three of the clues

༡	མི་གསར་པ་ཐུག་ཡས།	**mi̲ sārpa thūk-yä**
༢	ལྷ་མོ་ལ་བཤད་ཡས་དེ།	**lhāmo-la shǟ'-yä the̲**
༣	མགྲོན་ཁང་ལ་བསྡད་ཡས།	**ṭö̲nkhang-la tä̲-yä**
༤	མ་བསྟན་ཡས་དེ་ཚོ།	**ma-tǟn-yä the̲ntsho**
༥	མི་ལ་སྐྱོན་འཛུགས་ཡས།	**mi̲-la kyȫn tsūk-yä**
༦	ངུ་ཡས།	**ngu̲-yä**
༧	མགྱོགས་པོར་བཤད་ཡས།	**kyōkpo shǟ'-yä**

Language point

7 Phrases with fixed auxiliaries

Careful attention must normally be paid to the choice of auxiliary verb, but some standard phrases have auxiliaries that are frozen; the same one, **re̲'** (or its negation, **ma-re̲'**) is used, irrespective of time or person. Occasionally **yo̲re'** can be substituted, but not the other auxiliaries. The phrases are 'to be important', using the term **khä̲l-chēnpo** (Unit 10); 'to be all right', with **chōkpa** and 'to be okay/all right', with **ṭ̱i̱kpa** (both in Unit 14, Dialogue 1); and 'to be allowed', using **chōkpa** (this unit, Dialogue 1).

The phrases are used when talking about whether it is all right, important, etc. to do a particular action. But the way that these phrases are attached to the action verbs they refer to varies. Before doing Exercise 7, it would be best to check the examples of these phrases in the units mentioned. No. 6 requires some creative thinking; 'important' never appears attached to an action verb in the text.

Exercise 7

Translate:

1 We can come to collect you!
2 Is it all right if I wait here?
3 One's not allowed to sit like that.
4 Is it all right for me to take this if it has no owner?
5 Am I allowed to speak with these people?
6 One can't wear those clothes at the monastery.
7 Eating tsampa is important for Tibetans.

Language point

8 Thoughts, wishes and opinions

འདོད་པ། – mainly for expressing longer-term wishes and desires, rather than immediate ones. As in Dialogue 2, add **tö̱'** straight after an action verb, to make a phrase like **ca̱ng-tö̱'** ('wish to study'), or **la̱p-tö̱'** ('wish to tell'). Finish the sentence with a verb of existence. When action verbs which end with vowel sounds have **tö̱'** added, they gain a **n** 'suffix'-sound; e.g. **ṭo̱n-tö̱'** ('desire to go'), **ṭä̱n-tö̱'** ('desire to stay').

བསམ་ཚུལ། **sāmtshul** – an opinion or view formed over time, not an immediate reaction.

བསམ་པ་ལ་། **sāmpa-la** – preceded by 'my', 'her', etc.; for expressing thoughts and views on some matter, either longer-term, or more immediate.

…ཟེར་ན…། **. . . s̱erna . . .** preceded by a name or personal pronoun (often with the agentive particle, especially when a single syllable): followed, like **sāmpa-la**, by some thought or view. As the use of **s̱erna** suggests, the view, etc. is something articulated, so this is often used for reporting what others have expressed, e.g. 'according to Yeshe' ('Yeshe says').

Exercise 8

(For this final exercise, no transliteration is provided.)

Expand these into sentences which express the thoughts and views of these characters on the matters or people listed; e.g. for no.1, what does Lisa think is 'important'? The answer section has some suggestions, but neither they nor the dialogues give the whole picture. These characters certainly haven't expressed everything they think and feel, and may sometimes have got carried away, and said things that they don't really mean.

1	ལི་ས་ཟེར་ན……	གལ་ཆེན་པོ།
2	རྡོ་རྗེ་ཟེར་ན……	གྲོགས་པོ།
3	རྡོ་རྗེ……(+འདོད།)	ལས་འགན།
4	ཡེ་ཤེས་ཀྱི་བསམ་པ་ལ……	རིག་གཞུང་།
5	རྡོ་རྗེའི་བསམ་པ་ལ……	ཡེ་ཤེས… ཡིན་ནའང……།
6	ལི་སའི་བསམ་པ་ལ……	རྡོ་རྗེ… ཡིན་ནའང……།
7	རྡོ་རྗེ་ཟེར་ན……	ལི་ས… ཡིན་ནའང……།
8	ཡེ་ཤེས་ཀྱི་བསམ་པ་ལ……	རྡོ་རྗེ… ཡིན་ནའང……།

Oh, and finally, of course:

ཁྱེད་རང་ཟེར་ན……།

Grammar section

- Grammar summary
- Technical grammar points
- What has and has not been covered

Grammar summary

Tone (a reminder)

Tibetan is a tonal language. The system is relatively straightforward. Basically, syllables are either toned or neutral, and toned syllables are either high or low tone. Those unaccustomed to tonal systems may initially find modulating their voice uncomfortable. But it is not an optional feature; it is essential for any genuine communication.

Word order

Unlike English, the verb is always at the end of the sentence. So the arrangement is something like: 'this Tibetan is', and 'I tourist am'. When one word qualifies another, the order is essentially opposite to English. Thus adjectives go after the thing they describe (like 'people many') and demonstratives come after things they refer to (i.e. 'girl this', 'boy that').

Gender and number

Nouns have no gender and require no article (equivalents to 'a/an' etc.). Words do not indicate number; a noun has one form, used both for single and plural items. The situation is similar with verbs; the same form of a verb is used, irrespective of whether one is saying something like 'I am', or 'we are'.

Basic verb division

There is no one verb 'to be'. Basic sentences assert something either about *identity* or *existence*, so the copula verbs they use fall into either of these two categories. Identity here generally refers to more fixed features of a person or thing. Included in the existence category are the location and various temporary or subjective features of the person or thing. Copula verbs (both those of identity and existence) have no conjugation. The time-frame is understood either by context or by the addition of temporal adverbs.

Questions

There are two main ways to formulate questions: using a question-word – equivalents to 'what?', 'who?' etc. – or adding a question-particle after the verb. There are various question-particles; the one used depends on the verb. When asking a question, one follows the *rule of anticipation*. The rule is that the question must use the verb which is expected in the answer. If English had such a rule, the answer 'Yes, I am Jane.' would be preceded by the question 'Am you Jane?'

Affirmation and negation

There is no direct equivalent of the word 'yes'. To affirm something, you use the verb – as though responding 'am' to an enquiry about whether you are the Tibetan student. Likewise, there are no negation words equivalent to 'no', or 'not'. To negate something, you modify the verb, by adding the consonant **m**. The form this takes depends upon the verb, but the **m** will either be incorporated into the verb itself, or form part of a separate syllable, placed before it.

Verb features

Copula verbs basically join subjects with properties to form sentences, and vary according to the subject (i.e. whether it is I, you, etc.). But in addition, these verbs reveal something about the source of the information, the evidence for making a statement etc. ('evidentiality'). One aspect of this (featuring in the book) is that some verbs indicate that the speaker has witnessed what he or she is talking about first-hand, whereas others do not.

Implied subjects

It is extremely common to miss out the subject from a sentence (i.e. instead of 'he is here', saying something more like 'is here'). In many cases it will be clear from the auxiliary verb who or what the subject is, but context also has a large part to play.

Grammatical 'case'

Nouns don't inflect to show their grammatical function in a sentence: instead, particles are affixed to them. These work, for instance, like prepositions, such as 'to', 'at', and 'from' in English. But unlike the English, these follow rather than precede the words they refer to. So the order is more like 'Lhasa to' than 'to Lhasa'.

Action verbs - structure

Action verbs (equivalents of 'to go', 'to do', etc.) have only limited conjugation. But they are generally grouped together at the end of a sentence with a supporting ('auxiliary') verb, to form a *verb-unit*. The words used as auxiliary verbs are almost all the same as those used as copula verbs. It is the verb-units, and particularly the auxiliary verbs within them, that provide grammatical information about when and by whom the action is performed, as well as other details (e.g. evidentiality).

Action verbs - main division

The main division of action verbs is that between those showing *intentional* and *non-intentional* actions. The latter refers not just to actions done unintentionally, but also to many things counted as states or conditions in English, such as feelings, moods and impressions, over which one has no direct control. The auxiliary verbs used with the two classes of verbs differ (mainly in the first person).

Action verbs - secondary division

The second most important division of action verbs is akin to the transitive–intransitive distinction. An unusual characteristic of Tibetan (from an English perspective) is that the subject (the person or thing doing the action) is marked out in the sentence, when the action verb is transitive, by having a particle known as the *agentive particle* attached to it.

Technical grammar points

This section expands upon certain things appearing in the text, dealing with some formal grammar rules (required mainly for the written sentence), as well as certain generalisations and observations about the language.

Some particle forms

In the written sentence, the genitive particle (**telta**), introduced in Unit 3, takes different forms, depending on the final suffix of the word it is attached to:

After suffixes	འབྲེལ་སྒྲ། *form*
ད་བ་ས།	ཀྱི as a separate syllable
ག་ང།	གི ,, ,, ,, ,,
ན་མ་ར་ལ།	གྱི ,, ,, ,, ,,
འ། (and suffixless syllables)	འི། incorporated into the syllable

These rules are observed throughout the book, so there are numerous examples to refer to.

As mentioned in Unit 7, the rules of use for the agentive particle (**che̱ṭa**) are very similar:

After suffixes	བྱེད་སྒྲ། *form*
ད་བ་ས།	ཀྱིས as a separate syllable
ག་ང།	གིས ,, ,, ,, ,,
ན་མ་ར་ལ།	གྱིས ,, ,, ,, ,,
འ། (and suffixless syllables)	ས། incorporated into the syllable

Likewise, the word for 'also' varies its form:

After suffixes	*Particle form*
ག་ད་བ་ས།	ཀྱང as a separate syllable
ང་ན་མ་ར་ལ།	ཡང ,, ,, ,, ,,
འ། (and suffixless syllables)	འང incorporated into the syllable

Modal verbs (a summary of features)

Generally, these verbs:

1 have no conjugation
2 are attached to intentional verbs
3 transform the whole sentence structure into a non-intentional one
4 are not used in combination with the agentive particle
5 may have fixed auxiliaries (see Unit 15).

The rule of the 'essential' verb

Conjunctions (joining together clauses) and some other words are constructed around verbs. The conjunction **yi̱nnä:** ('but') for instance, is based on the verb **yi̱n**. As copula or auxiliary verbs, **yi̱n** and **yö̱'** are generally used only for the first person, whereas **re̱'**, **tu̱'**, etc. are used when the subject is a second or third person. However, **yi̱nnä:** is used for all persons, not just the first. This demonstrates a general pattern; **yi̱n** and **yö̱'** are the most fundamental or 'essential' verbs for expressing the concepts of identity and existence. They, or their negative forms, are the ones used to construct conjunctions (equivalents of 'if', 'when', etc.) and other words, including nouns and adjectives (e.g. **shāme'**, 'vegetarian'). Other verbs can't have particles or other words attached to them like this, so don't have the same range of functions.

Verb conjugation

As mentioned earlier, when rendering a spoken sentence in written form, you observe the written conventions. This includes the conjugation of action verbs, which plays a minor role in speech. Granted, there are sometimes variations in an action verb: with the actions of eating, watching, etc. you *hear* a difference between the past and present-future forms of the verbs. But distinguishing between these two time-frames is an isolated case. The verb-unit, and specifically the auxiliary, is obviously far more important than the main verb in indicating time (as well as aspect, evidentiality and some features of modality).

The fact that some verb-units are not limited to a single time-frame (some may be used to indicate either the past or present, for instance) means that they should not be directly equated with tenses.

The agentive particle

In line with the character of this series, the text aims to provide the learner with practical information about where the particle should be used (rather than exploring the whole range of its functions). However, a few more details here can help to develop the profile of the particle.

The transitive–intransitive distinction of verbs in English is based upon whether or not a direct object is taken. There is a similar two-fold division of action verbs in Tibetan. But the direct object is only one factor in this division. Another primary consideration is whether or not an agent is overtly involved in the action. It marks this agent with the **che̱ṭa** (agentive particle). Related to this, Tibetan is described as an 'ergative language'.

Native speakers are aware that some action verbs should, generally speaking, be used in conjunction with an agentive particle, whilst others should not (the Tibetan–English glossary will help the learner distinguish which verb is which). However, this alone cannot guarantee correct use of the agentive particle. First, as remarked in the text, even with transitive verbs, the particle is used infrequently in the present or future (and is not even used with complete consistency with transitive verbs in the past). We also saw that it has other functions, such as in the volunteering structures (Unit 10), and that in these, the transitive–intransitive distinction is irrelevant, as it is used with both transitive and intransitive verbs.

There are a few more functions, not discussed in the text, of which the learner should be aware. In sentences set in the present or future, the particle most commonly occurs when the speaker wishes to single out the one who is doing or will do the action, e.g. 'that is something that *she* will do' (as opposed to you). See also Unit 13, Exercise 8, when Duho talks about Akhu Thubten offering to take Tashi's things: '*He* says he'll do it . . .'.

As mentioned in Unit 7, the agentive particle is not just for people. The last line of Dialogue 1, Unit 11 asserts that it is the *medicine* (with an agentive particle) that will help. Linked to this, the particle also has an instrumental function. That is, it often marks the thing someone used to do an action *with*, in for example, 'they beat him with *sticks*' or 'they're eating with *their hands*'.

Of course, further subtleties of use for the agentive particle await discovery by the learner. But this summary hopefully provides a reasonable outline of the essentials.

First-person negation

On the few occasions that the negative of the first-person auxiliary for a past action does appear in written form, the preference is for writing མེད། rather than མིན། (although the sounds are hardly distinguishable). As the negation of ཡིན།, it would seem more logical to write མིན། here. The spelling མེད། aligns it more with present perfect structures. But these are not covered in the book. In using མེད། here I am simply following consensus.

Honorific terms – formation and structure

Nouns and action verbs are the two most important classes of word for expressing honorific language. Understanding some basic patterns can help in getting to grips with the register.

■ Nouns – generally follow one of two patterns:

(a) Where the honorific term is quite different from the ordinary level one – most notably the parts of the body (Unit 11), e.g. for 'eye', **cā̲n** vs. **mīk**.

(b) Where the honorific term is formed by adding one of a small number of honorific prefix-words to the ordinary one – most obvious with items of food and drink (Unit 9), e.g. for 'tea' **sō̲lcha** vs. **cha̲**.

■ Action Verbs – again, there are two patterns:

(a) With two-syllable action verbs in particular, the honorific form is often quite different from the ordinary form, e.g. 'to say', **sūngwa** vs. **la̲pa**.

(b) Compound action verbs are most often made into honorific ones by taking the appropriate honorific noun, then adding one of the main honorific verbalisers (see Unit 14).

It is sometimes also the case that one honorific verb serves as the polite form for a number of ordinary level action verbs: more than one action, for instance, is denoted by the honorific verbs ཕེབས་པ། and གཟིགས་པ།.

This book has focused upon honorific vocabulary in three areas: polite requests (Unit 5), eating and drinking (Unit 9), and the parts of the body (Unit 11). These pinpoint the areas that learners should concentrate upon. The verbs used in polite requests are probably the most commonly heard Tibetan honorific words, whereas when forming both honorific nouns and verbs, the stock vocabulary most commonly drawn from is that related to (1) parts of the body, and (2) eating and drinking.

Limitations of the transliteration

The transliteration system's job is to represent those sounds that the learner needs to know in order to communicate. Not wanting to further complicate the system, I chose not to include certain finer sound distinctions. However, these distinctions do warrant a note. In time (and with the help of the audio) the learner will hopefully come to appreciate them:

(a) In ཡོད་རེད། **yo̲re'** the vowel-sound of the first syllable is distinct, neither **o** nor **ö**.
(b) Again, neither **o** nor **ö**, but slightly different from the above, the vowel-sound in དགོས། **kö̲'** ('to want/need': Unit 9) and the first syllables in སྔོན་པོ། **ngȫnpo** and དངོས་གནས། **ngȫnä'** is a distinct sound.
(c) Nasalisation – of the type noted in Unit 2, with མིན། – is a widespread phenomenon, occurring mainly at the end of syllables ending with ན in the written form, e.g. ཡིན།.
(d) Tone contours: within the high or low tones, more subtle variations, where the sound either remains flat, rises, or falls can also, with practice, be discerned. Listen out, for example, to the contour (falling then rising) of tone in 'sorry!' (དགོངས་དག).
(e) The difference between ཨ and འ is not simply tonal: འ has some qualitative distinction to it which eludes capture in standard transliteration.

Instead of continuing with such points I shall end with an appeal to learners to appreciate the limits of a transliteration system. Sounds represented as **p** or **k** in the system may seem more like **b** and **g** to some listeners, depending on their language background. The transliteration is only a rough description.

Similarly, tone is a very real feature of Tibetan. But Tibetan has neither a formal presentation, nor a vocabulary to describe it. Tibetans may speak and hear tones perfectly, but they have not been educated to believe that the sounds of their language must accord with the high, low or neutral-tone scheme. A learner must certainly refer to this scheme, but as familiarity with the language grows, a good deal more tonal variation than it suggests probably awaits discovery.

Most importantly, the transliteration system is not prescriptive. It is not there to set boundaries for the sounds of the language. It is simply a tool, and one that should definitely be discarded at some point, if you want to experience the full richness and uniqueness of the language's sound.

The remaining numbers

As Unit 3 explained, the tens (30–90) are formed by adding 'ten' (**cū**) after each of the numbers from 3 to 9. But note the slight variations in spelling:

30 – སུམ་ཅུ། **sūmcū**	70 – བདུན་ཅུ། **tü̱ncū**
40 – བཞི་བཅུ། **shi̱pcū**	80 – བརྒྱད་ཅུ། **kyä̱cū**
50 – ལྔ་བཅུ། **ngāpcū**	90 – དགུ་བཅུ། **ku̱pcū**
60 – དྲུག་ཅུ། **ṭhu̱kcū**	

That is: the first syllables are spelt the same way as the cardinal numbers (3–9), except that the **sūm** in 30 loses its prefix. The rule for the second syllable (**cū**) is: when following a suffixless first syllable, **cū** has a prefix, but when following a first syllable with a suffix, **cū** has no prefix.

■ 100 and beyond

100 –	བརྒྱ།	**kya̱**	1000,000 –	ས་ཡ།	**sāya**
1000 –	སྟོང་ཕྲག།	**tōngṭhak**	10,000,000 –	བྱེ་བ།	**che̱wa**
10,000 –	ཁྲི།	**ṭhī**	100,000,000 –	དུང་ཕྱུར།	**thu̱ngchur**
100,000 –	འབུམ།	**pu̱m**			

When forming numbers above 100, there are two features to note:

1 The occasional use of དང་། **thang** (similar to 'and' in English numbers)
2 The occasional reversal of order

So, for exact numbers (without tens, units, etc.), one adds a cardinal number (1–9) after the thousand, million, etc., to indicate how many one means; for example:

1000 – སྟོང་ཕྲག་གཅིག **tōngṭhak-cīk**, 7,000,000 – ས་ཡ་བདུན། **sāya-tü̱n**

The exception is the hundreds. 100 is just **kya̱**, but numbers 2-9 use the reverse of the usual order (i.e. they go in front of the hundred). In the case of 200 and 300, the 2 and 3 lose their prefixes: ཉིས་བརྒྱ། **nyi̱kya**, སུམ་བརྒྱ། **sūmkya**.

Whenever the first syllable of these hundred-words has no suffix, a **p**-sound appears (from the second syllable), e.g. བཞི་བརྒྱ། **shi̱pkya**, ལྔ་བརྒྱ། **ngāpkya**, and དགུ་བརྒྱ། **ku̱pkya**.

For less exact higher numbers (with tens, units, etc.), from 101–199, **kya̱** is followed by དང་། **thang**; e.g. བརྒྱ་དང་དགུ། **kya̱-thang ku̱** (109), བརྒྱ་དང་སུམ་ཅུ་སོ་ལྔ་། **kya̱-thang sūmcu-sōnga** (135).

For numbers 201-999, དང་། **thang** is not used; e.g. ཉིས་བརྒྱ་ལྔ་བཅུ། **nyi̱kya-ngāpcū** (250). Numbers 1,001–9,999 commonly use the reverse order, and 1,000 is abbreviated to སྟོང་། **tōng**. 2 and 3 change their spelling, as with 200 and 300, and 1 also changes (to ཅིག **chīk**), e.g. སུམ་ཁྲི་གསུམ་སྟོང་། **sūmṭhī-sūmtōng** (33,000), ཅིག་སྟོང་དགུ་བརྒྱ་ལྔ་བཅུ་ང་བརྒྱད། **chīktong ku̱pkya ngāpcu-ngapkyä̱'** (1,958). This is also the way to say the year 1958.

For numbers from 100,001 and above, the usual order, rather than the reverse order is used. དང་། **thang** is also inserted, after the highest number:

འབུམ་བཞི་དང་ཁྲི་བདུན།	**pu̱m-shi̱-thang ṭhī-tü̱n**	(470,000)
ས་ཡ་ལྔ་དང་སྟོང་ཕྲག་དྲུག	**sāya-ngā-thang tōngṭhak-ṭhu̱k**	(5,006,000)

What has and has not been covered

Verbs: a framework

The following diagram illustrates the broad divisions and structure underlying the verbs:

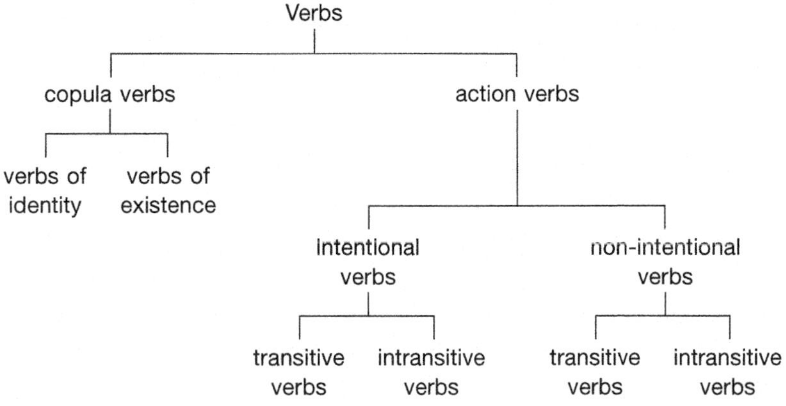

Verb choices

To clarify the point made in the introduction about the selection of material for this book: the learner needs to begin with a core group of sentence structures upon which to build. Too many choices at the start can hamper gaining command of this core group. This book is a 'Complete Course' in that it teaches more than enough for someone wishing to engage in conversations of basic and medium level. As with any standard guide to a language, it teaches the basic range of statements, questions, interjections, etc.

A learner obviously faces the normal challenges regarding the selection of sentence structure and vocabulary. But she or he is also called upon to make a number of choices that are not required in English, namely:

1 Is this something that I have first-hand experience of, or not? (the evidential perspective)
2 Is this something that I should express certainty about, or not? (see below)
3 Should I use honorific language or not?

Underlying these questions is one of this book's most fundamental lessons: that is, the answer to the question 'how do I say this in Tibetan?' is, in the majority of cases, *it depends*; further clarification about who is being spoken to (and/or about), and the speaker's relation to the content of the speech (i.e. its source, etc.) is required in most situations. All three of the above choices to some extent centre upon which verbs to use.

The major choices that this book does not ask the learner to make also represent two major perspectives within the spoken language, related to:

(a) the degree of certainty
(b) expressing newly acquired information

These are both expressed through choices of verb auxiliaries. In the case of (a), Unit 12 teaches one way that a speaker can express things to show that he or she is less than certain about them. This is perfectly adequate for many situations, but the language actually has many more degrees than this. Tibetan also has a separate form of expression for (b) a phenomenon technically known as 'mirativity'.

This is a perspective distinct from that of evidentiality, and one sometimes has to choose which of the two perspectives to take on a sentence (even though of course, the English 'translations' would be the same in both cases).

Quite aside from these two perspectives, there are numerous other aspects of the language which have not been discussed here; they will have to wait until another book.

Key to exercises

Unit 1

Exercise 1

1 1, 2 1, 3 2 (e-ni), 4 3 (shi-ka-tse), 5 2 (la-me), 6 2 (phö-kä'), 7 2 (ya-ya), 8 2 (ṭha-ṭik)

Exercise 2

(*Corrected versions in brackets*) 1 *Correct*; 2 *Incorrect* (yok-po); 3 *Correct*; 4 *Incorrect* (mang-po); 5 *Correct*; 6 *Incorrect* (shuk-chen-po); 7 *Incorrect* (ngo-shen-pa); 8 *Incorrect* (u-tang-wa); 9 *Incorrect* (nyung-nyung)

Exercise 3

(a) phām (b) ma̱ng (c) kīl (d) ngo̱m (e) lu̱ng (f) chēm (g) o̱ng

Exercise 4

1 རུལ། rü̱l; 2 ཨོན། ȫn; 3 ངས། ngä̱'; 4 ཞོན། shö̱n; 5 ཁལ། khǟl; 6 དུལ། thü̱l; 7 ཇུས། chü̱'; 8 བོལ། phö̱l; 9 ཡུན། yü̱n

Exercise 5

tāng si̱n kȫl ngä̱l tha̱ng chī' tsūm chi̱k yül hēp
ཏང་། ཟིན། ཀོལ། ངལ། དང་། ཆིས། ཙུམ། ཆིག ཡུལ། ཧེབ།:
chī' could be written: ཆིད།

Exercise 6

1 གླ། ཟླ། 2 སུང་། སྲུང་། 3 ཀྭ། ཀ། 4 ཞུར། སྦྱུར། 5 ཟློ། སློ། 6 ཙ། ཛྱ། 7 གྭ། དྲ། 8 ཚོད། ཕྱོས།
9 ཛ། ཛྱ།

Exercise 7

ས། ག ང་། པ། ཛ། ད།

Exercise 8

ko̱ ṭǟl ku̱r ngȫ’ yūk sȫl ko̱ng khyōr kāk

Exercise 9

ṭha̱ng ṭa̱ng ta̱ sǖn kya̱ co̱k tā ṭi̱ tōk kyü̱n lōng kū lāp

Exercise 10

shōk pār o̱ sēr tshȫl kǟ’ ta̱ shu̱: tȫ’ sa̱wa chīnpa
ṭä̱’ lēpa hrūk she̱pa ṭo̱wa cī ṭi̱kpa nyūng ngāte
yȫnchok mȫpa ci̱kpa ṭǖnpa tshēring phȫkä’ nāmṭhu
to̱ce nga̱nyī’ chūtshö’

Unit 2

Exercise 1

1 བསོད་ནམས་བོད་པ་རེད། sȫnam phö̱pa re̱’. Sönam is Tibetan; 2 ང་ (your name) ཡིན། nga̱ (X) yi̱n. I am (X); 3 ཁྱེད་རང་ལི་ས་རེད། khyērang li̱sa re̱’. You are Lisa; 4 མོ་རང་ཕྱི་རྒྱལ་བ་རེད། mo̱rang chīkyälwa re̱’. She is a foreigner; 5 ཁོ་རང་བསོད་ནམས་མ་རེད། khōrang sȫnam ma-re̱’. He is not Sönam.

Exercise 2

(a) ང་ཏུ་ཧོ་ཡིན། nga̱ tu̱ho yi̱n.; (b) ཁྱེད་རང་བསོད་ནམས་རེད། khyērang sȫnam re̱’.; (c) ཁོང་ལི་ས་རེད། khōng li̱sa re̱’.; (e) ཕུན་ཚོགས་བུ་མོ་མ་རེད། ཁོང་བུ་རེད། phǖntshok phu̱mo ma-re̱’. khōng phu̱ re̱’.; (f) བསོད་ནམས་ནང་པ་རེད། ཁ་ཆེ་མ་རེད། sȫnam na̱ngpa re̱’, khāche ma-re̱’.

Exercise 3

ཡིན། yi̱n; ཡིན་པས། yi̱n-pä; རེད་པས། re̱’-wä; མིན་པས། me̱-pä; མ་རེད་པས། ma-re̱’-wä; རེད། re̱

Exercise 4

(a) ཁྱེད་རང་། khyērang དེ། the̲ (b) *Adding* tsho *to words that end in a vowel sound creates an extra* n *suffix-sound in them.*

Exercise 5

2 and 4 can be translated using a verb of identity; the remainder cannot.

Exercise 6

(b) ཡ་གི་དེ་ཁང་པ་རེད། ya̲ki-the khāngpa re̲'. (c) འདི་ཚོ་མི་རེད། ti̲n-tsho mi̲ re̲'. (d) དེ་ས་རེད། the̲ sā re̲'. (e) མ་གི་དེ་འབུ་རེད། ma̲ki-the pu̲ re̲'.

Exercise 7

1 (a) That is a window. (b) You are not Phuntshok. (c) They are doctors. (d) You are Tibetan. 2 (a) དེ་སྒེའུ་ཁུང་རེད་པས། the̲ ke̲khung re̲'-wä. (b) ཁྱེད་རང་ཕུན་ཚོགས་མིན་པས། khyērang phǖntshok me̲-pä. (c) ཁོང་ཚོ་སྨན་པ་རེད་པས། khōng-tsho mǟnpa re̲'-wä. (d) ཁྱེད་རང་བོད་པ་ཡིན་པས། khyērang phö̲pa yi̲n-pä.

Unit 3

Exercise 1

(a) Person from Amdo; (b) Lhasan; (c) Mongolian; (d) Indian; (e) German; (f) Bhutanese

Exercise 2

2 ང་ཚོའི་གྲོགས་པོ། nga̲ntshö: ṭho̲kpo 3 ཁོང་གི་དགེ་རྒན། khōng-ki ke̲kän 4 ཁོང་ཚོའི་ཁྱི། khōng-tshö: khyī 5 དེ་ཁྱེད་རང་ཚོའི་དེབ་རེད། the̲ khyērang-tshö: the̲p re̲'. 6 དེ་ཚོ་ང་ཚོའི་མ་རེད། the̲ntsho nga̲ntshö: ma-re̲'.

Exercise 3

(a) ཉི་ཤུ་རྩ་གསུམ། (nyi̲shū-tsaksūm); (b) བཞི་བཅུ་ཞེ་བརྒྱད། (shi̲pcu-shepkyä̲'); (c) བརྒྱད་ཅུ་གྱ་ལྔ་། (kyä̲cu-kyangā); (d) དྲུག་ཅུ་རེ་དྲུག (ṭhu̲kcu-reṭhu̲k); (e) བདུན་

ཅུ་དོན་བདུན། (tü̱ncu-thöntü̱n); (f) ལྔ་བཅུ་ང་གཉིས། (ngāpcu-nganyī’); (g) དགུ་བཅུ་གོ་དགུ། (ku̱pcu-koku̱)

Exercise 4

1 ལྷ་ས་བ་དེ། lhāsawa the̱ 2 མོ་ཊ་དཀར་པོ་འདི། mo̱ṭa kārpo ti̱ 3 ཁམས་པ་འདི་ཚོ། khāmpa ti̱ntsho 4 སྨྱུ་གུ། nyūku 5 ཆུ་གཙང་མ་དེ། chū tsāngma the̱ 6 ལུང་པ་དེ་ཚོ། lu̱ngpa the̱ntsho

Exercise 5

1 *Sönam’s teacher* 2 *Nyima’s camera* 3 བུ་དེའི་ཁང་པ། phu̱ thä̱: khāngpa 4 མི་ཕྱུགས་པོ་དེའི་ཁང་པ། mi̱ chūkpo thä̱: khāngpa 5 ཇ་འདིའི་མིང་། cha̱ ti̱: mi̱ng

Exercise 6

(a) རེད་པ། re̱’-wa; (b) རེད་པ། re̱’-wa; (c) རེད་པ། re̱’-wa; (d) མ་རེད་པ། ma-re̱’-wa; (e) ཡིན་པ། yi̱n-pa

Exercise 7

གཟའ་ཕུར་བུ།

Unit 4

Exercise 1

2 *in India* རྒྱ་གར་ལ། kya̱kar-la; 3 *in/at this shop* ཚོང་ཁང་འདི་ལ/འདིར། tshōngkhang ti̱-la/tä̱:; 4 *at/in the two restaurants* ཟ་ཁང་གཉིས་ལ། sa̱khang nyī’-la; 5 *in that country* ལུང་པ་དེ་ལ་/དེར། lu̱ngpa the̱-la/thä̱:; 6 *in/at Lhamo’s home* ལྷ་མོའི་ནང་ལ། lhāmö:-na̱ng-la

Exercise 2

1 ང་བལ་ཡུལ་ལ་ཡོད། nga̱ phä̱lyül-la yö̱’. 2 བསོད་ནམས་འདིར་མི་འདུག sönam tä̱: min-tu̱’. 3 ལྷ་མོ་ཚོང་ཁང་ལ་འདུག་གས། lhāmo tshōngkhang-la tu̱’-kä. 4 ང་ཚོ་ནང་ལ་མེད། nga̱ntsho na̱ng-la me̱’. 5 ཁོང་ཇ་ཁང་ལ་འདུག་གས། khōng

cha̱khang-la tu̱’-kä. 6 ཁྱེད་རང་གྲོགས་པོ་མཉམ་དུ་ཡོད་པས། khyērang ṭho̱kpo nyāmtu yö̱’-pä.

Exercise 3

The subject (Tashi) is implied in lines 2, 3, 4, 6, 7, and part of 5.

Exercise 4

1 ཁྱེད་རང་ག་པར་ཡོད། khyērang kha̱wa: yö̱’. 2 མེད། ཁས་ས་ང་ཚོ་ནང་ལ་མེད། me̱’, khā̆sa nga̱ntsho na̱ng-la me̱’. 3 དེ་རིང་བཀྲ་ཤིས་ལས་ཁུངས་ལ་འདུག་གས། the̱ring ṭāshi lä̱khung-la tu̱’-kä. 4 ད་གིན་འདིར་མི་ལྔ་འདུག ད་ལྟ་མི་བཞི་འདུག tha̱ncin tä̱: mi̱ ngā tu̱’. tha̱nta mi̱ shi̱ tu̱’. 5 དེ་དུས་ཁྱེད་རང་གི་གྲོགས་པོ་ག་པར་འདུག thethü̱’ khyērang-ki ṭho̱kpo kha̱wa: tu̱’.

Exercise 5

2 སྨན་ཁང་དངུལ་ཁང་གི་རྒྱབ་ལོགས་ལ་འདུག ṭa̱khang ngūlkhang-ki kya̱plo-la tu̱’. 3 དགོན་པ་རིའི་རྒྱབ་ལོགས་ལ་འདུག ko̱mba ri̱: kya̱plo-la tu̱’. (*i.e. partly obscured by smaller hill*) 4 ཟ་ཁང་དངུལ་ཁང་གི་འཁྲིས་ལ་འདུག sa̱khang ngūlkhang-ki ṭhī-la tu̱’. 5 གླང་འཁོར་འབབ་ཚུགས་མགྲོན་ཁང་གི་མདུན་ལ་འདུག lāngkhor-pa̱ptshuk ṭö̱nkhang-ki tü̱n-la tu̱’.

Exercise 6

(a) སྨན་ཁང་ལ་ཕེབས། ṭa̱khang-la phēp. (b) དངུལ་ཁང་ལ་ཕེབས། དེ་ཟ་ཁང་གི་འཁྲིས་ལ་འདུག ngūlkhang-la phēp. the̱ sa̱khang-ki ṭhī-la tu̱’. (c) ཕ་གིར་མགྲོན་ཁང་འདུག་ག ཚོང་ཁང་དེའི་རྒྱབ་ལོགས་ལ་འདུག phākä: ṭö̱nkhang tu̱’-ka. tshōngkhang the̱: kya̱plo-la tu̱’. (d) ཕ་གིར་རི་འདུག་ག ཁོང་གི་ཁང་པ་དེའི་སྒང་ལ་འདུག phākä: ri̱ tu̱’-ka. khōng-ki khāngpa the̱: ka̱ng-la tu̱’.

Exercise 7

(b) ཏུ་ཧོ་ལ་ཁ་དཔར་/སྨྱུ་གུ་/ཆུ་ཡོད་རེད། tu̱ho-la khāpa/nyūku/chū yo̱re. (c) ཏུ་ཧོ་ལ་ཀོ་རི་ཡའི་གྲོགས་པོ་ཡོད་རེད། tu̱ho-la kōriyä: ṭho̱kpo yo̱re. (d) ཚོང་པ་དེ་ལ་བུ་/ཚོང་ཁང་/ཟ་ཁང་ཡོད་རེད། tshōngpa the̱-la phu̱/tshōngkhang/sa̱khang yo̱re’.

Exercise 8

(a) ཇོ་ལགས། chọla: (b) བུ་མོ། phụmo (c) ཁོང་། khōng (d) *A kinship term should not be used; for the appropriate address, see Unit 14.*

Unit 5

Exercise 1

(a) དགེ་རྒན། kẹkän + སློབ་ཕྲུག lōpṭhuk; རྒན་འཁོགས། kạ̈nkhōk + གཞོན་གཞོན། shọ̈nshön; ཕ་མ། phāma + ཕྲུ་གུ། phūku (b) *teachers to students – orders, e.g.* ཤོག shōk; *students to teachers – formal, e.g.* རོགས་གནང་། rọ-nāng; *elders to young – orders or neutral; young to elders – neutral or formal; parents to children – orders or neutral; children to parents – neutral or formal.*

Exercise 2

1 ནང་ལ་ཕེབས་རོགས། nạng-la phēp-rọ. 2 དངུལ་ང་ལ་བསྟན་ཨང་། ngǖl ngạ-la tǟn-a. 3 ཕ་གིར་མ་འགྲོ phākä: ma-ṭọ. 4 འདིར་བཞུགས། tạ̈: shụ: 5 འདི་བཞེས་རོགས་གནང་། tị shẹ-rọ-nāng.

Exercise 3

བཀྲ་ཤིས་དེར་འདུག ṭāshi thạ̈: tụ'.; ཁོ་རང་ལ་ཁ་ལག་འདུག khōrang-la khālak tụ'.; ཁ་ལག་དེ་ཞིམ་པོ་འདུག khālak-the shịmpo tụ'.; ཚ་པོ་འདུག tshāpo tụ'.' ཇ་ལ་འབུ་འདུག chạ-la pụ tụ'.

Exercise 4

2 རྒྱགས་ག། kyạka རྒྱགས་ཤོས། kyạkshȫ' 3 ལས་སླ་པ། lạ̈lāwa/lạ̈lā: ལས་སླ་ཤོས། lạ̈lāshȫ' 4 སྐྱིད་པ། kyīwa སྐྱིད་ཤོས། kyīpshȫ' 5 དྲོ་པ། ṭhọwa དྲོ་ཤོས། ṭhọshȫ' 6 ཤུགས་ཆེ་པ། shūk-chē: ཤུགས་ཆེ་ཤོས། shūk-chēshȫ'

Exercise 5

1 Sönam is older than Tashi. 2 The hotel is further than the monastery. 3 There are fewer chairs than people. 4 There are more people in

China than in America. 5 The outside of that building is more attractive than the inside.

Exercise 6

(a) *1 requires a verb of identity;* tu̱' *cannot be used: 2 and 4 could use* tu̱'. (b) *Using* tu̱' *in 2 and 4 would tell us that the speaker has discovered the things reported (probably recently), through first-hand experience.*

Exercise 7

(a) ཕུ་ཆུང་རྣམ་རྒྱལ་ལས་ལོ་ཆུང་ང་རེད། phu̱chung nāmkyäl-lä lo̱-chūngnga re̱'. (b) རྣམ་རྒྱལ་ཕུ་ཆུང་ལས་ལོ་ཆེ་བ་རེད། nāmkyäl phu̱chung-lä lo̱-chē: re̱'. (c) བློ་གྲོས་ལོ་ཆེ་ཤོས་རེད། lōṭhö' lo̱-chēshö' re̱'. (d) བློ་གྲོས་རྣམ་རྒྱལ་ལས་གཟུགས་པོ་རིང་ང་འདུག lōṭhö' nāmkyäl-lä su̱kpo-ri̱ngnga tu̱'. (e) རྣམ་རྒྱལ་བློ་གྲོས་ལས་གཟུགས་པོ་ཐུང་ང་འདུག nāmkyäl lōṭhö'-lä su̱kpo-thūngnga tu̱'. (f) ཕུ་ཆུང་གཟུགས་པོ་རིང་པོ་མི་འདུག phu̱chung su̱kpo-ri̱ngpo min-tu̱'.

Unit 6

Exercise 1

1 ང་ཁོ་ལ་དགའ་པོ་ཡོད། nga̱ khō-la ka̱po yö̱'. 2 ང་ཚོ་ལས་ཀ་ལ་དགའ་པོ་མེད། nga̱ntsho lä̱ka-la ka̱po me̱'. 3 ཁྱེད་རང་སུ་ལ་དགའ་བ་ཡོད། khyērang sū-la ka̱: yö̱'. 4 ཁྱེད་རང་ཁང་མིག་ཆེ་བ་ལ་དགའ་བ་ཡོད་པས། khyērang khāngmik chē:-la ka̱: yö̱'-pä. 5 བསོད་ནམས་ས་ཆ་ཁུ་སིམ་པོ་ལ་དགའ་པོ་ཡོད་རེད། བཀྲ་ཤིས་(ས་ཆ་ཁུ་སིམ་པོ་ལ་)དགའ་པོ་ཡོད་མ་རེད། sȫnam sācha khūsimpo-la ka̱po yo̱re'. ṭashi (sācha khūsimpo-la) ka̱po yo̱ ma-re̱'. 6 ཁྱེད་རང་བོད་ཇ་ལ་དགའ་པོ་ཡོད་པས། khyērang phö̱cha-la ka̱po yö̱'-pä.

Exercise 2

1 What/which colour do you like? 2 What colour is your chair? 3 How many colours are there in this book?

Exercise 3

This song (both); Indian food (ka̱po); *large hotels* (ka̱po); *today's picnic (adjective-tu̱'); this book (both); Tashi's paternal aunt (both)*

Exercise 4

ང་ཁ་ལག་འདི་ལ་དགའ་པོ་ཡོད། nga̱ khālak-ti̱-la ka̱po yö̱'/དགའ་པོ་ཏོག་ཙམ་ཡོད། ka̱po tēts yö̱'/དགའ་པོ་ཞེ་དྲག་ཡོད། ka̱po she̱ṭhak yö̱'; ཁ་ལག་འདི་ག་འདྲ་ཞིམ་པོ་འདུག khālak-ti̱ kha̱nṭa shi̱mpo tu̱'.

ང་མི་དེ་ལ་དགའ་པོ་མེད། nga̱ mi̱-the̱-la ka̱po me̱'/དགའ་པོ་ཙ་ནས་མེད།/ka̱po tsa̱nä me̱'/མི་དེ་ག་འདྲ་སྡུག་ཆགས་འདུག mi̱-the̱ kha̱nṭa tu̱kcāk tu̱.

Exercise 5

1 *These days that man is a civil servant.* 2 *Lhamo has so many children!* 3 *Tenzin was in Kham when he was five.* 4 སྔོན་མར་ང་གཉིས་ཀ་སློབ་གྲྭ་དེ་ལ་ཡོད། ngǟnma nga̱ nyī'ka lōpṭha the̱-la yö̱'. 5 ང་སྔོན་མར་རྒྱ་མིའི་ཁ་ལག་ལ་དགའ་པོ་མེད། ཡིན་ནའང་འདི་ཞིམ་པོ་ཞེ་དྲག་འདུག nga̱ ngǟnma kya̱mi: khālak-la ka̱po me̱'. yi̱nnä ti̱ shi̱mpo she̱ṭhak tu̱'. 6 སྔོན་མར་ཉི་མ་ལ་ཨ་རིའི་དགའ་པོ་ཡོད་རེད། ngǟnma nyi̱ma-la āri: ka̱po yo̱re'. 7 ད་གིན་ཁྱེད་རང་དངུལ་ཁང་ལ་མེད་པས། tha̱ncin khyērang ngǖlkhang-la me̱'-pä. 8 ཕ་གིར་མི་གཅིག་འདུག་ག སྔོན་མར་ཁོ་རང་སྐད་གྲགས་ཆེན་པོ་རེད། phākä: mi̱ cīk tu̱'-ka, ngǟnma khōrang kǟṭhak-chēnpo re̱'.

Exercise 8

1 No, we don't. 2 Two: Tashi and Dölma. 3 It's difficult for the speaker to spend time with his best friend, Tashi. 4 Dölma, who goes out with Tashi, was once the speaker's girlfriend, but now she doesn't like him. This makes meeting Tashi difficult.

Exercise 9

The picnic yesterday was good. Many of my friends and acquaintances were there, but Tashi wasn't. Tashi is my best friend. [Things] are more fun when Tashi's there. When we were children, we were always together. But these days Tashi has a new girlfriend. Her name is ‘Dölma’. I used to have a girlfriend. And her name? . . . Yes, ‘Dölma’. Tashi’s new girlfriend used to be my girlfriend. And now, Dölma doesn’t like me. I am Tashi’s best friend. But these days it’s a little difficult.

Unit 7

Exercise 1

ང་…ཡོང་མེད། nga̱ . . . yo̱ng-me̱; ལྟ་བ་…མ་ཡོང་བ་རེད། ta̱wa . . . ma-yo̱ngwa-re̱’; ང་ཚོ་…ཉལ་བ་ཡིན། nga̱ntsho . . . nyä̱lwa-yi̱n; ཡེ་ཤེས་དང་སྒྲོལ་མ་…བསྡད་པ་རེད། ye̱shē’ thang ṭö̱lma . . . tä̱wa-re’; ཁྱེད་རང་ཚོ་…བསྡད་པ་ཡིན་པས། khyērang-tsho . . . tä̱wa-yi̱n-pä

ཕྱིན་པ་མེད། chīnpa-me̱ is false

Exercise 2

1 I stayed in a hotel. 2 She went to the Tibetan restaurant. 3 Why did you come early? 4 Don’t sit on the ground! 5 Where did you sleep last night?

Exercise 3

Underlined – verbs in Tibetan. Bold – first-hand experience verbs.

> *“Last night I got back home early. Yeshe* ***came*** *to my place at about seven. He also came to my place the night before, but I was not there. My neighbour saw him, and* ***told*** *me he had been there. Last night Yeshe (****drank****) and I drank tea and talked for a while. I asked if he would go to see Sönam later. But he* ***said*** *he was not well. He* ***went*** *home. At least that is where he* ***said*** *he was going. . . . .”*

Exercise 4

1 I didn’t go home. 2 Did you [plural] go to China? 3 At whose place did that man sleep? 4 I stayed yesterday, didn’t I? 5 Did you go for a stroll? 6 I didn’t go in the mountains.

(a) 3 and 5 are also wrong. (b) 1 མེད། me̱; 3 རེད་/སོང་། re̱'/sōng; 5 ཕྱིན་པ་ཡིན་པས། chīnpa yi̱n-pä. (c) 1 because it's a first-person action (past: negation); 3 because it's a third-person action. Depending on whether the person asked is assumed to have experienced it first-hand or not, there are two alternatives; 5 because the question, posed to a second person, follows the rule of anticipation.

Exercise 5

1 ཁྱེད་རང་གུང་སེང་ལ་ག་དུས་ཕྱིན་པ་ཡིན། khyērang ku̱ngseng-la kha̱thü' chīnpa-yi̱n. 2 ཁས་ས་ང་དེར་བསྡད་པ་ཡིན། ཡིན་ནའང་དེ་རིང་བསྡད་མེད། khǟsa nga̱ thä̱: tä̱wa-yi̱n. yi̱nnä the̱ring tä̱-me̱. 3 ཁང་པ་སྙིང་པ་དེའི་ནང་ལ་མ་འགྲོ། khāngpa nyīngpa the̱: na̱ng-la ma-ṭo̱. 4 ལམ་ཁ་ཡག་པོ་མི་འདུག ང་ཚོ་ཕྱིན་མེད། la̱mkha ya̱kpo min-tu̱', nga̱ntsho chīn-me̱. 5 བཀྲ་ཤིས་ཁོ་རང་གི་ཨ་ཅག་གི་རྩ་ལ་ཉལ་བ་རེད། ṭashi khōrang-ki āca-ki tsā-la nyä̱lwa-re̱'. 6 ང་ལས་ཀ་ལ་ཕྱིན་མེད། གཟའ་སྤེན་པ་རེད། nga̱ lä̱ka-la chīn-me̱ sa̱-pēnpa re̱'.

Exercise 6

(a) *Duho doesn't use the responses when telling Yeshe that they arrived just the day before, nor when answering Yeshe's next question. This is because the responses described are mainly for 'yes' or 'no'-type questions. Yeshe's questions aren't like this.* (b) *Duho adds* ལགས། la: *to one answer. In another, he uses the polite* གསུངས།.

Exercise 7

Dialogue 1 – none; Dialogue 2 – 'to give', 'to explain/describe', 'to work'.

Exercise 8

1 ཁྱེད་རང་གིས། khyērang-ki̱' 2 ང་ཚོས། nga̱ntshȫ' 3 ང་ཚོའི་ཕ་མས། nga̱ntshö: phāmǟ:' 4 གཞུང་གིས། shu̱ng-ki̱' 5 མོ་ཊ་དེས། mo̱ṭa-the̱' 6 ལྟ་བ་དང་ཕུན་ཚོགས་ཀྱིས། ta̱wa-thang phǖntshok-ki̱'

Unit 8

Exercise 1

1 I shan't stay at home tomorrow. 2 Where will your friend go? 3 Who's sleeping in the smallest room? 4 When will you (plural) return? 5 That person won't give/pay the money.

Exercise 2

(a) ཆུ་ཚོད་བརྒྱད་པ་ཡོལ་ནས་སྐར་མ་ལྔ། chūtshö kyäpa yöl-nä kārma ngā; (b) ཆུ་ཚོད་ལྔ་དང་སྐར་མ་སུམ་ཅུ་སོ་ལྔ། chūtshö ngā-thang kārma sūmcu-songā; (c) ཆུ་ཚོད་དྲུག་པ་ཡོལ་སོང་། chūtshö ṭhukpa yöl-sōng; (d) ཆུ་ཚོད་གཉིས་པ་ཡོལ་ནས་སྐར་མ་ཉི་ཤུ། chūtshö nyīpa yöl-nä kārma nyishu. (e) ཆུ་ཚོད་བཅུ་གཅིག་ཙམ། chūtshö cūcīk-ts.

Exercise 3

1 མོ་རང་(གིས་)ད་ལྟ་ག་རེ་བྱེད་ཀྱི་འདུག moranq(-ki') thanta khare chiki-tu'. 2 ཁོང་ཚོས་ང་སྐད་བཏང་སོང་། ཡིན་ནའང་ང་ཕྱིན་མེད། khōng-tshȫ' nga kǟ tāng-song. yinnä nga chīn-me. 3 ཁོ་རང་ཚོས་སྐད་ག་རེ་རྒྱག་གི་འདུག khōrang-tshȫ' kǟ' khare kyaki-tu'. 4 མོ་ཊ་ལ་ང་ཁྱེད་རང་མཉམ་དུ་བསྡད་ཀྱི་ཡིན། moṭa-la nga khyērang nyāmtu täki-yin. 5 བསྟན་འཛིན་འདིར་མི་འདུག་གས། འོ་ན་ང་བསྒུག་གི་ཡིན། tēntsin tä: min-tu'-kä. ona nga kuki-yin. 6 ཉོ་ཆ་ཁྱེད་རང་གིས་བརྒྱབ་པ་རེད། ཁ་ལག་ང་རང་བཟོ་གི་ཡིན། nyopcha khyērang-ki' kyapa-re'. khālak ngarang soki-yin.

Exercise 4

(a) ཆུ་ཚོད་བཅུ་པ་ལ་…ང་ལས་ཀ་བྱེད་ཀྱི་ཡིན། chūtshö' cūpa-la . . . nga läka cheki-yin. (b) ཆུ་ཚོད་བཅུ་གཅིག་དང་ཕྱེད་ཀ་ལ་…ཁྱེད་རང་ཁ་ལག་བཟའ་གི་རེད། chūtshö' cūcīk-thang chēka-la . . . khyērang khālak saki-re'. (c) ཆུ་ཚོད་ལྔ་པ་ཡོལ་ནས་སྐར་མ་བཅུ་ལ་…ང་ཚོ་འདིར་མེད། chūtshö' ngāpa yöl-nä kārma cū-la . . . ngantsho tä: me'. (d) ཆུ་ཚོད་གཉིས་པ་ལ་…ཟླ་བ་ཟ་ཁང་ལ་ཕྱིན་པ་རེད། chūtshö' nyīpa-la . . . tawa sakhang-la chīnpa-re'. (e) ད་ལྟ་…ཁྱེད་རང་འདིར་ཡོང་གི་ཡིན་པས། thanta . . . khyērang tä: yōngki-yin-pä. (f) དགོང་དག་ཆུ་ཚོད་བཅུ་གཅིག་ལ་…ནང་ལ་རྒྱུགས། kongthak chūtshö' cūcīk-la . . . nang-la kyuk.

Exercise 5

1 ང་ཁྱེད་རང་གི་ལས་ཁུངས་ལ་ཡོང་གི་ཡིན། nga̱ khyērang-ki lä̱khung-la yo̱ngki-yi̱n. ཆུ་ཚོད་གཉིས་པ་ཡོལ་ནས་སྐར་མ་བཅོ་ལྔ་ལ་ཡོང་གི་ཡིན། chūtshö' nyīpa yö̱l-nä kārma cōngā-la yo̱ngki-yi̱n. དེའི་བར་དུ་ལས་ཀ་བྱེད་ཀྱི་ཡིན། the̱: pha̱rthu lä̱ka che̱ki-yi̱n. 2 དེ་རིང་ང་ལ་དུས་ཚོད་མེད། the̱ring nga̱-la thü̱tshȫ' me̱'. སང་ཉིན་ཞོགས་པར་ང་ནང་ལ་བསྡད་ཀྱི་ཡིན། sāngnyin sho̱kpa nga̱ na̱ng-la tä̱ki-yi̱n. ཆུ་ཚོད་བཅུ་གཅིག་ལ་ཕེབས་ཤོག chūtshö' cūcīk-la phēp-shōk. 3 ང་ད་ལྟ་ཟ་ཁང་ལ་ཡོད། nga̱ tha̱nta sa̱khang-la yö̱'. ང་ངོ་ཤེས་པ་གཅིག་མཉམ་དུ་ཡོད། nga̱ ngo̱shēnpa cīk nyāmtu yö̱'. ཆུ་ཚོད་བདུན་པའི་སྔོན་ལ་ཤོག chūtshö' tü̱npä: ngȫn-la shōk.

Exercise 6

(a) ང་མགྲོན་ཁང་ཆེན་པོ་དེ་ལ་བསྡད་ཀྱི་མེད། གང་ཡིན་ཟེར་ན། དེ་གོང་ཆེན་པོ་རེད། nga̱ ṭö̱nkhang chēnpo the̱-la tä̱ki-me̱:, kha̱ngyin-se̱rna the̱ ko̱ngchēnpo re̱'. (b) ང་གྲོགས་པོའི་རྩ་ལ་འགྲོ་གི་ཡིན། གང་ཡིན་ཟེར་ན། ང་ལ་དུས་ཚོད་སྟོང་པ་ཡོད། nga̱ ṭho̱kpö: tsa̱-la ṭo̱ki-yi̱n, kha̱ngyin-se̱rna nga̱-la thü̱tshȫ' tōngpa yö̱'. (c) ང་གླིང་ཁ་ལ་འགྲོ་གི་ཡིན། གང་ཡིན་ཟེར་ན། དེ་རིང་གུང་སེང་རེད། nga̱ līngka-la ṭo̱ki-yi̱n, kha̱ngyin-se̱rna the̱ring ku̱ngseng re̱'. (d) ང་བསྟན་འཛིན་ལ་དངུལ་དེ་སྤྲད་ཀྱི་མེད། གང་ཡིན་ཟེར་ན། ང་ལ་དངུལ་མེད། nga̱ tēntsin-la ngǖl-the̱ ṭǟki-me̱:, kha̱ngyin-se̱rna nga̱-la ngǖl me̱'. (e) ང་བོད་ཀྱི་ཟ་ཁང་དེ་ལ་ཁ་ལག་བཟའ་གི་ཡིན། གང་ཡིན་ཟེར་ན། ང་བོད་ཀྱི་ཁ་ལག་ལ་དགའ་པོ་ཡོད། nga̱ phö̱ki-sa̱khang the̱-la khālak sa̱ki-yi̱n, kha̱ngyin-se̱rna nga̱ phö̱ki-khālak-la ka̱po yö̱'.

Exercise 7

1 *There was confusion about why Duho was going to the airport; Tshering Dolkar assumed he was catching a flight.* 2 *Duho either misheard or mistook the phrase* āle-tha̱ngpo *as a reference to a specific time. Tshering Dolkar decides that a face-to-face conversation might lead to less confusion, and suggests Duho visit the office.*

Suggestions: (a) Rather than just stating his destination, Duho should perhaps have volunteered more information about the purpose of his trip. (b) Duho probably needs to pay a bit more attention.

Exercise 8

(a) དགོང་དག་ཆུ་ཚོད་བདུན་དང་ཕྱེད་ཀ་ལ་ཨེ། ko̲ngthak chūtshö' tü̲n-thang chēka-la-ē. (b) རླངས་འཁོར་འབབ་ཚུགས་ལ་ཨེ། lāngkhor pa̲ptshuk-la-ē. (c) འབབ་ཚུགས་ཀྱི་མདུན་ལ་ཨེ། pa̲ptshuk-ki tü̲n-la-ē.

Unit 9

Exercise 1

1 ཁྱེད་རང་ལ་རྐུབ་བཀྱག་དགོས་པས། khyērang-la kūpkyak kö̲'-pä. 2 ང་ལ་ཁོང་ཆུང་ང་དེ་དགོས། nga̲-la kho̲ng-chūngnga the̲ kö̲'. 3 ཁྱེད་རང་ལ་(ཁ་ལག་)འདི་ཏོག་ཙམ་དགོས་པས། ཞིམ་པོ་འདུག khyērang-la (khālak) ti̲ tēts kö̲'-pä. shi̲mpo tu̲'. 4 *Do you want help (can I help you)?* 5 *I don't want a separate room.*

Exercise 2

(a) ཁྱེད་རང་ལ་ག་རེ་དགོས། khyērang-la kha̲re kö̲'. (b) འབྲས་བརྗོས/ཞོ་/ཇ་འདུག་གས། ṭä̲ngȫ'/sho̲/cha̲ tu̲'-kä. (c) ང་ལ་འབྲས་དང་ཞོ་དགོས། nga̲-la ṭä̲'-thang sho̲ kö̲'.

Exercise 3

(a) ང་རོགས་པ་བྱེད་གར་ཡོང་གི་ཡིན། nga̲ ro̲kpa-che̲ka yo̲ngki-yi̲n. *I'm coming to help*. (b) ཁོ་རང་གིས་ཁ་ལག་མངགས་ནས་བཟས་སོང་། khōrang-ki̲' khālak ngāk-nä sä̲-song. *He ordered food then ate*. (c) གནམ་གྲུ་ཁས་ས་བབ་ནས་དེ་རིང་འཕུར་བ་རེད། nāmṭhu khä̆sa pha̲p-nä the̲ring phīrwa-re̲'. *The plane landed yesterday, and took off [again] today*. (d) ང་མ་ཉལ་ནས་འགྲོ་གི་ཡིན། nga̲ ma-nyä̲l-nä ṭo̲ki-yi̲n. *I'm going without having slept [i.e. foregoing sleep]*. (e) ངས་དངུལ་མ་སྤྲད་ནས་ཟློས་གར་ཁང་(གི་)ནང་ལོགས་ལ་ཕྱིན་པ་ཡིན། ngä̲' ngü̆l ma-ṭä̆-nä tö̲karkhāng(-ki) na̲nglo-la chīnpa-yin. *I went into the theatre without giving money/paying*.

Exercise 4

1 ཁོས་གང་ཡང་མ་ལབ་ནས་ཕྱིན་/འགྲོ་སོང་། khȫ' khä̱: ma-la̱p-nä ṭo̱/chīn-song. 2 ང་ཚོ་ཟ་ཁང་ལ་བསྡད་ནས་སྐད་ཆ་བཤད་པ་ཡིན། nga̱ntsho sa̱khang-la tä̱-nä kǟcha shǟpa-yi̱n. 3 ང་མགྲོན་ཁང་བཙལ་གར་འགྲོ་གི་ཡིན། nga̱ ṭö̱nkhang tshǟlka ṭo̱ki-yi̱n. 4 ང་ལ་ཁ་ལག་མི་དགོས། ངས་གཅིག་བཟས་ནས་(འདིར་)ཡོང་བ་ཡིན། nga̱-la khālak mo-kö̱'. ngä̱' cīk sä̱-nä (tä̱:) yo̱ngwa-yi̱n. 5 ཉི་མས་ཐུག་པ་གཉིས་མངགས་ནས་གཅིག་ང་ལ་སྤྲད་སོང་། nyimä̱' thūkpa nyī' ngāk-nä cīk nga̱-la ṭǟ'-sōng.

Exercise 5

1 Tibetans don't like meat – false 2 Tibetans prefer (drinking) tea to milk – true 3 Tibetans make beer in their homes – true 4 Tibetans never eat with their hands – false 5 Tibetans don't eat many sweet things – true 6 Tibetans have more yoghurt than (Han) Chinese – true

Exercise 6

1 *Decline politely, such as with* ལགས་མིན། la̱-me̱: *(and probably an excuse).* 2 ཞལ་ལག་མཉེས་པོ་གནང་གོ། shä̱lak nyēpo nāng-ko. 3 འགྲིགས་སོང་ལགས། ṭi̱k-sōng la:. 4 *One might say* འགྲིགས་སོང་། ṭi̱k-sōng, *but if things are very informal,* མི་དགོས། mo-kö̱' *or even* ང་བཟའ་གི་མིན། nga̱ sa̱ki-me̱: *would be acceptable.* 5 འོ་ཡ། o̱ya. 6 *There is no special response; one might say something like* འོ་ཡ། o̱ya, *but not* ཐུགས་རྗེ་ཆེ། thūce-chē.

Exercise 7

1 Some foreigners. 2 **A.** What are they eating? **B.** It's called 'salad'. **A.** 'Salad' is it? **B.** Yes, foreigners eat a lot of green vegetables. **A.** I see. They aren't tasty for us Tibetans, are they? **B.** No. In our area we give that sort of vegetation to the animals. **A.** And what are they drinking? **B.** That's a soft drink (*lit.* 'sweet water'). **A.** Why are they drinking children's drinks? **B.** No idea! 3 The two mentioned just prior to Exercise 5.

Unit 10

Exercise 1

2 ཇ་གཅིག་ལ་སྐོར་མོ་ལྔ་རེད། cha-cīk-la kormo ngā re'. 3 དེ་མི་དགོས། ལྕང་ཀུ་དེ་ལ་ག་ཚོད་རེད། the mo-kö'. canku the-la khatshȫ' re'. 4 འདི་ང་ལ་འཚོང་རོགས་བྱེད། ti nga-la tshōng ro-chi'. 5 ཐུག་པ་ལ་ངས་སྐོར་མོ་བཅུ་བཞི་སྤྲད་པ་ཡིན། thūkpa-la ngä' kormo cūpshi ṭā̈pa-yin. 6 ཅོག་ཙེ་དེ་(སྐོར་མོ་)ག་ཚོད་ལ་བཙོང་གི་ཡིན། cōktse the (kormo) khatshȫ'-la tsōngki-yin. 7 ཁོ་རང་གི་མོ་ཊ་ཉིན་མ་གཉིས་ལ་གཡར་བ་ཡིན། khōrang-ki moṭa nyima nyī'-la yārwa-yin.

Exercise 2

1 ཡིན། yin, མི min *I'll buy noodles, because we don't have any at home.* 2 ཀར། ka, ལས་ lä *I'm not going (out) to buy that now, because I have work.* 3 སྔོན་པོ་ ngōnpo, ཡོད། yö' *I didn't buy the blue one, because I don't like blue. I prefer red.* 4 མེད། me:, ཤ་ shā *I'm not going to buy them shaphaklep, because they don't eat meat.* 5 ནས་ nä, ཆུང་ང་། chūng-nga *I'm going to buy from him, because his things are cheaper.*

Exercise 3

(a) Today I went to the market, to do some shopping. I bought some pork for Tashi, because Tashi especially likes pork. I also bought some good vegetables. I paid 6 yuan for some carrots. After shopping, I went to borrow a film. They charge (take) seven yuan a day for each film. But when I went, they did not have any good ones; I didn't borrow any. (b) 1 ཁྲོམ་ལ་ – *'to' (location)*; 2 བཀྲ་ཤིས་ལ་ – *'for' (a person)*; 3 ཕག་ཤ་ལ་ – *marking the object for 'like'*; 4 ཀུང་ལ་ཐུག་ལ་ – *'for' (rate)*; 5 ཉིན་མ་གཅིག་ལ་ – *'for' (time period)*; 6 ཁོ་ཚོ་ལ་ལྟད་མོ་ – *indicating the person who 'has'*.

Exercise 4

(a) I'll tell Phuntshok! (b) I'll give it at seven o'clock! (c) I'll give them a ring! (d) Let me help you! (e) I don't have time today. I'll go tomorrow!

Exercise 5

1 ད་ང་(ནང་ལ་)ལོག་གི་ཡིན། tha̱ nga̱ (na̱ng-la) lo̱ki-yi̱n. 2 ངས་བླུག་དགོས། ngä̱’ lūk-ko̱. 3 ང་ཉོ་གི་མིན། nga̱ nyo̱ki-me̱:. 4 ད་ང་འགྲོ་གི་ཡིན། tha̱ nga̱ ṭo̱ki-yi̱n. 5 ངས་བསྡད་དགོས། ngä̱’ tä̱-ko̱.

Exercise 6

1 (ཁྱེད་རང་གིས་)དེ་སུའི་རྩ་ནས་ཉོས་པ་ཡིན། (khyērang-ki̱’) the̱ sǖ: tsa̱-nä nyö̱wa-yi̱n. 2 ཚོང་པ་ལ་བསིལ་མ་མི་འདུག ཁྱེད་རང་ལ་ཡོད་པས། tshōngpa-la sīlma min-tu̱’. khyērang-la yö̱’-pä. 3 ཅ་ལག་འདི་གཞན་དག་དེ་ཚོ་ལས་གོང་ཁེ་པ་རེད། cālak ti̱ shä̱nthak the̱ntsho-lä kho̱ng-khe̱wa re̱’. 4 ཁོ་རང་ཚོ་དེ་ག་ཚོད་ལ་འཚོང་གི་ཡོད་རེད། khōrangtsho the̱ kha̱tshȫ’-la tshōngki-yo̱re’. 5 ངས་དེབ་དེ་ཉོས་མེད། གོང་ཆེན་པོ་ཞེ་དྲག་འདུག ngä̱’ the̱p-the nyö̱-me̱ khōng-chēnpo she̱thak tu̱’. 6 ཕོར་པ་འདི་ཚོ་ཚང་མ་འདྲ་པོ་འདུག phōrpa ti̱ntsho tshāngma ṭa̱po tu̱’. 7 ཕྱུ་པ་ག་གི་ཉོ་གི་ཡིན། chūpa kha̱khi nyo̱ki-yi̱n.

Exercise 7

2 རྡུ་ཧོ་ཕྱུ་པ་རྩ་ནས་གྱོན་གྱི་ཡོད་མ་རེད། tu̱ho chūpa tsā-nä kö̱nki yo̱-ma-re̱’. 3 སྤེན་པ་མཚམས་མཚམས་(ལ་)རྩམ་པ་ཉོ་གི་ཡོད་རེད། pēnpa tshāmtshām(-la) tsāmpa nyo̱ki-yo̱re’. 4 རྡུ་ཧོ་ནམ་རྒྱུན་ཀོ་རི་ཡ་ལ་སྡོད་ཀྱི་ཡོད་རེད། tu̱ho na̱mkyun kōriya-la tä̱ki-yo̱re’. 5 རྡུ་ཧོ་མཚམས་མཚམས་(ལ་)ཁྲོམ་ནས་དུག་སློག་ཉོ་གི་ཡོད་རེད། tu̱ho tshāmtshām(-la) ṭhōm-nä thu̱klōk nyo̱ki-yo̱re’. 6 ནམ་རྒྱུན་རྒྱ་མིའི་ཚོང་པ་བོད་སྐད་རྒྱག་གི་ཡོད་མ་རེད། na̱mkyun kya̱mi: tshōngpa phö̱kǟ’ kya̱ki yo̱-ma-re̱’.

Exercise 8

(a) *With a friend, the request-endings* རོགས་བྱེད། ro-chi̱, དང་། thang, *and* ཨང་། a *are likely. What follows is for the sake of practice – one probably wouldn’t actually add a request-ending after every instruction, or say* the̱-nä *each time.*

1 དང་པོར་སྒྲོལ་མའི་རྩ་ལ་འགྲོ་རོགས་བྱེད། མོ་རང་ལ་སྐོར་མོ་དགུ་བཅུ་སྤྲོད། tha̱ngpo ṭö̱lmä: tsā-la ṭo̱-ro-chi̱. mo̱rang-la ko̱rmo ku̱pcu ṭǟ’. 2 དེ་ནས་མི་ལྔ་ལ་བག་ལེབ་ཉོ་དང་། the̱-nä mi̱ ngā-la pha̱klep nyo̱-thang. 3 དེ་ནས་ཀུ་ཤུ་ཀི་ལོ་གཅིག་

ཉོ་དང་། the̲-nä kūshu kīlo-cīk nyo̲-thang. 4 དེ་ནས་འབྲས་ཀི་ལོ་གཉིས་ཉོ་དང་། the̲-nä ṭä̲' kīlo nyī' nyo̲-thang. 5 དེ་ནས་ཤ་ཡག་པོ་འདུག་མི་འདུག་ལྟ་ཨང་། the̲-nä shā ya̲kpo tu̲' min-tu̲' tā-a. 6 དེ་ནས་ཚེམ་ཁང་ནས་ངའི་སྟོད་ཐུང་དེ་ལེན་རོགས་བྱེད། the̲-nä tshēmkhang-nä ngä̲: tȫthung-the le̲n-ro-chi̲.

(b) *The first is* དེའི་རྗེས་ལ། thä̲: ce̲-la *('after that'). The second is* ནས། nä, *which would allow one to link some of the sentences together, for example*: སྒྲོལ་མའི་རྩ་ལ་ཕྱིན་ནས་མོ་རང་ལ་སྒོར་མོ་དགུ་བཅུ་སྤྲད། ṭö̲lmä: tsā-la chīn-nä mo̲rang-la ko̲rmo ku̲pcu ṭǟ'.

Unit 11

Exercise 1

1 གི་རེད། -ki-re̲' 2 སོང་། sōng 3 གྱི་ཡིན། -ki-yi̲n 4 སོང་། sōng 5 གི་ཡིན། -ki-yi̲n 6 གི་འདུག -ki-tu̲' 7 མ་སོང་། ma-sōng 8 སོང་། sōng.

Exercise 2

Reception – to contract; to receive. **Perception** – to forget; to hear. **Occurrence** – to happen/occur; to be ill (honorific); to be ill (non-honorific); to have a headache; to cough; to be helpful; to have a cold; to depend; to have a fever; to have a sore throat; to feel dizzy; to vomit; to fall asleep; to itch; to fall over; to recover; to find.

Exercise 3

		རེད།	ཡིན།	འདུག	ཡོད།	ཡོད་རེད།	སོང་།
I	Int.	✗	✓	✗	✓	✗	✗
	Non-int.	✓	✗	✓	✗	✗	✓
You	Int.	✓	✗	✓	✗	✓	✓
	Non-int.	✓	✗	✓	✗	✓	✓
He/she	Int.	✓	✗	✓	✗	✓	✓
	Non-int.	✓	✗	✓	✗	✓	✓

Exercise 4

(a) *Question*: ཁྱེད་རང་ཕྱག་སྙུང་གི་འདུག་གས། khyērang chāk nyūngki tu̱’-kä. *Answer*: ང་ལག་པ་ན་གི་འདུག nga̱ la̱kpa na̱ki-tu̱’. (*For (b) and (c), replace what’s in the boxes for (a) with these*): (b) *Q*: སྤྱན་ cā̈n *A*: མིག་ mīk; (c) *Q*: ཞབས། sha̱p *A*: རྐང་པ། kāngpa; (d) *Q*: ཁྱེད་རང་དབུ་དང་སྐུ་སྟོད་སྙུང་གི་འདུག་གས། khyērang ū thang kūtȫ’ nyūngki tu̱’-kä. *A*: ང་མགོ་དང་སྒལ་པ་ན་གི་མི་འདུག nga̱ ko̱ thang kä̱lpa na̱ki min-tu̱’. (e) *Q*: ཁས་ས་ཁྱེད་རང་དབུ་བསྙུངས་སོང་ངས། khā̈sa khyērang ū nyūng sōng-ngä. *A*: ཁས་ས་ང་མགོ་ན་མ་སོང་། khā̈sa nga̱ ko̱ na̱ ma-sōng.

Exercise 5

2 ཚ་གི་འདུག tshāki-tu̱’. 3 ཁྱེད་རང་ཨ་མཆོག་ན་གི་མི་འདུག་གས། khyērang āmcok na̱ki-min-tu̱’-kä. 4 ང་ཁ་སྐོམ་གྱི་འདུག ང་གཉིས་གཅིག་འཐུང་གར་འགྲོ nga̱ khākomki-tu̱’. nga̱-nyī’ cīk thūngka ṭo̱. 5 ང་ཚོ་ཚང་མ་གྲོད་ཁོག་ཞེ་དྲག་ལྟོགས་ཀྱི་འདུག གང་ཡིན་ཟེར་ན། ང་ཚོས་ཉིན་གུང་ཁ་ལག་བཟས་མེད། nga̱ntsho tshāngma ṭho̱khok she̱ṭhak tōki-tu̱’. kha̱ngyin-se̱rna nga̱ntshȫ’ nyi̱nkung-khālak sä̱-me̱. 6 ང་གཡེར་མ་ཟ་དུས་ལྕེ་ལེ་སྦྲིད་ཀྱི་འདུག nga̱ ērma sa̱-thü’ cēle pi̱:ki-tu̱’. 7 ཁས་ས་ཕྲུ་གུ་མང་པོ་གྲོད་ཁོག་བཤལ་སོང་། khā̈sa phūku ma̱ngpo ṭho̱khok shā̈l-song.

Exercise 6

2 ང་གཅིག་ཟ་དགོས་ཡོད། nga̱ cīk sa̱ kö’ yö̱’. 3 ཁྱེད་རང་སྨན་ཟ་དགོས་རེད། khyērang mā̈n sa̱ kö’ re̱’. 4 ང་གསང་སྤྱོད་ལ་འགྲོ་དགོས་ཡོད། nga̱ sāngcö’-la ṭo̱ kö’ yö̱’. 5 ང་གྲོགས་པོ་ལ་རོགས་པ་བྱེད་དགོས་ཀྱི་འདུག nga̱ ṭho̱kpo-la ro̱kpa che̱ kö’-ki tu̱’. 6 ང་གུང་སེང་ལ་འགྲོ་དགོས་ཡོད། nga̱ khu̱ngseng-la ṭo̱ kö’ yö̱’. 7 ཁྱོད་རང་ཚོ་ཉལ་དགོས་རེད། khyērang-tsho nyä̱l kö’ re̱’.

Exercise 7

(a) a strikethrough marks an incorrect verb. (b) replacement verbs are in bold.

ཆམ་པ་~~རག་~~**བརྒྱབ**་སོང་། chāmpa ~~ra̱k~~-**kya̱p** song; ཆམ་པ་~~རག་~~**རྒྱག**་གི་ཡོད་རེད། chāmpa ~~ra̱k~~-**kya̱p**-ki-yo̱re'; སྨན་~~རྙེད་~~**འཚོལ**་(**བཙལ**་)ཀར་ mān ~~nyē'~~-**tshä̱l**-ka; སྨན་~~ལེན་པ་ཡིན་~~**རག་སོང**་། mān ~~le̱npa-yi̱n~~ **ra̱k-song**; གློ་རྒྱག་གི་~~ཡོད་~~**འདུག** lō kya̱pki ~~yö'~~ **tu̱'**; ཆམ་པ་~~བསྣུང་~~**བརྒྱབ**་སོང་། chāmpa ~~si̱m~~ **kya̱p**-song.

(c) My mother got a cold. I went to buy (her) some cold-medicine. But I didn't get any, because many people have been getting colds in this village, and are buying all the medicine. Yesterday, I went to another village, to find some medicine. They had some cold-medicine there, and I got some. But now I'm also coughing. I've caught the cold!

Exercise 8

2 ང་དེ་རིང་ཁྲོམ་ལ་ཕྱིན་པ་ཡིན། nga̱ the̱ring ṭhōm-la chīnpa-yi̱n. 4 ཡིན་ནའང་ཡེ་ཤེས་ཡོད་རེད། yi̱nnä: ye̱shē yo̱re'. 5 ཁྱེད་རང་ཨེམ་ཆི་བསྟེན་པ་ཡིན་པས། khyērang ēmchi tēnpa yi̱n-pä. 6 ང་རིའི་སྒང་ལ་འགྲོ་དུས་མགོ་ཡུ་འཁོར་གྱི་འདུག nga̱ ri̱: ka̱ng-la ṭo̱-thü' ko̱yu khōrki-tu̱'.

Unit 12

Exercise 1

1 མོ་ཊ་དེ་གསར་པ་ཡིན་ས་རེད། mo̱ṭa-the sārpa yi̱n-sa re̱'. 2 ཟ་ཁང་འདི་ལ་ཤ་མེད་ཁ་ལག་ཡོད་ས་མ་རེད། sa̱khang ti̱-la shāme' khālak yö̱'-sa ma-re̱'. 3 གནམ་གྲུ་ཐང་འདི་ནས་ཐག་རིང་པོ་ཡོད་ས་རེད། nāmṭhuthāng ti̱-nä thā-ri̱ngpo yö̱'-sa re̱'. 4 ང་ཚོ་ཆུ་ཚོད་བཅུ་པ་ལ་སླེབ་ས་མ་རེད། nga̱ntsho chūtshö' cūpa-la lēp-sa ma-re̱'. 5 མོ་ཊ་དེ་ལ་མི་མང་པོ་ཡོད་ས་རེད། mo̱ṭa the̱-la mi̱ ma̱ngpo yö̱'-sa re̱'. 6 གླངས་འཁོར་དེར་འགྲོ་ས་མ་རེད། lāngkhor thä̱: ṭo̱-sa ma-re̱'. 7 ང་ཚོའི་ཁ་ལོ་པ་དེས་ཨ་རག་འཐུང་གི་ཡོད་ས་རེད་པས། nga̱ntshö: khālowa the̱' ārak thūngki yö̱'-sa re̱'-wä.

Exercise 2

1 *Today it will rain.* 2 *I should think it'll rain tonight.* 3 *I shouldn't think it'll be sunny this morning.* 4 ཆར་པ་གཏོང་གི་འདུག་གས། chārpa tāngki tu̱'-kä.

5 ཁས་ས་གྲང་མོ་འདུག ཡིན་ནའང་གངས་བཏང་མ་སོང་། khä̆sa ṭha̱ngmo tu̱', yi̱nnä kha̱ng tāng ma-sōng. 6 ང་ཚོ་ལྷ་ས་ལ་འགྲོ་དུས་སེར་བ་བརྒྱབ་སོང་། nga̱ntsho lhāsa-la ṭo̱-thü' sēra kya̱p-song. 7 ཡ་གིར་གངས་རྒྱག་གི་ཡོད་ས་རེད། ya̱kä: kha̱ng kya̱ki yö̱'-sa re̱'.

Exercise 3

1 ···ཀྱི་རེད། . . . ki-re̱' *We'll be able to come at one o'clock.* 2 ···ས་རེད། . . . sa-re̱' *I should think I'll be able to drive this large vehicle.* 3 ···སོང་། . . . sōng *He was able to take three people.* 4 ···མ་སོང་། . . . ma-sōng *I wasn't able to drink all (of it).* 5 ···ཀྱི་མི་འདུག . . . ki-min-tu̱' *I can't close the door.* 6 ···ས་རེད་པས། . . . sa-re̱'-wä *Do you think you'll be able to carry those things?* 7 ···ཀྱི་རེད། . . . ki-re̱' *They can sit in the front of the car.*

Exercise 4

(b) ཤུགས་ཆེན་པོ་བྱས་ནས་བསྡད་པ། shūk-chēnpo-chä̱nä tä̱wa – *to sit down heavily*; (c) དྲོ་པོ་བྱས་ནས་གྱོན་པ། ṭho̱po-chä̱nä khö̱npa – *to wear warmly (i.e. to wrap up warmly)*; (d) ལྟད་མོ་སྐྱིད་པོ་བྱས་ནས་ལྟ་བ། tēmo kyīpo-chä̱nä tāwa – *to watch a show happily/with pleasure*; (e) སྐྱིད་པོ་བྱས་ནས་ཉལ་བ། kyīpo-chä̱nä nyä̱lwa – *to sleep comfortably/contentedly*; (f) ལས་སླ་པོར་འགོ་བ། lä̱lāpo ko̱wa – *to catch (an illness) easily/easily-contractible*; (g) ཁ་ལག་ལྷོད་ལྷོད་བྱས་ནས་ཟ་བ། khālak lhö̆lhö'-chä̱nä sa̱wa – *to eat in a relaxed fashion*

Exercise 5

(a) མོ་ཊ་གཞན་དག་མ་ཡོང་ན་ང་ཚོ་རྒྱལ་རྩེ་ལ་འགྲོ་ཐུབ་ཀྱི་མ་རེད། mo̱ṭa shä̱nthak ma-yo̱ng-na nga̱ntsho kya̱ntse-la ṭo̱ thūp-ki ma-re̱'. (b) *(as in A)* ང་ཚོ་མགྲོན་ཁང་ལ་(ལོག་)འགྲོ་ཐུབ་ཀྱི་མ་རེད། *(as in A)* nga̱ntsho ṭö̱nkhang-la (lo̱k-)ṭo̱ thūp-ki ma-re̱'. (c) *(as in A)* ང་ཚོ་རོགས་པ་འཚོལ་གར་འགྲོ་དགོས་རེད། *(as in A)* nga̱ntsho ro̱kpa tshä̆lka ṭo̱ kö' re̱'. (d) ང་ཚོ་རོགས་པ་འཚོལ་གར་འགྲོ་ན་ང་ཚོ་ལ་འདོགས་ཁྲིས་སོ་བརྒྱག་ས་རེད། nga̱ntsho ro̱kpa tshä̆lka ṭo̱-na nga̱ntsho-la to̱kkhyi' sō-kya̱p sa re̱'. (e) ཇག་པ་ཡོང་ན་ང་ཚོ་ག་རེ་བྱེད་དགོས་རེད། cha̱kpa y̲ong-na nga̲ntsho kha̲re che̲' kö' re̲'. (f) ང་ཚོ་ལ་ཆུ་མ་རག་ན་ཁ་སྐོམ་གྱི་རེད། nga̲ntsho-la chū ma-ra̲k-na khākōmki-re̲'. (g) ང་ཚོ་ལ་ཟ་ཡས་མ་རག་ན་གྲོད་ཁོག་ལྟོགས་ཀྱི་རེད། nga̲ntsho-la sa̲yä ma-ra̲k-na ṭho̲khok tōki-re̲'. (h) ཨེ་ནི་ང་ཚོ་ལ་ཆུ་མ་རག་ན་ང་ཚོ་ཤི་ས་རེད། ēni nga̲ntsho-la chū ma-ra̲k-na nga̲ntsho shī-sa re̲'. (i) ཨེ་ནི་ང་ཚོ་ལ་ཟ་ཡས་མ་རག་ན་ང་ཚོ་ཤི་ས་རེད། ēni nga̲ntsho-la sa̲yä ma-ra̲k-na nga̲ntsho shī-sa re̲'.

Exercise 6

1 The road was also very bad (i.e. potholed). 2 No. 3 They've been unable to extract the jeep from the rut. 4 No. 5 He's bored, but probably what bothers Duho more is Sönam's reluctance to talk.

Translations:

DUHO The road was really bad. But the driver didn't drive carefully. There was a rut in the road, but because he was talking so much, he didn't see it. And our jeep went into the rut. Nothing happened to us, and there was no damage to the jeep. But we've been unable to get the jeep out of the rut. We need help. We'll get help if other vehicles come along, but they aren't coming. I'm annoyed with the driver, and Sönam isn't really talking with me. I'm fed up.

SÖNAM Many foreigners act like Duho. I suppose it's a foreign custom. Sometimes unfortunate things just happen. But how does it help if one immediately blames one's companions? It's not pleasant.

Exercise 7

1 He doesn't seem to blame either the driver, or the road, particularly. He seems to accept that unfortunate things occasionally occur. 2 He doesn't seem to appreciate Duho's complaints and criticisms. 3 Yes; in the dialogue he seems more concerned with calming Duho. Privately, he isn't happy with the way Duho's reacting. 4 Probably he means being quick to voice criticisms, and more generally, to complain. 5 Duho apparently wants to analyse the situation in terms of where the faults lie. Sönam, having accepted the situation, is more concerned with ensuring that there's no bad feeling amongst the travellers. 6 Probably forbearance, stoicism, and camaraderie.

Exercise 8

Duho: 5, 6, 7, and 8. *Sönam*: 1, 2, and 4. *Driver*: definitely 3 and 9; he might also be thinking any of 1, 2, 4, 6, or 8, but he's probably not giving the other two so much thought.

Unit 13

Exercise 1

(b) ✓ (c) ✗ (d) ✓ (e) ✓ (f) ✓ (g) ✓ (h) ✓

Exercise 2

2 He'll say he didn't do it. 3 She (etc.) says she'll go by plane. 4 Thubten says he'll come to your place in the evening. 5 Who says those (two) aren't friends? 6 Dölma said that if Sönam doesn't stay, neither will she. 7 He (etc.) says that the weather's good there. 8 She (etc.) says she'll explain later. 9 He (etc.) says he's busy (i.e. has work) now, and you should come (to see him) at four o'clock.

Exercise 3

2 ཆང་འཐུང་མཁན་དེ། chāng thūng-khän-the̱ 3 ཕྱི་ལོགས་ལ་སྐད་ཆ་བཤད་མཁན་དེ་ཚོ། chīlo-la kăcha shā̆'-nyän-the̱ntsho 4 ནང་ལ་མ་ལོག་མཁན་དེ་ཚོ། na̱ng-la ma-lo̱k-nyän-the̱ntsho 5 ཐུག་སློག་དཀར་པོ་གྱོན་མཁན་དེ། thuklōk kārpo khö̱n-nyän the̱ 6 ཕ་མ་མེད་མཁན་ཕྲུ། phāma me̱'-khän phu̱ 7 ཀང་པ་རིང་པོ་ཡོད་མཁན་དེ་ཚོ། kāngpa ri̱ngpo yö̱'-nyän-the̱ntsho 8 སློབ་སྦྱོང་མ་བྱེད་མཁན་ཕྲུ་གུ་དེ་ཚོ། lōpcong ma-che̱'-nyän phūku-the̱ntsho

Exercise 4

1 Yeshe, 2 Tenpa, 3 Sönam, 4 Tenzin (boy), 5 Tashi, 6 Lhamo, 7 Duho

Exercise 5

2 Type 2; 3 Type 1; 4 Type 2; 5 Type 2; 6 Type 1; 7 Type 2; 8 Type 2; 9 Type 2; 10 Type 2.

Exercise 6

1 ང་ཚོ་སྐལ་བཟང་གི་སྐོར་ལ་སྐད་ཆ་བཤད་དགོས་ཀྱི་འདུག nga̱ntsho kālsang-ki kōr-la kācha shā' kö'-ki tu̱'. 2 ཁྱེད་རང་ལས་ཀ་ལ་ཡོད་རེད་བསམས་སོང་། khyērang lä̱ka-la yo̱re' sām-song. 3 དེ་རིང་བཀྲ་ཤིས་འདིར་འདུག་མི་འདུག་ངས་ཧ་གོ་གི་མེད། the̱ring ṭāshi tä̱: tu̱' min-tu̱' ngä̱' hākho̱ki-me̱'. 4 མོ་རང་གིས་དངུལ་(གི་)ཐོག་ལ་སྐད་ཆ་དྲིས་མ་སོང་། mo̱rang-ki̱' ngūl(-ki) thōk-la kācha ṭhi̱' ma-sōng. 5 སྨན་པ་དེ་བོད་སྐད་ཤེས་ཀྱི་ཡོད་མེད་ཁྱེད་རང་(གིས་)ཧ་གོ་གི་ཡོད་པས། mānpa the̱ phö̱kā' shīnki yö̱'-me̱' khyērang(-ki̱) hākho̱ki yö̱'-pä. 6 ཁྱེད་རང་ངའི་གྲོགས་པོ་རེད་བསམས་སོང་། khyērang ngä̱: ṭho̱kpo re̱' sām-song. 7 མི་དེ་ངོ་ཤེས་ཀྱི་ཡོད་པས། mi̱-the ngo̱shīnki yö̱'-pä. 8 ང་འགྲོ་གི་མ་རེད་བསམས་སོང་ངས། nga̱ ṭo̱-ki ma-re̱' sām song-ngä. 9 མོ་ཊ་ཆུ་ཚོད་ག་ཚོད་ལ་ཡོང་གི་རེད་ཧ་གོ་གི་ཡོད་པས། mo̱ṭa chūtshö' kha̱tshö'-la yo̱ngki-re̱' hākho̱ki yö̱'-pä.

Exercise 7

Q1 ཁྱེད་རང་(གི་)མཚན་ལ་ག་རེ་ཞུ་གི་ཡོད། khyērang(-ki) tshān-la kha̱re shu̱ki-yö̱'. Q2 ག་རེ་ལབ་པ་ཡིན། kha̱re la̱pa-yi̱n. Q3 བོད་སྐད་(ཀྱི་)ཐོག་ལ་དེ་ལ་ག་རེ་ཟེར་གྱི་ཡོད་རེད། phö̱kā'(-ki) thōk-la the̱-la kha̱re se̱rki-yo̱re'. Q4 དབྱིན་(ཇིའི་)སྐད་ལ་སློབ་ཕྲུག་ག་འདྲ་ཟེར་ལབ་དགོས་རེད། īn(ji:) kā'-la lōpṭhuk kha̱nṭäs la̱p-kö' re̱'. Q5 རྒྱ་སེ་ཟེར་ན་ག་རེ་རེད། kya̱se se̱r-na kha̱re re̱'. Q6 བོད་སྐད་(ཀྱི་)ཐོག་ལ་སྐད་ཆ་བཤད་མ་ཐུབ་མཁན་ལ་ག་རེ་ལབ་ཀྱི་ཡོད་རེད། phö̱kā'(-ki) thōk-la kācha shā' ma-thūp-nyän-la kha̱re la̱pki-yo̱re'.

Exercise 8

(a) Yes. (b) No. (c) He starts off quite confidently. But he falters towards the end, because he realises there's one detail he's not sure about, and has to guess. (d) Duho gets the name of the speaker wrong; it was Tshewang Norbu, not Tshering Norbu. More importantly, he doesn't pass on correctly the detail about how Tashi's things are meant to get to Akhu Thubten's place. (e) Duho was mostly right. But because he suggested that Tashi's things will be collected (instead of that he must take them to Akhu Thubten's place himself, soon, as Tshewang Norbu actually said) there's a danger that the arrangement won't work, unless Tashi decides to check.

Translation: On my way here I met an acquaintance of yours. His name is Tshering Norbu. He asked me to give you this message: He said that he is not going to the capital tomorrow, but that Akhu Thubten is going. He said that Akhu Thubten says he will take those things of yours. And what else was there? I should think that Tshering Norbu or Akhu Thubten will come to collect the things, because Tshering Norbu said that you don't have to go.

Unit 14

Exercise 1

Either ཁོ་ཚོ། khōtsho *(which is not polite) or* ང་། nga̱ + ཕེབས་པ། phēpa, མཆོད་པ། chȫpa, སྙུང་བ། nyūngwa, *or* བཞེས་པ། she̱pa *(i.e. with general honorifics); special individual* + འགྲོ་བ། ṭo̱wa, སྣོམ་པ། nūmpa, ལོག་པ། lo̱kpa, ཀློག་པ། lōkpa, *or* ཁ་སྐོམ་པ། khā-kōmpa *(i.e. ordinary level words).* རོགས་གནང་། ro-nāng *doesn't belong here; it's neither a person nor a verb.*

Exercise 2

1 b; 2 b; 3 c; 4 d (but most likely a mixed with some b); 5 d (but most likely, again a, perhaps mixed with some b); 6 b; 7 d (but preferably b).

Exercise 3

(a) *He said he has a bad head.* (b) *Does the teacher say that he/she is going/coming?* (c) *He (etc.) won't say (admit) that he doesn't know.* (d) *They (etc.) told us they won't go to look (at it).* (e) ཁོང་(གིས་)གནང་གི་ཡིན་ཟེར་གསུངས་སོང་། khōng(-kī') nāngki-yi̱n-s sūng-song. (f) ཁོང་ཚོ་སང་ཉིན་འདིར་ཕེབས་ཀྱི་མིན་ཟེར་གསུངས་སོང་། khōng-tsho sāngnyin tä̱: phēpki-me̱:-s sūng-song. (g) ཁོང་(གིས་)ང་ཚོ་ལ་ཞལ་དཔར་གནང་གི་ཡིན་ཟེར་གསུངས་སོང་ངས། khōng(-kī') nga̱ntsho-la shä̱lpar nāngki-yi̱n-s sūng sōng-ngä. (h) ཚེ་རིང་ལགས་སྙུང་གི་འདུག་ཟེར་གསུང་གི་འདུག ཡིན་ནའང་ཞལ་ལག་ཡག་པོར་མཆོད་ཀྱི་འདུག tshēring-la: nyūngki-tu̱k-s su̱ngki-tu̱'. yi̱nnä shä̱lak ya̱kpo chȫki-tu̱'. (i) ཁོང་(གིས་)ང་ཚོ་མཉམ་དུ་ཁ་རེ་བྱས་ནས་བཞུགས་ཀྱི་མིན་ཟེར་གསུངས་སོང་། khōng(-kī') nga̱ntsho nyāmtu kha̱re-chä̱nä shu̱ki-me̱:-s sūng-song.

Exercise 4

1 ང་དེ་(ཁྱེད་རང་ལ་)རྗེས་ལ་ལབ་ན་འགྲིག་གི་རེད་པས། nga̱ the̱ (khyērang-la) ce̱-la la̱p-na ṭi̱kki-re̱'-wä. 2 *(Doesn't work; it's asking another person to do something.)* 3 དགོང་དག་ངའི་གྲོགས་པོ་འདིར་ཡོང་ན་འགྲིག་གི་རེད་པས། ko̱ngthak ngä̱: ṭho̱kpo tä̱: yo̱ng-na ṭi̱kki-re̱'-wä. 4 ད་ལྟ་ཁོ་རང་ཚོ་ལ་དངུལ་མེད་ཟེར་ལབ་ཀྱི་འདུག སང་ཉིན་སྡད་ན་འགྲིག་གི་རེད་པས། tha̱nta khōrangtsho-la ngǖl me̱'-s la̱pki-tu̱'. sāngnyin ṭā̈'-na ṭi̱kki-re̱'-wä. 5 *(Doesn't work; as with no. 2).* 6 ང་ཚྭ་འདི་ལེན་ན་འགྲིག་གི་རེད་པས། nga̱ tshā ti̱ le̱n-na ṭi̱kki-re̱'-wä.

Exercise 5

1 correct; 2 incorrect (should be shu̱wa); 3 correct; 4 incorrect (should be nāngwa); 5 correct; 6 incorrect (see Unit 15).

Exercise 6

1 ལག་ཤུབས། la̱kshup, 2 ཕག་ཤ། phāksha, 3 དངུལ། ngǖl, 4 སྨན་པ། mā̈npa.

Exercise 7

1 ང་འདིར་སླེབས་ནས་ཟླ་བ་དྲུག་ཕྱིན་སོང་། nga̱ tä: lēp-nä ta̱wa ṭhu̱k chīn-song. 2 ཡི་གེ་མ་འབྲི་གོང་ལ་བསམ་བློ་ཡག་པོར་གཏོང་། yi̱ke ma-ṭi̱ kho̱ng-la sāmlo ya̱kpo tāng. 3 དེབ་འདི་ཨེ། ང་འདི་མ་ཀློག་ནས་ལོ་མང་པོ་ཕྱིན་སོང་། the̱p ti̱-ē, nga̱ ti̱ ma-lōk-nä lo̱ ma̱ngpo chīn-song. 4 ས་ཆ་དེ་མཐོ་པོ་རེད། མ་འགྲོ་གོང་ལ་གྲ་སྒྲིག་ཡག་པོར་བྱེད་དགོས་ཀྱི་འདུག sācha-the̱ thōpo re̱'. ma-ṭo̱ kho̱ng-la ṭha̱ṭīk ya̱kpo che̱ kö̱-ki tu̱'. 5 ཁྱེད་རང་(གིས་)རྒྱ་སྐད་སྦྱངས་ནས་ག་ཚོད་ཕྱིན་སོང་། khyērang(-ki) kya̱kā̈' ca̱ng-nä kha̱tshȫ' chīn-song. 6 Q. མོ་ཊ་འདི་ག་དུས་བཟོས་པ་རེད། mo̱ṭa-ti̱ kha̱thü' sö̱wa-re̱'. A. བཟོས་ནས་ལོ་མང་པོ་ཕྱིན་པ་རེད། sö̱'-nä lo̱ ma̱ngpo chīnpa-re̱'. 7 ཉི་མས་མོ་རང་གི་ཅོ་ཅོ་མ་མཐོང་ནས་ཉིན་མ་གསུམ་འགྲོ་སོང་ཟེར། nyima̱' mo̱rang-ki cōco ma-thōng-nä nyi̱ma sūm ṭo̱-song-sa̱.

Exercise 8

Dialogue 1

1 Mainly the manager; he wants to be sure there'll be a vehicle to take the abbot. 2 It seems a member of Dönthup's family was

supposed to have picked the abbot up. 3 Either the vehicle didn't come on time, or it didn't come at all. 4 The manager needs reassuring, but it's obviously Dönthup who feels worse about what happened previously.

Dialogue 2
1 Tenpa is received warmly. 2 To look after his mother, and later because he didn't have the confidence to face his teacher. 3 It seems that Gen Wangdu (Tenpa's former teacher) has passed away. 4 Gen Pasang shows no signs of this; but Tenpa definitely feels bad about what happened.

Verbs: Dialogue 1. (མོ་ཏ།) མ་ཡོང་བ།
Dialogue 2. (ཀྲན་དབང་འདུས།) དགོངས་པ་རྫོགས་པ།
Feeling: Dialogue 1. ངོ་ཚ་བ། shame
Dialogue 2. འགྱོད་པ་སྐྱེ་བ། to regret

Unit 15

Exercise 1

2 གནང་བ། nāngwa, 3 འབུལ་བ། phǖlwa, 4 ཞུ་བ། shu̱wa 5 གནང་བ། nāngwa, 6 ཞུ་བ། shu̱wa, 7 འབུལ་བ། phǖlwa

Exercise 2

(a) ཁ་དུས་ཡོང་བ་ཡིན། → ཁ་དུས་ཡོང་པ། kha̱thü' yo̱ngwa-yi̱n. → kha̱thü' yo̱ngpa.; ཁ་རེ་བྱས་ནས་ཡོང་མེད། → ཁ་རེ་བྱས་ནས་མ་ཡོང་པ། kha̱re-chä̱nä yong-me̱. → kha̱re-chä̱nä ma-yong-pa. (b) ཁ་རེ་བཟའ་གི་ཡིན། → ཁ་རེ་བཟའ་ག kha̱re sa̱ki-yi̱n. → kha̱re sa̱ka. (c) གཟིགས་ཀྱི་ཡིན་པས། → གཟིགས་གས། si̱ki-yi̱n-pä'. → si̱kä. (d) སྨན་དེ་ཉོས་པ་ཡིན་པས། → སྨན་དེ་ཉོས་པས། mǟn-the nyö̱wa-yi̱n-pä. → mǟn-the nyö̱pä; ད་ག་པར་འགྲོ་གི་ཡིན། → ད་ག་པར་འགྲོ་ག tha̱ kha̱wa ṭo̱ki-yi̱n. → tha̱ kha̱wa ṭo̱ka. (e) གནང་གི་ཡིན་པས། → གནང་གས། nāngki-yi̱n-pä. → nāngkä.

Exercise 3

(a) Let's (us two) go! (b) Are you going to make beer? (c) Be careful! (d) I'll tell (him)! (e) Didn't you speak (with them)? (f) Go quickly! (g) Will you post the letter? (h) (Incorrect) (i) Do you want vegetables?

Exercise 4

1 ཕར། phār; 2 ཕར། phār; 3 མི་དེས་ཚུར་མགོ་སྐོར་གཏང་ས་རེད། mi̱-the̱' tshūr ko̱kor tāng-sa re̱'; 4 ཚུར་བཀྲ་ཤིས་བདེ་ལེགས་ལབ་ཀྱི་འདུག་ག ཕར་བཀྲ་ཤིས་བདེ་ལེགས་ལབ། tshūr ṭāshi-te̱le' la̱pki-tu̱'-ka, phār ṭāshi-te̱le' la̱p; 5 ཚུར། tshūr.

Exercise 5

1 གནམ་གྲུ་མར་འབབ་ཀྱི་འདུག nāmṭhu ma̱r-pa̱pki-tu̱'. 2 ཡར་ལངས་ནས་ཁྱོད་ཀྱི་དྲི་བ་དེ་ཕར་གཏང་། ya̱r-la̱ng-nä khyō̈'-ki ṯiwa-the̱ phār tāng. 3 ཕར་ཁ་པར་མ་གཏང་། (ཁོ་རང་ཚོས་)ཚུར་གཏང་ཆོག་གི་རེད། phār khāpar ma-tāng, khōrang-tshō̈' tshūr tāng chōki-re̱'. 4 གླང་འཁོར་གཅིག་ལྷ་ས་ལ་ཕར་འགྲོ་གི་རེད། གཅིག་ལྷ་ས་ནས་ཚུར་ཡོང་གི་རེད། འདི་ཁ་གི་རེད། lāngkhor cīk lhāsa-la phār ṭo̱ki-re̱'. cīk lhāsa-nä tshūr yo̱ngki-re̱'. ṯi kha̱khi re̱'. 5 ཕར་ཤེས་ཞུས་ན་ཚུར་ཤེས་(སྐྱོན་)བརྒྱུག་གི་རེད། phār she̱sa shü̱'-nä tshūr she̱sa (kyō̈n)kya̱ki-re̱'. 6 ཟླ་ཉིན་ངས་ཁྱེད་རང་ལ་ཕར་དངུལ་གཡར་བ་ཡིན། ད་ལྟ་ང་ལ་ཚུར་སྤྲད་དང་། ta̱nyin ngä̱' khyērang-la phār ngǖl yārwa-yi̱n, tha̱nta nga̱-la tshūr ṭā̈-thang.

Exercise 6

(a) 1 *Meeting new people*; 2 *The* thing *that's to be said to Lhamo*; 3 *Staying in hotels*; 4 *Those* (things) *which won't be shown*; 5 *Criticising others*; 6 *Crying*; 7 *Speaking quickly* (b) *The use of: demonstratives* (ṯi *etc.*), *the pluraliser* (tsho), *or the inclusion of a person's name, all suggest things. Something like no. 6 could only really be an activity; it's difficult to think of a thing which might be described as 'a crier'.*

Exercise 7

1 ང་ཚོ་ཁྱེད་རང་ལེན་ཀར་ཡོང་ཆོག་གི་རེད། nga̱ntsho khyērang le̱nka yo̱ng-chōki-re̱'. 2 ང་འདིར་བསྒུགས་ན་འགྲིག་གི་རེད་པས། nga̱ tä̱: ku̱k-na ṯikki-re̱'-wä. 3 འདི་

འདྲ་སྡོད་ཆོག་གི་མ་རེད། tiṇṭä tä' chōki-ma-re'. 4 འདི་ལ་བདག་པོ་མེད་ན་ང་ལེན་ན་འགྲིག་གི་རེད་པས། ti-la takpo me'-na nga len-na ṭikki-re'-wä. 5 ང་མི་འདི་ཚོ་ལ་སྐད་ཆ་བཤད་ཆོག་གི་རེད་པས། nga mi tintsho-la kăcha shă' chōki re'-wä. 6 དགོན་པ་ལ་དུག་སློག་འདི་ཚོ་གྱོན་ན་འགྲིག་གི་མ་རེད། kompa-la thuklōk tintsho khön-na ṭikki-ma-re'. 7 རྩམ་པ་ཟ་ཡས་བོད་པ་ལ་གལ་ཆེན་པོ་ཡོད་རེད། tsāmpa sayä phöpa-la khäl-chēnpo yore'.

Exercise 8

1 ལེ་ས་ཟེར་ན་བོད་ཀྱི་ཆོས་དང་རིག་གཞུང་གལ་ཆེན་པོ་རེད། 2 རྟུ་ཧྲོ་ཟེར་ན་གྲོགས་པོ་མཉམ་དུ་དུས་ཚོད་བསྐྱལ་ན་སྐྱིད་པོ་ཡོད་རེད། 3 རྟུ་ཧྲོ་བོད་པ་མཉམ་དུ་སྡོད་དུས་ལས་འགན་གྱི་ཐོག་ལ་བསམ་བློ་གཏོང་འདོད་ཡོད་མ་རེད། 4 ཡེ་ཤེས་ཀྱི་བསམ་པ་ལ་བོད་ཀྱི་རིག་གཞུང་བོད་པའི་རིག་གཞུང་རེད། ཕྱི་རྒྱལ་མིའི་རིག་གཞུང་མ་རེད། 5 རྟུ་ཧྲོའི་བསམ་པ་ལ་ཡེ་ཤེས་ཁོ་རང་གི་གྲོགས་པོ་རེད། ཡིན་ནའང་མཚམས་མཚམས་ལ་སྐད་ཆ་བཤད་སྟངས་ཡག་པོ་ཡོད་མ་རེད། 6 ལེ་སའི་བསམ་པ་ལ་རྟུ་ཧྲོ་མི་ཡག་པོ་ཡོད་རེད། ཡིན་ནའང་དུས་ཚོད་ཡག་པོ་བྱས་ནས་བེད་སྤྱོད་གཏོང་གི་ཡོད་མ་རེད། 7 རྟུ་ཧྲོ་ཟེར་ན་ལེ་ས་ཡག་པོ་ཡོད་རེད། ཡིན་ནའང་མཚམས་མཚམས་ལ་བསམ་བློ་སྡུག་སྒྲུབ་དོག་པོ་ཡོད་རེད། 8 ཡེ་ཤེས་ཀྱི་བསམ་པ་ལ་རྟུ་ཧྲོ་མི་ཨའུ་ཚམ་རེད། ཡིན་ནའང་ཁོ་ལ་འཕྱ་ལས་བརྒྱབ་ན་སྐྱིད་པོ་ཡོད་རེད།

Translations of dialogues (Units 8–15)

Unit 8

Dialogue 1

SÖNAM *Hey Duho, what are you doing?*

DUHO *I'm not doing anything special at the moment.*

SÖNAM *Duho, there's a show at the theatre tonight. Let's go!*

DUHO *At what time?*

SÖNAM *The show is at seven o'clock.*

DUHO *What time is it now?*

SÖNAM *It's about five. You don't have anything to do at the moment, do you? Let's first go to the market. Get ready. I'll come to your place.*

DUHO *Sönam wait! Between six and six-thirty I don't have time. Someone is coming here.*

SÖNAM *But after that are you free?*

DUHO *Yes.*

SÖNAM *Well then I'll go home first. I'll come after six-thirty.*

Dialogue 2

DUHO *Is that Gangseng Travel Agency?*

TSERING *Yes.*

DUHO *I am calling from Ka̱ṭö guesthouse. Are you Tsering Dölkar?*

TSERING *Yes, I am.*

DUHO *Hello Tsering Dölkar. My name is Duho. I am a friend of Phuntshok's.*

TSERING	*Oh, hello.*
DUHO	*Tsering Dölkar, I'll be going to the airport the day after tomorrow. But the bus leaves really early. So I am looking for a car [to hire].*
TSERING	*We don't have our own car. But there are several drivers I know. What time does the flight leave?*
DUHO	*It is not flying, it is landing.*
TSERING	*How is that? Aren't you going by plane?*
DUHO	*No, my friend is travelling by plane.*
TSERING	*First please come to the office.*
DUHO	*At one o'clock, was that?*
TSERING	*No, come whenever you like.*

Unit 9

Dialogue 1

LHADZOM	*What are you going to eat? I'm going to have [*lit. *drink] thukpa.*
DEKYI	*The weather is cold, isn't it? I'm also going to have thukpa. Tenzin, what do you want?*
TENZIN	*I want momo.*
LHADZOM	*This child! He always eats the most expensive [dish]. Dekyi, call that boy [worker] over there, and order the food. I'm going to look for the bathroom.*
DEKYI	*Boy/son, give us two [bowls of] thukpa. And are there momos?*
WORKER	*[They're] making momos at the moment. They'll take about 15 minutes.*
DEKYI	*About 15 minutes? Well don't bring the thukpa just yet. Once the momos are finished bring everything together.*
WORKER	*All right. Drinks?*
DEKYI	*Two teas. Tenzin, do you want a drink?*
TENZIN	*I don't want a drink. [My] mother would say something [i.e. would complain].*

Dialogue 2

MOTHER	*Yes, here, please take a seat. First have a tea. I'm going to get the momos.* (she returns) *The food we have here isn't great [i.e. this is a modest offering], but please enjoy what there is.*
YESHE	*Duho, be careful when you eat the momos; they're hot!*
MOTHER	*Have some tea. How are the momos?*
DUHO	*Really tasty, thanks!*
MOTHER	*Have some salad as well. I have many more momos in the kitchen. Have some more tea. Isn't it cold?*
DUHO	*No more tea for me thanks, 'elder sister'* (she leaves the room) *Yeshe, your mother is pouring me so much tea! I really don't want any more. But she won't listen. Help me out!*
YESHE	*It doesn't matter. It's a tradition.* (she returns)
MOTHER	*Here, have some hot momos.*
DUHO	*Elder sister, I've really had enough.*
MOTHER	*Just have a few more!*
YESHE	*Duho, you speak Tibetan like a Tibetan. Now you should eat momos like a Tibetan. Don't hold back! Eat more!*
DUHO	*I am not holding back. Ow, my stomach!*
YESHE	*Oh, those poor foreigners . . .*

Unit 10

Dialogue 1

PENPA	*'Elder sister', do you have any khata [scarves]?*
SHOPKEEPER	*Yes, I do.*
PENPA	*Please show me. How much are those?*
SHOPKEEPER	*These are the better quality ones. They're fifty rupees each. [Do you want] to buy?*
PENPA	*Any chance of a reduction?*
SHOPKEEPER	*Buy two; I'll sell them for ninety rupees.*
PENPA	*Okay, I'll buy two. Have you also got tsampa?*
SHOPKEEPER	*Yes, I have tsampa.*

PENPA *How much does a kilo cost?*

SHOPKEEPER *A kilo costs eighty rupees.*

PENPA *Eighty rupees! Last year I bought some for sixty.*

SHOPKEEPER *These days everything is going up. It's also difficult for the traders. There used to be many Tibetan shops in this place. But these days I'm alone here. Tsampa is especially important for Tibetans. That's why I sell it. There's hardly any profit.*

PENPA *You are right, elder sister, tsampa is really important.*

Dialogue 2

DUHO *There was a shirt like this one in that shop just before. But that one was more expensive.*

TASHI *It is similar, but not the same.*

DUHO *What's the difference?*

TASHI *That one just before was better material. But try [this one] on. I'll have a look [to see] whether or not it suits you. Does it fit? It's not too tight, is it?*

DUHO *It's not too tight. How is it [on me]?*

TASHI *It suits you. Duho, do you sometimes wear a chupa?*

DUHO *A chupa? No, I don't wear [chupas]. Oh, this glove is also nice. But the pair isn't here. Where is the other one? I'll ask the trader.*

TASHI *How? There's no way he'll speak Tibetan. These traders only speak Chinese. You stay here. I'll ask.* (he leaves)

DUHO *What did he say?*

TASHI *He says there's only one of the pair.*

DUHO *Who's going to buy one glove?*

TASHI *Some people only have one hand, don't they?*

DUHO *Ridiculous!*

Unit 11

Dialogue 1

DOCTOR *Take a seat. Aren't you feeling well?*

TASHI *I have a fever, doctor, and a bad head.*

DOCTOR *Apart from that, is there nothing else?*

TASHI *I'm coughing a lot when I get up in the morning.*

DOCTOR *What happens when you cough?*

TASHI *I get a sore throat and feel dizzy.*

DOCTOR *I should think that it's a cold. Many people have colds at present.*

TASHI *And you doctor, haven't you got ill?*

DOCTOR *Doctors don't get colds. It is the rule for physicians! No, I'm just joking. But it really is the case that we don't catch many illnesses.*

TASHI *You're very fortunate, doctor.*

DOCTOR *It also depends on general health and hygiene.*

TASHI *Yes.*

DOCTOR *I'm writing the name of two medicines here. They'll help a little.*

Dialogue 2

LHAMO *Tenzin, I rang you just before. Didn't you hear?*

TENZIN *No, I didn't hear. Just before I was at the pharmacy.*

LHAMO *Did you buy my medicine?*

TENZIN *Yes.*

LHAMO *That's good. How many pills do I have to take?*

TENZIN *The man told me when I bought them. Then I immediately wrote it on some paper. But . . .*

LHAMO *What is it?*

TENZIN *Hold on, I'm thinking! I thought it was three pills [a day]; two in the morning and one in the evening.*

LHAMO *Are you sure? Otherwise it could be dangerous. This medicine is strong.*

TENZIN *Now I can't remember.*

LHAMO *Anyway, where is the piece of paper? Show me. Now where are you going?*

TENZIN *I need to go to the pharmacy again to ask.*

LHAMO *And the paper?*

TENZIN *I left the paper at the pharmacy.*

LHAMO *Oh no, what an individual!*

Unit 12

Dialogue 1

DRIVER *Come on over!*

DUHO *That doesn't seem like the man from yesterday.*

SÖNAM (to the driver) *Yesterday we made plans with another driver.*

DRIVER *He's my colleague. But he can't go to Gyantse today. He sent me in his place.*

DUHO *We should be careful. This man could con us.*

SÖNAM *Don't worry Duho. Let me do the talking.* (to the driver) *We already fixed a price with your colleague yesterday.*

DRIVER *I don't know anything about this. I wasn't here yesterday. But I'll take you for 300 Yuan.*

SÖNAM *You're familiar with your way, aren't you? How many hours will it take?*

DRIVER *It'll take about four hours.*

SÖNAM *Take us for 250 Yuan.*

DRIVER *That's not enough. I'll take you for 300. You aren't likely to get another jeep now.*

SÖNAM *Duho, I should think that's true. We're unlikely to get another jeep. Let's go with him!*

Dialogue 2

DUHO *That man didn't drive well, did he? I had my doubts about him from the start.*

SÖNAM *It wasn't the driver's mistake.*

DUHO *Then whose fault was it? What are we going to do if no other vehicles come?*

SÖNAM *Don't worry! Another vehicle will come.*

DUHO *But I shouldn't think any will come soon. And then if it snows . . .*

SÖNAM *So what if it snows? Jeeps can go in the snow.*

DUHO *But we don't have much to eat. And the place is high up. I can't breathe that well.*

SÖNAM *Duho, there's nothing we can do. We have to stay here and wait. And we're unlikely to freeze to death [*lit. *die from the cold] or die from altitude sickness. But if you talk in this way so much it won't help, and definitely creates more tension. Don't think so much. Stay calm!*

Unit 13

Dialogue 1

TSHENOR *Hello! You're Tashi's friend, aren't you? Are you likely to meet Tashi today?*

DUHO *I'm going to Tashi's place right now.*

TSHENOR *That's perfect! Do you think that you can take Tashi a message?*

DUHO *I'll take the message. What's your name 'elder brother'?*

TSHENOR *I'm called Tsewang Norbu. Please tell Tashi this: I [had] said that I would transport those things of Tashi's to the capital tomorrow. But something has cropped up at home, and I don't think I can go tomorrow. But 'Uncle' Thubten is going tomorrow. He says he'll transport those things. And [Tashi] needs to take them to his [Thubten's] place soon, because he says that he's going early tomorrow. Please tell Tashi this.*

DUHO *Hold on a minute please. You've said a lot, elder brother. I haven't got it all. What are the things [you mentioned]?*

TSHENOR *This isn't important. Tashi will know.*

DUHO *Well who is the one who said that he'd transport those things? Is it elder brother or uncle Thubten?*

TSHENOR *First, I said I'd transport them. But now uncle Thubten says he will.*

DUHO *So Tashi doesn't need to go [anywhere] does he?*

TSHENOR *Please listen carefully. Uncle Thubten is the one going to the capital, not Tashi. But Tashi's things have to be taken to uncle Thubten's place. If they're not taken there, uncle Thubten won't be able to transport them, will he?*

DUHO *Now I've understood! I'll deliver Tashi that exact same message.*

TSHENOR (as Duho walks away) *I wonder . . .*

Dialogue 2

LHAKPA *Hey Tshering; what are you thinking about?*

TSHERING *I'm not thinking. You see those two people behind us. I'm listening to them talking.*

LHAKPA *What language are they speaking in?*

TSHERING *I don't know. First I thought that it was Chinese. But hold on . . .*
(he listens again) *I think that it's probably Japanese.*

LHAKPA *I wonder what they're talking about.*

TSHERING *How should I know? I don't know Japanese. Oh, they're looking at us.*

TOURIST ta-si the-re.

LHAKPA *What? What did he say?*

TSHERING *You fool! He's saying 'hello' [ṭāshi-te̱le'] to us, isn't he? Say 'hello' back to them.*

LHAKPA *Hello, where are you from?*

TSHERING *What? They're foreigners. Of course they're not going to understand Tibetan.*

LHAKPA *No. Our language and theirs are quite similar. Kelzang told me that there's hardly any difference between the ways we count.*

TSHERING *That's fine then; you can sit there counting together!*

LHAKPA *Don't make fun of me.*

Unit 14

Dialogue 1

MANAGER *Are you making the arrangements with the car, Dönthup?*

DÖNTHUP *That goes without saying ['Manager'].* That's our responsibility. You shouldn't concern yourself with that. Listen; the abbot has said that he'll go as soon as the assembly is over tomorrow, didn't he? If that's the case, I'll bring the car here early in the morning and wait. Is it all right if I leave it by the [monastery] gate?*

MANAGER *Yes, that's fine.*

DÖNTHUP *All right; and at what time does the abbot say he [wants to] come back here?*

MANAGER *This I don't know. Dönthup, do you know the abbot's main attendant?*

DÖNTHUP *Yes, I do.*

MANAGER *Please ask him. Apart from that, if you're not able to make the arrangements with the vehicle tomorrow Dönthup, it doesn't matter. We can send the monastery vehicle.*

DÖNTHUP *Please don't say that. You shouldn't worry at all about the car. Tomorrow my brother/relation won't be involved; he is totally unreliable. He embarrassed the whole family before. If it doesn't work out well this time . . .*

* Some titles won't be translated in these final dialogues; there is no comfortable way to render them in English.

Dialogue 2

TENPA *May I come in? Haven't you recognised me? I'm Tenpa. I used to be Gen Wangdu's disciple . . .*

GEN PASANG *Tenpa? Oh yes. We haven't met for so many years. Now you arrive out of the blue . . . What is this?*

TENPA *This is something for 'teacher' [i.e. you].*

GEN PASANG *Are you giving it to me? Okay.*

TENPA *I haven't been to the monastery for about ten years.*

GEN PASANG *What happened back then? You went home. Then why didn't you come back?*

TENPA *At that time the situation at home was difficult. Mother was old. In fact she needed help [a companion], and there were no other relatives [there]. Before I left the monastery, I should have told Gen Wangdu about this situation. But I thought Gen Wangdu wouldn't grant me permission to leave, so I didn't tell him. I stayed helping my mother for two years. But then she died. I thought that if I came back to the monastery, I wouldn't be readmitted. I should have gone to visit Gen Wangdu, but I was embarrassed. But now it is too late. I really regret it.*

GEN PASANG *That's in the past. There's nothing that can be done about it now. What are you doing these days? Have you got a wife?*

TENPA *I am doing a little trading. I've been married for four years. And we have a daughter.*

GEN PASANG *This isn't a good time [i.e. things are bad]. But Tenpa, act kindly. Treat your child and wife well. When you trade, act honestly. And when you have time, make religious offerings.*

Unit 15

Dialogue 1

GEN ZÖPA *'Madam' tell me. The government worker . . .* (two young monks burst in) *Hey, you two, behave!*

LADY *Oh, a new monk. Where's he from? What is your name?*

THUPTEN *My name . . . my name is Thupten.**

JINPA *Hahaha, this youngster is really amusing.*

GEN ZÖPA *Be quiet! I suppose you taught him that.* (To the woman) *poor thing! They don't have honorific in their dialect. He doesn't know how to speak it. The other young monks mock him. They purposely teach him incorrect honorifics. Jinpa, did you teach him that?*

JINPA *I didn't teach him. I told him this: he should listen when seniors speak, and imitate them. Isn't that right?*

GEN ZÖPA *Don't be cheeky! Jinpa, you've got things to do at the market haven't you? Go and do them! There are some things on that table over there. They're to take to Uncle Pema's. And there are letters to collect from him. Now go!*

JINPA *There's lots of things to be taken, aren't there? I should think I'll need a helper. Am I allowed to take him? Please!*

GEN ZÖPA *Him? If you are planning to take him, you'll need to request permission from the disciplinarian. And come straight back! Don't go wandering off anywhere!*

JINPA *Yes. Thupten, would you do me the honour of accompanying and assisting?*

THUPTEN *I assist . . . I go . . .* co̱-cu̱ yä̱.

GEN ZÖPA *Don't speak your dialect here, people won't understand. Jinpa, teach him the language properly!*

* He accidentally uses honorific language for himself.

Dialogue 2

YESHE *Oh, so you two had a quarrel?*

DUHO *I didn't quarrel with her. The one quarrelling was Lisa. I met a foreigner yesterday. He says he buys old Tibetan things here, and then sells them abroad. He doesn't know Tibetan, so I helped him when he bought some things. But when I told Lisa, she lost her temper, and spoke harshly to me.*

YESHE *What did she say?*

DUHO *She said many things. For example, she said that those people are conning poor Tibetans. And helping them is damaging to Tibetan culture. And if one knows Tibetan well, one should use it wisely. Yeshe, I assisted him. That's being helpful to someone, isn't it?*

YESHE *Why are you saying that?*

DUHO *I like to have fun. I like to spend time with friends. But according to Lisa, I'm wasting all my time. Yeshe, what type of person would you say I am?*

YESHE *I'd say you're happy-go-lucky.*

DUHO *Lisa wants to study Tibetan religion and culture. But me . . . Yeshe, drinking and talking with one's companions; isn't that also Tibetan culture?*

YESHE *It's custom.*

DUHO *She said this: if one knows the language, one has a responsibility to study the religion and culture. Yeshe, what's your opinion about that?*

YESHE *I don't have any opinion about that. But what I think is that the beer doesn't taste so good if you go on about such things.*

DUHO *I can hear something outside. There is shouting, and I think someone is crying.*

YESHE *Ignore it. There's nothing we can do. Sit down and have some more beer . . .*

Tibetan–English glossary

The number after each entry is the unit in which the word is introduced.

Verb key

I – intentional; NI – non-intentional
S – used with the agentive particle (**che̱ṭa**)
H – general honorific; hu-H – 'humble' honorific; hi-H – high honorific (verbs not marked with H, etc. belong to the ordinary register)

Following tradition, verbs are listed under their present form (there is no concept of an infinitive). If only one form is listed, the verb's past, present, and future forms are the same. The past form (when differing from the present) is listed next. The future form of many verbs is identical to the present one; when it differs, this future form appears last.

Word order key

Entries are arranged according to the alphabet, but not in a left to right order. They are primarily listed according to their first syllable's *central letter*. The elements are then introduced, in cycles, in this order: suffix – vowel marker – subscript – prefix – superscript. So when words with the central letter alone are exhausted, those with just a central letter and suffix are introduced. Next, those with a central letter, suffix, and vowel marker are introduced, etc.

ཀ།

ཀི་ལོ། **kīlo** kilogram (from English) 10

ཀུ་ཤུ། **kūshu** apple 9

ཀོ་ཙེ། **kōtse** chopsticks 9

ཀྱི། **ki** (genitive-particle) 7

ཀྲིན་མོག **ṭīmo** steamed bread 9

ཀླད་ཀོར། **lā̃kor** zero 3

ཀློག་པ། **lōkpa** to read
བཀླགས་པ། བཀླག་པ། (S/I) 11

དཀའ་ལས་ཁག་པོ། **kāle-khākpo** difficult 10

དཀར་པོ། **kārpo** white 6

དཀར་ཡོལ། **kāryöl** porcelain cup/bowl 9

དཀྱིལ(་ལ)། **kyīl** centre of/amidst 12

བཀའ་འདྲི་གནང་བ། **kānṭi-nāngwa** to ask (H/S/I) 14

བཀའ་སློབ། **kālop** advice (H) 15

བཀའ་སློབ་གནང་བ། **kālop-nāngwa** to bestow advice (H/S/I) 15

བཀའ་སློབ་ཞུ་བ། **kālop-shu̱wa** to request/accept advice (hu-H/S/I) 15

བཀྲ་ཤིས་བདེ་ལེགས། **ṭāshi-te̱le'** 'hello'/greetings 2

རྐང་། **kāng** piece/item (measure word) 9

རྐང་པ། **kāngpa** foot/leg 11

རྐང་བཙུགས་ནས། **kāngtsuk-nä** on purpose 15

རྐུན་མ། **kūma** thief 11

རྐུབ་བཀྱག **kūpkyak** chair 5

ལྐུགས་པ། **kūkpa** fool/idiot (*lit.* mute) 13

སྐད་གྲགས་ཆེན་པོ། **kā̃ṭhak-chēnpo** famous/prominent 3

སྐད་རྒྱག་པ། **kā̃-kya̱pa** to shout (S/I) 8

སྐད་ཆ་ཅི་གྲོས་མོལ་གྲོས།
kā̃cha-cīṭömö̱lṭö' banter 6

སྐད་ཆ་འདྲི་བ། **kā̃cha-ṯiwa** to ask (S/I) 10

སྐད་ཆ་བྱེད་པ། **kā̃cha-che̱pa** to negotiate/discuss a plan (S/I) 12

སྐད་ཆ་བཤད་མཁན། **kā̃cha shā̃-nyän** the one who speaks/the speaker 13

སྐད་གཏོང་བ། **kā̃-tāngwa** to call to; invite (S/I) 8

སྐར་མ། **kārma** minute 4/8

སྐུ་མཁྱེན། **kūkyi** please! (usually when pleading) 15

སྐུ་སྟོད། **kūtö̃'** back (of body; H) 11

སྐུ་ཞབས་ལགས། **kūsho'-la:** (address for monks and some officials) 14

སྐུ་གཟུགས། **kūsuk** body (H) 11

སྐོར། **kōr** about 9

སྐྱིད་པོ་གཏོང་བ། **kyīpo-tāngwa** to have a good time (S/I) 15

སྐྱུག་པ་སྐྱུག་པ། **kyūkpa-kyūkpa** to vomit
····བསྐྱུགས་པ། ····བསྐྱུག་པ། (S/NI) 11

སྐྱེ་དམན། **kyēmän** woman; wife 4

སྐྱེལ་བ། **kyelwa** to transport/carry
བསྐྱལ་བ། (S/I) 12

སྐྱོན། **kyö̃n** fault; defect/harm 12

སྐྱོན་པ། **kyö̃npa** (honorific version of the verbaliser རྒྱག་པ། **kya̱pa**) 14

སྐྱོན་འཛུགས་པ། **kyȫn-tsūkpa** to criticise/blame ···བཙུགས་པ། ···གཟུགས་པ། (S/I) 12

སྐྲ། **ṭā** hair 11

ཁ

ཁ། **khā** mouth 11

ཁ་སྐོམ་པ། **khā-kōmpa** to be thirsty (NI) 11

ཁ་ཆེ། **khāche** Muslim 2

ཁ་བཏགས། **khāta** Tibetan silk 'scarf' (gen. white, signifying auspiciousness) 10

ཁ་དཔར། **khāpar** phone 2

ཁ་དཔར་གཏོང་བ། **khāpar-tāngwa** to phone (S/I) 8

ཁ་བ། **khāwa** to smell (NI) 11

ཁ་ལག **khālak** food (meal) 5

(མོ་ཊའི་)ཁ་ལོ་པ། **(moṭä:) khālowa** driver 8

ཁ་ཤས། **khāshä'** several 4

ཁག་ཁག **khāka** different 4

ཁག་པོ། **khākpo** difficult 6

ཁང་པ། **khāngpa** house/building 2

ཁང་མིག **khāngmik** room 5

ཁམས། **khām** the Tibetan province 3

ཁུ་སིམ་པོ། **khūsimpo** quiet 4

ཁུག་ཀྱོག **khūkyok** isolated 6

ཁེ་བཟང་། **khēpsang** profit/gain 10

ཁེ་གཙང་། **khētsang** en suite/separate 5

ཁོ་རང་། **khōrang** he (non-polite) 2

ཁོ་རང་གི། **khōrang-ki** his 3

ཁོང་། **khōng** he; she (polite); (polite address, for attracting someone's attention) 2

ཁོང་གི། **khōng-ki** his; hers (polite) 3

ཁོང་ཚོའི། **khōng-tshö:** their; theirs (polite) 3

ཁྱད་པར། **khyēpar** difference 10

ཁྱི། **khyī** dog 2

ཁྱེད་རང་། **khyērang** you (polite) 2

ཁྱེད་རང་གི། **khyērang-ki** your/yours (singular) 3

ཁྱེད་རང་གཉིས། **khyērang-nyī'** you (two) 3

ཁྱེད་རང་ཚོའི། **khyērang-tshö:** your/yours (plural) 3

ཁྱོ་ག **khyōka** husband 4

ཁྱོད། **khyȫ'** you (non-polite or intimate) 2

ཁྱོན་ནས། **khyȫnnä** (emphatic; negation) 14

ཁྲལ། **ṭhǟl** tax/duty 11

ཁྲོམ། **ṭhōm** market 8

ཁྲོམ་ས། **ṭhōmsa** market-place 6

མཁན། **nyän/khän** the one who . . . 13

མཁན་པོ། **khǟnpo** abbot 14

མཁྱེན་པ། **khyēnpa** to know/to understand (H/S/NI) 14

འཁྱག་པ། **khyākpa** to feel cold (persons) འཁྱགས་པ། (NI) 12

འཁྱམས་འཁྱམས། **khyāmkhyam** a wander/stroll around 7

འཁྱེར་བ། **khyērwa** to carry/take ཁྱེར་བ། (S/I) 9

འཁྲིད་པ། **ṭhīwa** to bring/take ཁྲིད་པ། (S/I) 14

འཁྲིས། **ṭhī'** beside/next to 4

འཁྲུག་པོ། **ṭhūkpo** lively/exciting 6

ག

ག་གི། **kha̱ki** which? 3

ག་དུས། **kha̱thü'** when? 2

ག་འདྲ། **kha̱nṭa** how? 5

ག་འདྲ་སེ། (or ག་འདྲ་ཟེར།) **kha̱nṭäs** how? (for actions) 8

ག་ནས། **kha̱nä** where from? 3

ག་པར། **kha̱wa:** where? 4

ག་པར། **kha̱:wa** (*lit.* 'where?' used to deny or call into doubt an assertion) 10

ག་པར་ག་པར། **kha̱:wa-kha̱wa** (emphatic denial) 7

ག་ཚོད། **kha̱tshȫ'** how many/how much? 3

ག་རེ། **kha̱re** what? 2

ག་རེ་བྱས་ནས། **kha̱re-chä̱nä** why? 7

ག་རེ་ཟེར། **kha̱re-sa̱** (speech-filler); what does he/she/it say? 13

ག་ལེ། **kha̱le** gently/leisurely 5

ག་ལེར་ཕེབས། **kha̱le:-phēp** goodbye! (wished by someone staying) 5

ག་ལེར་བཞུགས། **kha̱le:-shu̱:** goodbye! (wished by someone departing) 5

གང་། **kha̱ng** one 9

གང་ཡང་། **khä̱:** nothing (with neg. verb); anything/any (with affirm. verb) 6

གང་ཡིན་ཟེར་ན། **kha̱ngyin-se̱rna** because 8

གང་ཤེས། **kha̱ngshē'** I've no idea! 6

གངས་རྒྱག་པ། **kha̱ng-kya̱pa** to snow (NI) 12

གངས་གཏོང་བ། **kha̱ng-tāngwa** to snow (NI) 12

གད་མོ་སློང་བ། **khä̱mo-lāngwa** to amuse

···བསླངས་པ། ···བསློང་བ། (S/I) 15

གར། **ka** (conjunction) 9

གལ་ཆེན་པོ། **khä̱l-chēnpo** important 10

གས། **kä** (question-particle for **tu̱'**) 4

གི། **ki** (genitive-particle) 7

གུང་ལ་ཕུག **khu̱ng-laphūk** carrots 9

གུང་སེང་། **ku̱ngseng** holiday 7

གུས་ཞབས། **khu̱shap** respect 14

གོ། **kho** (number-particle for 91–99) 3

གོ་བ། **kho̱wa** to hear (S/NI) 11

གོང་ཁེ་པོ། **kho̱ng-khēpo** cheap 10

གོང་སྒྲིག་པ། **kho̱ng-ṭi̱kpa** bargaining/settling a price (S/I) 10

གོང་ཆེན་པོ། **kho̱ng-chēnpo** expensive 4

གོང་ཚད། **kho̱ngtshä'** price 10

གོས་ཐུང་། **khö̱thung** trousers 10

གྱ། **khya** (number-particle for 81–89) 3

གྱི། **ki** (genitive-particle) 7

གྱོང་། **khyo̱ng** loss (financial, etc.) 10

གྱོན་པ། **khö̱npa** to wear (S/I) 10

གྲ་སྒྲིག་བྱེད་པ། **ṭha̱ṭik-che̱pa** make preparations/get ready (S/I) 8

གྲ་མ་སྒྲིག **ṭa̱:-maṭi̱k** unfortunate events/mishaps 12

གྲང་མོ། **ṭha̱ngmo** cold 5

གྲང་ཚལ། **ṭha̱ngtshäl** salad 9

གྲངས་ཀ་རྒྱག་པ། **ṭha̱ngka-kya̱pa** to count (S/I) 13

གྲི། **ṭhi̱** knife 9

གྲོགས་པོ། **ṭho̱kpo** friend 3

གྲོང་ཁྱེར། **ṭho̱ngkhyer** town 6

གྲོང་གསེབ། **ṭho̱ngsep** village 6

གྲོད་ཁོག **ṭho̱khok** stomach 9

གྲོད་ཁོག་རྒྱགས་པ། **ṭho̱khok-kya̱kpa** to be full (stomach) ''' བརྒྱགས་པ། ''' བརྒྱག་པ། (NI) 11

གྲོད་ཁོག་ལྟོགས་པ། **ṭho̱khok-tōkpa** to be hungry (NI) 11

གྲོད་ཁོག་བཤལ་བ། **ṭho̱khok-shā̃lwa** to have diarrhoea (NI) 11

གྲོལ་བ། **ṭhö̱lwa** to end (for gatherings: NI) 14

གྲྭ་པ། **ṭha̱wa** monk 6

གླ་བ། **lāwa** to hire གླས་པ། **lā̃wa** (S/I) 12

གླང་ཤ། **lāngshā** beef 9

གླིང་ཁ། **līngka** picnic 6

གློ་རྒྱག་པ། **lō-kya̱pa** to cough (NI) 11

དགའ་པ། **ka̱:** prefer 6

དགའ་པོ། **ka̱po** to like 6

དགའ་པོ། **ka̱wo** partner (boyfriend/girlfriend) 3

དགའ་ཤོས། **ka̱shö'** favourite 6

དགུ། **ku̱** nine 3

དགེ་སྐོས། **ke̱kö̃'** monastery disciplinarian 15

དགེ་རྒན། **ke̱kän** teacher 2

དགེ་ཕྲུག **ke̱ṭhuk** disciple 14

དགེ་བཤེས། **ke̱shē'** (person with specific monastic degree) 14

དགོང་དག **ko̱ngthak** evening/night 8

དགོངས་དག **ko̱ng:tha** sorry! 6

དགོང་དྲོའི་ཁ་ལག **ko̱ngṭhö:-khālak** evening meal 9

དགོངས་པ་གནང་བ། **ko̱ngpa-nāngwa** to grant permission (H/S/I) 14

དགོངས་པ་ཞུ་བ། **ko̱ngpa-shu̱wa** to request permission (hu-H/S/I) 15

དགོངས་པ་རྫོགས་པ། **ko̱ngpa-tso̱kpa** to die (hi-H/NI) 14

དགོན་པ། **ko̱mba** monastery 4

དགོས་པ། **kö̱pa** to need/want (modal verb) 9

མགོ། **ko̱** head 11

མགོ་སྐོར་གཏོང་བ། **ko̱kor-tāngwa** to deceive (S/I) 12

མགོ་ན་བ། **ko̱-na̱wa** to have a headache (NI) 11

མགོ་ཡུ་འཁོར་བ། **ko̱yu-khōrwa** to feel dizzy (NI) 11

མགྱོགས་པོ(ར)། **kyo̱kpo** quickly/soon 12

མགྲོན་ཁང་། **ṭö̱nkhang** hotel/guesthouse 4

འགོ་ནས། **ko̱nä** again 11

འགོ་བ། **khö̱pa** to contract (illness) གོས་པ། (NI) 11

འགོར་བ། **ko̱rwa** to take time (NI) 9

འགྱོད་པ་སྐྱེ་བ། **kyö̱pa-kyēwa** to regret (NI) 14

འགྲམ། **ṭa̱m** next to 14

འགྲུལ་སྐྱོད། **ṭü̱lkyö'** travel 12

འགྲོ་བ། **ṭo̱wa** to go ཕྱིན་པ། **chīnpa** (I) 7

འགྲོངས་པ། **ṭho̱ngwa** to die གྲོངས་པ། (H/NI) 14

རྒན་འཁོགས། **kä̱nkhōk** elderly/old (person) 4

རྒན་པ། **kä̱npa** elder; older

རྒན་ལགས། **kä̱n-la:** (address for teacher) 14

རྒྱ་གར། **kya̱kar** India 3

རྒྱ་ཐུག **kya̱thuk** type of noodles/soup 9

རྒྱ་ནག **kya̱nak** China 3

རྒྱ་མ། **kya̱ma** (a measure of weight: about 500g/1.1 pounds) 10

རྒྱ་མི། **kya̱mi** Chinese (person) 3

རྒྱ་རིགས། **kya̱rik** Chinese (Han) 3

རྒྱ་སེ། **kya̱se** rose 13

རྒྱག་པ། **kya̱pa** (verbaliser) བརྒྱབ་པ། བརྒྱག་པ། (I) 8

རྒྱག་པ། **kya̱pa** (verbaliser) བརྒྱབ་པ། རྒྱག་པ། (NI) 8

རྒྱབ། **kya̱p** behind 4

རྒྱབ་འདྲེ་རྒྱག་པ། **kya̱mṭe-kya̱pa** to quarrel (S/I) 15

རྒྱབ་ལོགས། **kya̱plo:** behind 4

རྒྱལ་ཁབ། **kyä̱lkhap** country 3

རྒྱལ་སྒོ། **kyä̱lko** gate 14

རྒྱལ་རྩེ། **kya̱ntse** a Tibetan town 12

རྒྱལ་ས། **kyä̱lsa** capital city 13

རྒྱུ་ཆ། **kyu̱pcha** material(s) 10

(རྒྱུ་)ཕྱུག་པོ། **(kyu̱-)chūkpo** wealthy 3

རྒྱུགས། **kyu̱k** go! 7

རྒྱུགས་སྤྲོད། **kyu̱kṭö'** test/exam 6

རྒྱུས། **kyü̱'** familiar with 12

སྒང་། **ka̱ng** on top/above 4

སྒལ་པ། **kä̱lpa** back 11

སྒུག་པ། **ku̱kpa** to wait (S/I) 8

སྒེའུ་ཁུང་། **ke̱khung** window 2

སྒོ། **ko̱** door 2

སྒོ་རྒྱག་པ། **ko̱-kya̱pa** to close the door (S/I) 12

སྒོ་ང་། **ko̱nga** egg 9

སྒོར་མོ། **ko̱rmo** (denomination of money) 5

སྒྲིག་ཁྲིམས། **ṭ̱ikṭhim** rule(s) 11

སྒྲིག་འཛུགས། **ṭ̱iktsu̱k** rules/regime 6

འགྲིམ་འགྲུལ་ཁང་། **ṭ̱imṭul-kha̱ng** travel agent 8

འགྲོ། **ṭo̱** let's go! 7

བརྒྱད། **kyä̱'** eight 3

ང

ང་། **nga̱** I/me 2; **nga̱** (number-particle for 51–59) 3

ང་གཉིས། **nga̱-nyī'** we/us (two) 3

ང་ཚོ། **nga̱ntsho** we/us 2

ང་ཚོའི། **nga̱n-tshö:** our/ours 3

ང་རང་། **nga̱rang** I/me 2

ང་ལ། **nga̱-la** for me 5

ངའི། **ngä̱:** my/mine 3

ངུ་བ། **ngu̱wa** to cry ངུས་པ། (I) 15

ངོ་མཁྱེན་པ། **ngo̱khyēnpa** to know/recognise a person (H/S/NI) 14

ངོ་ཚ་བ། **ngo̱tshāwa** shame 14

ངོ་ཚ་པོ་བཟོ་བ། **ngōtshāpo-sö̱wa** to embarrass/shame (S/I) 14

ངོ་ཤེས་པ། **ngōshēnpa** acquaintance 3; **ngo̱-shēpa** to recognise/know someone (S/NI) 13

དངངས་སྐྲག་བྱེད་པ། **ngāmṭak-che̱pa** to be anxious (NI) 12

དངོས་གནས། **ngȫnä'** really; seriously; real 3

དངོས་གནས་བྱས་ན། **ngȫnä-chä̱na** in fact 14

མངག་པ། **ngākpa** to order (food, etc.) མངགས་པ། (S/I) 9

མངར་མོ། **ngārmo** sweet (taste); sweet dishes (desserts, etc.) 9

ལྔ། **ngā** five 3

ལྔ་བཅུ། **ngāpcu** fifty 3

སྔ་པོ་ནས། **ngāpo-nä** early on 14

སྔ་པོ། **ngāpo** early 7

སྔ་མ། **ngāma** former 7

(སྔོ་)ཚལ། **(ngō-)tshǟl** vegetable 9

སྔོན་པོ། **ngȫnpo** blue (but also the colour of vegetation) 6

སྔོན་ལ། **ngǟn-la** before 8

ཅ

ཅ་ལག **cālak** thing (manmade, mainly small items) 10

ཅོ་ཅོ། **cōco** elder brother 4

ཅོག་ཙེ། **cōktse** table 5

གཅིག **cīk** one 3; something/someone/somewhere 6/8

གཅིག་གཉིས་ཙམ། **cīknyī'-ts** one or two 5

གཅིག་པ། **cīkpa** the same 10

གཅོར་བ། **cārwa** to approach (used for visiting) བཅར་བ། གཅར་བ། (hu-H/I) 14

བཅུ། **cū** ten 3

བཅུ་དགུ། **cūrku̱** nineteen 3

བཅོ་བརྒྱད། **cōpkyä̱'** eighteen 3

བཅོ་ལྔ། **cōngā** fifteen 3

བཅུ་གཅིག **cūcik** eleven 3

བཅུ་གཉིས། **cūnyī'** twelve 3

བཅུ་དྲུག **cūṭhu̱k** sixteen 3

བཅུ་བདུན། **cūptü̱n** seventeen 3

བཅུ་བཞི། **cūpshi** fourteen 3

བཅུ་གསུམ། **cūksūm** thirteen 3

ལྕམ་སྐུ་ཞབས། **cām kūsho'** (address: for women of aristocratic origin) 15

ལྕེ་ལེ། **cēle** tongue 11

ཆ

ཆ། **chā** pair 10

ཆ་ཚང་། **chātshang** complete/all 5

ཆང་། **chāng** beer 6

ཆང་ཁང་། **chāngkhang** pub/drinking place 6

ཆང་ས་རྒྱག་པ། **chāngsa-kya̱pa** to get married (S/I) 8

ཆམ་པ། **chāmpa** a cold 11

ཆམ་པ་རྒྱག་པ། **chāmpa-kya̱pa** to have a cold (NI) 11

ཆར་པ་རྒྱག་པ། **chārpa-kya̱pa** to rain (NI) 12

ཆར་པ་གཏོང་བ། **chārpa-tāngwa** to rain (NI) 12

ཆིབས་བསྐྱུར་གནང་བ། **chīpkyur-nāngwa** to come/go (hi-H/I) 14

ཆུ། **chū** water 2

ཆུ་ཁང་། **chūkhang** bathroom 5

ཆུ་ཚོད། **chūtshö'** hour; timepiece (clock, watch, etc.) 8

ཆུ་ཚོད་དྲུག་པ། **chūtshö'-ṭhu̱kpa** six o'clock 8

ཆུང་ཆུང་། **chūngchūng** small 5

ཆུང་དྲག **chūng-ṭhak** too small 10

ཆེ་དྲག **chē-ṭhak** too large 10

ཆེ་བ། **chē:** bigger/larger/greater 5

ཆེན་པོ། **chēnpo** large/major/great 4

ཆོག་པ། **chōkpa** to be all right 14; allowed (modal verb) 15

ཆོས་ལགས། **chȫ'-la:** (polite address to nun) 14

མཆོད། **chȫ'** please eat!/please drink! 5

མཆོད་འབུལ་ཞུ་བ། **chȫnpü̱l-shu̱wa** to make religious offerings (S/I) 14

འཆི་བ། **shīwa** to die ཤི་བ། འཆི་བ། (NI) 12

ཇ

ཇ། **cha̱** tea 3

ཇ་ཁང་། **cha̱khang** teahouse 4

ཇ་དམ། **cha̱tham** thermos 6

ཇག་པ། **cha̱kpa** robber/bandit 12

ཇུས་གཏོགས་བྱེད་པ། **chu̱tōk-che̱pa** to interfere; to be involved (S/I) 14

ཇོ་ལགས། **chōla:** elder brother 4

མཇལ་བ། **cä̱lwa** to meet (hu-H/NI) 14

མཇལ་གར་བཅར་བ། **cä̱lka-cārwa** to go to meet (hu-H/I) 14

མཇལ་ཡོང་། **cä̱l-yong** see you! 8

འཇོག་པ། **sha̱kpa** to put བཞག་པ། གཞག་པ། (S/I)

རྗེད་པ། **ce̱'pa** to forget བརྗེད་པ། (S/NI) 11

ལྗང་གུ། **ca̱nku** green 6

ལྗགས། **ca̱k** tongue (H) 11

ཉ

ཉ། **nya̱** fish (live)

ཉ་ཤ། **nya̱shā** fish (flesh) 9

ཉན་པ། **nyä̱npa** to listen མཉན་པ། (S/I) 9

ཉལ་བ། **nyä̱lwa** to lie down (particularly for sleep: I) 7

ཉི་གདུགས། **nyi̱tuk** umbrella 15

ཉི་མ། **nyi̱ma** sun 2

ཉི་མ་སྟོན་པ། **nyi̱ma-tä̃npa** to be sunny (NI) 12

ཉི་ཤུ། **nyi̱shū** 3

ཉི་ཧོང་གི་སྐད། **nyi̱hong-ki kä̃'** Japanese (language) 13

ཉིན་གུང་ཁ་ལག **nyi̱nkung-khālak** lunch 9

ཉིན་མ། **nyi̱ma** day 3

ཉུང་ཉུང་། **nyu̱ngnyu̱ng** few 5

ཉེན་ཁ། **nye̱nkha** danger/risk 11

ཉོ་ཆ་རྒྱག་པ། **nyo̱pcha-kya̱pa** to shop (S/I) 8

ཉོ་བ། **nyo̱wa** to buy ཉོས་པ། **nyöwa** (S/I) 10

ཉོབ་པ། **nyo̱pa** to be bored/listless (NI) 12

གཉིད་ཁུག་པ། **nyī' khūkpa** ''''ཁུགས་པ། to fall asleep (NI) 11

གཉིས། **nyī'** two 3

གཉིས་ཀ། **nyī'ka** both 4

གཉིས་པ། **nyī'pa** second 8

གཉེར་པ། **nyērpa** 'manager' 14

མཉམ་དུ། **nyāmtu** together 4

སྙིང་པ། **nyīngpa** old 5

རྙེད་པ། **nyēpa** to find (NI) 11

སྙད་གཙེ་བ། **nyā̃'-tsēwa** to ridicule ····གཙེས་པ། (S/I) 13

སྙན་པོ། **nyā̃npo** pleasant (sounding) 6

སྙན་མཆོག **nyēncok** ear (H) 11

སྙིང་རྗེ་པོ། **nyīng-ce̱po** attractive 5

སྙིང་རྗེ། **nyīngcē:** exclamation of sympathy) 9

སྙུང་བ། **nyūngwa** to be ill བསྙུངས་པ། བསྙུང་བ། (H/NI) 11

ཏ

ཏག་ཏག **tākāk** exact/precisely 13

ཏོག་ཙམ། **tēts** slightly; a bit 4

གཏན་གཏན། **tā̃ntän** definitely 12

གཏོང་བ། **tāngwa** to send བཏང་བ། གཏང་བ། (S/I); verbaliser 8

གཏོང་གནང་བ། **tāng-nāngwa** (honorific of verbaliser གཏོང་བ།) 14

ལྟ་བ། **tāwa** to watch/look at བལྟས་པ། **tā̃wa** བལྟ་བ། (S/I) 10/11

ལྟད་མོ། **tā̃mo** spectacle/performance (either live or seen on screens) 8

ལྟོས། **tō̃'** look! 6

སྟངས། **tāng** the way/style (of doing something) 13

སྟབས་བདེ་པོ། **tāpte̱po** convenient 4

སྟེན་པ། **tēnpa** to consult བསྟེན་པ། (S/I) 11

སྟོང་པ། **tōngpa** empty; free (for time and availability) 5/8

སྟོད་ཐུང་། **tō̃thung** shirt/blouse 10

སྟོན་པ། **tā̃npa** to show བསྟན་པ། (S/I) 11

བརྟན་པོ། **tā̃npo** reliable 14

ཐ

ཐག་ཉེ་པོ། **thā-nye̱po** near 4

ཐག་རིང་པོ། **thā-ri̱ngpo** far 4

ཐང་ཆད་པ། **thāng-chä̱pa** to be tired (NI) 12

ཐབ་ཚང་། **thāptsang** kitchen 9

ཐུག་པ། **thūkpa** noodles and noodle dishes; soup and broth 9

ཐུག་པ། **thūkpa** to meet (NI) 13

ཐུགས་ཁྲལ་གནང་བ། **thūkṭhäl-nāngwa** to worry/concern oneself (H/NI) 14

ཐུགས་རྗེ་ཆེ། **thūce-chē** 'thank you' 2

ཐུང་ཐུང་། **thūngthūng** short 5

ཐུབ་པ། **thūpa** to be able/can (modal verb) 12

ཐུར་མ། **thūrma** spoon 9

ཐོག **thōk** in (i.e. a language); about 13

ཐོག་ཀ **thōka** upstairs 5

ཐོག་རྐྱག **thōkyap** all of a sudden 14

ཐོག་ལ། **thōk-la** on/by (for transport) 8

མཐུན་རྐྱེན། **thūnkyen** facilities 5

མཐོ་པོ། **thōpo** high 5

མཐོང་བ། **thōngwa** to see (S/NI) 11

འཐུང་བ། **thūngwa** to drink བཏུངས་པ། བཏུང་བ། (S/I) 9

འཐུང་ཡས། **thūngyä** a drink 9

འཐེན་ཐུག **thēnthūk** soup (with flattened noodles) 9

འཐོན་པ། **thōnpa** to leave/depart
ཐོན་པ། (I) 14

ད

ད། **tha̱:** so/now (speech-filler) 9/10
ད་གིན། **tha̱ncin** just before/just now 4
ད་ལྟ། **tha̱nta** now/at present 4
ད་ལན། **tha̱län** this time 14
ད་ལོ། **tha̱lo** this year 7
དང་། **thang** ‘and’ 4
དང་། **thang** (affix for requests, etc.) 5
དང་པོ། **tha̱ngpo** first 8
དང་པོ་ནས། **tha̱ngpo-nä** from the start 12
དམ་པོ། **tha̱mpo** strict; tight 6
དུག་སློག། **thu̱klōk** clothes 10
དུས། **thü’** when 6
དུས་ཚོད། **thü̱tshō’** time 8
དུས་ཚོད་སྐྱེལ་བ། **thü̱tshō’-kyālwa** to spend time ·····བསྐྱལ་བ། (S/I) 15
དེ། **the̱** that; the 2
དེ་ག་རང་། **tha̱ka-rang** quite right! 10
དེ་འདྲ། **the̱nṭä** like that/that way 7
དེ་ཚོ། **the̱n-tsho** those 2
དེབ། **the̱p** book 2
དེབ་ཚོང་ཁང་། **the̱p-tshōngkhang** bookshop 4
དེའི་སྔོན་ལ། **the̱: ngān-la** before that 8
དེའི་རྗེས་ལ། **thä̱: ce̱-la** after that 8
དེའི་རྩ་ལ། **the̱: tsā-la** next to that 4
དེར། **thä̱:** there 4
དོ། **tho̱** two 9
དོ་དགོང་། **tho̱kong** this evening 8
དོ་པོ། **tho̱po** baggage 5
དོགས་པ་ཟ་བ། **tho̱kpa-sa̱wa** to have doubts/suspicions (NI) 12
དོན། **thön** (number-particle for 71–79) 3
དྲག་པ། **ṭha̱kpa** recover (NI) 11
དྲག(་པ)། **ṭha̱k’** too 10
དྲང་པོ། **ṭha̱ngpo** honest 13
དྲང་པོ་བྱེད་པ། **ṭha̱ngpo-che̱pa** to act honestly (S/I) 14
དྲན་པ། **ṭhä̱npa** to remember; to think (S/NI) 11
དྲི་བ་གཏོང་བ། **ṭhi̱wa-tāngwa** to ask a question (S/I) 13
དྲི་མ། **ṭhi̱ma** smell 11
དྲུག **ṭhu̱k** six 3
དྲོ་པོ། **ṭho̱po** warm 5
གདོང་པ། **to̱ngpa** face 11
བདག་པོ། **ta̱kpo** owner 3
བདུན། **tü̱n** seven 3
བདུན་ཕྲག **tü̱nṭhak** week 3
བདེ་པོ། **te̱po** well 2
བདེན་པ། **te̱npa** true 3
མདང་དགོང་། **ta̱ngkong** last night/yesterday evening 7
མདུན། **tü̱n** front 4
འདི། **ti̱** this 2
འདི་འདྲ། **ti̱nṭä** like that/in that way 12
འདི་ནས། **ti̱nä** from here 4
འདི་བར། **ti̱wa:** around here 4
འདི་ཚོ། **ti̱n-tsho** these 2

འདིར། **tä̱:** here 4
འདུག། **tu̱'** (verb of existence) 4
འདུག་ག། **tu̱'-ka** (tag form of **tu̱'**) 4
འདུག་མི་འདུག། **tu̱' min-tu̱'** whether 10
འདོགས་ཁྱི། **to̱kkhyi** Tibetan Mastiff 12
འདོད(་པ)། **tö̱'(-pa)** to wish/to want (modal verb) 15
འདོན་པ། **tö̱npa** to extract བཏོན་པ། གདོན་པ། (S/I) 12
འདྲ་པོ། **ṭa̱po** alike/similar 10
འདྲ་མི་འདྲ། **ṭa̱-minṭa̱** all sorts 6
སྡུག་ཅགས། **tu̱kcāk** terrible 6
སྡེ་དགེ། **te̱rge** Derge (a Tibetan town) 7
སྡེར་ཙེ། **te̱rtse** plate 9
སྡོད་པ། **tä̱pa** to stay/live; sit བསྡད་པ། (I) 7
བསྡད་ས། **tä̱sa** place to stay, etc. 6

ན

ན། **na** if 12
ན་ཚ། **na̱tsha** illness 11
ན་བ། **na̱wa** to be ill (NI) 11
ནག་པོ། **na̱kpo** black 3
ནང་། **na̱ng** inside 4; home 3
ནང་མི། **na̱ngmi** family 13
ནང་པ། **na̱ngpa** Buddhist 2
ནང་བཞིན། **na̱ngshin** the same as 9
ནང་ལོགས། **na̱nglo:** inside 5
ནད་པ། **nä̱pa** patient/sick person 11
ནམ་རྒྱུན། **na̱mkyun** usually/normally 10
ནས། **nä** from 3; (conjunction) 9
ནོར་འཁྲུལ། **no̱rṭhül** mistake/error 12
ནོར་ཀྱོག། **no̱rkyok** mistaken 15
གནང་། **nāng** (affix for requests, etc.) 5
གནང་བ། **nāngwa** to do (H/S/I); to give (H/S/I); (honorific version of verbaliser བྱེད་པ། **che̱pa**) 14
གནངས་ཉིན་ཁ། **nāngnyinkha** day after tomorrow 8
གནམ་གྲུ། **nāmṭhu** airplane 8
གནམ་གྲུ་ཐང་། **nāmṭhuthāng** airport 8
གནམ་གཤིས། **nāmshi'** weather 9
གནས་སྟངས། **nä̃tang** situation 14
གནས་ཚུལ། **nä̃tshul** situation 14
གནས་ཚུལ་ཐོན་པ། **nä̃tshül-thö̱npa** something has cropped up 13
གནོད་པ། **nö̃'pa** to harm/damage (NI) 15
སྣ་ཁུང་། **nāku** nose 11
སྣང་བ་སྐྱིད་པོ། **nāngwa-kyīpo** carefree 15
སྣེ་ལེན་པ། **nēlenpa** receptionist 5
སྣོམ་པ། **nūmpa** to smell བསྣམས་པ། བསྣམ་པ། (S/I) 11

པ

པཱ་ལགས། **pāla:** father 3
པར་ཆས། **pārche** camera 2
པས། **pä/wä** (question-particle) 2
དཔེ། **pē:** exceptionally 6
དཔེར་ན། **pērna** for example 15
སྤུན་སྐྱ། **pīnkyak** relation/sibling 4
སྤུས་ཀ། **pū̃ka** quality 10
སྤོ་(སྤོ་)ལགས། **pō(po)la:** grandfather 4
སྤྱན། **cä̃n** eye (H) 11

སྤྱི་ཟླ། **cīnta** month (of general calendar) 8

སྤྲུལ་སྐུ། **ṭūlku** recognised 'incarnate' 14

སྤྲོ་འཆམ་པ། **ṭōchāmpa** tourist 13

ཕ

ཕ་གི། **phāki** that (over there) 2

ཕ་གིར། **phākä:** over there 4

ཕ་མ། **phāma** parents 4

ཕ་ཡུལ། **phāyül** (person's) area/land of origin 3

ཕ་ཡུལ་སྐད། **phāyül-kā̃'** regional dialect 15

ཕག་ཤ། **phāksha** pork 9

ཕན་ཐོགས་པ། **phā̃nthokpa** to be helpful/useful (NI) 15

ཕན་པ། **phā̃npa** to be helpful/beneficial (NI) 11

ཕར། **phār** there/away (from here) 14/15

ཕལ་ཆེར། **phā̃lcher** probably 13

ཕེབས། **phēp** come in! (H) 5

ཕེབས་པ། **phēpa** to go; to come (H) 7

ཕོར་པ། **phōrpa** bowl 9

ཕྱག **chāk** arm/hand (H) 11

ཕྱག་ཚོད། **chāktshö'** o'clock (H) 14

ཕྱག་མཛུབ། **chāktsuk** finger (H) 11

ཕྱག་རོགས་གནང་བ། **chākrok-nāngwa** to help (H/S) 15

ཕྱག་ལས་གནང་བ། **chāklä-nāngwa** to work (H/S) 15

ཕྱི་རྒྱལ། **chīkyäl** foreign/abroad 7

ཕྱི་རྒྱལ་བ། **chīkya̱lwa** foreigner 2

ཕྱི་ཚེས། **chītshe'** date (general calendar) 8

ཕྱི་ལོགས། **chīlo:** outside 4

ཕྱུ་པ། **chūpa** traditional Tibetan dress (having male and female versions) 10

ཕྱུར་བ། **chūra** cheese 9

ཕྱེད་ཀ། **chēka** half 8

ཕྲུ་གུ། **phūku** child 4

འཕྱ་ལད་རྒྱག་པ། **chālä-kya̱pa** to mock (S/I) 15

འཕྲོ་བརླག་གཏོང་བ། **ṭhōla'-tāngwa** to waste (S/I) 15

འཕྲོད་བསྟེན་དང་གཙང་སྦྲ། **ṭhö̃ten thang tsāngṭa** health and hygiene 11

བ

བག་ལེབ། **pha̱klep** bread 9

བར། **pha̱r** between 4

བར་དུ། **pha̱rthu** until 8

བལ་ཡུལ། **phä̱lyül** Nepal 3

བུ། **phu̱** boy; 2 son (when preceded by possessive pronoun, etc.) 3

བུ་མོ། **phu̱mo** girl 2; daughter (as above)

བུད་མེད། **phü̱me'** woman 8

བེད་སྤྱོད་གཏོང་བ། **phe̱cö̃-tāngwa** to use (S/I) 15

བོད། **phö̱'** Tibet 3

བོད་སྐད། **phö̱kā̃'** spoken Tibetan 8

བོད་སྐད་རྒྱག་པ། **phö̱kā̃'-kya̱pa** to speak Tibetan (S/I) 8

བོད་ཇ། **phö̱cha** Tibetan tea 6

བོད་པ། **phö̱pa** Tibetan (person) 2

བོད་ཚེས། **phö̱tshe'** date (Tibetan calendar) 8

བོད་ཟླ། **phö̱nta** month (Tibetan calendar) 8

བོད་ཡིག **phö̱'-yi̱k** written Tibetan 13

བོད་རིགས། **phö̱rik** Tibetan (ethnic group) 3

བྱ་ཤ། **cha̱shā** chicken (meat) 9

བྱས་ནས། **chä̱nä** (adverbial phrase) 12

བྱེད་སྒྲ། **che̱ṭa** (agentive particle: with the forms ཀྱིས་གིས་གྱིས་ས།) 7

བྱེད་པ། **che̱pa** བྱས་པ། to do (S/I); verbaliser (I/NI) 8

བྲོ་བ། **ṭho̱wa** taste (of food, etc.) 15

བླ་མ། **lāma** lama 14

བླུག་པ། **lūkpa** to pour/put in (S/I) 9

དབུ། **ū** head (H) 11

དབུ་སྐྲ། **ūṭa** hair (H) 11

དབུགས་གཏོང་བ། **ūk-tāngwa** to breathe (I) 12

དབུས་གཙང་། **ǖ'-tsang** Central Tibet 3

དབྱིན་(ཇིའི་)སྐད། **īn(chi:-)kǟ'** English (language) 13

དབྱིན་ཡུལ། **īnyül** England 3

དབྱིན་ལན། **īnlän** England 3

འབབ་པ། **pa̱ppa** to land བབ་པ། (NI) 8

འབུ། **pu̱** small creature/bug 2

འབུལ་བ། **phülwa** ཕུལ་བ། དབུལ་བ། to offer (hu-H/S/I) 14

འབྲས། **ṭä̱'** rice 9

འབྲས་བརྗོས། **ṭä̱ngȫ'** fried rice 9

འབྲི་བ། **ṭi̱wa** write བྲིས་པ། བྲི་བ། (S/I) 11

འབྲུག་ཡུལ། **ṭu̱kyül** Bhutan 3

འབྲེལ་སྒྲ། **ṭe̱lṭa** (genitive-particle) 3/7

སྦད་དེ། **pä̱t** extremely 5

སྦ་སི། **pa̱si** bus (from English) 4

སྦྲུག་སུབ་དོག་པོ། **bu̱ksup-tho̱kpo** narrow

སྦྲུག་སུབ་དོག་པོ་བཟོ་བ། **bu̱ksup-tho̱kpo-so̱wa** to make a situation tense (S/I) 12

སྦྱོང་བ། **ca̱ngwa** to study/train སྦྱངས་པ།/སྦྱང་བ། (S/I) 10

སྦྲག་ཁང་། **ṭa̱khang** post office 4

སྦྲིད་པ། **pi̱:wa** to feel numb/to lack sensation (NI) 11

མ

མ། **ma** (negating particle) 2

མ་གི། **ma̱ki** that (down there) 2

མ་གིར། **ma̱kä:** down there 4

མ་འགྲོ། **ma-ṭo̱** don't go! 7

མ་གཏོགས། **matōk** only 10

མ་གཞི་ནས། **ma-shi̱nä** anyway 4

མ་རེད། **ma-re̱'** is/are not 2

མང་པོ། **ma̱ngpo** many/much 3

མང་ཙམ། **ma̱ngtsa** some more 9

མར། **ma̱r** butter 9; down 15

མི། **mi̱** person 2; someone/anyone 4

མི། **mi̱n** (negating particle for **tu̱'**) 4

མིག **mīk** eye 11

མིང་། **mi̱ng** name 2

མིད་པ་ཚ་བ། **mi̱pa-tshāwa** to have a sore throat (NI) 11

མེན། **me̱:** (negation of **yi̱n**) 2/7

སྨུ་མེན། **mu̱men** purple 6

མེ། **me̱** fire

མེ་འཁོར། **me̱khor** train (railway)

མེ་ཏོག། **me̱tok** flower 11

མེད། **me̱'** (negation of **yö̱'**) 4

མོ་རང་། **mo̱rang** she (non-polite) 2

མོ་རང་གི། **mo̱rang-ki** (non-polite) hers 3

མོ་ཊ། **mo̱ṭa** car (from English) 2

མོ་ཊ་གཏོང་བ། **mo̱ṭa-tāngwa** to drive (S/I) 8

མོག་མོག། **mo̱mo** (a food: parcels of dough, encasing meat, etc.) 9

དམའ་པོ། **māpo** low 5

དམར་མོ་/པོ། **mārmo/po** red 6

དམིགས་བསལ། **mīksäl** special/particular 8

རྨོ་མོ་ལགས། **mōmola:** རྨོ་ལགས། **mōla:** grandmother 4

སྨན། **mǟn** medicine 11

སྨན་པ། **mǟnpa** doctor 2

སྨན་ཚོང་ས། **mǟn-tshōngsa** chemist/pharmacy 11

སྨུག་པ་འཁོར་བ། **mūkpa-khōrwa** to be misty/foggy (NI) 12

སྨྱུ་གུ **nyūku** pen 2

ཙ

ཙམ། **tsa** around/approximately 8

གཙང་མ། **tsāngma** clean 3

རྩ། **tsā** place (home, etc. of a person) 7; (number-particle for 21–29) 3

རྩ་ནས། **tsānä** (emphatic negation) 6

རྩམ་པ། **tsāmpa** roasted barley grain flour (Tibetan staple food) 9

རྩིས་རྒྱག་པ། **tsī'-kya̱pa** to calculate (S/I)

རྩུབ་པོ། **tsūpo** rough; harsh 15

རྩེད་ཁང་། **tsēkhang** gaming centre 6

རྩེད་མོ། **tsēmo** game 6

རྩེད་མོ་རྩེ་བ། **tsēmo-tsēwa** to play; to joke ····བརྩེས་པ། ····བརྩེ་བ། (S/I) 11

ཚ

ཚ་གློག། **tshālok** heating 5

ཚ་པོ། **tshāpo** hot 5

ཚ་བ། **tshāwa** to have a stinging or burning sensation (NI) 11

ཚ་བ་འབར་བ། **tshāwa-pa̱rwa** to have a fever (NI) 11

ཚ་བོ། **tshāwo** nephew 4

ཚ་མོ། **tshāmo** niece 4

ཚང་མ། **tshāngma** all/everything 4

ཚབ། **tshāp** replacement/instead of 12

ཚར་བ། **tshārwa** to finish (NI) 9; already (modal verb: NI) 12

ཚལ། **tshäl** vegetables 9

ཚིག་པ་ཟ་བ། **tshīkpa-sa̱wa** to be angry/annoyed (NI) 12

ཚུད་པ། **tshǖpa** to be (re-)admitted (NI) 14

ཚུར། **tshūr** back to (here, me, etc.) 14/15

ཚུར་ཕྱོགས། **tshūr-cho'** this side 4

ཚུར་ཤོག། **tshūr-shōk** come back! 15

ཚེམ་(བུ་)ཁང་། **tshēm(pu)-khāng** the tailors 10

ཚེམས། **tshēm** tooth (H) 11

ཚེས་པ། **tshēpa** calendar date 8

ཚོགས། **tshōk** prayer assembly (for monks or nuns) 14

ཚོང་མཁན། **tshōngkhǟn** shopkeeper/seller 10

ཚོང་ཁང་། **tshōngkhang** shop 3

ཚོང་རྒྱག་པ། **tshōng-kyapa** to trade (S/I) 8

ཚོང་པ། **tshōngpa** trader/business person 3

ཚྭ། **tshā** salt 14

མཚན་(མོ)། **tshǟn(mo)** night 5

མཚམས་མཚམས་(ལ)། **tshāmtsham(la)** sometimes 10

མཚོན་མདོག **tshöntok** colour 6

འཚོང་བ། **tshōngpa** to sell བཙོངས་པ། བཙོང་བ། (S/I) 10

འཚོལ་བ། **tshǟlwa** to search for བཙལ་བ། (S/I) 8/9

ཛ

མཛངས་བྱེད་པ། **tsang-chepa** to practise restraint (through politeness; S/I) 9

མཛུབ་མོ། **tsuku** finger/toe 11

འཛིན་པ། **simpa** to catch བཟུང་བ། གཟུང་བ། (S/I) 11

འཛུལ་བ། **tsülwa** to enter (I) 12

ཛིག་པོ། **tsikpo** impressive/majestic 6

ཝ

ཝེ། **we** hey! (informal greeting) 7

ཞ

ཞབས། **shap** foot/leg (H) 11

ཞལ། **shǟl** mouth (H) 11

ཞལ་དཔར་(གཏོང་)གནང་བ། **shǟlpar (tāng-)nāngwa** to phone (H/S/I) 14

ཞལ་རས། **shǟlrä'** face (H) 11

ཞལ་ལག **shǟlak** food (H) 9

ཞི་བདེ། **shite** peace 6

ཞིག **shik** a (used infrequently) 13

ཞིམ་པོ། **shimpo** tasty/aromatic 5

ཞུ་བ། **shuwa** ཞུས་པ། **shüwa** (honorific for verbaliser བྱེད་པ། **chepa**; hu-H/S/I) 14

ཞེ། **she** (number-particle for 41–49) 3

ཞེ་དྲག **shethak** very; a lot 5; too 10

ཞེ་ས། **shesa** honorific language 14

ཞེད་པ། **shepa** to be scared (NI) 12

ཞོ། **sho** yoghurt 9

ཞོགས་ཀས། **shokä** morning 11

ཞོགས་ཇ། **shokcha** 'breakfast' (actually meaning 'morning tea') 9

ཞོགས་པ། **shokpa** morning 8

ཞྭ་མོ། **shamo** hat 10

གཞན། **shǟn** otherwise 11

གཞན་དག **shǟnthak** other; another 4; other than that 11

གཞས། **shǟ'** song 6

གཞུང་། **shung** government; authority 4

གཞོན་གཞོན། **shönshön** young 3

བཞག **shak** put down! (see འཇོག་པ།) 5

བཞི། **shi** four 3

བཞུགས། **shu:** sit down!; wait! (H) 5

བཞུགས་པ། **shu:pa** to sit; stay/live (H/I) 5

བཞེངས་པ། **shangwa** to stand up; arise (H/I) 14

བཞེས། **she'** take! (esp. for food or drink: H) 5

ཟ

ཟ་ཁང་། **sakhang** restaurant 3

ཟ་ཕྲུག་ལང་བ། **sapthuk-langwa** to itch ····ལངས་པ། (NI) 11

ཟ་བ། **sawa** to eat བཟས་པ། **säwa** བཟའ་བ། (S/I) 9

ཟ་ཡས། **sayä** food/foodstuffs 6

ཟམ་པ། **sampa** bridge

ཟིང་སྐྱ། **singkya** pink 6

ཟིན་པ་ལ། **sinpa-la** to (o'clock) 8

ཟུག་རྒྱག་པ། **suk-kyapa** to ache (NI) 11

ཟེར། **se/-s** (speech-marker) 13

ཟེར་མཁན་གཅིག **sekhän** one called 4

···ཟེར་ན···། **. . . serna . . .** according to 15

ཟེར་བ། **serwa** to say (S/I) 13

ཟླ་ཉིན། **tanyin** last year 7

ཟླ་བ། **tawa** month; moon 8

ཟློས་གར་ཁང་། **tökarkhāng** theatre 8

གཟབ་གཟབ་བྱེད་པ། **sapsap-chepa** to be careful/act carefully (S/I) 9

གཟབ་གཟབ་བྱས་ནས། **sapsap-chänä** carefully 12

གཟའ། **sa** day (in weekday names) 3

གཟའ་ཉི་མ། **sa-nyima** Sunday 3

གཟའ་པ་སངས། **sa-pāsang** Friday 3

གཟའ་སྤེན་པ། **sa-pēnpa** Saturday 3

གཟའ་ཕུར་བུ། **sa-phūrpu** Thursday 3

གཟའ་མིག་དམར། **sa-mikmār** Tuesday 3

གཟའ་ཟླ་བ། **sa-tawa** Monday 3

གཟའ་ལྷག་པ། **sa-lhākpa** Wednesday 3

གཟིགས་པ། **sikpa** to look; to buy (S/H) 10 to see (S/NI) 14

གཟུགས་པོ། **sukpo** body 5

གཟུགས་པོ་ཐུང་ཐུང་། **sukpo-thūngthūng** short (for people) 5

གཟུགས་པོ་རིང་པོ། **sukpo-ringpo** tall (for people) 5

བཟོ་བ། **sowa** to make བཟོས་པ། **söwa** (S/I) 8

འ

འོ། **o** ah/oh! 2

འོ་ན། **ona** so/well then 4

འོ་མ། **oma** milk 9

འོ་ཡ། **oya** okay 4

འོ་རེད། **o-re'** oh yes! 6

འོག **ok** below/under 4

འོག་ཐོག **oktho'** lower/ground floor 5

འོག་མ། **okma** younger brother or sister 4

འོང་། **ong** yes/okay 7

ཡ

ཡ་གི། **yaki** that (up there) 2

ཡ་གིར། **yakä:** up there 4

ཡ་གཅིག **ya-cīk** one of a pair 10

ཡ་མེད་གཏོང་བ། **yame'-tāngwa** to ignore (S/I) 15

ཡ་ཡ། **ya:ya** (response indicating agreement, acceptance, etc.) 7/14

ཡག་པོ། **yakpo** good 5

ཡག་པོ་བྱས་ནས། **y̱akpo-chä̱nä** well (describing actions) 12

ཡག་པོར། **y̱akpo** well (describing actions) 12

ཡག་པོ་བྱེད་པ། **y̱akpo-che̱pa** to treat well 14

ཡག་བྱུང་། **y̱akchung** (expression: somewhere between 'that's good!' and 'thanks!') 11

ཡག་ཤོས། **y̱ak-shō̱'** best 5

ཡང་། **yä** also 2; neither (with negation) 4

ཡང་མིན་ན། **y̱angme̱:na** or/alternatively 13

ཡར། **ya̱r** up 15

ཡར་ཕེབས། **ya̱r-phēp** come in! 15

ཡར་འཕར་བ། **ya̱r-phārwa** to increase (NI) 10

ཡར་ལང་བ། **ya̱r-la̱ngwa** to arise (I) 11

ཡས **yä** (particle; also spelt ཡ།, ཡག།, ཡས།) 14/15

ཡི་གེ **yi̱ke** letter

ཡིན། **yi̱n** (verb of identity: 'am', etc.) 2

ཡིན་དང་ཡིན། **yi̱n-tayi̱n** of course! 5

ཡིན་ནའང་། **yi̱nnä:** but 3

ཡིན་པ། **yi̱n-pä** (question tag) 3

ཡིན་ས་རེད། **yi̱n-sa-re'** I should think it is . . . (identity) 11/12

ཡུལ་ལྗོངས། **yu̱lcong** scenery 6

ཡོང་ང་། **yo̱ngnga** okay! 10

ཡོང་བ། **yo̱ngwa** to come (I) 7; to happen (NI) 12

ཡོད། **yö̱'** (verb of existence: 'am', etc.) 4

ཡོད་པ། **yö̱-pa** (question tag) 7

ཡོད་རེད། **yo̱re'** (verb of existence: 'is', etc.) 4

ཡོད་ས་རེད། **yö̱'-sa re̱'** I should think that . . . (existence) 12

ཡོལ་ནས། **yö̱l-nä** past (o'clock) 8

གཡག **yāk** yak 1

གཡར་བ། **yārwa** to borrow; to lend (S/I) 10

གཡས་པ། **yǟpa** right(-hand)

གཡེར་མ། **ērma** Szechuan pepper 11

གཡོན་པ། **yȫnpa** left(-hand)

ར

ར། **ra̱** goat

རག་པ། **ra̱kpa** receive (NI) 11

རག་ལས་པ། **ra̱kläpa** to depend (NI) 11

རང་། **ra̱ng** just/really (emphatic) 7

རི། **ri̱** hill/mountain 4

རི་ལི། **ri̱li** train; railway (from English) 13

རིག་གཞུང་། **ri̱kshung** culture 15

རིང་པོ། **ri̱ngpo** long/tall 5

རིན་པོ་ཆེ། **ri̱npochē** (address: mainly for recognised 'incarnate' figures) 14

རིལ་བ། **ri̱lwa** to fall over (NI) 11

རིལ་བུ། **ri̱lpu** pill 11

རེ། **re̱** (number-particle for 61–69) 3

རེ་རེ། **re̱re** each 10

རེད། **re̱'** (verb of identity: 'is', etc.) 3

རེད་པ། **re̱'-wa** isn't it? (tag question) 3

རོགས། **ro̱'** (affix for requests, etc.) 5

རོགས་གནང་། **ro̱-nāng** (affix for requests, etc.) 5

རོགས་པ། **ro̱kpa** companion; associate 3

རོགས་པ་བྱེད་པ། **ro̱kpa-che̱pa** to help (S/I) 8

རླུང་ལང་བ། **lūng-la̱ngwa** to lose one's temper ···ལངས་པ། (NI) 15

རླངས་འཁོར། **lāngkhor** automobile/bus 4

རླངས་འཁོར་འབབ་ཚུགས། **lāngkhor-pa̱ptshuk** bus station 4

ལ

ལ། **la** at/in; to; for (**la̱thön**-particle) 4

ལ་དུག་རྒྱག་པ། **la̱thuk-kya̱pa** to have altitude sickness (NI) 12

ལ་དོན། **la̱thön** (particle: see entry for ལ།) 4

ལག་པ། **la̱kpa** arm/hand 9/11

ལག་ཤུབས། **la̱kshup** gloves 10

ལགས། **la:/la** (polite expression: added to names and responses); 'pardon' 2/8

ལགས་སོ། **la̱:so** (expression of assent/agreement) 9

ལང་བ། **la̱ngwa** to stand up; to arise ལངས་པ། (I)

ལད་ཟློས་བྱེད་པ། **lä̱ntö'-che̱pa** to imitate (S/I) 15

ལན་སྐྱེལ་མཁན། **lä̱n-kyēl-nyän** messenger 13

ལན་སྐྱེལ་བ། **lä̱n-kyēlwa** to pass on/deliver a message ···བསྐྱལ་བ། (S/I) 13

ལན་རྒྱག་པ། **lä̱n-kya̱pa** to answer (S/NI) 13

ལན་པོ། **lä̱npo** becoming/to suit 10

ལབ་པ། **la̱pa** to tell/say (S/I) 9/13

ལམ་ཁ། **la̱mkha** road/path 4

ལམ་སང་། **la̱msāng** immediately 11

ལས། **lä** than (comparative) 5

ལས་ཀ། **lä̱ka** work 6

ལས་ཀ་བྱེད་པ། **lä̱ka-che̱pa** to work (S/I) 8

ལས་ཁུངས། **lä̱khung** office 4

ལས་འགན། **lä̱nkän** responsibility 14

ལས་བྱེད། **lä̱'che'** civil servant/office worker 3

ལས་མི། **lä̱mi** worker 9

ལས་རོགས། **lä̱rok** colleague 4

ལི་ཝང་། **li̱wang** orange (colour) 6

ལུགས་སྲོལ། **lu̱ksȫl** custom/tradition 4

ལུང་པ། **lu̱ngpa** country/area 3

ལུས་པ། **lä̱wa** to accidentally leave something (NI) 11

ལེན་པ། **le̱npa** to take/collect/get བླངས་པ། བླང་པ། (S/I) 9

ལོ། **lo̱** year 3

ལོག་པ། **lo̱kpa** to go back/return (for people: I) 7

ལོག་འགྲོ་པ། **lo̱kṭowa** (same as above) ལོག་ཕྱིན་པ། (I) 7

ཤ

ཤ། **shā** meat 6

ཤ་ཕག་ལེབ། **shāphaklep** fried, meat-filled flattened 'breads' 9

ཤ་མེད། **shāme'** vegetarian (food) 6

ཤ་མེད་(པའི་)ཁ་ལག
shāme'(-pä:)khālak vegetarian (*lit.* 'meatless') food 9

ཤངས་། **shāng** nose (H) 11

ཤོད་པ། **shǟ'pa** to say/explain/ describe བཤད་པ། **shǟpa** 7/13

ཤི་བ། (see འཆི་བ།) 12

ཤུགས། **shūk** power/strength 5

ཤེས་པ། **shēpa** to understand/know (S/NI) 13

ཤོག **shōk** (affix for requests, etc.) 5

ཤོག **shōk** come! 7

ཤོག་གུ། **shūku** paper 11

ཤོང་བ། **shōngwa** to fit (NI) 10

ཤོས། **shȫ'** '-est' (superlative) 5

ས

ས། **sā** ground 2; (agentive particle) 7

ས་ཀོང་། **sākong** rut 12

ས་ཆ། **sācha** place 6

སང་ཉིན། **sāngnyin** tomorrow 8

སུ། **sū** who? 2

སུའི། **sǖ:** whose 3

སུད་སི། **sǖsi** Switzerland 3

སུམ་བརྒྱ། **sūmkya** three hundred 12

སུམ་ཅུ། **sūmcū** thirty 3

སེམས། **sēm** mind 6

སེམས་ཁྲལ། **sēmṭhäl** worry/concern 6

སེམས་ཅན། **sēmcän** animal 6

སེམས་པ། **sāmpa** to think བསམས་པ། བསམ་པ། (NI) 11

སེམས་པ་བཟང་པོ་བྱེད་པ།
sēmpa-sa̱ngpo-che̱pa to act kindly 14

སེར་པོ། **sērpo** yellow 6

སེར་བ་རྒྱག་པ། **sēra-kya̱pa** to hail (NI) 12

སོ། **sō** tooth 11; (number-particle for 31–39) 3

སོ་རྒྱག་པ། **sō-kya̱pa** to bite (S/I) 12

སོག་ཡུལ། **sōkyül** Mongolia 3

སོང་། **sōng** (auxiliary verb) 7

གསང་སྤྱོད། **sāngcö'** toilet 5

གསན་པ། **sǟnpa** to listen (H/S/I) 13

གསར་པ། **sārpa** new 5

གསུང་བ། **sūngwa** to say/tell གསུངས་པ། (H/S) 13

གསུངས། **sūng** speak! (H) 5

གསུམ། **sūm** three 3

གསོལ་ཇ། **sȫlcha** tea (H) 9

གསོལ་ཁྲོད། **sȫlṭhö'** stomach (H) 11

གསོལ་དཔོན། **sȫlpön** main attendant 14

བསམ་ཚུལ། **sāmtshul** opinion 15

བསམ་བློ་གཏོང་བ། **sāmlo-tāngwa** to think (S/I) 11

བསིལ་མ། **sīlma** change (i.e. coins) 10

བསོད་བདེ་ཆེན་པོ། **sōte-chēnpo** fortunate (person) 11

སྲང་ལམ། **sānglam** street 4

སྲུ་མོ། **sūmo** aunt (maternal) 4

སླེབ་པ། **lēpa** to arrive སླེབས་པ། (NI) 12

སློབ་པ། **lāpa** to teach བསླབས་པ། བསླབ་པ། (S/I) 15

སློབ་ཕྲུག **lōpṭhuk** student 2

སློབ་སྦྱོང་བྱེད་པ། **lōpcong-chẹpa** to study (S/I) 8

སློབ་ཚན། **lōptshän** lesson 6

ཧ

ཧ་གོ་བ། **hākhọwa** to understand/know (S/NI) 13

ཧ་ལས་པ། **hāläwa** to be surprised/shocked (NI) 12

ལྷགས་པ་རྒྱག་པ། **lhākpa-kyạpa** to be windy (NI) 12

ལྷོད་ལྷོད་བྱེད་པ། **lhȫlhö'-chẹpa** to take it easy (I) 12

ཨ །

ཨ། **ā** what? 3

ཨ་ཁ། **ākha** (exclamation) that's a shame! 7

ཨ་ཁུ། **ākhu** uncle (paternal) 4

ཨ་ཅག **āca** elder sister 4

ཨ་མཆོག **āmcok** ear 11

ཨ་མདོ། **āmto** Eastern Tibetan province 3

ཨ་ནེ། **āne** aunt (paternal) 4; nun 14

ཨ་ཕ། **āpha** father 4

ཨ་མ། **āma** mother 4

ཨ་ཙི། **ātsi:** (exclamation: surprise, etc.) 7

ཨ་ཞང་། **āshang** uncle (maternal) 4

ཨ་ཡོ། **āyo** (exclamation: weariness or discontent) 11

ཨ་ར། **āra** ow! 9

ཨ་རི། **āri** America (USA) 3

ཨ་རིའི་སྒོར་མོ། **āri:-kọrmo** US dollar 5

ཨ་ལས། **ālä** oh, I see 2

ཨ་རག **ārak** spirits (alcohol) 2

ཨ་ལེ་དང་པོ། **āle-thạngpo** anyway/but first 8

ཨང་། **ā** (affix for requests, etc.) 5

ཨའུ་ཙམ། **āü:-ts** not bad/passable 8

ཨེ། **ē** (question-particle) 8

ཨེ་ནི། **ēni** and/so 2

ཨེན་ཆུང་། **ēnchung** young monk 15

ཨེམ་ཆི། **ēmchi** doctor 11

English-Tibetan glossary

Words which equate to action verbs in Tibetan are listed, in their present form, as either intentional (I) or non-intentional (NI).

The number after each entry shows the unit where the word first occurs.

'' indicates that the word only loosely equates to the Tibetan entry.

abbot མཁན་པོ། **khā̈npo** 14
able to ཐུབ་པ། **thūpa** 12
about ཐོག **thōk** 13; སྐོར། **kōr** 9
above སྒང་། **ka̲ng** 4
ache ཟུག་རྒྱག་པ། **su̲k-kya̲pa** (NI) 11
acquaintance ངོ་ཤེས་པ། **ngo̲shēnpa** 3
after རྗེས་ལ། **ce̲-la** 8
again འགོ་ནས། **ko̲nä** 11
airplane གནམ་གྲུ། **nāmṭhu** 8
airport གནམ་གྲུ་ཐང་། **nāmṭhuthāng** 8
all ཚང་མ། **tshāngma** 4
allowed ཆོག་པ། **chōkpa** 15
also ཡང་། **yä** 2
altitude sickness ལ་དུག **la̲thuk** 12
'am' ཡིན། **yi̲n** 2; ཡོད། 4
America (USA) ཨ་རི། **āri** 3
'and' དང་། **thang** 4; ཨེ་ནི། **ēni** 2
angry ཚིག་པ་ཟ་བ། **tshīkpa-sa̲wa** (NI) 12
animal སེམས་ཅན། **sēmcän** 6
another གཞན་དག **shā̲nthak** 4
answer ལན་རྒྱག་པ། **lā̲n-kya̲pa** (I) 13
anxious དངངས་སྐྲག་བྱེད་པ། **ngāmṭak-che̲pa** (NI) 12
any(thing) གང་ཡང་། **khā̲:** 6
anyway མ་གཞི་ནས། **ma-shi̲nä** 4
apple ཀུ་ཤུ། **kūshu** 9
arise ལང་བ། **la̲ngwa** (I) 11
arm ལག་པ། **la̲kpa** 9
around (approximately) ཙམ། **ts** 5
arrive སླེབ་པ། **lēpa** (NI) 12
ask སྐད་ཆ་འདྲི་བ། **kā̈cha-ti̲wa** 10; དྲི་བ་གཏོང་བ། **ṭhi̲wa-tāngwa** (I) 13
at ལ། **la** 4
attractive སྙིང་རྗེ་པོ། **nyīng-ce̲po** 5
aunt (maternal) སྲུ་མོ། **sūmo** 4
aunt (paternal) ཨ་ནེ། **āne** 4

bank དངུལ་ཁང་། **ngṻlkhang** 4
banter སྐད་ཆ་ཅི་གྲོས་མོལ་གྲོས། **kā̈cha-cīṭömö̲lṭö'** 6

bargain གོང་སྒྲིག་པ། **kho̲ng-t̲ikpa** (l) 10
bathroom ཆུ་ཁང་། **chūkhang** 5
because གང་ཡིན་ཟེར་ན། **kha̲ngyin-se̲rna** 8
bed ཉལ་ཁྲི། **nyä̲lṭhī**
beef གླང་ཤ། **lāngshā** 9
beer ཆང་། **chāng** 6
before སྔོན་ལ། **ngȫn-la** 8
behind རྒྱབ(་ལོགས)། **kya̲p(lo:)** 4
below འོག **o̲k** 4
beside འཁྲིས། **ṭhī'** 4
best ཡག་ཤོས། **ya̲kshȫ'** 5
between བར། **pha̲r** 4
Bhutan འབྲུག་ཡུལ། **ṭu̲kyül** 3
bite སོ་རྒྱག་པ། **sō-kya̲pa** (l) 12
black ནག་པོ། **na̲kpo** 3
blue སྔོན་པོ། **ngȫnpo** 6
body གཟུགས་པོ། **su̲kpo** 11
book དེབ། **the̲p** 2
bookshop དེབ་ཚོང་ཁང་། **the̲p-tshōngkhang** 4
bored ཉོབ་པ། **nyo̲pa** (Nl) 12
borrow གཡར་བ། **yārwa** (l) 10
both གཉིས་ཀ། **nyī'ka** 4
bowl ཕོར་པ། **phōrpa** 9
boy བུ། **phu̲** 2
bread བག་ལེབ། **pha̲klep** 9
breathe དབུགས་གཏོང་བ། **ūk-tāngwa** (l) 12
bridge ཟམ་པ། **sa̲mpa**
bring འཁྲིད་པ། **ṭhīwa** (l) 14
broth (and some soups) ཐུག་པ། **thūkpa** 9
brother (elder) ཅོ་ཅོ། **cōco**; ཇོ་ལགས། **chōla:** 4
Buddhist ནང་པ། **na̲ngpa** 2
bug/small creature འབུ། **pu̲** 2
building ཁང་པ། **khāngpa** 2
bus སྦ་སི། **pa̲si**; (སྤྱི་སྤྱོད་)གླངས་འཁོར། **(cīcȫ'-)lāngkhor** 8
bus station གླངས་འཁོར་འབབ་ཚུགས། **lāngkhor pa̲ptshuk** 4
but ཡིན་ནའང་། **yi̲nnä:** 3
butter མར། **ma̲r** 9
buy ཉོ་བ། **nyo̲wa** (l) 10
by (for transport) ཐོག་ལ། **thōk-la** 8

call (out to someone) སྐད་གཏོང་བ། **kǟ'-tāngwa** (l) 8
camera པར་ཆས། **pārche** 2
can ཐུབ་པ། **thūpa** 12
capital city རྒྱལ་ས། **kyä̲lsa** 13
car མོ་ཊ། **mo̲ṭa** 2
(act) carefully གཟབ་གཟབ་བྱེད་པ། **sa̲psap-che̲pa** (l) 9
carrot གུང་ལ་ཕུག **khu̲ng-laphūk** 9
carry འཁྱེར་བ། **khyērwa** (l) 9
catch འཛིན་པ། **si̲mpa** (l) 11
centre དཀྱིལ། **kyīl** 12
chair ཀུབ་བཀྱག **kūpkyak** 5
change (coins) བསིལ་མ། **sīlma** 10
cheap གོང་ཁེ་པོ། **kho̲ng-khēpo** 10
cheese ཕྱུར་བ། **chūra** 9
chemist (pharmacy) སྨན་ཚོང་ས། **mǟn-tshōngsa** 11
chicken (meat) བྱ་ཤ། **cha̲shā** 9
child ཕྲུ་གུ། **phūku** 4

China རྒྱ་ནག **kya̱nak** 3
Chinese (Han) རྒྱ་རིགས། **kya̱rik** 3
Chinese (language) རྒྱ་སྐད། **kya̱kǟ'** 10
chopsticks ཀོ་ཙེ། **kōtse** (from Chinese) 9
clean གཙང་མ། **tsāngma** 3
clock (or watch) ཆུ་ཚོད་། **chūtshö'** 8
close (a door) སྒོ་རྒྱག་པ། **ko̱-kya̱pa** (I) 12
clothes དུག་སློག **thu̱klōk** 10
cold གྲང་མོ། **ṭha̱ngmo** 5
have a cold ཆམ་པ་རྒྱག་པ། **chāmpa-kya̱pa** (NI) 11
(work) colleague ལས་རོགས། **lä̱rok** 4
colour མཚོན་མདོག **tshȫntok** 6
come ཡོང་བ། **yo̱ngwa** (I) 7
companion རོགས་པ། **ro̱kpa** 3
consult (esp. doctors) སྟེན་པ། **tēnpa** (I) 11
convenient སྟབས་བདེ་པོ། **tāpte̱po** 4
cough གློ་རྒྱག་པ། **lō-kya̱pa** (NI) 11
count གྲངས་ཀ་རྒྱག་པ། **ṭha̱ngka-kya̱pa** (I) 13
country རྒྱལ་ཁབ། **kyǟlkhap**; ལུང་པ། **lu̱ngpa** 3
criticise སྐྱོན་འཛུགས་པ། **kyȫn-tsūkpa** (I) 12
cry ངུ་བ། **ngu̱wa** (I) 15
culture རིག་གཞུང་། **ri̱kshung** 15
cup (porcelain) དཀར་ཡོལ། **käryöl** 9

danger ཉེན་ཁ། **nye̱nkha** 11
date (day of month) ཚེས་པ། **tshēpa** 8
daughter བུ་མོ། **phu̱mo** 2
day ཉི་མ། **nyi̱ma** 3
deceive མགོ་སྐོར་གཏོང་བ། **ko̱kor-tāngwa** (I) 12
definitely གཏན་གཏན། **tǟntän** 12
depend རག་ལས་པ། **ra̱kläpa** (NI) 11
(regional) dialect ཕ་ཡུལ་སྐད། **phāyül-kǟ'** 15
diarrhoea གྲོད་ཁོག་བཤལ་བ། **ṭho̱khok-shǟlwa** (NI) 11
die འཆི་བ། **shīwa** (NI) 12
difference ཁྱད་པར། **khyēpar** 10
different ཁག་ཁག **khāka** 4
difficult ཁག་པོ། **khākpo** 6; དཀའ་ལས་ཁག་པོ། **kāle-khākpo** 10
disciple དགེ་ཕྲུག **ke̱ṭhuk** 14
dizzy མགོ་ཡུ་འཁོར་བ། **ko̱yu-khōrwa** (NI) 11
do བྱེད་པ། **che̱pa** (I) 8
doctor སྨན་པ། **mǟnpa** 2; ཨེམ་ཆི། **ēmchi** (from Mongolian) 11
dog ཁྱི། **khyī** 2
door སྒོ། **ko̱** 2
down མར། **ma̱r** 15
drink འཐུང་ཡས། **thūngyä** 9
drink འཐུང་བ། **thūngwa** (I) 9
drive མོ་ཊ་གཏོང་བ། **mo̱ṭa-tāngwa** (I) 8
driver (མོ་ཊའི་)ཁ་ལོ་བ། **(mo̱ṭä:-) khālowa** 8

each རེ་རེ། **re̱re** 10
ear ཨ་མཆོག **āmcok** 11
early སྔ་པོ། **ngāpo** 7
eat ཟ་བ། **sa̱wa** (I) 9

egg སྒོ་ང་། **konga** 9

eight བརྒྱད། **kyä'** 3

eighteen བཅོ་བརྒྱད། **cōpkyä'** 3

eleven བཅུ་གཅིག **cūcik** 3

empty སྟོང་པ། **tōngpa** 5

end (a gathering) གྲོལ་བ། **ṭhölwa** (NI) 14

England དབྱིན་ཡུལ། **īnyül**; དབྱིན་ལན། **īnlän** 3

English (language) དབྱིན་(ཇིའི་)སྐད། **īn(chi:)-kä'** 13

enjoy oneself སྐྱིད་པོ་གཏོང་བ། **kyīpo-tāngwa** (I) 15

enter འཛུལ་བ། **tsülwa** (I) 12

evening དགོང་དག **kongthak** 8

evening meal དགོང་དྲོའི་ཁ་ལག **kongṭhö:-khālak** 9

everything ཚང་མ། **tshāngma** 6

exact ཏག་ཏག **tākāk** 13

exam རྒྱུགས་སྤྲོད། **kyukṭö'** 6

expensive གོང་ཆེན་པོ། **khongchēnpo** 4

extract འདོན་པ། **tönpa** (I) 12

eye མིག **mīk** 11

face གདོང་པ། **tongpa** 11

facilities མཐུན་རྐྱེན། **thūnkyen** 5

fall རིལ་བ། **rilwa** (NI) 11

fall asleep གཉིད་ཁུག་པ། **nyī'-khūkpa** (NI) 11

family ནང་མི། **nangmi** 13

famous སྐད་གྲགས་ཆེན་པོ། **kǟṭhak-chēnpo** 3

far ཐག་རིང་པོ། **thā-ringpo** 4

father ཨ་ཕ། **āpha**; པཱ་ལགས། **pāla:** 4

fault སྐྱོན། **kyȫn** 12

favourite དགའ་ཤོས། **kashö'** 6

fever ཚ་བ་འབར་བ། **tshawa-parwa** (NI) 11

few ཉུང་ཉུང་། **nyungnyung** 5

fifteen བཅོ་ལྔ། **cōngā** 3

fifty ལྔ་བཅུ། **ngāpcu** 3

find རྙེད་པ། **nyēpa** (NI) 11

finger མཛུབ་མོ། **tsuku** 11

finish ཚར་བ། **tshārwa** (NI) 9

fire མེ། **me**

first དང་པོ། **thangpo** 8

fish (animal) ཉ། **nya**; (flesh) ཉ་ཤ། **nyashā**

fit (clothes etc.) ཤོང་བ། **shōngwa** (NI) 10

five ལྔ། **ngā** 3

flower མེ་ཏོག **metok** 11

foggy སྨུག་པ་འཁོར་བ། **mūkpa-khōrwa** (NI) 12

food ཟ་ཡས། **sayä** 6; (meals) ཁ་ལག **khālak** 5

fool སྐུགས་པ། **kūkpa** 13

foot རྐང་པ། **kāngpa** 11

for ལ། **la** 5

foreign ཕྱི་རྒྱལ། **chīkyäl** 7

foreigner ཕྱི་རྒྱལ་བ། **chīkyälwa** 2

forget བརྗེད་པ། **cepa** (NI) 11

four བཞི། **shi** 3

fourteen བཅུ་བཞི། **cūpshi** 3

Friday གཟའ་པ་སངས། **sa-pāsang** 3

friend གྲོགས་པོ། **ṭhokpo** 3

from ནས། **nä** 3

front མདུན། **tü̱n** 4

full (stomach) གྲོད་ཁོག་རྒྱགས་པ། **ṭho̱khok kya̱kpa** (NI) 11

game རྩེད་མོ། **tsēmo** 6

gate རྒྱལ་སྒོ། **kyä̱lko** 14

girl བུ་མོ། **phu̱mo** 2

give སྤྲོད་པ། **ṭȫ'pa** (I) 7

gloves ལག་ཤུབས། **la̱kshup** 10

go འགྲོ་བ། **ṭo̱wa** (I) 7

goat ར། **ra̱**

good ཡག་པོ། **ya̱kpo** 5

goodbye! ག་ལེར་ཕེབས། **kha̱le:-phēp** (to someone leaving) 5

goodbye! ག་ལེར་བཞུགས། **kha̱le:-shu̱** (to someone staying) 5

government གཞུང་། **shu̱ng** 4

grandfather སྤོ་(སྤོ་)ལགས། **pō(po)la:** 4

grandmother སྨོ་(མོ་)ལགས། **mō(mo)la:** 4

green ལྗང་གུ། **ca̱nku** 6

ground ས། **sā** 2

hail སེར་བ་རྒྱག་པ། **sēra-kya̱pa** (NI) 12

hair སྐྲ། **ṭā** 11

half ཕྱེད་ཀ། **chēka** 8

hand ལག་པ། **la̱kpa** 9

harm གནོད་པ། **nȫ'pa** (NI) 15

hat ཞྭ་མོ། **sha̱mo** 10

have (no direct equivalent) 4

he (polite) ཁོང་། **khōng**; (non-polite) ཁོ་རང་། **khōrang** 2

head མགོ། **ko̱** 11

headache མགོ་ན་བ། **ko̱-na̱wa** (NI) 11

hear གོ་བ། **kho̱wa** (NI) 11

heating ཚ་གློག **tshālok** 5

'hello' བཀྲ་ཤིས་བདེ་ལེགས། **ṭāshi-te̱le'** 2

help རོགས་པ་བྱེད་པ། **ro̱kpa-che̱pa** (I) 8

here འདིར། **tä̱:** 4

her/s (polite) ཁོང་གི། **khōng-ki**; མོ་རང་གི། **mo̱rang-ki** 3

high མཐོ་པོ། **thōpo** 5

hire གླ་བ། **lāwa** (I) 12

his (polite) ཁོང་གི། **khōng-ki**; (non-polite) ཁོ་རང་གི། **khōrang-ki** 3

holiday གུང་སེང་། **ku̱ngseng** 7

home ནང་། **na̱ng** 3

homeland ཕ་ཡུལ། **phāyül** 3

honest དྲང་པོ། **ṭha̱ngpo** 13

honorific language ཞེ་ས། **she̱sa** 14

hot ཚ་པོ། **tshāpo** 5

hotel མགྲོན་ཁང་། **ṭö̱nkhang** 4

hour ཆུ་ཚོད། **chūtshö'** 8

house ཁང་པ། **khāngpa** 2

how? ག་འདྲ། **kha̱nṭa** 5; (about actions) ག་འདྲ་བྱེར། **kha̱nṭäs** 8

how many/much? ག་ཚོད། **kha̱tshȫ'** 3

hundred བརྒྱ། **kya̱** 5

hungry གྲོད་ཁོག་ལྟོགས་པ། **ṭho̱khok-tōkpa** (NI) 11

husband ཁྱོ་ག **khyōka** 4

I/me ང་། **nga̱** 2

if ན། **na** 12

ignore ཡ་མེད་གཏོང་བ། **ya̱me-tāngwa** (I) 15

ill ན་བ། **na̱wa** (NI) 11

illness ན་ཚ། **na̱tsha** 11

immediately ལམ་སེང་། **la̱msāng** 11
important གལ་ཆེན་པོ། **khä̱l-chēnpo** 10
in (a language) ཐོག **thōk** 13
India རྒྱ་གར། **kya̱kar** 3
inside ནང་། **na̱ng** 4
interfere ཛུས་གཏོགས་བྱེད་པ། **chu̱tōk-che̱pa** (I) 14
invite སྐད་གཏོང་བ། **kä̃'-tāngwa** (I) 8
'is' རེད། **re̱'**; འདུག **tu̱'** etc. 2/4
isolated ཁུག་ཀྱོག **khūkyok** 6
itch ཟ་ཕྲུག་ལང་བ། **sa̱pṭhuk-la̱ngwa** (NI) 11

Japanese (language) ཉི་ཧོང་གི་སྐད། **nyi̱hongki-kä̃'** 13

Kham (Tibetan province) ཁམས། **khām** 3
kilograms ཀི་ལོ། **kīlo** (from English) 10
kitchen ཐབ་ཚང་། **thāptsang** 9
know ཧ་གོ་བ། **hākho̱wa**; ཤེས་པ། **shēpa** (NI) 13

lama བླ་མ། **lāma** 14
land འབབ་པ། **pa̱ppa** (NI) 8
large ཆེན་པོ། **chēnpo** 4
leave (depart) འཐོན་པ། **thö̃npa** (I) 14
leave (something accidentally) ལུས་པ། **lä̱wa** (NI) 11
left(-hand) གཡོན་པ། **yö̃npa**
leg རྐང་པ། **kāngpa** 11
lend གཡར་བ། **yārwa** (I) 10
lesson སློབ་ཚན། **lōptshän** 6
lie down (esp. to sleep) ཉལ་བ། **nyä̱lwa** (I) 7
like དགའ་པོ། **ka̱po** 6
listen ཉན་པ། **nyä̱npa** (I) 9
live སྡོད་པ། **tä̱wa** (I) 7
lively འཁྲུག་པོ། **ṭhūkpo** 6
long རིང་པོ། **ri̱ngpo** 5
loss (financial, etc.) གྱོང་། **khyo̱ng** 10
low དམའ་པོ། **māpo** 5
lunch ཉིན་གུང་ཁ་ལག **nyi̱nkung-khālak** 9

make བཟོ་བ། **so̱wa** (I) 8
man མི། **mi̱**
many མང་པོ། **ma̱ngpo** 3
market ཁྲོམ། **ṭhōm** 8
market-place ཁྲོམ་ས། **ṭhōmsa** 6
marry ཆང་ས་རྒྱག་པ། **chāngsa-kya̱pa** (I) 8
material(s) རྒྱུ་ཆ། **kyu̱pcha** 10
meat ཤ། **shā** 6
medicine སྨན། **mä̃n** 11
meet ཐུག་པ། **thūkpa** (NI) 13
milk འོ་མ། **o̱ma** 9
mind སེམས། **sēm** 6
minute སྐར་མ། **kārma** 4
mistake ནོར་འཁྲུལ། **no̱rṭhül** 12
monastery དགོན་པ། **ko̱mba** 4
Monday གཟའ་ཟླ་བ། **sa̱-ta̱wa** 3
money དངུལ། **ngül** 4; (denomination) སྒོར་མོ། **ko̱rmo** 5
Mongolia སོག་ཡུལ། **sōkyül** 3
monk གྲྭ་པ། **ṭha̱wa** 6

month ཟླ་བ། **t̲awa** 8
moon (and personal name) ཟླ་བ། **t̲awa** 7
morning ཞོགས་པ། **sho̲kpa**; ཞོགས་ཀས། **sho̲kä** 11
mother ཨ་མ། **āma** 4
mountain རི། **ri̲** 4
mouth ཁ། **khā** 11
Muslim ཁ་ཆེ། **khāche** 2
must དགོས(་པ།) **kö̲'pa** (NI) 11
my/mine ངའི། **ngä̲:** 3

name མིང་། **mi̲ng** 2/3
near ཐག་ཉེ་པོ། **thā-nye̲po** 4
need དགོས། **kö̲'** 9
Nepal བལ་ཡུལ། **phä̲lyül** 3
nephew ཚ་བོ། **tshāwo** 4
new གསར་པ། **sārpa** 5
niece ཚ་མོ། **tshāmo** 4
night མཚན(་མོ)། **tshä̲n(mo)** 5
nine དགུ། **ku̲** 3
nineteen བཅུ་དགུ། **cūrku̲** 3
no/not (no direct equivalents) 2
noodles and noodle dishes ཐུག་པ། **thūkpa** 9
nose སྣ་ཁུང་། **nāku** 11
now ད་ལྟ། **tha̲nta** 4
numb སྦྲིད་པ། **pi̲:wa** (NI) 11
nun ཨ་ནེ། **āne** 14

offer འབུལ་བ། **phūlwa** (H/I) 14
office ལས་ཁུངས། **lä̲khung** 4
okay! ཡོང་ང་། **yo̲ngnga** 10; འོང་། **o̲ng** 7

old རྙིང་པ། **nyīngpa** (objects) 5
old རྒན་འཁོགས། **kä̲nkhōk** (people) 4
on སྒང་། **ka̲ng** 4
one གཅིག། **cīk** 3
opinion བསམ་ཚུལ། **sāmtshul** 15
or ཡང་མིན་ན། **ya̲ng-me̲:na** 13
orange (colour) ལི་ཝང་། **li̲wang** 6
order (food, etc.) མངག་པ། **ngākpa** (I) 9
organise གྲ་སྒྲིག་བྱེད་པ། **ṭhaṭik-che̲pa** (I) 8
other གཞན་དག། **shä̲nthak** 4
our/ours ང་ཚོའི། **nga̲ntshö:** 3
outside ཕྱི་ལོགས། **chīlo:** 4
owner བདག་པོ། **ta̲kpo** 3

pair ཆ། **chā** 10
paper ཤོག་བུ། **shūku** 11
parents ཕ་མ། **phāma** 4
partner (boy/girlfriend) དགའ་པོ། **ka̲wo** 3
passport/permit ལག་འཁྱེར། **la̲khyer**
peace ཞི་བདེ། **shi̲te** 6
pen སྨྱུ་གུ **nyūku** 2
person མི། **mi̲** 2
phone ཁ་པར། **khāpar** 2
phone ཁ་པར་གཏོང་བ། **khāpar-tāngwa** (I) 2
picnic གླིང་ཁ། **līngka** 6
pill རིལ་བུ། **ri̲lpu** 11
pink ཟིང་སྐྱ། **si̲ngkya** 6
place ས་ཆ། **sācha** 6
plate སྡེར་ཚེ། **te̲rtse** 9
please (no direct equivalent) 5

pork ཕག་ཤ། **phāksha** 9
post office སྦྲག་ཁང་། **ṭa̱khang** 4
pour བླུག་པ། **lūkpa** (I) 9
power ཤུགས། **shūk** 5
prefer དགའ་པ། **ka̱:** 6
price གོང་ཚད། **kho̱ngtshä'** 10
probably ཕལ་ཆེར། **phālcher** 13
profit ཁེ་བཟང་། **khēpsang** 10
pub ཆང་ཁང་། **chāngkhang** 6
purposely ཀྲང་བཙུགས་ནས། **kāngtsu̱k-nä** 15
purple སྨུ་མེན། **mu̱men** 6
put འཇོག་པ། **sha̱kpa** (I) 5

quality སྤུས་ཀ། **pǖka** 10
quarrel རྒྱབ་འདྲེ་རྒྱག་པ། **kya̱mṭe-kya̱pa** (I) 15
quickly མགྱོགས་པོར། **kyo̱kpo** 12
quiet ཁུ་སིམ་པོ། **khūsimpo** 4

rain ཆར་པ་གཏོང་བ། **chārpa-tāngwa** (NI) 12
read ཀློག་པ། **lōkpa** (I) 11
real དངོས་གནས། **ngȫnä'** 3
receive རག་པ། **ra̱kpa** (NI) 11
receptionist སྣེ་ལེན་པ། **nēlenpa** 5
recognise ངོ་ཤེས་པ། **ngo̱-shēpa** (NI) 13
recover དྲག་པ། **ṭha̱kpa** (NI) 11
red དམར་མོ་/པོ། **mārmo/po** 6
region ལུང་པ། **lu̱ngpa** 3
relation (sibling, etc.) སྤུན་སྐྱ། **pīnkyak** 4
reliable བརྟན་པོ། **tǟnpo** 14
remember དྲན་པ། **ṭhä̱npa** (NI) 11
replacement ཚབ། **tshāp** 12
responsibility ལས་འགན། **lä̱nkän** 14
restaurant ཟ་ཁང་། **sa̱khang** 3
return (come back) ལོག་པ། **lo̱kpa** (I) 7
rice འབྲས། **ṭä̱'** 9
right(-hand) གཡས་པ། **yǟpa**
road/path ལམ་ཁ། **la̱mkha** 4
robber ཇག་པ། **cha̱kpa** 12
room ཁང་མིག **khāngmik** 5
rose རྒྱ་སེ། **kya̱se** 13
rough རྩུབ་པོ། **tsūpo** 15
rules/regime སྒྲིག་འཛུགས། **ṭi̱ktsuk** 6
rut ས་ཀོང་། **sākong** 12

salad གྲང་ཚལ། **ṭha̱ngtshäl** 9
salt ཚྭ། **tshā** 14
same གཅིག་པ། **cīkpa** 10
Saturday གཟའ་སྤེན་པ། **sa̱-pēnpa** 3
say ལབ་པ། **la̱pa**; ཟེར་བ། **se̱rwa** (I) 13
scared ཞེད་པ། **she̱pa** (NI) 12
school སློབ་གྲྭ། **lōpṭha** 13
search འཚོལ་བ། **tshǟlwa** (I) 8
second གཉིས་པ། **nyī'pa** 8
see མཐོང་བ། **thōngwa** (NI) 11
sell འཚོང་པ། **tshōngpa** (I) 10
send གཏོང་བ། **tāngwa** (I) 8
seven བདུན། **tü̱n** 3
seventeen བཅུ་བདུན། **cūptün** 3
several ཁ་ཤས། **khāshä'** 4
she (polite) ཁོང་། **khōng**; (non-polite) མོ་རང་། **mo̱rang** 2
shirt སྟོད་ཐུང་། **tȫthung** 10
shop ཚོང་ཁང་། **tshōngkhang** 3

shop ཉོ་ཆ་རྒྱག་པ། **nyo̱pcha-kya̱pa** (I) 8
short ཐུང་ཐུང་། **thūngthūng** 5
should དགོས(་པ།) **ko̱'pa** (NI) 11
shout སྐད་རྒྱག་པ། **kǟ'-kya̱pa** (I) 8
show སྟོན་པ། **tǟnpa** (I) 11
similar འདྲ་པོ། **ṭa̱po** 10
sister (elder) ཨ་ཅག **āca** 4
sit སྡོད་པ། **tä̱wa** (I) 7
situation གནས་ཚུལ། **nǟtshul** 14
six དྲུག **ṭhu̱k** 3
sixteen བཅུ་དྲུག **cūṭhu̱k** 3
slightly ཏོག་ཙམ། **tēts** 4
small ཆུང་ཆུང་། **chūngchūng** 5
smell དྲི་མ། **ṭhi̱ma** 11
smell ཁ་བ། **khāwa** (NI) 11
snow གངས་རྒྱག་པ། **kha̱ng-kya̱pa** (NI) 12
something (someone, somewhere) གཅིག **cīk** 6/8
sometimes མཚམས་མཚམས(་ལ)། **tshāmtsham(-la)** 10
son བུ། **phu̱** 3
song གཞས། **shä̱'** 6
soon མགྱོགས་པོ། **kyo̱kpo** 12
sorry! དགོངས་དག **ko̱ng:tha** 6
speak Tibetan བོད་སྐད་རྒྱག་པ། **phö̱kǟ'-kya̱pa** (I) 8
special དམིགས་བསལ། **mīksäl** 8
spirits (alcohol) ཨ་རག **ārak** 2
spoon ཐུར་མ། **thūrma** 9
stand ལང་བ། **la̱ngwa** (I)
stay སྡོད་པ། **tä̱wa** (I) 7
stomach གྲོད་ཁོག **ṭho̱khok** 9
street སྲང་ལམ། **sānglam** 4
strength ཤུགས། **shūk** 5
student སློབ་ཕྲུག **lōpṭhuk** 2
study སློབ་སྦྱོང་བྱེད་པ། **lōpcong-che̱pa** (I) 8
sun (and personal name) ཉི་མ། **nyi̱ma** 2
Sunday གཟའ་ཉི་མ། **sa̱-nyi̱ma** 3
sunny ཉི་མ་སྟོན་པ། **nyi̱ma-tǟnpa** (NI) 12
surprised ཧ་ལས་པ། **hāläwa** (NI) 12
sweet (taste) མངར་མོ། **ngārmo** 9
Switzerland སུད་སི། **sǖsi** 3

table ཅོག་ཙེ། **cōktse** 5
tailor ཚེམ་(བུ་)ཁང་། **tshēm(pu)-khāng** 10
take ལེན་པ། **le̱npa**; འཁྱེར་བ། **khyērwa** 9; འཁྲིད་པ། **ṭhīwa** (I) 14
take (time) འགོར་བ། **ko̱rwa** (NI) 9
tall རིང་པོ། **ri̱ngpo** 5
taste བྲོ་བ། **ṭho̱wa** 15
tasty ཞིམ་པོ། **shi̱mpo** 5
tax ཁྲལ། **ṭhǟl** 11
tea ཇ། **cha̱** 3
teach སློབ་པ། **lāpa** (I) 15
teacher དགེ་རྒན། **ke̱kän** 2
teahouse ཇ་ཁང་། **cha̱khang** 4
tell ལབ་པ། **la̱pa** (I) 9
ten བཅུ། **cū** 3
'thanks' ཐུགས་རྗེ་ཆེ། **thūce-chē** 2
that/the དེ། **the̱** 2
theatre ཟློས་གར་ཁང་། **tö̱kärkhang** 8
their/s ཁོང་ཚོའི། **khōng-tshö:** 3
there དེར། **thä̱:**, ཕ་གིར། **phākä:** 4

thermos ཇ་དམ། **cha̱tham** 6
these འདི་ཚོ། **ti̱n-tsho** 2
thief རྐུན་མ། **kūma** 11
thing (manmade item) ཅ་ལག **cālak** 10
think བསམ་བློ་གཏོང་བ། (l); སེམས་པ། **sāmpa**; དྲན་པ། **ṭ̱änpa** (Nl) 11
thirsty ཁ་སྐོམ་པ། **khā-kōmpa** (Nl) 11
thirteen བཅུ་གསུམ། **cūksūm** 3
thirty སུམ་ཅུ། **sūmcū** 3
this འདི། **ti̱** 2
those དེ་ཚོ། **the̱n-tsho** 2
three གསུམ། **sūm** 3
throat མིད་པ། **mi̱pa** 11
Thursday གཟའ་ཕུར་བུ། **sa̱-phūrpu** 3
Tibet བོད། **phö̱'** 3
Tibetan (person) བོད་པ། **phö̱pa** 2
Tibetan (spoken) བོད་སྐད། **phö̱kǟ'** 8
Tibetan (written) བོད་ཡིག **phö̱'yik** 13
Tibetan tea བོད་ཇ། **phö̱cha** 6
time དུས་ཚོད། **thü̱tshȫ'** 8
tired ཐང་ཆད་པ། **thāng-chä̱pa** (Nl) 12
to ལ། **la** 4
toe (རྐང་པའི་)མཛུབ་མོ། **(kāngpä:-) tsu̱ku** 11
together མཉམ་དུ། **nyāmtu** 4
toilet གསང་སྤྱོད། **sāngcö'** 5
tomorrow སང་ཉིན། **sāngnyin** 8
tongue ལྕེ་ལེ། **cēle** 11
too དྲགས(་པ)། **ṭ̱hak(-pa)** 10
tooth སོ། **sō** 11
tourist སྤྲོ་འཆམ་པ། **ṭōchāmpa** 13
town གྲོང་ཁྱེར། **ṭ̱hongkhyer** 6

trade ཚོང་རྒྱག་པ། **tshōng-kya̱pa** (l) 8
trader ཚོང་པ། **tshōngpa** 3
tradition ལུགས་སྲོལ། **lu̱ksȫl** 4
train (railway) མེ་འཁོར། **me̱khor**; རི་ལི། **ri̱li**
train སྦྱོང་བ། **ca̱ngwa** (l) 10
transport སྐྱེལ་བ། **kyēlwa** (l) 12
travel agent འགྲིམ་འགྲུལ་ཁང་། **ṭ̱imṭ̱ul-kha̱ng** 8
trousers གོས་ཐུང་། **khö̱thung** 10
true བདེན་པ། **te̱npa** 3
Tuesday གཟའ་མིག་དམར། **sa̱-mikmār** 3
twelve བཅུ་གཉིས། **cūnyī'** 3
twenty ཉི་ཤུ། **nyi̱shū** 3
two གཉིས། **nyī'** 3

umbrella ཉི་གདུགས། **nyi̱tuk** 15
uncle (maternal) ཨ་ཞང་། **āshang** 4
uncle (paternal) ཨ་ཁུ། **ākhu** 4
under འོག **o̱k** 4
understand ཧ་གོ་བ། **hākho̱wa**; ཤེས་པ། **shēpa** (Nl) 13
until བར་དུ། **pha̱rthu** 8
up ཡར། **ya̱r** 15
upstairs ཐོག་ཀ **thōka** 5
use བེད་སྤྱོད་གཏོང་བ། **phe̱cȫ-tāngwa** (l) 15
usually ནམ་རྒྱུན། **na̱mkyun** 10

various འདྲ་མི་འདྲ། **ṭ̱a-minṭ̱a** 6
vegetables (སྔོ་)ཚལ། **(ngō-)tshǟl** 9
vegetarian (food) ཤ་མེད་(ཁ་ལག) **shāme'(-khālak)** 6

very ཞེ་དྲག། **she̱ṭhak** 5
village གྲོང་གསེབ། **ṭho̱ngsep** 6
vomit སྐྱུག་པ་སྐྱུག་པ། **kyūkpa-kyūkpa** (NI) 11

wait སྒུག་པ། **ku̱kpa** (I) 8
want དགོས། **kö̱'** 9; འདོད(་པ)། **tö̱'(-pa)** 15
waste འཕྲོ་བརླག་གཏོང་བ། **ṭhōlak-tāngwa** (I) 15
watch ལྟ་བ། **tāwa** (I) 10
water ཆུ། **chū** 2
we/us ང་ཚོ། **nga̱n-tsho** 2
wealthy (རྒྱུ་)ཕྱུག་པོ། **(kyu̱-)chūkpo** 3
wear གྱོན་པ། **khö̱npa** (I) 10
weather གནམ་གཤིས། **nāmshi'** 9
Wednesday གཟའ་ལྷག་པ། **sa̱-lhākpa** 3
week བདུན་ཕྲག **tü̱nṭhak** 3
weigh རྒྱ་མ་བརྒྱག་པ། **kya̱ma-kyakpa** (I) 10
well བདེ་པོ། **te̱po** 2
what? ག་རེ། **kha̱re** 2
when དུས། **thü'** 6
when? ག་དུས། **kha̱thü'** 2
where? ག་པར། **kha̱wa:** 4
where from? ག་ནས། **kha̱nä** 3
which? ག་གི **kha̱ki** 3

white དཀར་པོ། **kārpo** 6
who? སུ། **sū** 2
whose སུའི། **sǖ:** 3
why? ག་རེ་བྱས་ནས། **kha̱re-chä̱nä** 7
wife སྐྱེ་དམན། **kyēmän** 4
window སྒེའུ་ཁུང་། **ke̱khung** 2
windy ལྷགས་པ་རྒྱག་པ། **lhākpa-kya̱pa** (NI) 12
woman བུད་མེད། **phü̱me'**; སྐྱེ་དམན། **kyēmän** 4
work ལས་ཀ། **lä̱ka** 6
work ལས་ཀ་བྱེད་པ། **lä̱ka-che̱pa** (I) 8
write འབྲི་བ། **ṭi̱wa** (I) 11

yak གཡག **yāk** 1
year ལོ། **lo̱** 3
yellow སེར་པོ། **sērpo** 6
yes (no direct equivalent) 2
yoghurt ཞོ། **sho̱** 9
you (polite) ཁྱེད་རང་། **khyērang**; (non-polite) ཁྱོད། **khyȫ'** 2
young གཞོན་གཞོན། **shö̱nshön** 3
your/s (singular) ཁྱེད་རང་གི། **khyērang-ki** 3
your/s (plural) ཁྱེད་རང་ཚོའི། **khyērang-tshö:**

zero ཀླད་ཀོར། **lä̱kor** 3

Index